To Read a Poem

SECOND EDITION

Donald Hall

Harcourt Brace Jovanovich College Publishers

Fort Worth   Chicago   San Francisco   Philadelphia
Montreal   Toronto   London   Sydney   Tokyo

Publisher	Ted Buchholz
Acquisitions Editor	Michael Rosenberg
Development Editor	Stacy Schoolfield
Design/Project Editor	Publications Development Company
Production Manager	Kathleen Ferguson
Cover Art/Design Supervisor	Serena B. Manning
Cover Design	Pat Sloan
Composition	Publications Development Company

Cover Image: Edward Hopper. *Lighthouse Hill.* 1927. Oil on canvas. Dallas Museum of Art, gift of Mr. and Mrs. Maurice Purnell.

Address Editorial Correspondence to: 301 Commerce Street, Suite 3700, Fort Worth, TX 76102.

Address Orders to: 6277 Sea Harbor Drive, Orlando, FL 32887
1-800-782-4479, or 1-800-433-0001. (in Florida)

Acknowledgments start on page 387.

Printed in the United States of America

Library of Congress Cataloging-in-Publication Data

Hall, Donald, 1928–
    To read a poem / Donald Hall. — 2nd ed.
       p.   cm.
    Rev. ed. of: To read poetry. c1982.
    Includes index.
    ISBN 0-03-055539-6
    1. English poetry. 2. American poetry. I. Hall, Donald, 1928–
To read poetry. II. Title.
PR1175.H258 1991
808.1—dc20   91-5062
                                                             CIP

2 3 4 016 9 8 7 6 5 4 3 2 1

To Read a Poem

Also by Donald Hall

POETRY

Exiles and Marriages
The Dark Houses
A Roof of Tiger Lilies
The Alligator Bride: Poems New and Selected
The Yellow Room
A Blue Wing Tilts at the Edge of the Sea
The Town of Hill
Kicking the Leaves
The Happy Man
The One Day
Old and New Poems

PROSE

String Too Short to Be Saved
Henry Moore
Writing Well
Dock Ellis in the Country of Baseball
Goatfoot Milktongue Twinbird
Remembering Poets
Ox-Cart Man
To Keep Moving
The Weather for Poetry
The Man Who Lived Alone
Fathers Playing Catch with Sons
The Ideal Bakery
Poetry and Ambition
Seasons at Eagle Pond
Here at Eagle Pond

EDITIONS

Contemporary American Poets
A Choice of Whitman's Verse
The Oxford Book of American Literary Anecdotes
Claims for Poetry
The Oxford Book of Children's Verse in America

PLAYS

An Evening's Frost
Bread and Roses
The Bone Ring

To the Student

Reasons for Reading Poems

This book introduces poetry—maybe the oldest, certainly the most intense of literature's genres.

When we learn to read poems, we acquire a pleasure and a resource we never lose. Although literary study is impractical in one sense—few people make their living reading poems—in another sense it is almost as practical as breathing. Literature records and embodies centuries of human thought and feeling, preserving for us the minds of people who lived before us, who were like us and unlike us, against whom we can measure our common humanity and our historical difference. When we read our contemporaries, they illuminate a world we share. Whatever we claim for literature in general we must especially claim for poetry, which concentrates the virtues we attribute to drama and fiction. If we learn to read poems first, we will begin the study of literature as literature itself began—with the most concentrated and intense of its utterances.

When we read great poetry, something changes in us that stays changed. Poetry remembered becomes material to think with, and no one who has absorbed Shakespeare or Keats is quite the same again. Reading poetry adds tools by which we observe, measure, and judge the people and the properties of our universe—inside and outside.

In the fable of the ant and the grasshopper, the wise ant builds his storehouse against winter and prospers; the foolish grasshopper saves nothing and perishes. Anyone who dismisses the study of poetry on the ground that it will not be useful—to a chemist or an engineer, to a foreman or an x-ray technician—imitates the grasshopper. When we shut from our lives everything except food and shelter, part of us starves to death. Food for this hunger is music, painting, film, plays, stories, novels—and poems. Reading the poems of our language (there is more great poetry in the English language than in the literature of any other language), we take into ourselves the greatness of Chaucer and Shakespeare, of romantics like Blake, Keats, and Wordsworth, of Dickinson, of the grandparents of modern poetry. We respond knowledgeably to the contemporary poets who visit our colleges to read their poems. If there is a poetry reading at your school while you are studying poetry, do not miss it.

There is pleasure and understanding to take from the poetry of our language, if one first learns how to read it. No one expects to walk up to a computer and be able to program it without first learning something about computers. We have needed to learn skills in order to ride a bicycle, drive a car, play a guitar, shoot baskets, or typewrite. For some reason—perhaps because we are familiar with words from childhood and take them for granted—we tend to think that a quick glance at a poem should reward us, and that, if we do not find instant satisfaction, the work is beyond us, or not worth it, or irrelevant, or boring.

There are other problems for the beginning student of poetry. The ideas we derive from literature can seem confusing. Equally great poems may contradict each other in the generalizations we derive from them. One poem may recommend solitude, another society. One may advise us to seize the moment, another to live a life of contemplation. For that matter, two good readers may disagree about the implication of any work and each may argue persuasively, with detailed references to the poem, in support of different interpretations. A complex work of literature like a poem cannot be reduced to a simple, correct meaning. In an elementary arithmetic text, the answers may be printed in the back of the book. There are no answers to be printed in the back of this book.

Such nebulousness or ambiguity disturbs some students. After an hour's class discussion of a poem, with varying interpretations offered, they want the teacher to supply the answer to "But what *does* it mean?" We must admit that literature is inexact, and that the truth of poetry is not easily verifiable. Probably the poem means several things *at once* and not one thing at all. This is not to say, of course, that it means anything that anybody finds in it. Although differing, equally defensible opinions are common, error is even more common.

When modern people speak of truth, they usually mean something scientific or tautological. Arithmetic contains the truth of tautology; two and two make four because our definitions of *two* and *four* say so. In laboratories, we encounter the truth of statistics and the truth of observation. If we smoke cigarettes heavily, we have one chance in four to develop lung cancer. When we heat copper wire over a Bunsen burner, the flame turns blue.

But there is an older sense of truth in which statements that are apparently opposite can both be valid. In this older tradition, truth is dependent on the agreement of sensible men and women—like the "Guilty" or "Not guilty" verdict of a jury. A poem may be true when its characters behave according to probability within a context that is highly hypothetical. Because this literary (or philosophical, or legal, or historical) truth is inexact, changeable, and subject to argument, poetry can seem nebulous to minds accustomed to arithmetical certainty.

Let me argue this: If poetry is nebulous or inexact, if it is impossible to determine with scientific precision the value or the meaning of a work of art, this inexactness is the price literature pays for representing whole human beings and for embodying whole human feelings. Human beings themselves, in their feelings and in the wanderings of their short lives, are ambiguous and ambivalent, shifting mixtures of permanence and change, direction and disorder. Because literature is true to life and true to the complexities of human feeling, different people will read the same work with different responses. Literary art will sometimes affirm that opposite things are both true *because they are*. Such a condition is not tidy and it is perhaps regrettable—but it is human nature.

The Definition of Poetry

Before we attempt to define poetry, we must admit that a definition is impossible. Some words are more definable than others. If we do not know what a grommet or an ampersand is, a dictionary will tell us. If we do not know what love is, a definition will not help. *Poetry* is almost as difficult to define as *love*. With words like these, a definition is useful as a starting point for discussion—but only when we have experienced what we discuss. Once we have experienced poetry firsthand, we can think about it by trying to define it. Here is a useful exercise while you study poetry: at the end of each week, write a one-sentence definition of poetry as you understand it at that point; keep your changing definitions as testimony of the range of poetry.

Many definitions of poetry center on the delight of reading it. "Poetry," says a contemporary poet, "is a pleasure, like making love." John Milton (1608–1674) compared poetry to philosophical discourse and found it "more simple, sensuous and passionate." Samuel Taylor Coleridge (1772–1834) said that poetry's "proper and immediate object" was "the communication of immediate pleasure." Defining poetry by naming its components, Coleridge called the art "the best words in the best order." Matthew Arnold (1822–1888) made *best* more particular: "Poetry is simply the most beautiful, impressive and wisely effective mode of saying things . . . ." When he combined *beautiful* with *wisely effective,* Arnold sounded like Robert Frost (1874–1963), who claimed that poetry "begins in delight and ends in wisdom." The Roman poet Horace (65–8 B.C.) declared that poetry instructs while it pleases.

William Wordsworth (1770–1850) defined poetry as "the spontaneous overflow of powerful feelings" and said that it "takes its origin from emotion recollected in tranquility." This definition derives from an idea of the poet's creative process. Probably most definitions, like Milton's, describe the effect on the reader. John Keats (1795–1821): "Poetry should surprise by a fine excess, and not by singularity. It should strike the reader as a wording of his own highest thoughts, and appear almost as a remembrance." Or A. E. Housman (1859–1936): "Experience has taught me, when I am shaving of a morning, to keep watch over my thoughts, because, if a line of poetry strays into my memory, my skin bristles so that the razor ceases to act . . . ." If, after this barrage of definitions, any student feels confused, let me add one more confusion: Carl Sandburg (1878–1967) said "Poetry is a synthesis of hyacinths and biscuits."

Confusing, yes; but every one of these definitions makes its own sense when you have a broad experience of poems. Sandburg has fun with his definition—making a tongue-twister, among other things—but he is serious also: Poetry combines and reconciles within the same object things seemingly irreconcilable, like the flower with the Greek name and the simple product of the American kitchen. Metaphor brings together things that do not seem as if they could be brought together, as when Robert Frost says, "The petal of the rose / It was that stung . . . ," bringing together the soft rose petal and the bee's stinger. Metaphor is essential to poetry and a clue to its nature, for poetry juxtaposes things that really belong together but seem not to—love and hate, passion and indifference. Once again I must say: Poetry does this amalgamating because poetry is true to life, and in our lives we continually experience the simultaneous presence of opposing forces. We are not always aware of our ambivalence; poetry helps us understand the reality of our lives.

On the other hand, Poetry is words, and it is words arranged usually in lines, so that the right-hand side of the page is jagged. This definition is not so silly as it sounds: poems are not statements (the worst thing you can do to a poem is to reduce it to a rephrasing of its ideas) but objects, like paintings or sculptures, that include statements as *part* of their materials. The sound of a poem, controlled in large part by its lines, gives it an object's shapeliness and contributes to both pleasure and wisdom. The sound of a poem captures us—or perhaps we must surrender to it—and allows us access to its interior, which is perhaps why, in T. S. Eliot's words, "Genuine poetry can communicate before it is understood."

It can. But then, with close attention, it can be *understood as well*—and become an even greater pleasure.

The Words Themselves

Poetry is words. So far, I have talked as if poetry were the feelings and thoughts we derive from reading poems, but feelings and thoughts are not poetry's medium. Whatever poetry accomplishes in us it accomplishes by words. As paint and canvas form the medium of painting, and as sequences and combinations of sound different in pitch, duration, and quality form the medium of music, so the right words in the right order make poetry.

A Japanese named Basho wrote this haiku about three hundred years ago:

The morning glory—
another thing
that will never be my friend.

Basho reminds us that the natural world is separate from us, that we may not shoulder our way into it, like invading troops of the imagination, and assume that we are intimate with everything. The American poet Robert Bly translated these lines. Here are three other versions:

A. The morning glory
   is a separate being
   and I can never know it intimately.

B. The morning glory
   is yet another object
   with which I will never become closely acquainted.

C. The morning glory—
   something else
   that won't call me companion.

To understand and appreciate how these four versions differ from one another is to become sensitive to the words that make literature. In a general
way, they all mean the same thing. After the identical first lines, the translations differ in diction (the kinds of words chosen) and in rhythm (the pace
and tempo of the words). Versions A and B are dry, stiff, and unnatural.
Separate being sounds pretentious compared to *another thing. Yet another
object* is finicky with its *yet another,* and *object* is more scientific-sounding
than the casual *thing. With which I will never become closely acquainted* is
formal and distant, rhythmically slow. *And I can never know it intimately*
lacks interest or surprise in its words. The simplicity of *that will never be
my friend,* coming to rest on the surprise of the last word, makes Bly's
translation blossom in its final word. In version C, on the other hand, we
have a translation nearly as pleasing as the original one. *Something else* has
its own casual simplicity, and the little action of *call me companion—*
where the morning glory is imagined capable of speech—has some of the
surprise that the original translation found in *friend.*
     The difference is the words and their order.

What's Good, What's Bad

The claims I make for poetry are large: that it alters and enlarges our minds,
our connections with each other past and present, and our understanding of
our own feelings. These claims apply only to excellent poems. Some poems
are better than others—and some verse is not poetry at all. Even if judgments
are always subject to reversal, even if there is no way we can be certain of
being correct, evaluation lives at the center of literary study. It is never easy,
even after a lifetime of literary study, to explain, in words that will persuade
anyone who disagrees, why one poem is better than another. Still, the struggle is worth it. The struggle to name reasons for value—to evaluate works of
art—is lifelong, and although we may never arrive at satisfactory explanations, the struggle makes the mind more sensitive, more receptive to the next
work of literature it encounters.
     And as the mind becomes more sensitive and receptive to poetry, it may
become more sensitive and receptive to all sorts of things.

The Organization of This Book

In reading a poem, we respond to poetry's elements: images, metaphors, tones of voice, and allusions. For the sake of the ultimate pleasure of reading poems, this book explores these elements, types, and forms of poetry. Then we collect many poems by five poets—John Keats, Emily Dickinson, Robert Frost, Theodore Roethke, and Adrienne Rich. After reading the work of these few poets in depth, we gather a few poems by many poets, for further reading in the poetry of our language.

But before we take a separate look at poetry's elements, in the first chapter we will discuss two poems as a whole. Because eventually we wish to arrive at a sense of the poem as a whole, it makes sense to begin with models of such reading.

. . . and to the Instructor

In making selections and in writing the text for this collection, I have tried to serve one purpose: to help students read poetry with intelligence, gusto, and discrimination.

This book begins the study of poetry by examining whole poems, emphasizing that the goal of reading is not the analysis of parts but the understanding of wholes. For a fuller definition of poetry's elements, later chapters concentrate on parts.

Selections are frequently modern or contemporary; students best begin literary study without the distraction of an unfamiliar vocabulary, and without the handicap of historical ignorance. It would be silly to let this principle cheat us of Shakespeare or Wordsworth, but I feel that, at the beginning, when the students are shyest, it is best to assign contemporary examples, then gradually introduce examples from poetry's past.

I intend the text to be readable and entertaining while it remains serious. Because everyone is curious about the lives of authors (whether we ought to be or not), I have included biographical notes on all poets. My emphasis is esthetic—neither biographical nor historical; I mean to examine the way poetry works.

Footnotes and glosses translate foreign-language material, provide essential identifications, and define words not available in many dictionaries or words used in an archaic sense. The Appendix, Writing about Poems, should provide guidance for students preparing papers.

I've taken advice from several hundred American teachers of literature. When this book was only a notion, several years back, many people answered a questionnaire about what it should include. I am grateful; I have followed many suggestions.

Other professors read portions of the manuscript and commented in detail. I should like to thank Christopher P. Baker, Walter L. Barker, Sylvan Barnet, Ronald Baughman, R. S. Beal, Gary Blake, John Boni, Larry Champion, Barbara J. Cicardo, Paul Davis, R. H. Deutsch, Richard Dietrich, Donald Drury, John L. Fell, Art Goldsher, Randolph Goodman, William J. Gracie, Jr., Barnett Guttenberg, Nancy J. Hazelton, Michael Hogan,

Woodrow L. Holbein, John Huxhold, Henry E. Jacobs, Robert C. Johnson, John J. Keenan, Mike Keene, X. J. Kennedy, Hannah Laipson, Bette B. Lansdown, Robert Leggett, James MacKillop, James Moody, William W. Nolte II, Byron Petrakis, Anne Pidgeon, Doris Powers, William C. Pratt, Victoria Price, Jules Ryckebusch, Dennis Rygiel. H. Miller Solomon, Joe Sperry, William Stull, Cathy Turner, Ralph Voss, Martha Weathers, and James D. Welch, who reviewed the first edition. I also want to thank those who read the text and made helpful comments for the second edition: Gilbert Allen; Margaret Freeman, Los Angeles Valley College; Linda Merians, La Salle University; William Nicoloet, Southeastern Massachusetts University; and Sherry Zivley, University of Houston. At Harcourt Brace Jovanovich, I would like to thank the following people: Michael Rosenberg, Stacy Schoolfield, Molly Shepard, and Kathy Ferguson.

Finally, let me thank my own helpers in New Hampshire, in Ann Arbor, and in Santa Monica: Lois Fierro, Sharon Giannotta, Dorothy Foster, Pat Wykes, and Frank Barham—not to mention Jane Kenyon.

D.H.

Contents

CHAPTER ONE

Good Poems

Robert Frost, "Stopping by Woods on a Snowy Evening"

Here is a detailed reading of a poem by Robert Frost, "Stopping by Woods on a Snowy Evening." A close reading is called an **explication**, which someone has defined as "an explanation with complications." A pure explanation might first paraphrase the poem, turning its lines into words of prose. An explication goes further: it tries to account for the whole poem by attending to its sounds, its minute suggestions of meaning, its shapeliness. No explication will equal the poem itself, but in a good explication we can feel that we have come close to noticing and naming everything in the poem that affects us.

Stopping by Woods on a Snowy Evening   (1923)

Whose woods these are I think I know.
His house is in the village though;
He will not see me stopping here
To watch his woods fill up with snow.

My little horse must think it queer
To stop without a farmhouse near
Between the woods and frozen lake
The darkest evening of the year.

He gives his harness bells a shake
10 To ask if there is some mistake.
The only other sound's the sweep
Of easy wind and downy flake.

The woods are lovely, dark and deep,
But I have promises to keep,
And miles to go before I sleep,
And miles to go before I sleep.

1

Read this poem aloud, separating the lines with slight pauses but keeping your sense of whole sentences. Different lengths of pause between the lines affect a poem's rhythm. The pause you make at the end of the first line, where Frost ends the sentence with a period, should be longer than the pauses between lines in the second stanza, where there is no punctuation until the end. When we hear a poem or read it aloud, we encounter its body. Unless we feel a poem in our own bodies, we are apt to consider it merely an idea; we are apt to confuse a poem with its paraphrase.

Still, a good way to begin talking about a poem is to paraphrase or summarize it, to see if we are discussing the same poem. (A paraphrase finds different words for each of the poem's phrases. A **summary** is a short, simple report of the plot, like *TV Guide*'s descriptions of television shows.) Once we have paraphrased or summarized the poem, we can talk about its body and its soul. Here, summary is easy: *A man driving a horse-drawn cart or sleigh pauses beside a forest to watch the snow falling on it; the horse seems to want to keep moving, and the man decides he ought to move on, although the scene is pretty, and even inviting.*

Frost used to define poetry as what gets left out in a translation. You might as well say, instead, what gets left out in a summary; there's a gap the size of New Hampshire between Frost's sixteen lines and my forty-four words. But a summary helps at the start of an explication. When you've read a poem two or three times—slowly and quickly, silently and aloud—and when you have arrived at a tentative paraphrase, you are ready to go back to the poem and look at it bit by bit, as if you were taking apart a machine in order to understand how it works.

Start with the title. Sometimes titles give information we need to understand a poem's wholeness. This title, "Stopping by Woods on a Snowy Evening," is a description or label; it tells us what we're going to see, and then gives us the means to see it. This particular title requires little work on the reader's part.

In his first line—"Whose woods these are I think I know"—Frost switches the normal word order, which would have us say something like "I think I know whose woods these are." By moving *woods* to the start of the sentence, Frost gives it more prominence or power. We might say "What *nerve* you've got, heaven only knows!" for a similar emphasis.

In the second line, "His house is in the village though," the last word makes no logical sense; *though* or *although* should make some sort of contradiction or qualification to the statement that *I* know who owns this woodlot. But Frost writes as we usually speak—and *though* qualifies something left out. To understand *though,* we might paraphrase the whole statement, bracketing what is implicit: "I know who owns this land [and I would feel self-conscious if the owner saw me standing and staring into space this way] but he doesn't live out here, and therefore he won't see me pausing to gaze idly." The word *though* implies more than its one syllable would seem able to contain.

At the same time *though* implies something, it rhymes with the word that ends the first line. A rhyme word must feel natural or the poet will seem to have chosen it for the sake of rhyming. Looking to the rest of the stanza, we see that Frost doesn't rhyme the next line with anything nearby but rhymes the fourth line with the first and the second, tying the stanza together. Because we have the word *snowy* in the title, the idea of snow is important to this poem before we start reading it. Then the word *snow* ends a three-line sentence that makes snow the object of our attention. The last two lines of the stanza are a natural, inevitable journey to the culminating word *snow*. As soon as we get there, we realize that this is where we had to go, all the time. This inevitability is underlined by the rhyme, where *know* and *though* build up a sound-expectancy to culminate in *snow*.

Maybe the speaker's self-consciousness is the most important element in the first stanza. (I say "the speaker"—though it feels awkward—because I don't want to say "Robert Frost." *I* in a poem does not necessarily mean the poet.) To sense some embarrassment is to catch the tone of voice.* We all learn to catch the tone of people talking, when we understand the hundreds of small signals that tell us whether the person's tone is ironic or straight-forward, conniving or sincere.

As the stanza ends, we learn something besides the speaker's embarrassment; we learn the motive for stopping: "To watch his woods fill up with snow." Frost's language here is plain, but it could be plainer or flatter still; *I* could have said "to see it snow on his trees" or "to look at the snow falling on his forest." Saying *fill up* contributes to the image* or picture made by the poet; *his woods* becomes a container—empty or partly empty—which *snow* can fill.

As mentioned before, *here* doesn't rhyme with anything around it. If we hold the sound of the word in our ears, however, we are rewarded when we read the first line of the second stanza. We find pleasure in linking with something begun earlier; the experience is similar to the moment in a piece of music when a theme (or a phrase or a chord) returns. Rhyme holds parts of this poem together, linking stanzas more firmly than many poems try to do. The third line of each stanza, unrhymed to the lines near it, rhymes with three of the lines in the stanza following. The first three stanzas together are like groups of four dancers doing the same dance, with one member of each foursome holding hands with the group beyond it.

If it's a dance, it must move to a tune. **Rhythm** is an approximate recurrence or repetition in the pacing of sound; rhythm can be fast or slow, staccato or flowing. **Meter**, which is a measure or count of something, puts its own mark on certain rhythms. "Stopping by Woods" is written in meter, and this meter helps define the rhythm of the poem. If we pronounce *evening* as two syllables, we have, in every line, even-numbered syllables (two, four, six, and eight) that are louder than the odd-numbered syllables. Not all the even syllables are loud, but they are louder than the one, three, five, seven syllables. In *promises, prom-* is louder than the *have* before it, and *-ses* is louder than the *-i-* (just barely louder; you cannot say *prom*-IH-*ses*). This alternation of louder and softer syllables is the meter of the poem. Meter is not the only contributor to differing lengths of pause at lines' ends. A poet can manipulate punctuation

---

* Tone and image as elements of poetry are subjects of later chapters.

to accelerate rhythm or to slow it down. In prose, if we said that we stopped between the woods and a frozen lake, the darkest evening of the year, we would put a comma after lake, as I do in this sentence. But Frost uses the line's pause and avoids a comma, which would slow the stanza down more than he wants it slowed. On the other hand, in prose he wouldn't need a comma if he were telling us that he had promises to keep and miles to go before he slept— but here the poet slows his rhythm at the measured ending of the poem, and he puts a comma after *keep*. Notice that Frost manipulates commas only where commas in prose would be optional.

The second stanza, picking up the *here* rhyme, tells us that the *little* horse (*little* sounds affectionate; this person seems to care about his horse's feelings) *must think it queer*. Consider the word *must* as we use it in speech. If we know that it's raining, we say "It's raining"; if we only think so—because of forecasts or the distant sound of falling water—we say "It *must* be raining." We claim that something must be true only if we don't know it for certain. When Frost writes "My little horse must think it queer," he uses the doubtful *must;* he knows a human cannot mindread his horse. The speaker in the poem attributes doubts to his horse because he himself believes it weird or eccentric to stop one's horse for no good reason, out in the middle of nowhere, to watch snow falling in the darkness. This man's uneasiness shows in his self-mockery: even his horse *must* think he's crazy.

As this stanza continues, ostensibly telling what the horse must think queer, the poet gives us more information, in images that carry feelings on their backs. The road, we learn, passes between *the woods*—which are like a container filled with snow—and the *frozen lake*. Sometimes an image informs us by what it omits. *Frozen* adds cold to the poem (an image records not just pictures but *any* experience of the senses, like cold). The line also increases the solitude of the scene: the lane runs between wood and lake only; no houses or factories here, no inns or filling stations; just these cold and natural things, on "The darkest evening of the year."

This last detail (if we read clearly enough, looking for the implications of words) is strange if we take it literally—and when we read a poem, we ought to try at first to take the wording literally. We cannot conclude that this man has determined scientifically, using some instrument that measures light, that this clouded, moonless, starless night contains fewer candlepower units than any other night in the preceding twelve months. We could take it, in a roundabout way, that tonight is December 22, the longest night of the year, and insist with some logic that the length of its darkness aggregates more darkness and that therefore this is indeed the "darkest evening of the year." But poetry usually works by common sense, not on riddles that ingenuity must solve. It's just too complicated to explain this line as telling us that tonight is the winter solstice. Probably we do best to take the line as an expressive exaggeration, the way people always talk about the weather: "There's enough snow out there to bury the barn." "It hasn't rained so much since Noah." "It's the darkest night of the whole damned year."

In the third stanza, the little horse does what horses do; he shudders or shakes, standing still in the cold night. To the driver, who still feels foolish pausing to gaze at snow in the woods, the horse's jingling harness bells seem like the horse's reproach. The jingling is another image—so far we've had images of sight (*to watch*), of touch (*frozen lake*), and of sound (*bells*)—and now the sound images multiply: "the sweep / Of easy wind and downy flake." Notice that images often appeal to more than one sense. If *frozen* is an image of cold in *frozen lake,* it is also an image of sight and touch, because we know what a frozen lake looks like and feels like. And *the sweep* is a swooshing sound, but it's also (at least distantly) a visual broom moving.

The phrase *easy wind* is not an image at all. We could not draw (or play on an instrument, or hear) an easy wind as opposed to a difficult wind or an uneasy one. Does it mean anything at all to call the wind easy? First, let us paraphrase, using alternative words. Perhaps this wind is light and gentle— *easy* as "full of ease," like the softness of *downy* that *easy* is parallel to. If this paraphrase is accurate, someone might ask why the poet doesn't call the wind "light and gentle" or, to keep line length the same, just "gentle." We answer that *gentle* is not the same as *easy* and *easy* does it better; the paraphrase is only intellectual, and *easy* says it better because of its sound. It is a long and luxuriant word. That long *e* stretches itself out like a big cat on a sofa, and then the *z*-sound (spelled with an *s*) slinks sensuously and stretches again into the shorter *e*-sound of the *y*. These two syllables take longer to say than half a line elsewhere in the poem.

I would not argue that, in this word, "sound imitates sense" the way the sound of *drop* or *squish* is similar to the meanings of those words. (When sound imitates sense, we call it **onomatopoeia**.) I am not sure that a light wind speaks in long *es* or in *zs*. But I am sure that the grateful tongue delights in this word, picking up the long *e* of *sweep* and looking ahead to the long *e* that ends *downy,* and that these words, giving us in our minds the qualities of the scene, at the same time give us a sound-pleasure. We have two pleasures at once, one in our minds as we assent to a description, the other in our mouths as the poet arranges vowels and consonants, much as a chef arranges flavors for our pleasure.

We have concentrated on *easy. Downy* gives pleasure also. The *y* picks up the line's earlier *e* sound; the *ow* picks up a vowel from *sounds* in the line before. (This repetition of vowel sounds is called **assonance**.) If you don't know the word *downy,* look it up. (Always look up words you are not certain of.) *Down* means a good many things; among others it means goosefeathers, soft and white, and *downy* is an adjective made from the noun *down.* Because down is soft (touch) and white (vision), it gives us two kinds of image at once, and perhaps also distantly gives us an image of the snow as a great white bird. It is also a rural image, connected with barnyard and countryside. If Frost had tried comparing the whiteness of the snow to the whiteness of a sailboat's sails, his comparison would have gone far from the poem's world. Finally, the word *down* works its power on us for at least one more reason: it reminds us of the direction in which, relentlessly, snow must fall.

By the end of the third stanza, the poem has erected a dramatic conflict, like a story or a play. The conflict lives in the mind of the speaker, who attributes one side of his feeling to his horse; of course, it is the speaker who thinks it queer to pause where he pauses; at the same time, it is the speaker who stops to gaze into the *lovely* beauty of the wood, exercising the other side of his feeling. He is "of two minds about it," in the old expression. In the final stanza, mind 1 writes the first line and mind 2 answers with the second, third, and fourth; the mind with the most lines has the last word.

In our daily lives, we are often ambivalent—of two minds, and sometimes of three or four—about what we do. Often, two desires are in conflict; the woods are lovely, but I have duties; the scoop of ice cream will taste good, but I will get fat; I want to see this movie, but I want to pass that test. Human beings are ambivalent by nature: we often find ourselves headed in two directions at the same time. In our deepest selves, we are never one-hundred percent *anything,* neither loving nor hating, and if we tell ourselves we are pure, we fool ourselves.

Poetry expresses human ambivalence. That's one reason poetry is complicated—because people are complicated, and because poetry is true to people. Bad poems are often bad—lying, distorted, phony, sentimental—exactly because they deny ambivalent feeling. This poem is excellent (here is one criterion for excellence in poetry) because it embodies with honest clarity true human ambivalence. This poem is almost *about* ambivalence and its conflicts; at least it acts out a particular ambivalence with so much clarity that the poem in the reader's mind can stand for other conflicts. What for Frost's speaker was a quarrel between woods and duties can translate, in our lives, into a quarrel between birdwatching or writing a letter. When one set of particulars can stand in for another set of relationships, we have a **symbol**.

Symbols raise another subject: in interpreting a poem, where does the reader stop? Many people find further complexities—"levels," "meanings"—in this poem. Some readers have found this poem suicidal and claimed that it contains a wish to die. People have often tended to look for a death wish in Frost's work because, in his lifetime, Frost spoke about suicidal feelings. But should we *therefore* consider that when Frost's speaker looks into the woods, he takes the woods as a symbol for death and longs for the darkness of his own death? Not *therefore,* at any rate, for then we would be leaping from life to poem as if it were always possible to make equations between the facts of the life and the facts of the poem.

What can we say, finally, about the meaning of this poem—looking only at the poem itself? Meaning is not paraphrase, nor is it singling out words for their special effects, nor is it accounting for rhythm and form. It is all these things, and it is more. Meaning is what we try to explicate: the whole impression of a poem on our minds, our emotions, and our bodies. We can never wholly explicate a poem, any more than we can explicate ourselves, or another person—but we can try to come close. The only way to stretch and exercise our ability to read a poem is to try to understand and to name our whole response.

Then how shall we understand this last stanza, and the implications of the whole poem? Implication is the word I want to use. Although I may understand what is said on the surface, another voice speaks from underneath the poem—not a "hidden meaning," implying that the poet is a riddler or an Easter-egg-hider, but a second language of the poem, which exists underneath the first language. This is the quiet voice of implication, the poet's psyche speaking to the reader's psyche in a language just underneath the common-sense words, a language only these words in this order could manage to imply.

A poet makes a contract with the reader: I agree to use words as thoroughly as I can; you agree to read them the same way. Because this is a poem, we shall do well to examine even the simplest words. First, we have the bald statement of attraction: "The woods are lovely, dark, and deep." The word *lovely* has the word *love* in it, as *downy* included *down*. So the woods pertain somehow to love. *Dark* and *deep* go together, not just for their **alliteration** (the repetition of initial consonants). The woods are dark in this evening, filling up with snow (by definition, white); and they are deep, like a vessel with room for the filling. The woods are mysterious, perhaps a place suitable for hiding, and this sensation of mystery has an attraction like the attraction people feel for each other; so the woods are *lovely*. *Dark and deep* work together as a double adjective, explaining the *kind* of "lovely." How different the line would be if Frost had punctuated it differently and used a comma after *dark*. "The woods are lovely, dark, and deep"—pronounced as punctuated—makes a different sound, and even a different *meaning*: the extra comma makes the three adjectives enumerate separate qualities of the woods; in the line as Frost wrote it, instead of enumerated qualities we have a rush of feeling. Such difference a comma makes!

Apparently, the feelings in this poem are universal, and all of us find in ourselves, on occasion, a desire to abandon the track of everyday duty and embrace the peace of nothingness. Perhaps I go too far, in trying to name the unnameable, with the paraphrase "the peace of nothingness." My naming is not so good as Frost's naming and some readers will prefer their own different naming. "The peace of nothingness" attempts to paraphrase a feeling that, for some people, apparently seems suicidal—and for others merely sleepy. My inadequate phrase attempts to bring together the two sides.

Different readings can be valid—but *not all readings*. There are limits to the validity of interpretations, and these limits are set by the poem. One reader tells me that the poem indicates a desire to put a bullet through one's head. Another says the poem implies that Frost wants to move to Arizona and escape the winter. The suicidal reading is only a little askew. If all of us sometimes desire what we might call peace or oblivion, such feeling is not entirely alien to the desire to die. Perhaps sleep—"death's second self," as Shakespeare called it—will satisfy the desire. The speaker in this poem expresses a taste for darkness that resembles the wish to die but does not duplicate it; to find a death wish in this poem is only an exaggeration, like calling the pain of a stubbed toe "excruciating agony." On the other hand, the reader who finds Frost on his way to Arizona simply misreads; there is nothing like it in the poem. Presumably, the cold of the poem made the reader think of a warm climate and then attribute the thought to Frost's poem. To avoid misinterpretation, always take care to distinguish the source of a notion: does Phoenix happen in the poem or in your own head?

After talking about one poem for so many pages, I think of Whitman's little poem about listening to the "Learn'd Astronomer," who spoke in scientific terms about astronomical data. Whitman's response is to go outside the lecture hall and look up "in perfect silence at the stars." Read again Robert Frost's simple, pleasurable, universal poem:

Stopping by Woods on a Snowy Evening

Whose woods these are I think I know.
His house is in the village though;
He will not see me stopping here
To watch his woods fill up with snow.

My little horse must think it queer
To stop without a farmhouse near
Between the woods and frozen lake
The darkest evening of the year.

10   He gives his harness bells a shake
To ask if there is some mistake.
The only other sound's the sweep
Of easy wind and downy flake.

The woods are lovely, dark and deep,
But I have promises to keep,
And miles to go before I sleep,
And miles to go before I sleep.

Questions and Exercises

1. What happens when Frost repeats a line?

2. Whose feet these are I think I know.
   His head's beneath a T-shirt though.
   He will not mind an ice cube here . . .

   Complete a fourth line.

3. Rewrite the poem, staying as close to the original as you can, but change all the important words. Use a thesaurus or a dictionary of synonyms, if you like. Let *whose* and *I* and *his* remain; change *woods, know, horse,* and so forth. You could begin "Whose forest this is, I recognize . . ." Compare different versions in class, deciding which is closest to the original, and which most ingenious. Compare the class versions with Frost's original. (Sometimes it works best to concentrate on one stanza only or to divide the class into four sections, each doing one stanza.)

William Carlos Williams, "so much depends"

Robert Frost was a traditional poet, writing in rhyme and meter. During Frost's lifetime, the slightly younger William Carlos Williams made a different sort of poem. Williams was born in Rutherford, New Jersey, where he practiced medicine for more than forty years, after his education in Switzerland, at the University of Pennsylvania, and in Germany. He wrote free verse, lines of poetry strong in rhythm but free of the regular repetitions of meter. He is another good poet; his poems force us to acknowledge kinds of excellence foreign to Frost's excellence. Williams invents original shapes in his poems and forces us to become aware of a poem as a made object. He was a poet of images, of the *eye;* but, as we will see, he wrote also for the *ear* and placed his words for our maximum pleasure in their sound.

So much depends upon a red wheelbarrow, glazed with rainwater, beside the white chickens.

This sentence is unlikely to elicit much response. It seems nonsensical, unworthy of attention. In a way, attention is exactly the problem. This poem by William Carlos Williams is printed above not as a poem but as a one-sentence paragraph in which the words have not been *attended to. Attention,* which Williams brings to bear by his use of *lines,* is exactly what we miss.

When someone asks the difference between poetry and prose, I like to answer. "Poetry is jagged on the right-hand side of the page." Poetry is written in lines, and lines make a big difference. Lines act like musicians' notations. They tell us how to say a poem aloud, or how to hear it. Yet, most beginning readers of poetry read either as if lines didn't exist at all or as if the sense always stopped at the lines' ends.

Knowing that the wheelbarrow sentence is really a poem, let us try putting it into lines, starting with the most obvious arrangement:

So much depends upon
a red wheelbarrow
glazed with rainwater
beside the white chickens.

I call this arrangement obvious, because the lines break where the phrases pause. If you were saying the prose sentence aloud and had to pause three times because you were out of breath, you would pause where these lines end. As it happens, these linebreaks are not the poet's—but if they were, let us see what we could find in them. Putting the sentence into these lines must affect the meaning of the sentence, if we take "meaning" to be the words' total impact on the reader. In search of meaning, let us first try paraphrase: "These things are really important: a small red cart with wheels on it, with water on it from a rainshower, next to the poultry." (I cannot paraphrase the simplicities of *red* and *white.*) When I asserted that meaning must be changed by the line arrangement, my claim was not grand; putting these clauses into lines slows down the sentence, adding pauses greater than the pauses we would make if we spoke the sentence as prose. The pauses isolate the clauses within brackets of time, made visible on poetry's page by the white spaces around the poem. The results are focus, intensity, concentration, and emphasis.

In the lines quoted, the last three make visual images, and the first line insists on the importance of what follows—therefore, on the importance of the visual. To isolate these lines, by pauses and spaces, is to emphasize the singularity of each unit and to draw closer attention to the redness of the wheelbarrow, to the wetness of the rain, to the whiteness of the chickens. The greater emphasis of these lines *intensifies* meaning.

But not sufficiently for William Carlos Williams. Here is the poem as he actually wrote it:

> so much depends
> upon
>
> a red wheel
> barrow
>
> glazed with rain
> water
>
> beside the white
> chickens

By this arrangement, meaning is further enhanced, sound is released, and the poem is made exact, fixed, permanent—like a carving. The prose sentence from page 9 is repeated exactly, but, by breaking the words into these lines, Williams makes an object; and his object enforces a meaning.

First, *look* at the poem William Carlos Williams wrote. Look at its shape on the page, without reading or understanding a word; the poem already begins to make a statement, saying "I am orderly; I am arranged on purpose; there is nothing sloppy or careless or inadvertent in me; I will reward careful reading." The visual statement of a poem on the page may be the least of poetry's sensuous qualities, but it exists.

The visual shape suggests an audible performance, behaving like musical notation. In its true form, the poem has more pauses than it had in the four-line version, and more variety in the pauses; generally, the pause between the lines of each two-line stanza is short—like the pause between *wheel* and *barrow*—and the pause that leaps the larger white space between stanzas is longer. But there are degrees of difference within this generalization. Syntax and sense require that the pause between *rain* and *water* be shorter than the pause between *white* and *chickens.* With seven places for pauses at line-ends, the poem calls for seven different degrees of pause.

More pause creates still more emphasis, a more concentrated focus. We see this most clearly in *wheelbarrow: wheel / barrow,* where a linebreak gives us two nouns for one, shows us the original parts of a compound word, and makes a statement about the importance of observing the physical world. This linebreak gives us twice as much *thingness,* making us recognize wheels as separate, barrow as separate, and wheelbarrow as a synthesis of the two, which is also a third thing. In *rainwater,* we see the same act repeated. The first line's *depend / upon* splits a verb phrase into its parts (like the later splitting of compound nouns) and hangs the preposition from a verb that originally meant "hang from." In the last stanza, splitting *white* from *chickens* gives us at least a little more attention to the quality of the color than we get if *white chickens* is printed on one line.

But the poem's arrangement does more than intensify meaning and more than make a pretty shape. It releases varied sounds, two assonances in particular, that grant the reader a pleasure equivalent to the eye's pleasure in seeing *red, rain,* and *white.* In the four-line arrangement, the third line was "glazed with rainwater." When the poet did it his way, the fifth line of the poem becomes "glazed with rain," and the long diphthong *āi* bursts twice into bloom. The flowering of the diphthong alters the pace of the line, for when the reader comes to *rain* and tastes the pleasure of the repeated sound, he or she stretches it a little; the *n* of "rain" allows the sound to be held on the tongue and savored.

The next pair of lines gives the same pleasure to the mouth alerted to assonance. The long-*i* diphthong in the second syllable of *beside* finds itself mirrored and repeated in the vowel of *white,* buried midline in the earlier version. Both times the word stretched and exalted is a sensuous and meaningful word, *rain* describing the sources of *water, white* the color of chickens; insofar as sound specifies more attention given to a word, assonance impinges upon our understanding, and the coincidence of vowel sounds contributes to meaning.

This little poem by William Carlos Williams is not a vessel loaded with philosophical or intellectual content; it does not resemble the works of Plato or Thomas Jefferson. The poem does have meaning, but its statement belongs more to the area of sensation than to the area of thought.

Feelings and ideas happen at the same time; ideas carry feelings with them, and feelings imply ideas. If Williams's poem insists on the importance of the physical world, the *insistence* is an emotional value placed on a philosophical idea. And the poem makes its statement not by generalizing but by giving a particular example—something of the world, visible, stared at, and held to. The visual details are perceived with passion and necessity, as if they were railings on a narrow bridge, onto which we hold in order not to fall into the chasm below. The intensity of this experience, which makes the poem valuable, derives largely from the poet's skill in manipulating sounds. Here it is again:

so much depends
upon

a red wheel
barrow

glazed with rain
water

beside the white
chickens

Exercise

Using different words, imitate the shape and sound of Williams's poem. A form is anything done a second time. The first time somebody wrote a sonnet, it was not a sonnet; the second time somebody wrote one, and the third—then we began to call them sonnets. Consider that you are writing a newly discovered form of poetry called a wheelbarrow. You can define a wheelbarrow as four two-line stanzas; each first line has three words, each second line has one word; each one-word second line has two syllables; each three-word first line has either three or four syllables.

Here's one student's wheelbarrow:

it is extremely
serious

to watch the
teacher

writing long words
in chalk

on blackboards
all morning

Which lines fit the form? Which don't?

Wallace Stevens, "Disillusionment of Ten O'Clock"

A third example of a good poem is one by Wallace Stevens, who was a friend of William Carlos Williams when they were both young and who met Robert Frost in Florida when both poets were old. After graduation from Harvard and the New York University Law School, Stevens practiced law in New York City; he lived in Greenwich Village and spent much time with other writers who gathered there. In his late thirties, he became associated with the Hartford Accident and Indemnity Company, serving as a vice-president for the last decade of his life.

Disillusionment of Ten O'Clock   (1915)

The houses are haunted
By white night-gowns.
None are green,
Or purple with green rings,
Or green with yellow rings,
Or yellow with blue rings.
None of them are strange,
With socks of lace
And beaded ceintures.
10 People are not going
To dream of baboons and periwinkles.
Only, here and there, an old sailor,
Drunk and asleep in his boots,
Catches tigers
In red weather.

With this poem I will not provide an explication; instead, I will ask questions, hoping to suggest ways of arriving at an explication. Read the poem several times, slowly, before you begin to read the questions.

Questions

1. In the title, is *ten o'clock* A.M. or P.M.? What in the poem suggests one or the other?

2. Think of the word *disillusionment*. Take it apart. What might this word have to do with the hour of ten o'clock? Are there illusions or disillusions in the body of the poem?

3. Does *haunted* tell you anything about the title? How?

4. There is a ghost in the word *haunted*. Ordinarily, there would be no ghost in the word *night-gown*. What word makes *haunted* go with *night-gown*?

5. Do you know whether there are bodies inside these nightgowns?

6. In lines 3 through 6, the poet presents images in the negative. Can we learn anything from being told that something does *not* exist? What do these negatives imply? What is missing from these houses?

7. In line 7, *strange* can be a vague and imprecise word; in this context, do other words define *strange* and make it less vague?

8. A *ceinture* is a belt, and the word was already unusual when Stevens published the poem in 1915. Why would a poet use a word most readers would have to look up? Can a poet mean something simply by using an outlandish word?

9. In line 10, we finally hear of people. Are these the people whose houses are haunted by white nightgowns? How can you tell?

10. Stevens could have broken his lines differently:

People are not
Going to dream of baboons . . .

or:

People are not going to dream
Of baboons . . .

Can you think of why it was a good idea to break the line where Stevens broke it?

11. In this poem, baboons and periwinkles are examples that are parallel to other examples. What words in this poem are they parallel to? Why?

12. What is the relationship of the last four lines of the poem to the lines that came earlier?

13. Why is the sailor drunk? What is he doing? How do these details contrast with the main scene of the poem?

14. Someone has said that in this poem Stevens was eating his cake and having it too. Comment.

15. Frost's poem was written in metrical four-line stanzas. Williams's poem was tightly structured free verse. Characterize sound and rhythm in this poem, pointing out particular effects. Can you find assonance? Alliteration?

To find other poems by these poets, check the index.

CHAPTER TWO

Poems Are Made of Words

Apoem is single, whole, and seamless, but, to discuss it, we need to treat it as if we could take it apart and examine its elements as we can examine elements of a machine: this is a carburetor, which mixes air and fuel; this is a spark plug. . . . The parts of an internal-combustion engine, however, are genuinely separate; in a poem, you cannot detach rhythm from imagery except by paying attention to the one element rather than to the other; within a poem, rhythm and imagery are properties of the same words.

Before we concentrate on the elements of poetry, let us look at the medium of poetry, which is words. Many people assume that poetry's materials are emotions and ideas. Emotions and ideas exist *in* poems or *through* poems, and we must account for them in paraphrase when we explicate, but they are not poetry's material. If we argued that emotions and ideas are poetry's material, we would have to claim that trees and mountains are the medium of landscape painting. Canvas and paint are the painter's material, and poems are made of words.

Reading poetry, we read words used with the greatest *energy* and *fixity*.

Fixity is the unique correctness and immovability of a word in its place. If you change almost any word in a long novel, you change the novel very little; if you change a word in a good poem, you change the poem considerably: "His house is in the hamlet though" would change Frost's poem by substituting *hamlet* for *village*. This fixity is partly a function of size, but not entirely; it is a measure of relative exactness in use. Poetry does not acknowledge synonyms. *Roget's Thesaurus* or any other dictionary of synonyms lists words that resemble each other in their meaning, but a poet makes poems by manipulating the small differences in meaning between synonyms; think of the differences between *hamlet* and *village,* or the many differences among *hide, conceal, cover up, secrete, screen, obscure, suppress, veil, disguise, camouflage, shroud.*

Energy comes from the efficiency with which the poet uses language; poems are made of words used efficiently. When I write this sentence, I sound like an engineer—and I want to. An efficient machine turns energy received into a nearly equal amount of energy put out. Sloppy language

14

wastes energy, often by failing to say what it means; at best, it uses more words than are necessary, perhaps three vague words in place of the precise one. "Glazed with rain / water" is better than "covered all over with dampness as a result of precipitation." *Good poetry is the perfect machine of language.*

To use words most efficiently, the writer must be aware of their wholeness, of their dictionary senses or **denotations**, and of **connotations**—the associations not usually found in a dictionary. The poet uses the history of a word, its family, its origins, its associations. *Snow* carries "whiteness" with it, a connotation. Other connotations for snow include cold and winter. Further associations can become less universal and more particular. For a Northerner, *snow* may include "skiing"; for a Sun Belt resident, *snow* may include the notion of travel. If the associations of *snow* include not only travel but a three-day drive in a Plymouth that uses too much oil, connotation has given way to private association. Much connotation is public enough for use not only by poets and not only for literature. Real estate agents do not sell *houses;* they sell *homes*—the same buildings, but connoting comfort, warmth, and a dog sleeping in front of the fireplace. A *sanitation engineer* may do the same work a plumber used to do, but the title sounds more impressive. If poets use connotations to tell us honest feelings, politicians and lobbyists can use connotations for deceit. *Honorarium* sounds better than *payment, payment* better than *bribe.* All three words are heavy with connotation.

Concepts of denotation and connotation are useful, but we need to understand that they don't tell us everything. The *con*notation of *wheelbarrow* does not include its compoundness, revealed only when a poet splits it back into two words: *wheel barrow.* And when a word has different *de*notations or dictionary meanings, the peripheral definitions of the word in the poem hover around the central ones.

Poets do not always use every potential meaning of a word. By their context, they can employ some connotations or unused denotations and shut off others. Thomas Hardy's poem "During Wind and Rain" includes the line

How the sick leaves reel down in throngs.

A dictionary may tell us that to reel is to be thrown off balance, to stagger, to move in a circle, to dance a reel, or to pull in a fishing line. In the context of the poem, not every meaning becomes active. Because the word before *leaves* is *sick, reel,* as in "stagger"—like a sick person too weak to walk— becomes strengthened by context. Earlier in this poem, Hardy speaks of music: "They sing their dearest songs . . . / Treble and tenor and bass / And one to play . . . ," and although the songs may be hymns or folk songs, the "dance" part of *reel* shows signs of life. (All of these meanings are related: *reel* originally meant a kind of spool, and evolved into all sorts of circular motions.) Connotations interweave, and peripheral denotations act like connotations. In this poem's context, the stagger-meaning is foremost, the dance-meaning acts like a strong connotation, and the fishing-meaning hovers unused in the distance. If a reader, when first glancing at this line, thought of *reel* as fishing reel, the line would remain obscure until the reader looked for another denotation of *reel*.

When leaves are compared to dancers, the poet has made a metaphor. We should mention one other matter connecting word and metaphor. Many readers leap to interpret a word as metaphor when the poet has used it literally. The insistence on the fanciful, at the expense of the plain, is a common source of misreading. Edwin Arlington Robinson begins a stanza about a dying man

> Blind, with but a wandering hour to live . . .

Many readers see the word *blind* and think that Robinson means "obtuse" in the common metaphorical use of the word—as in "Good grief! Are you *blind?*" But the rest of the stanza reveals that the man is sightless. Readers who hold on to the "obtuse" meaning find the poem highly obscure. It is wise to remember a rule of thumb: take poems literally until they make you take them figuratively. "Sightless" is the denotation of the word *blind*. *Blind* has meant "sightless" for a long time; the first citation in the *Oxford English Dictionary* (*OED,* that wonderful, enormous dictionary that quotes words in contexts as they change over history) is dated A.D. 1000. The first citation of *blind* as "obtuse" is also A.D. 1000; the metaphorical use is as ancient as the literal.

Reading old poems, we need the *OED* to let us know how poets used words—efficiently, with energy and fixity—in their own times, for words change. When the eighteenth-century poet Alexander Pope spoke of *science* he did not mean physics or chemistry but knowledge in general; our word *science* comes from *scio,* Latin for "I know."

Reading new poems, we can use the *OED* also, because many poets— seeking the energy that comes from using words in their wholeness—refer by their context to a word's history, its old or original meanings. Richard Wilbur is a contemporary American who likes to play with **etymology**, the study of word origins and history. In his poem "Lamarck Elaborated," he pretends to believe genetic theories that say that genes transmit acquired characteristics.* The theory is untrue, but, with his imagination, Wilbur tries out a world in which the things of the world created our bodies. The sun, for instance, made our eyes. Wilbur writes a stanza of complicated wordplay:

> The yielding water, the repugnant stone,
> The poisoned berry and the flaring rose
> Attired in sense the tactless finger-bone
> And set the taste-buds and inspired the nose.

Paraphrased, the stanza says that we acquired touch, taste, and smell by acts of touching, tasting, and smelling. Water, which gives to the touch, and stone,

---

* French naturalist Jean Baptiste Pierre Antoine de Monet, Chevalier de Lamarck (1744– 1829). His flawed theory of evolution was nevertheless an important forerunner of the work of Charles Darwin.

which doesn't—which pushes it back, which is what *repugnant* means—
attired (clothed) *in sense* (in our senses) *the finger-bone,* which had formerly
been clumsy or without tact; *tact* comes from the word for "touch," as in
tactile, so *tactless* by etymology means "untouching": before it was clothed in
sensation, the fingerbone was without touch. The *berry* that poisons us, which
we distinguish by taste, *sets* our taste buds, the way a gardener sets out plants.
The flaring rose (flared like a nostril to smell) *inspired* our noses. *Inspired,* in
one common usage, means "invented" ("Monday Night Football was the inspi-
ration of Roone Arledge") but actually comes from a Latin word that means "to
breathe in."

Here are a few poems—with questions intended to sharpen your sensitivity
to the manipulation of words.

Hogwash   (1944)

The tongue that mothered such a metaphor
Only the purest purist could despair of.

Nobody ever called swill sweet but isn't
Hogwash a daisy in a field of daisies?

What beside sports and flowers could you find
To praise better than the American language?

Bruised by American foreign policy
What shall I soothe me, what defend me with

But a handful of clean unmistakable words—
10 Daisies, daisies, in a field of daisies?
                    —*Robert Francis**

Questions

  1. In the first line, what happens if you remove *mothered* and substitute "fathered"?
    "conjured"? "created"? "gathered"? "mounted"? "built up"? "constructed"? What
    are the associations of *mothered* and of the substitute words?

  2. How does the word *swill* find its way into this poem? Would "junk" be just as
    good? "Garbage"?

  3. Look up the word *daisy* to check on its ancestry. What are the insides of *daisy*? If
    you used "tulip," how would its different history match the rest of the poem? Is
    daisy better for this poem, or just different? If the word were "flower," would the
    poem be less than it is?

* See page 235 for a note about Robert Francis. Brief biographical notes on poets whose
work is included in this book precede their poems in "A Gathering of Poems," which begins on
page 182. For rapid location of dates and other information about any author represented in this
volume, look for the italicized page number following the entry for his or her name in the index.

4. Does *defend,* in its associations, relate to other words in this poem?

5. In the last stanza, what sort of *handful* would you have if your hand were full of words? A handful of swill? What does the poet compare words to?

During Wind and Rain   (1917)

They sing their dearest songs—
He, she, all of them—yea,
Treble and tenor and bass,
    And one to play;
With the candles mooning each face. . . .
    Ah, no; the years O!
How the sick leaves reel down in throngs!

They clear the creeping moss—
Elders and juniors—aye,
Making the pathway neat
    And the garden gay;
And they build a shady seat. . . .
    Ah, no; the years, the years;
See, the white storm-birds wing across!

They are blithely breakfasting all—
Men and maidens—yea,
Under the summer tree,
    With a glimpse of the bay,
While pet fowl come to the knee. . . .
    Ah, no; the years O!
And the rotten rose is ript from the wall.

They change to a high new house,
He, she, all of them—aye,
Clocks and carpets and chairs
    On the lawn all day,
And brightest things that are theirs. . . .
    Ah, no; the years, the years;
Down their carved names the rain-drop ploughs.
              —*Thomas Hardy*

Questions

1. Consider the associations of *creeping.* Which are used? Which unused? Does the word make a comparison?

2. In line 21, Hardy uses the word *ript.* Substitute *pulled* and consider the differences. Substitute "descends" for *is ript.* Discuss the differing associations of the words. Discuss the differing grammar.

3. In line 22, try these substitutes for *high:* "tall," "white," "brand," "dark," and "low." Is difference in image a difference in value?

4. The last word of the poem is *ploughs.* How do its denotation, connotations, sound, and grammar—the whole word, family associations and all—contribute to this poem? Does the whole word *conclude* the poem?

good times   (1969)

my daddy has paid the rent
and the insurance man is gone
and the lights is back on
and my uncle brud has hit
for one dollar straight
and they is good times
good times
good times

10 my mama has made bread
and grampaw has come
and everybody is drunk
and dancing in the kitchen
and singing in the kitchen
oh these is good times
good times
good times

oh children think about the
good times
                    —*Lucille Clifton*

Questions

1. The speaker in *good times* uses a different English. Discuss the import of *is* instead of *are.*

2. How do words change when we repeat them? What is the effect of repeating *good times?*

3. Does this poem make you think of music? How?

Silence   (1935)

My father used to say,
"Superior people never make long visits,
have to be shown Longfellow's grave
or the glass flowers at Harvard.
Self-reliant like the cat—
that takes its prey to privacy,
the mouse's limp tail hanging like a shoelace from its mouth—
they sometimes enjoy solitude,
and can be robbed of speech
10 by speech which has delighted them.

The deepest feeling always shows itself in silence;
not in silence, but restraint."
Nor was he insincere in saying, "Make my house your inn."
Inns are not residences.

—Marianne Moore

Questions

1. In the second line, the poet uses the word *superior.* Make a list of words that might be considered synonyms and that would make sense in this context. Discuss the difference each substitution would make to the poem.

2. Longfellow's grave is in Cambridge, Massachusetts, a city that also contains Harvard University, which shows in a museum some remarkably realistic glass reproductions of flowers—a favorite stop for tourists. What is the connection of the sentence containing these objects with the sentences that make the rest of this poem? In lines 3 and 4, what words provide the implicit connection?

3. In this poem, where does the idea of silence enter, after the title?

4. What do you make of this cat? Have you known cats who liked to show off their prey, who are not reticent at all? If you have, does the knowledge bother you in reading this poem? Do you feel that the cat somehow seems more important to the poem than its use as an illustrative simile could warrant? How?

5. How does the author show that although *Superior people* enjoy being by themselves, they are equipped to encounter others?

6. "Not in silence, but restraint." What is the difference? Why does the author say one thing and then correct it? What is the effect of using two words instead of one?

7. The last two lines make a distinction by means of definitions. How does this verbal contrast grow out of earlier lines of the poem?

When President John F. Kennedy was inaugurated in 1961, he invited Robert Frost to read a poem as part of the ceremony. Frost recited this poem, which he had written years before.

The Gift Outright   (1942)

The land was ours before we were the land's.
She was our land more than a hundred years
Before we were her people. She was ours
In Massachusetts, in Virginia,
But we were England's, still colonials,
Possessing what we still were unpossessed by,
Possessed by what we now no more possessed.
Something we were withholding made us weak
Until we found out that it was ourselves
10 We were withholding from our land of living,
And forthwith found salvation in surrender.
Such as we were we gave ourselves outright
(The deed of gift was many deeds of war)
To the land vaguely realizing westward,

But still unstoried, artless, unenhanced,
Such as she was, such as she would become.

Questions

1. Frost *almost* recited the poem as written. For the next-to-last word, he said *will* instead of *would*. How did this alter the meaning of the poem?

2. Distinguish different sorts of possession. Why does Frost use the same word when the reader must learn to distinguish different meanings for it? What allows you to find different meanings for one word in a single poem?

3. What sort of a phrase is *salvation in surrender?*

4. Does *realize* usually take an object? Does it here? How does the grammar help to define this use of the word?

5. Notice the many balances throughout the poem. List them.

Here's an old poem, written during Queen Elizabeth I's reign, with its spelling modernized. Ben Jonson was a great playwright, a rival and friend of Shakespeare. He wrote on the death of his firstborn son.

On My First Son   (1603)

Farewell, thou child of my right hand, and joy;
My sin was too much hope of thee, loved boy.
Seven years thou wert lent to me, and I thee pay,
Exacted by thy fate, on the just day.
O, could I lose all father now. For why
Will man lament the state he should envy?
To have so soon 'scaped° world's, and flesh's, rage,   escaped
And if no other misery, yet age?
Rest in soft peace, and, asked, say here doth lie
10 Ben Jonson, his° best piece of poetry.   Jonson's
For whose sake, henceforth, all his vows be such,
As what he loves may never like too much.

Questions

1. In the third line, Jonson's word order puts *I* next to *thee,* which we would not do. *Thee* is the object of *pay,* and we would say "And I pay thee" or "And I pay you." In what sense is *pay* used?

2. How can Jonson call the day *just?* What other words—or what ideas carried by what words—support *just?*

3. How would you paraphrase *all father?*

4. Look up the word *poetry* in an etymological dictionary. How can Jonson use the word to stand in for his son?

5. The poem works by a series of contrasted words. What does *lament* contrast with? *rage? world's?*

6. Describe the contrast in the last line.

CHAPTER THREE

Images

An **image** is language that speaks to our senses, recording a sensuous experience. Poetry abounds in visual images, directed to the sense of sight, like "white chickens" or ". . . woods fill up with snow." Poetry also includes images of touch, taste, smell, and hearing. Hot-and-cold is tactile, a form of touch; here is a poem made of images for heat:

Heat   (1925)

O wind, rend open the heat,
cut apart the heat,
rend it to tatters.

Fruit cannot drop
through this thick air—
fruit cannot fall into heat
that presses up and blunts
the points of pears
and rounds the grapes.

10 Cut the heat—
plough through it,
turning it on either side
of your path.
                    —*H.D.*

The American poet H.D. (Hilda Doolittle) was one of the Imagist poets, a group dedicated to writing vivid and precise natural description. When H.D. asks the wind to *rend open the heat,* she gives the invisible heat a bulk that can be *cut apart,* therefore making an image of heat as something thick, substantial. Then she tells us how bulky it is: "Fruit cannot drop / through this thick air." These lines imply a natural scene with fruit trees, and air so heavy that even a falling apple cannot penetrate it. H.D. communicates feeling through exaggeration; she does not merely render like a snapshot. She describes the heat as a pressure, antigravitational and upward, blunting the pears that would otherwise be sharp-angled; heat acts, by its constant pressure, to make the grapes round. Then the poet ends her poem by returning implicitly to the wind for help—meteorological reality, because breezes blow away hot air—and when she asks the wind to become a plow, she again evokes the thickness, weight, and density of the heat, comparing it to earth a plow turns.

Images of touch like H.D.'s are not as common as visual images. In this old poem, a male poet describes the appearance of a woman:

Upon Julia's Clothes   (1648)

Whenas in silks my Julia goes,
Then, then, methinks, how sweetly flows
That liquefaction of her clothes.

Next, when I cast mine eyes, and see
That brave vibration, each way free,
O, how that glittering taketh me!
                    —Robert Herrick

Herrick describes something seen, and his images are visual. We are invited to *see* Julia in motion, wearing a silk dress. We don't know the color of the silk, and we know nothing of Julia's appearance except for her dress. We have the watery image of *flows* and *liquefaction,* and, later, her sway from side to side and the silk's glitter. The poem gives us only a partial picture of Julia, but we feel Herrick's whole delight: the visual images embody Herrick's feeling.

Poets use images to embody feelings; they use images instead of abstract explanations. Here's a poem by Allen Ginsberg:

First Party at Ken Kesey's with Hell's Angels   (1968)

Cool black night thru redwoods
cars parked outside in shade
behind the gate, stars dim above
the ravine, a fire burning by the side
porch and a few tired souls hunched over
in black leather jackets. In the huge
wooden house, a yellow chandelier
at 3 A.M. the blast of loudspeakers
hi-fi Rolling Stones Ray Charles Beatles
10 Jumping Joe Jackson and twenty youths
dancing to the vibration thru the floor,
a little weed in the bathroom, girls in scarlet
tights, one muscular smooth skinned man
sweating dancing for hours, beer cans

bent littering the yard, a hanged man
sculpture dangling from a high creek branch,
children sleeping softly in bedroom bunks,
And 4 police cars parked outside the painted
gate, red lights revolving in the leaves.
—*Allen Ginsberg*

The poem starts with a word of skin-feelings, *cool,* and ends with a compelling visual image. With the phrases *cool black, shade, stars dim,* and *fire burning,* Ginsberg sets a scene of contrasts. Then the poet speaks of *souls hunched over,* and we feel a tiredness. Next in the poem we have an image of sound, then dancing; the dancing comes as a visual image, but the word's associations contain muscular feeling as well. Then the poem leads us through everything seen, in a list of images—litter, a sculpture, children sleeping—with a cinematic effect, as if a camera panned slowly over a static scene, recording frame after frame of reality. Finally, the camera settles on the ominous image of the police cars with lights revolving. The poem's effect comes entirely from its images; there is no commentary at all.

The reader is *shown,* not *told.* Modern poets usually avoid abstract language, using concrete details instead. At the end of this poem, Ginsberg might have written about fear or apprehensiveness or dread or ominousness. Using instead the images *police cars parked* and *red lights revolving,* he communicates feeling directly; abstractions would have communicated the *names* of feelings, or *ideas* about feelings, not the feelings themselves.

H.D.'s heat was tactile, using images of touch. Ginsberg's poem is mostly visual but also uses images of touch and hearing. When Robert Frost, in "Stopping by Woods on a Snowy Evening," wrote about "the sweep / Of easy wind . . . ," he used an image of sound. Poets use images of smell more rarely ("the acrid odor of maple") and also images of taste: when Keats longs for wine, he calls it "a draught of vintage that hath been / Cool'd a long time . . ."; he appeals to the touch-sense of the tongue, or taste.

Read this brief poem by Rita Dove.

Lint (1989)

Beneath the brushed wing of the mallard
an awkward loveliness.

Under the cedar lid a mirror
and a box in a box.

Blue is all around
like an overturned bowl.

What to do with this noise
and persistent lint,

the larder filled past caring?
10 How good to revolve

on the edge of a system—
small, unimaginable, cold.
                    —Rita Dove

Notice how she starts her poem with a visual image, in the first line, before she tells us about "awkward loveliness" in the second line. The image props up the words about the image; the poem expresses sensuous love for the physical world. Without images that embody beauty and the love of beauty—"Blue is all around/ like an overturned bowl."—the poem would merely editorialize.

Images describe real things, and these poems come from the world we live in. Here are more poems of our world, with questions that mostly call attention to their images.

Nantucket   (1938)

Flowers through the window
lavender and yellow

changed by white curtains—
Smell of cleanliness—

Sunshine of late afternoon—
On the glass tray

a glass pitcher, the tumbler
turned down, by which

a key is lying—And the
10 immaculate white bed
        —William Carlos Williams

Questions

   1. Most of these images are visual. Is there an exception?

   2. Is *changed* an image? Is it an idea?

   3. Do these images carry feeling? Can you name the feeling?

   4. Can you paraphrase this poem for its ideas?

Denise Levertov is an American poet who takes great pleasure in observation of the world outside: sight, sound, coolness—and soot from chimneys.

The World Outside   (1964)

i

On the kitchen wall a flash
of shadow:
          swift pilgrimage
of pigeons, a spiral
celebration of air, of sky-deserts.
And on tenement windows
a blaze
      of lustred watermelon:
stain of the sun
10 westering somewhere back of Hoboken.

ii

The goatherd upstairs! Music
from his sweet flute
roves from summer to summer
in the dusty air of airshafts
and among the flakes
of soot that float
in a daze from chimney
to chimney—notes
remote, cool, speaking of slender
20 shadows under olive-leaves. A silence.

iii

Groans, sighs, in profusion,
with coughing, muttering, orchestrate
solitary grief; the crash of glass, a low voice
repeating over and over, 'No.
    No. I want my key. No you did not.
    No.'—a commonplace.
And in counterpoint, from other windows,
the effort to be merry—ay, maracas!
—sibilant, intricate—the voices wailing pleasure,
30   arriving perhaps at joy, late, after sets
have been switched off, and silences
are dark windows?
               —Denise Levertov

Questions

1. How many images can you find in this poem, appealing to how many senses?

2. When the poet says *pilgrimage,* what world does she enter? Is it figurative or literal? What other words go with *pilgrimage?*

3. Is there any sort of connection between "a blaze / of . . . watermelon" and "notes / remote, cool . . ."?

Gary Soto, a young Chicano poet who grew up working in the fields of the San Joaquin Valley in California, uses images from his experience as a farm worker. This poem comes from a sequence called "The Elements of San Joaquin":

Sun   (1977)

In June the sun is a bonnet of light
Coming up,
Little by little,
From behind a skyline of pine.

The pastures sway with fiddle-neck
Tassels of foxtail.

At Piedra
A couple fish on the river's edge,
Their shadows deep against the water.
10 Above, in the stubbled slopes,
Cows climb down
As the heat rises
In a mist of blond locusts,
Returning to the valley.

—Gary Soto

Questions

1. Compare this poem with H.D.'s "Heat," p. 22.

2. Distinguish the different senses Soto's images appeal to.

3. What kind of action lies behind *sway* and connects it with *fiddle-neck?* What does the poet compare the foxtail to?

Latin Night at the Pawnshop   (1987)

Chelsea, Massachusetts
Christmas, 1987

The apparition of a salsa band
gleaming in the Liberty Loan
pawnshop window:

Golden trumpet,
silver trombone,
congas, maracas, tambourine,
all with price tags dangling
like the city morgue ticket
on a dead man's toe.

—Martín Espada

Questions

1. The poet begins this imagistic poem with an abstraction, *apparition*. Does this word influence the way you see the musical instruments?
2. This poem ends with a simile. Or is it an image? Or both?
3. What does the poet accomplish by his final comparison?

We have been reading poems that describe realities. Allen Ginsberg's dancers and police cars are really there—we accept his word for it. Herrick's Julia wears silk clothing. H.D.'s poem exaggerates, but it does not invent a bizarre world. William Carlos Williams and Denise Levertov describe an objective world in language that specifies the way they take it in. Martín Espada's pawnshop is real.

But some poems use fantastic images to create worlds previously uncreated, as if the poet were recounting a dream. Here's a dreamy poem by Gregory Orr called "Washing My Face":

Last night's dreams disappear.
They are like the sink draining:
a transparent rose swallowed by its stem.

The last image conjures up something imaginary—*a transparent rose*. Because we know what roses look like, and because we know what transparency means, we can assemble these words into an image of a transparent rose. Then we understand that the transparent rose resembles the water in the sink, when we wash our faces at waking; the water makes a swirling shape like petals, as it disappears down the drain. The tenuousness of last night's dreams makes *transparent* feel right; the pleasant word *rose* implies that these disappearing dreams were happy ones.

Many contemporary Americans write poems that include realistic as well as fantastic images. These poems may move back and forth from one sort of concrete detail to another, from the seen to the dreamed and back again. James Wright wrote many poems that combined the two ways of seeing— looking out and looking in. Here is one:

Lying in a Hammock at William Duffy's Farm in Pine Island, Minnesota   (1961)

Over my head, I see the bronze butterfly,
Asleep on the black trunk,
Blowing like a leaf in green shadow.
Down the ravine behind the empty house,
The cowbells follow one another
Into the distances of the afternoon.
To my right,

In a field of sunlight between two pines,
The droppings of last year's horses
10   Blaze up into golden stones.
I lean back, as the evening darkens and comes on.
A chicken hawk floats over, looking for home.
I have wasted my life.

—*James Wright*

The first time one reads the poem, the last line is a shock. Some people feel that the last line is not earned, that it comes out of nowhere, that the poem fails because of a trick ending. Other readers report that, although they are shocked by the ending, it feels right. The issue is whether the last line grows naturally out of what goes before. Granted that it is a surprise, is it a cheap surprise or is it a surprise that leads to clear understanding?

Look back at what the poet sees, as he lies in the hammock at William Duffy's farm in Pine Island, Minnesota.* Notice the lethargy and passivity, not only of lying in a hammock but also of the many enclosures of space—in a hammock which is on a farm, which is in a town, which is named after an island, which is in a state. There are many layers to this cocoon.

First, the poet sees a butterfly colored bronze. But bronze is not only a color, it is a metal. If a butterfly were bronze, it would be permanent and inorganic. One of the connotations of *butterfly,* on the other hand, is the fragility of a brief life. In the phrase *bronze butterfly,* fantastic when we think of the metal bronze, we find the paradox of evanescence and solidity, change and permanence. We also see the color of bronze in contrast to the tree trunk's color, and then we see the butterfly move, "Blowing like a leaf in green shadow," as if its fragility returned quickly and the vision of permanence were brief. In the dream world, images can change quickly. The first three lines give us an extended image of clear contrasting colors—and contrasting senses of permanence and change. In the next three lines we cannot see the cows but, hearing the cowbells, we can visualize the ravine where they walk. Some of these words carry feeling without carrying images. "Into the distances of the afternoon" is not a visual image, nor is it addressed to any other sense, but the line takes the cows away from us, and the increasing distance—together with the emptiness of the house in the line before—introduces loneliness. The next four lines give us another scene and an absence of horses. We begin to realize that most things in this poem are gone. The horses have left behind only their manure.

In this poem, nothing goes down and stays down; nothing comes up without going down again. Any perception calls forth its opposite; if a butterfly is bronze, it is also moving in the wind. Even when the poet talks of the cowbells (more frail and distant than cows) he has them *follow one another* (which is warm and companionable) *into the distances,* which are far, lonely, and separate. Now, like a playwright keeping our attention with dramatic

---

* This poem comes from a tradition and an historical moment when the reader properly assumes the identity of "I" and the poet.

contrast, the poet has built to something glorious—and shocks us with horse manure; then he shocks us again by making horse manure glorious: it blazes up "into golden stones," an image of fantasy. The more we look at these words, the more we realize the complications of feeling that control them. The poem is not intellectually complex; it is complex in feeling, an emotional density embodied in images.

In the next line, the poet at first departs from imaging the world around him, and says *I lean back,* as if in passive withdrawal. Then he observes the world again, *as the evening darkens and comes on.* This is not the absence of light but the gathering of darkness, something coming close to him as everything else leaves. Loneliness slides toward something more desperate, and the poet writes the line that brings everything together. The next-to-last line is the climax of the poem and the skeleton key to the feelings of the poem: "A chicken hawk floats over, looking for home." In the mind of this lonely speaker, the bird is going home; even this predator, killer of the homely chicken, has a home to look for. By implication of the whole poem, and especially of the last line, the speaker does not have a home to go to. Instead, he lies in a hammock on somebody else's farm, and everything he looks at reminds him of his solitude and his unworthiness. We sense that wherever the poet looks in the landscape, he cannot help but see his own troubles.

Once you have understood the psychological state of the poem's speaker, its images make their melancholy point. At first sight, the butterfly was transformed into solidity and value—the speaker *wants* his life to change—then it becomes fragile and transitory again; but it remains beautiful in its sleep, as he does not, in his passivity. The *empty house* is the home the speaker is exiled from, as he is exiled from cows' company. Wherever the cowbells move, we know that eventually in the afternoon the cows will go home to be milked; the bells remind us of a destination. While the speaker remains static, passive, unchanging, even horse droppings are glorified! All the speaker can think to do, under the ominous pressure of darkness, is give up.

Try reading another poem by James Wright and following the track of its different images.

A Blessing   (1961)

Just off the highway to Rochester, Minnesota,
Twilight bounds softly forth on the grass.
And the eyes of those two Indian ponies
Darken with kindness.
They have come gladly out of the willows
To welcome my friend and me.
We step over the barbed wire into the pasture
Where they have been grazing all day, alone.
They ripple tensely, they can hardly contain their happiness
10   That we have come.
They bow shyly as wet swans. They love each other.
There is no loneliness like theirs.

At home once more,
They begin munching the young tufts of spring in the d rkness.
I would like to hold the slenderer one in my arms,
For she has walked over to me
And nuzzled my left hand.
She is black and white,
Her mane falls wild on her forehead,
20 And the light breeze moves me to caress her long ear
That is delicate as the skin over a girl's wrist.
Suddenly I realize
That if I stepped out of my body I would break
Into blossom.

Questions

1. Which images describe a real world? Which are fantastic? Interpret the fantastic images.

2. Why is it appropriate that there be two ponies, instead of one or three?

3. In the second line, is the verb *bounds* an image? What sense does it bring you?

4. The poet puts together two sentences—"They love each other. There is no loneliness like theirs"—that would not normally seem to go together. Can you defend the juxtaposition?

5. Analyze the image *young tufts of spring.*

Other poetry goes further into fantasy than James Wright's, Sometimes a poet will use wholly bizarre images—without even the connection of rose to sink, or horse droppings to gold—to tell the truth of feeling. Chilean poet Pablo Neruda received the gift of a pair of socks hand-knitted by a peasant woman. He was pleased at this tribute, and wrote a poem that embodied his pleasure. Robert Bly translated it from the Spanish.

Ode to My Socks   (tr. 1974)

Maru Mori brought me
a pair
of socks
which she knitted herself
with her sheep-herder's hands,
two socks as soft
as rabbits.
I slipped my feet
into them
10 as though into
two
cases
knitted
with threads of
twilight

and goatskin.
Violent socks,
my feet were
two fish made
20 of wool,
two long sharks
seablue, shot
through
by one golden thread,
two immense blackbirds,
two cannons,
my feet
were honored
in this way
30 by
these
heavenly
socks.
They were
so handsome
for the first time
my feet seemed to me
unacceptable
like two decrepit
40 firemen, firemen
unworthy
of that woven
fire,
of those glowing
socks.

Nevertheless
I resisted
the sharp temptation
to save them somewhere
50 as schoolboys
keep
fireflies,
as learned men
collect
sacred texts,
I resisted
the mad impulse
to put them
in a golden
60 cage
and each day give them
birdseed
and pieces of pink melon.
Like explorers
in the jungle who hand

over the very rare
green deer
to the spit
and eat it
70 with remorse,
I stretched out
my feet
and pulled on
the magnificent
socks
and then my shoes.

The moral
of my ode is this:
beauty is twice
80 beauty
and what is good is doubly
good
when it is a matter of two socks
made of wool
in winter.

—Pablo Neruda

Questions

1. When Neruda writes that he "resisted / the mad impulse / to put them / in a golden / cage . . . ," is he using an image to describe the socks? Did this help you know what they look like? If an image does not describe an object, what else can it describe?

2. In rapid succession, Neruda says that his feet were "two fish made / of wool," "two long sharks," "two immense blackbirds," and "two cannons." What does this do to advice about trying to take poems literally?

3. Find other examples of the fantastic image in this poem and interpret them.

4. Contrast:

> Dear Maru Mori,
>
> Thank you ever so much for your kind gift of a pair of socks. They are very pretty. They are warm. They fit me perfectly. I will wear them all the time. Mrs. Neruda likes them too. Thank you again.
>
> Yours truly,
> *Pablo Neruda*

CHAPTER FOUR

Figures of Speech, Especially Metaphors

Figures of speech are extraordinary, original, nonliteral uses of language, common to lively speech and literature. It would be literal to say "She walked slowly across the field." To say "She walked across the field as slowly as a snail with a pulled muscle" uses a figure of speech called a **simile**, which makes an explicit comparison using *like* or *as* or a verb like *seems* or *appears*. A **metaphor**, like a simile, talks about one thing in terms of another, but a metaphor's comparison is implicit; it does not use *like* or *as, seems* or *appears:* "She snailed her painful way across the field." Poems abound in metaphors. This chapter deals mainly with metaphors and similes, but includes a few other figures of speech.

Here is another poem by Gregory Orr that uses simile:

All Morning   (1975)

All morning the dream lingers.
I am like thick grass
in a meadow, still
soaked with dew at noon.
           —*Gregory Orr*

The poet compares himself to grass, declaring that he shares a quality with it. The simile works through a visual image—we *see* grass soaked with dew— but it is not the picture that does the comparing: a set of relationships makes the comparison work. This simile, like many, can be expressed as an equation: dew is to grass as dreams are to me. The comparison *states* that my dreams remain with me for a while, the way dew clings to a blade of grass. Besides this statement, there are two implications to the simile: eventually the dream/dew will vanish/evaporate; because dew brings nourishment to grass, dreaming has value for me.

If we omitted *like* from Orr's poem, we would have:

All morning the dream lingers.
I am thick grass
in a meadow, still
soaked with dew at noon.

The last three lines would make a metaphor, not a simile. The terms compared—*I* to *thick grass,* dreams to persistent dew—would remain the same, but the manner of the comparison would change. The reader is led by the simile: "I am *like* thick grass"; when the line becomes "I am thick grass," the guiding hand disappears and the reader may not know where to go.

Often, metaphor is more powerful than simile. Apparently it is older and more primitive, and derives from "primary process thinking," as psychologists describe it, in which dissimilar things are perceived as identical. Metaphor is the poetic mode of thought, flying across barriers of logic to assert identities. When small children speak of the leg of a table or the hand of a clock, they perceive a flesh-and-blood leg and a hand; the table, in their language, has power to walk, the clock can gesture and point. For the child, such metaphors are alive; for the adult they are dead. When the adult mind thinks in metaphor, it regains lost power misplaced in the pursuit of maturity.

All language began as metaphor, and in many of our words is buried an image that unites dissimilar things: a daisy was once a day's eye. In casual speech, we use continual **personification** (a figure of speech by which we humanize the nonhuman): clouds frown, fires rage, distant mountains glower, meadows look cheerful, zippers prove recalcitrant, the sun smiles, and the horizon looks inviting.

Metaphors in poems often happen quickly; we are moved without knowing what has touched us; unless we are explicating, we do not even notice that the poet has used metaphor. One of Robert Frost's best poems, "To Earthward" (page 150), begins by saying that, when he was young, feelings came easily; a tiny stimulus produced a strong response: "The petal of the rose," he says, "It was that stung." We understand *stung* as "gave pain," with the consciousness that this pain derives from pleasure too exquisite; the pang of beauty is overwhelming and therefore painful. If we think about it, *stung* is a metaphor, because a rose does not ordinarily sting anything. What stings us? A thorn pricks, but it does not sting. When Frost writes "The petal of the rose / It was that stung," he compares the soft petal of a flower to the harsh sting of a bee. Metaphors work by contrast as well as by comparison; things compared in a metaphor must be unlike, and the poet makes them alike. Usually, difference affects us more than similarity; a poet who compares the seemingly incomparable wins us with energy of resolved contrast.

It is easy to see how *sting* and *petal* contrast. But how do they come together? A bee—never named, yet part of the connotations of *sting*—belongs in a garden. A poem often finds its metaphors within an area, and Frost's poem moves among flowers and gardens for its images and metaphors. Bees work in gardens for pollen. If Frost had substituted for *stung* an image of a dentist's office—"The petal of the rose / It was that drilled"—we would not have been able to follow him in his feeling. Coherence of metaphor makes Frost's words operate upon us, even if we do not know that we are operated upon. Coherence of *rose* and *stung,* by way of an unstated bee, develops the metaphor.

Many metaphors in poetry work almost subliminally, like Frost's *stung,* but we also find extended metaphors. In the following poem, William Shakespeare starts by asking if he might make a comparison:

(1609)

Shall I compare thee to a summer's day?
Thou art more lovely and more temperate:
Rough winds do shake the darling buds of May,
And summer's lease hath all too short a date.
Sometime too hot the eye of heaven shines,
And often is his gold complexion dimm'd;
And every fair° from fair sometime declines,   beautiful thing
By chance or nature's changing course untrimm'd.
But thy eternal summer shall not fade
10 Nor lose possession of that fair thou ow'st.°   ownest: possess
Nor shall Death brag thou wand'rest in his shade,
When in eternal lines to time thou grow'st;
   So long as men can breathe or eyes can see,
   So long lives this and this gives life to thee.
                —*William Shakespeare*

This poem follows the common poetic form of the **sonnet**, fourteen lines of rhymed iambic pentameter (see pages 92–93). In the course of his fourteen lines, Shakespeare compares relentlessly, always to the effect that A is greater than B. No, you are not like a summer's day, you are better. To prove his conclusion, he compares parts of wholes. He breaks a summer's day down into weather, temperature, and temperament. Weather is more changeable than you are; you remain the same when the weather does not. Even in May, when blossoms begin to show, the weather can be unpleasant—but not you. Summer is a tenant who has rented an estate for a short time only (Shakespeare's sonnets and plays are full of legal and financial metaphor) but your tenancy of beauty is longer than a mere summer. Notice that by the fourth line Shakespeare has established his comparison of *thee* and *summer* so thoroughly that he can introduce the further metaphor of tenancy without confusion.

If summer leases, summer resembles a human being. The fifth line introduces another personification, when we hear of *the eye of heaven,* and we identify the *eye* with the sun when we hear that this eye *shines.* Having established the sun, without speaking of it directly, Shakespeare describes *his gold complexion,* as if the yellow sun had skin, and makes a cloudy day the sun's loss. In contrast, his love is never lessened or dimmed. Notice how the connotations of precious metal work to flatter the day, and thus flatter the love that is greater than the day.

The first eight lines of the poem—the **octave** of a sonnet—carry out its implications. The **sestet**—the sonnet's last six lines—expands upon the unchanging quality of the love and ends by praising itself. Death shall not brag of keeping this person-summer's day in shade, because these lines of poetry give eternal life. Shakespeare is able to bring Death into his metaphor, because shade treats sun as death treats life.

Shakespeare's poem extends a series of linked metaphors through fourteen lines. Here is another example of a single-word metaphor, like Frost's *stung,* which I use in order to move on to another subject. At the end of "During Wind and Rain" (page 18), Thomas Hardy writes:

> Down their carved names the rain-drop ploughs.

A plow is a natural object in the rural scene of this poem—and thus belongs in this poem's metaphorical area—but this is not a literal plow; metaphor turns a raindrop into an agricultural implement: raindrop is to gravestone as plow is to earth. The metaphor of *ploughs* has implications central to the poem: if raindrop acts on granite as plow on meadow, by implication many years have passed. If, however, we read the line lazily, taking *ploughs* as if it meant "moves vigorously forward"—as in a dead metaphor like "the fullback plows through the line" or "the tugboat plows through the waves"—nothing happens at all.

We constantly use figures of speech that once enjoyed freshness and vitality but that we no longer hear as figures of speech. Declaring we feel immovable, we say "I am glued to my chair." If we picture what we have said, we have a comical scene. But with dead metaphors, neither speaker nor hearer pictures anything at all. In a dead metaphor, the old comparison or assertion of identity is what is dead. If we did not say that we were glued to the chair, we might have said that we were anchored to the spot and no one would see the old schooner in the harbor, its anchor played out behind it, caught in the coral of the harbor bottom. For that matter, "dead metaphor" is a dead metaphor; and if I say that the old comparison is buried, I make the same morbid assertion. Once these metaphors were alive; now they are decayed corpses. The first time anyone used the metaphor of "dead metaphor," he implied that a hole had been dug—six feet deep, six feet long, three feet across—in the dirt of the phrase, and that somebody had placed the body of a comparison in this hole and heaped dirt over the body.

Live metaphors embody feelings. Dead metaphors embody stock responses, clichés, and lethargy. Bad poetry uses dead metaphors as commonly as we do in speech. Good poetry invents new metaphors, making vivid comparisons.

People often mix their dead metaphors. "Then the hand of God stepped in . . . ." makes a wonderful anatomical mixture. Of course *the hand of God* was used as if it meant "fortuitous circumstance," and *stepped in* as if it meant "happened next." When I first taught writing, one of my students wrote in a poem "The door yawned and beckoned." By *yawned* she meant that it opened, by *beckoned* that it looked inviting. But the two dead metaphors together made an impossible anatomy again, in which a door was an open mouth from which a hand suddenly extended. (Journalists as well as poets are experts at mixing dead metaphors. Take this example: "Mushrooming insurance and energy costs represent a double-barreled shotgun pointed at New England's ski areas." The writer of this sentence developed the ability *not* to see, or the writer could not have turned a soft vegetable into a steel weapon.)

Forming the habit of taking things literally, a reader becomes increasingly sensitive to language. Reading literally, we do not read the word *blind* automatically as if it means "obtuse"—which is to use *blind* as a dead metaphor. When we read *blind,* we take it to mean "sightless" until we find out otherwise. Then we do not write a sentence like this one recently printed in a country weekly: "'American optometrists are blind to the advantages of small town living,' said Dr. Harvey Bagnold to the Rotary Club last Tuesday."

Taking words as literally as possible—until the poem forces us to understand that we are reading a metaphor—we read the metaphor that is there. When Hamlet talks about his problems, he says that one possibility is to "take arms against a sea of troubles." The *Encyclopaedia Britannica,* in an otherwise sensible entry on "Metaphor," cites this figure as a mixed metaphor because people do not bear weapons against the ocean. It is not a mixed metaphor. It is visual metaphor embodying an idea and the emotions appropriate to that idea. Hamlet acknowledges that his problems are as soluble as the sea is vulnerable to his assault. The image expresses his feelings of futility. Shakespeare has Hamlet reveal his feelings by making a metaphor that provides an image of someone taking arms—in the context of the play, a sword or dagger—against an ocean.

Besides personification, a subdivision of metaphor mentioned on page 35, and hyperbole, or extreme exaggeration ("That room was two miles wide!"), we need mention only two other forms of figurative language, not quite so common as metaphor and simile. In **synechdoche** we speak of something by naming only a part of it. A poet might refer to a naval fleet as "two hundred keels," for instance, and his audience would understand that *keel* stood for boat. It is a way of referring to boats without using the word, which has perhaps lost freshness through overuse. We use synechdoche in everyday speech if we say that, during the summer, Gloria acquired wheels—she bought a used Oldsmobile. The part of the car stands in for the whole of the car.

In **metonomy** we speak of the object in terms of something closely connected with it—not a part of it as in synechdoche, but a thing closely and legitimately associated with it. Thus we can refer to a stove as its heat, for heat is not a part of the stove but a quality of it, or an association. Charles Reznikoff writes:

> Holding the stem of the
> beauty she had
> as if it were still
> a rose.

The poet first uses *beauty* by metonomy, as a quality of flowers; then he makes the flower particular.

Here are some poems followed by questions about metaphor and other figures of speech.

(1609)

That time of year thou mayst in me behold
When yellow leaves, or none, or few, do hang
Upon those boughs which shake against the cold,
Bare ruin'd choirs[1] where late the sweet birds sang.
In me thou seest the twilight of such day
As after sunset fadeth in the west,
Which by and by black night doth take away,
Death's second self, that seals up all in rest.
In me thou seest the glowing of such fire
10 That on the ashes of his youth doth lie,
As the death-bed whereon it must expire,
Consumed with that which it was nourish'd by.
    This thou perceiv'st which makes thy love more strong,
    To love that well which thou must leave ere long.
                                    —*William Shakespeare*

Questions

1. Paraphrase the poem, summarize the content, and discern the structure.

2. Where do you find the first figure of speech? What sort of figure is it?

3. How are the three quatrains linked in idea? Is there metaphorical coherence? Imagistic coherence?

4. In the fourth line, are the birds literal or figurative or both?

5. In the eleventh and twelfth lines, does the analogy make a complex idea simpler? Or does it make a simple idea more difficult?

6. List and name all figures of speech in this sonnet.

Orchids   (1948)

They lean over the path,
Adder-mouthed,
Swaying close to the face,
Coming out, soft and deceptive,
Limp and damp, delicate as a young bird's tongue;
Their fluttery fledgling lips
Move slowly,
Drawing in the warm air.

[1] Choir lofts, the part of the church building where the choirboys sang during religious services

And at night,
10 The faint moon falling through whitewashed glass,
The heat going down
So their musky smell comes even stronger,
Drifting down from their mossy cradles:
So many devouring infants!
Soft luminescent fingers,
Lips neither dead nor alive,
Loose ghostly mouths
Breathing.

—Theodore Roethke

Questions

1. List the different things the orchids are compared to.

2. The poem moves from one metaphoric area to another. What are the areas? Does the poem cohere? What keeps its different parts together?

The Hill   (1962)

It is sometime since I have been
to what it was had once turned me backwards,
and made my head into
a cruel instrument.

It is simple
to confess. Then done,
to walk away, walk away,
to come again.

But that form, I must answer,
10 is dead in me, completely,
and I will not allow it
to reappear—

Saith perversity, the willful,
the magnanimous cruelty,
which is in me
like a hill.

—Robert Creeley

Questions

1. What are the connotations of *instrument?* Is the word a metaphor?

2. Note all the metaphors in this poem. Is there a dead metaphor here? A personification?

3. Note other figures of speech.

4. Does the final figure of speech have impact on the earlier word *me?*

November and Aunt Jemima   (1990)

We sit at the table and that is grace,
the way one commits the prelude to kowtowing
by folding into the chair.

Usually we eat as if on a subway,
among strangers, standing to avoid the
toilet seat. Today, though, is Thanksgiving

so guilt bibs us, an extra place
is set for Aunt Jemima, the pancake box
occupies the chair, the family resemblance

10 unmistakeable. Hips full as Southern Baptist
tents but of a different doctrine.
Teeth white as the shock of lynching, thirty-two

tombstones. Despite the headrag
neither she nor her sister that bore me
are mistaken for gypsies.

The color of corrosion, she is not called
classic. The syrup that is the liquid
version of her skin flows like the promised

milk and honey so once a year we welcome
20 her. Even Christ would not be welcome every
day. Especially Christ who cannot come

without judgment just as she cannot come
without pancakes, flat, humane stones
still thrown at her by those whose sins

being white are invisible as her pain, the
mix in the box after the grinding of bones.
                              —*Thylias Moss*

Questions

1. How are the verbs of the first stanza—including participles—related to each other?

2. In the twelfth line, do you like the construction of the simile? Why?

3. What is "the color of corrosion"? What does this phrase imply?

4. Discuss the final metaphor here. Is it also an image? How does it conclude the poem?

CHAPTER FIVE

Tone, with a Note on Intentions

A poem's **tone**, in common definition, reveals the writer's attitude toward a subject, an attitude that could include sarcasm or irony or awe. In conversation, we indicate tone by our manner of speaking or by our facial expression: "Great!" can be pronounced so that it is a compliment or an insult. When we discuss a poem's tone, we discuss the value we attribute to its statements. Wallace Stevens, in "Disillusionment of Ten O'Clock," wrote:

> People are not going
> To dream of baboons and periwinkles.

In the context of this poem, which has already told us about "houses . . . haunted / By white night-gowns," we hear the speaker's tone as ironic. **Irony** is the perception of incongruity of discrepancy—between statement and meaning, for instance. Because we know that these unimaginative people will dream colorless dreams, it is ironic to name the exotic *baboons and periwinkles* as possible subjects of their dreams. Other poems are explosive and angry in tone, like John Donne's line beginning "The Canonization":

> For Godsake hold your tongue and let me love!

Other poems reveal sarcasm, as in E. E. Cummings's lines from "Poem, or Beauty Hurts Mr. Vinal":

> take it from me kiddo
> believe me
> my country, 'tis of
>
> you, land of the Cluett
> Shirt Boston Garter and Spearmint
> Girl With The Wrigley Eyes (of you
> land of the Arrow Ide

and Earl &
Wilson
10   Collars) of you i
sing: land of Abraham Lincoln and Lydia E. Pinkham,
land above all of Just Add Hot Water and Serve—
from every B. V. D.

let freedom ring

These examples are relatively simple. Because most poems are complex, many-sided, and ambivalent, the tone of many poems is hard to name and easy to mistake.

When we speak of a poem's tone, we make a metaphor, speaking of a poem as if it were a person and could voice its own words. It can help, studying tone in poetry, to try out the analogy of poems-as-people. If we sometimes misunderstand tone in poems, it is also true that we can misunderstand personal tones of voice, even when we have body, pitch, gesture, and eyebrows to help us understand. In everyday life, we interpret people's tones every hour of the day, without noticing that we do it. When we are offended by someone, or when we are touched or pleased, it is often the tone that does the offending or the pleasing. Perhaps we live with someone, and after dinner one night someone says "I'll do the dishes." These four words, depending on their tone, could mean a great many things. They could mean "Of course I'm getting stuck with doing the dishes, you slob, the way I always do, and the way I get stuck with taking out the garbage and picking up the biology notes from Gerry and standing in line for the football tickets." Or, they could mean "I want to do the dishes because you look so tired, and I'm always happy to take on a little work on your behalf, because you do so much for me, and I'm grateful for you getting that book from the library." Or, they could mean "I'm about to ask a favor," or "I think you're mad at me," or "I'll get points this way," or "Here is something I can do in order to avoid doing homework," or "When you wash the dishes, they never get clean."

Usually, we can decode the tone of somebody's voice. For that matter, we decode the way someone crosses a room or closes a door or drinks a Coke. Decoding a roommate, we use a glossary of behavior that we have been learning since birth. Door slams mean anger, says this dictionary; deep sighs mean frustration. We receive signals through gestures and through words, and we respond in kind; we communicate by tones.

Readers of poetry learn a system of signals by which they understand the tone of a poem, just as everybody learns the tones of personal pitch and gesture. One of the contracts that a poet makes with readers stipulates that tone shall be ascertainable: an assured tone is one of the criteria of excellence in poetry. Sometimes, poems fail by not making tone clear enough. For instance, here is a portion of a poem by a talented student:

. . . on sour air, the bells
chimed season's greetings

> to the departed host
> of Christmas . . .

If you cannot decode the tone of this fragment, you are not alone. What is the poet's attitude toward the subject? The poet intended *season's greetings* to be highly ironic, even sarcastic. Reading it, one could not be certain; a potential irony floated, unanchored, two inches above the page. The poet might have anchored irony any number of ways, but it is worth saying that ironic clichés are difficult to control; sometimes a context that demands irony provides control, sometimes it will come from a structure that repeats and varies the same irony. This fragment fails to make the irony seem intentional.

A Note on Intentions

When most of us speak about poetry, we refer to an author's intentions without even noticing that we do it. Speaking of diction and idiom, metaphor and image, we couch our discoveries in terms of the poet's presumed wishes and endeavors. Interpreting meaning, we say "This is what the poet was trying to say." The last phrase is especially common—and it is unfortunate: it promotes a picture of the poet as a fumbling, inarticulate slob, unable to say what is meant. The expression suggests that we will help out the dolt standing there with mouth open; let us inform the grateful poet of what he or she was trying and failing to say.

Whenever we begin to speak of a poet's intentions, we ought to consider what we are *really* talking about. Surely, no one is so presumptuous as to believe that he or she *really* knows what was in Milton's mind before he wrote *Paradise Lost*—or what was in Robert Frost's mind before he wrote "Stopping by Woods on a Snowy Evening," for that matter. Common sense reveals our ignorance; we need no degrees in psychology. Everything that ever happened to Robert Frost—every poem he ever read, every conversation he ever took part in, every winter he ever lived through, every horse he ever drove—entered his poem. Or so I am free to suppose.

We never know, with anything like certainty, why we make important decisions in our own lives. If ignorance prevails about our own intentions, how can we possibly presume to know someone else's? The formula What was he trying to do? How well did he accomplish his purposes? presupposes a sort of knowledge we cannot claim. It is true that some poets have revealed their intentions to us—in autobiography, in letters to editors or to friends, and in answer to questions. I suggest that we should not believe them. We should *listen* to what they say—if the poem is good, the poet's talk about it is bound to be interesting, even if only for what the poet leaves out. But we should listen skeptically, with our minds alert for falsity; we should not listen naïvely, as if we were getting the words from the horse's mouth. Often, the most sophisticated people become naïve when artists claim to explain their work. When politicians explain that their motives are noble and selfless, nobody believes them. When poets do the same, people nod their heads. Really, there is every reason for artists to lie to us when they tell us about their work—because they have every reason to lie to themselves. Good poems by their nature reveal many sides of a person, including sides poets may wish to conceal. Robert Frost, for instance, revealed a dark side in many poems—fears of madness, longings for oblivion, notions of evil, intimations of meaninglessness—which was not the self he chose to reveal on the lecture platform. In speaking about his poems, he denied their darkness.

Some poets have the illusion that they intend whatever takes place in their poems. They are like people who, in an argument, defend the rightness of everything they have ever said or done. Other poets admit that they wrote this phrase, or that whole poem, without knowing exactly what they were saying. T. S. Eliot, for instance, proclaimed his innocence of intention in much of "The Waste Land." Probably more often, a writer will consciously intend something on the surface—and write something else underneath the surface. The writer may not be aware of the subsurface meaning until later, when somebody points it out. Some writers deny it even after it is pointed out. Some students and teachers talk in classrooms about "hidden meanings" in a poem, an unfortunate phrase that makes reading poems sound like detective work. If we must speak of "hidden meanings," we ought to acknowledge that poets frequently hide meanings from themselves, and not just from readers.

Maybe the word *intention* should be stricken from our critical vocabulary; we speak sometimes of "unconscious intentions," a phrase in which the noun contradicts the adjective. In our lives, we tend to judge by actions or results rather than intentions; if someone breaks our jaw while "only trying to help," we are smarter to remember the broken jaw than to warm ourselves over the avowed intention. With poems, we must pay no attention to intentions, or even to the idea of intentions, but look for actions and results. We must attend to what is there, *really there on the page,* and to the impingements of the words upon us.

Tone is easy to miss or misinterpret. Many readers seize on one notion of tone in a quick reading, and ignore or cannot accept alternative readings. Assuming one tone, they eliminate the possibility of others, or of tonal variation. This short poem, alive with tone, requires thoughtful reading.

Transformations (1917)

Portion of this yew
Is a man my grandsire knew,
Bosomed here at its foot:
This branch may be his wife,
A ruddy human life
Now turned to a green shoot.

These grasses must be made
Of her who often prayed,
Last century, for repose;
10 And the fair girl long ago

Whom I often tried to know
May be entering this rose.

So, they are not underground,
But as nerves and veins abound
In the growths of upper air,
And they feel the sun and rain,
And the energy again
That made them what they were!
                    —*Thomas Hardy*

First, let us agree on a summary. A man walks among the graves of people he has heard about or has known in life. He observes that all these bodies endure, at least as particles in graveyard plants.

This summary is as pale as a government bulletin, because I am trying to sanitize the tone of it. What, then, is the tone of Hardy's poem? Is it melancholy? Is the visitor happy in the graveyard? Does Hardy announce molecular immortality as a discovery of vast scientific and spiritual importance? At first glance, he may seem to do the last. One student, writing about this poem, said, at the end of a paper, "So after this depression about everybody dying Thos. Hardy shakes himself out of it. He decides to look on the bright side of things so he notices that everybody really lives and nobody really dies because the roses etcetera go on blooming year after year after year after year." These sentences run into trouble as a paraphrase, and describe a poem which, if Hardy had written it, would have been dishonest; this student has Hardy turn himself away from sadness by lying to himself and to his readers. And this poem is *almost* the one Hardy wrote; I don't think that this student's interpretation is far off. Still, it mistakes Hardy's tone.

"Transformations" begins with a physical scene. An old man—many clues, like trying to know a fair girl, and an acquaintance with someone "last century," hint that the speaker is male and is getting on—walks musing in a graveyard. At the beginning, he thinks of deaths remote from him, and the tone is quiet and contemplative. As the old man moves forward in time, closer to his own end, the tone shifts.

Notice that Hardy begins by implying that he is certain, and modifies his tone of certainty as the poem develops. The change in the degree and in the type of assertion makes the change in tone. The first two lines are plain statement: "Portion of this yew / Is a man my grandsire knew. . . ." Obviously, the speaker knows the truth of what he says, and we believe him; the yew tree must be adjacent to the grave, and we can accept this assertion scientifically. If someone is buried next to a tree, after a number of years it must be true that some of the tree's molecules contain atoms that were earlier part of that person's body. When the speaker goes on "Bosomed here at its foot," he moves into metaphor. The metaphor has resonance and secondary implication, but it also carries information: the man my grandsire knew is buried (his burial compared to a baby snuggled up to a breast) at the base of the tree.

The speaker then takes certainty as a starting point and adds fancy: "This branch *may be* his wife . . . ." He plays straight with us: he *admits* that when he begins to think of a particular part of the tree as composed of a particular person, he is *playing* with the possibilities of his scientific commonplace. If the wife (as we can assume) is buried beside her husband "here at its foot," it is common sense to assume that she also participates in the tree's molecules, but it is fanciful to think of her as a special new branch. (That she's thought of as a *green shoot* implies that she died more recently than her husband.) The speaker modestly admits a lack of knowledge or certainty, admits his playful fancy, by using the verb form *may be.*

The first line of the second stanza appears at first glance to make a definite assertion: "These grasses must be made . . . ." If *must be* in our usage meant "absolutely, incontrovertibly has to be," we would have a statement of certainty. But, with the typical oddity of our speech, *must be* encodes a lack of certainty. When Hardy writes "These grasses must be made," he uses *must be* the way we do when we say "It must be six o'clock." (Robert Frost, as we have seen, used the same idiom when he wrote "My little horse must think it queer. . . .") In Hardy's poem, we are allowed to understand that a woman (who "prayed / Last century for repose") is buried hereabouts, so her remains may well be part of the grasses here; on the other hand, the lines say, possibly they are not (because of the length of time? because of possible error about the gravesite?). In the second part of this stanza, Hardy reverts to the *may be* form of possibility, making the metaphor that is the high point of the poem: "the fair girl . . . / May be entering this rose." Her molecules promenade through the stem to the blossom. In the metaphor, the rose has doors or portals, like a house or church, and the pretty young woman in the shape of her molecules walks through the door.

So far the tone has been simple. Hardy told us a certainty followed by fancies and probabilities. We walk beside an old man though a churchyard, where he ruminates on the persistence of matter translated from one organism to another. In the third stanza, the tone changes entirely. We can perceive the change in the poem's grammar. In his verb forms, Hardy reverts from *must be* and *may be* to direct assertion. "So," the poem tells us, as a result of what has just been said, "they [the dead] *are* not underground."

But they are. Yes, some molecules of decay may have escaped, but the dead are not *really* "as nerves or veins" abounding "In the growths of upper air." We know that the poem tells us false when it says that they *abound* and that "they *feel* the sun and rain / And the energy again / That made them what they were!" The *tone* of this assertion is made loud by the exclamation point, a triumphant, almost ecstatic assertion of the survival of the dead. It is the *tone* of the exclamation that must concern the reader. The poem seems to argue that it has proved survival after death by what it has observed of plant life. The poem began by winning our trust with its scrupulous use of verbs moving from *is* to *may be* and *must be.* Now it seems to violate the trust, by asserting *are* when we must be aware that the idea depends on speculation, on fantasy, and on a scientific notion that deals with particles of human flesh, not with whole human beings.

Because the leap to assertion is such a grand leap, and because we have learned to trust the implicit reasonableness of the speaker, the leap to false assertion creates a tone of strong and urgent feeling, which speaks to us like unwritten lines of poetry, saying "I know this assertion to be false; I make it only because I must, because the mortality of bodies is unacceptable to me!" The poem, through its tone—accomplished mostly by variations in verbs— speaks to us eloquently of the dread and fear of death.

Hardy's intention, in writing the poem, is not known to the reader—not to me, not to you, not to Hardy's most devoted student or scholar. But, in its own words and in its slow and steady motion down the page, the poem makes its shape inevitable—if we read with a steady care, with attention, and with the sensitivity we use interpreting the gesture and pitch of a person we love.

Here are some poems to read for their tone.

Museum Piece   (1950)

The good grey guardians of art
Patrol the halls on spongy shoes,
Impartially protective, though
Perhaps suspicious of Toulouse.[1]

Here dozes one against the wall,
Disposed upon a funeral chair.
A Degas[2] dancer pirouettes
Upon the parting of his hair.

See how she spins! The grace is there,
10   But strain as well is plain to see.
Degas loved the two together:
Beauty joined to energy.

Edgar Degas purchased once
A fine El Greco,[3] which he kept
Against the wall beside his bed
To hang his pants on while he slept.
                    —*Richard Wilbur*

Questions

1. In the first line, what is the tone of the word *good?*

2. Alliteration is the repetition of consonant sounds, as in *good gray guardians.* Does alliteration in the first line contribute to the tone of the line?

[1] Henri de Toulouse-Lautrec Monfa (1864–1901) made notable paintings of Parisian life and characters, but is best known for his posters of nightclubs and entertainers. [2] Edgar Degas (1834–1917), one of the important French impressionists, is best known for his paintings and pastels of ballerinas. [3] El Greco (1548?–1614?), native of Crete and student of the Venetian master Titian, lived in Toledo from his late twenties and was the leading sixteenth-century mystical Spanish painter. His work often distorts the human form by elongating it.

3. Notice the rhyme in the first stanza. Can a rhyme contribute to tone? Does this rhyme?

4. Does the first stanza introduce a tone that remains the same throughout the poem? Where does the poem's tone change? How do you know?

5. What is the tone of the last line of the poem? Does it resolve the differing tones earlier in the poem?

Hay for the Horses   (1959)

He had driven half the night
From far down San Joaquin
Through Mariposa, up the
Dangerous mountain roads,
And pulled in at eight A.M.
With his big truckload of hay behind the barn.
With winch and ropes and hooks
We stacked the bales up clean
To splintery redwood rafters
10 High in the dark, flecks of alfalfa
Whirling through shingle-cracks of light,
Itch of haydust in the sweaty shirt and shoes.
At lunchtime under Black oak
Out in the hot corral,
—The old mare nosing lunchpails,
Grasshoppers crackling in the weeds—
'I'm sixty-eight,' he said,
'I first bucked hay when I was seventeen.
I thought, that day I started,
20 I sure would hate to do this all my life.
And dammit, that's just what
I've gone and done.'

—*Gary Snyder*

Questions

1. How would you characterize the tone of the first sentence of this poem? Do you trust it to be straightforward? Why?

2. In the poem's middle, does the tone change at all? Do you sense any change in the speaker's attitude toward the subject?

3. In the last part of the poem, the poet quotes another speaker. Does this new speaker have a characteristic tone? What do you know of him from his tone? What does the poet do to reveal his tone?

What I Heard at the Discount Department Store   (1988)

Don't touch that. And stop your whining too.
Stop it. I mean it. You know I do.

If you don't stop, I'll give you fucking something
to cry about right here
and don't you think I won't either.

So she did. She slapped him across the face.
And you could hear the snap of flesh against the flesh
halfway across the store. Then he wasn't whining anymore.
Instead, he wept. His little body heaved and shivered and wept.
10 He was seven or eight. She was maybe thirty.
Above her left breast, the pin said: Nurse's Aide.

Now they walk hand in hand down the aisle
between the tables piled with tennis shoes
and underpants and plastic bags of socks.

I told you I would. You knew I would.
You can't get away with shit like that with me,
you know you can't.
You're not in school anymore.
You're with your mother now.
20 You can get away with fucking murder there,
but you can't get away with shit like that with me.
Stop that crying now I say
or I'll give you another little something
like I did before.

Stop that now. You'd better stop.

That's better. That's a whole lot better.
You know you can't do that with me.
You're with your mother now.

                                                —*David Budbill*

Questions

1. How soon do you understand that a character, other than the poet, speaks this poem? What is her tone and how do you know it?

2. How can a title contribute to the tone of a poem?

3. Do you ever find this poem departing from the tone established at the start? Where?

Ends   (1963)

Loud talk in the overlighted house
That made us stumble past.
Oh, there had once been night the first,
But this was night the last.

Of all the things he might have said,
Sincere or insincere,
He never said she wasn't young,
And hadn't been his dear.

Oh, some as soon would throw it all
10 As throw a part away.
And some will say all sorts of things,
But some mean what they say.
                         —*Robert Frost*

Questions

1. Who is *us?*

2. What is overheard?

3. Do any overheard words have a tone to them that you trust? Distrust? What words give you your impressions?

4. What do you feel you know about the overheard people? Try to discover everything you can about them, and then decide how you know what you know.

5. What are these people arguing about? Do you know? Or do you know only the tone of the argument? Which is more important, the subject of an argument or its tone?

CHAPTER SIX

Symbols and Allusions

In "To Read a Story," a symbol was defined as a person, object, place, or event that comes to stand for something other than it is, usually something more than it is, and for a class of events or relationships. This definition can serve as a starter here. Again, we must make distinctions among kinds of symbolism: the **conventional** (or **traditional**) **symbol**, the **natural symbol**, and the **literary symbol**. We must speak as well about allusion and reference in poetry, devices that overlap when a poet refers or alludes to a traditional symbol and that resemble each other in the difficulty they cause for students.

It is easiest to speak first of *natural symbols*, which occur in literature but which tend toward cliché: night is a natural symbol of death, and so is autumn. Shakespeare and other geniuses have made great literature using natural symbols; remember "That time of year thou mayst in me behold . . ." (page 39), where both night and autumn are symbols of death. Because natural symbols tend to be trite, modern writers seldom use them, or use them in the negative, setting up the expectation of a stock response, and then disappointing it. The great modern poet T. S. Eliot began one of his first poems, "The Love Song of J. Alfred Prufrock," with

> Let us go then, you and I,
> When the evening is spread out against the sky . . .

appealing to stock responses, and to the natural symbolism of sunset as beauty or fulfillment. His audience, when he wrote the poem in 1911, might have expected him to go on:

> Like veils of painted gossamer on high . . .

Instead, he turned this expectation upside down with his actual third line:

> Like a patient etherized upon a table.

A natural symbol underwent a radical alteration.

The word *symbol* begins by meaning a simple sign, like a circle containing a cigarette, with a diagonal line crossing out the cigarette; everybody knows the sign or the symbol for NO SMOKING. We speak of *conventional symbols* like these signs and like national flags or the logos of sports teams. Another sort of conventional symbol (it would be better perhaps to speak of these as *traditional symbols*) are images or phrases that have acquired meaning over centuries of history or association, like the cross and the Star of David. A poet who uses an image of a cross can hardly avoid reference to Christ, Christianity, and suffering. Therefore, reference allies itself to traditional (and conventional) symbolism. We speak of conventional and traditional symbols together because the distinction between them is quantitative; "conventional" symbols are simple signs; "traditional" symbols are signs with long and complex associations.

Finally, there is the *literary symbol,* of which a fictional example was Chekhov's "Gooseberries." Here is a poem by William Blake:

The Sick Rose　(1794)

O Rose, thou art sick!
The invisible worm
That flies in the night,
In the howling storm,

Has found out thy bed
Of crimson joy,
And his dark secret love
Does thy life destroy.
　　　—William Blake

Reading this poem, let us as always first try the literal. A sick rose could suffer from a plant bacterium. But the second line of the poem reveals that we cannot continue to read on a literal level, because invisible worms fly only in the imagination. Back to the first line, then. *Rose* is capitalized, which may give us the sense that this flower is more than a flower, or that a real flower is addressed as if it embodied something beyond itself. To connect this flower with the notion of sickness seems a violation of the natural, as if we said that a mountain squeaked like a mouse. The contrast between *rose* and *sick* occurs at the levels of both sound and idea, as the full *os* of the first two syllables dwindle into the quick short *is* of *sick* and *invisible*.

"The Sick Rose" makes a literary symbol. When we ask what it is a symbol of, we ask the wrong sort of question. A literary symbol is not a figure or a riddle to which there exists a simple answer, or a correct interpretation. Instead, it is a series of words—creating image or event or character or fantasy or plot or scene—that is irreducible, that in itself is a formula for a complex set of feelings and ideas never before rendered in the same way. *The literary symbol cannot be translated or identified.* We can talk about it and we can talk around it, but the symbol will always sit in the center of our words, smiling enigmatically, content to be itself. A great French symbolist poet, Stéphane Mallarmé, made a metaphor for the symbol: he said it was "the new word." We can find this metaphor useful to our thinking about the literary symbol, because it cannot be defined or named by anything except itself. It resembles, then, a "new word," as if the poet invented the word *chair* for the first time, and there were no other word for chair but *chair*.

William Blake makes a symbol for a new thing. *The invisible worm* is not described in terms of horns and claws; it is a general "worm," with the particular attribute of invisibility—and with other attributes that associate feelings with this *new word*. This is a worm gifted with flight like a dragon, and gifted especially to fly in a darkness (night as a natural symbol is frightening, possibly the place of evil) and through a storm (destruction, possibly divine wrath) that makes a noise like the cries of someone in pain. The sick rose and its worm live in a place of terror and fear, are themselves instruments and victims of terror and fear. Syntax of subject and object, predator and victim, locates a scene in the second stanza. The worm has found "thy bed / Of crimson joy . . ." The word *joy* seems unambivalent, but it is not: crimson is blood-color, one of sin's colors, and dangerous; at least violent and extreme. One would expect malice from such a worm, and one hears *love* instead, but it is a *dark, secret* love, and it is a love that rhymes *joy* with *destroy*. When love is both dark and secret, adjectives like crimson complicate the wholeness of the noun; if they do not reverse love into hate, or joy into pain, or fondness into malice, they introduce elements of the negative into the positive; they make by their complexity a wholeness. It is a wholeness that is also a new, single thing: symbolist poem or "new word."

Many poems speak of roses, in many different ways—sometimes as traditional or literary symbols and sometimes not. Theodore Roethke's great contemporary poem, "The Rose" (pages 165–167), makes a literary symbol, another new word like William Blake's. But in Charles Reznikoff's four-line poem,

> Holding the stem of the
> beauty she had
> as if it were still
> a rose.

rose is not a symbol but a type, "a thing of beauty." When Shakespeare says "A rose by any other name would smell as sweet," or when Gertrude Stein tells us "A rose is a rose is a rose," these writers do not make new words, but, like Reznikoff, they use the rose as a type: a flower beautiful in its odor; a thing of this world.

The Problem of Allusion

Blake's "The Sick Rose" carries countless associations for the student of literature. If a contemporary poet wrote now about "the rose's worm"—he or she would make an **allusion** to "The Sick Rose," almost a quotation. Allusion works with ideas as well as with words. One critic reading Blake's "The Sick

Rose" believed that he found an allusion to Shakespeare's line "Lilies that fester smell far worse than weeds." It is now time for us to focus on allusion. Poems can allude to other poems and to history, to ideas, to fact, and to myth. All poems retelling old stories are allusive; a new version of "Casey at the Bat" would be an allusion to the old ballad; a new poem that tells about Oedipus or Hamlet must be based on allusions to the old plays.

Allusion has become a problem for modern readers, because people no longer share the same backgrounds. A century ago, an allusion to the Bible supposed no special knowledge; a century ago, among literate people, it was not obscure to speak of Greek deities like Apollo or Aphrodite; a century ago, even scientific knowledge was commonly held, partly because there was relatively little of it. Now we not only specialize in fields; we find specialties within specialties. The high-energy physicist cannot understand the physicist who studies the behavior of particles at low temperatures.

Allusion is common in poetry, and acts as a barrier to understanding. Sensitivity to allusion in poetry can only grow with extended reading. It is not an element of poetry that can be studied by exercise and thought; it is an element of poetry that can be named and introduced—but then it must be learned and practiced by much reading. No shortcut will solve the problem of allusion.

But one shortcut, obvious enough, will *help* with certain poems. Here is an epigram (a short, pithy poem; see pages 105–106) by Louise Bogan:

To an Artist, to Take Heart   (1941)

Slipping in blood, by his own hand, through pride,
Hamlet, Othello, Coriolanus fall.
Upon his bed, however, Shakespeare died,
Having endured them all.

—Louise Bogan

Bogan alludes to three Shakespearean heroes. The names of Hamlet and Othello will be familiar to most American students, though not always the stories that their names allude to. The name of Coriolanus will be new to most. Reading this poem, the student is forced to a dictionary or a reference book.* The problem of allusion is often a problem of vocabulary, especially

* Earlier, this book urged the use of the *Oxford English Dictionary* (page 16). In the pursuit of allusions, the student can use the whole reference room. For help with the proper names in Bogan's poem, the *Oxford Companion to English Literature* would perhaps be the best resource, in which entries for these names summarize plots and tell the tragic flaws of heroes. Oxford also prints a *Companion to American Literature,* and *Companions* to the literatures of other languages. The *Oxford Classical Dictionary* is very good on mythology, and there are classical dictionaries and companions from other publishers. The *Readers' Encyclopedia* is a useful volume, as are more specialized volumes of reference: the *Encyclopedia of American Biography. Webster's Biographical Dictionary, An Encyclopedia of World History,* and the *Encyclopaedia Britannica. The New Columbia Encyclopedia* is an excellent resource in one volume. Reference librarians will often point researchers in the right direction. With certain poets, especially highly allusive poets of the eighteenth century who refer to their own contemporaries by name and by pseudonym, it is useful to consult the notes of a scholarly edition of the poet's work, where the research has been done for us.

when it is a matter of proper names. To know that Hamlet is the hero of a play by Shakespeare called *Hamlet*—as a dictionary might tell us—would not help, even with this brief poem. But if we know enough of the story to remember that Hamlet died young and by violence, we can begin to understand the allusion and the poem. We cannot understand the poem without understanding the allusions.

Checking allusions in Louise Bogan's four lines, we learn that Coriolanus's tragic flaw was pride; we add this fact to Othello's suicide and Hamlet's death in a duel. We notice that the three phrases of Bogan's first line follow the order of the three heroes' names in the second line. We understand that the playwright who conceived them lived longer then they did, even if he suffered (*endured* has the connotation of survival with difficulty) and ended by dying in bed.

Because of the difficulties of allusion, certain great and allusive poets are underrepresented in this book, among them Milton, Dryden, and Pope. For the same reason, it is hard to choose poems that can give fair exercise in uncovering allusions. The poems that follow, and the questions that go with them, raise issues largely of symbolism. But not entirely.

Prout's Madeleine (1949)

Somebody has given my
Baby daughter a box of
Old poker chips to play with.
Today she hands me one while
I am sitting with my tired
Brain at my desk. It is red.
On it is a picture of
An elk's head and the letters
B.P.O.E.—a chip from
10 A small town Elks' Club. I flip
It idly in the air and
Catch it and do a coin trick
To amuse my little girl.
Suddenly everything slips aside.
I see my father
Doing the very same thing,
Whistling "Beautiful Dreamer,"
His breath smelling richly
Of whiskey and cigars. I can
20 Hear him coming home drunk
From the Elk's Club in Elkhart
Indiana, bumping the
Chairs in the dark. I can see
Him dying of cirrhosis
Of the liver and stomach
Ulcers and pneumonia,
Or, as he said on his deathbed, of

Crooked cards and straight whiskey,
Slow horses and fast women.
                —*Kenneth Rexroth*

Questions

1. Where does allusion begin in this poem? List and explain its allusions.

2. Does this poem use any sort of symbol?

Taking the hands of someone you love (1960)

Taking the hands of someone you love,
You see they are delicate cages . . .
Tiny birds are singing
In the secluded prairies
And in the deep valleys of the hand.
                —*Robert Bly*

Question

Compare this poem with the poem above by Kenneth Rexroth. Does this one invite you to look for symbolism? What sort of symbolism? Why?

The Draft Horse (1962)

With a lantern that wouldn't burn
In too frail a buggy we drove
Behind too heavy a horse
Through a pitch-dark limitless grove.

And a man came out of the trees
And took our horse by the head
And reaching back to his ribs
Deliberately stabbed him dead.

The ponderous beast went down
10 With a crack of a broken shaft.
And the night drew through the trees
In one long invidious draft.

The most unquestioning pair
That ever accepted fate
And the least disposed to ascribe
Any more than we had to to hate,

We assumed that the man himself
Or someone he had to obey
Wanted us to get down
20 And walk the rest of the way.
                —*Robert Frost*

Questions

1. Do you take this action literally?

2. Are there natural symbols here? Traditional or conventional symbols?

3. Does this poem make a "new word"? What in this poem gives you the suggestion that it might be symbolic?

The Monument   (1939)

Discuss w/ class

Now can you see the monument? It is of wood
built somewhat like a box. No. Built
like several boxes in descending sizes
one above the other.
Each is turned half-way round so that
its corners point toward the sides
of the one below and the angles alternate.
Then on the topmost cube is set
a sort of fleur-de-lys of weathered wood,
10 long petals of board, pierced with odd holes,
four-sided, stiff, ecclesiastical.
From it four thin, warped poles spring out,
(slanted like fishing-poles or flag-poles)
and from them jig-saw work hangs down,
four lines of vaguely whittled ornament
over the edges of the boxes
to the ground.
The monument is one-third set against
a sea; two-thirds against a sky.
20 The view is geared
(that is, the view's perspective)
so low there is no "far away,"
and we are far away within the view.
A sea of narrow, horizontal boards
lies out behind our lonely monument,
its long grains alternating right and left
like floor-boards—spotted, swarming-still,
and motionless. A sky runs parallel,
and it is palings, coarser than the sea's:
30 splintery sunlight and long-fibred clouds.
"Why does that strange sea make no sound?
Is it because we're far away?
Where are we? Are we in Asia Minor,
or in Mongolia?"
              An ancient promontory,
an ancient principality whose artist-prince
might have wanted to build a monument
to mark a tomb or boundary, or make
a melancholy or romantic scene of it . . .
40 "But that queer sea looks made of wood,

half-shining, like a driftwood sea.
And the sky looks wooden, grained with cloud.
It's like a stage-set; it is all so flat!
Those clouds are full of glistening splinters!
What is that?"

        It is the monument.
"It's piled-up boxes,
outlined with shoddy fret-work, half-fallen off,
cracked and unpainted. It looks old."
50 —The strong sunlight, the wind from the sea,
all the conditions of its existence,
may have flaked off the paint, if ever it was painted,
and made it homelier than it was.
"Why did you bring me here to see it?
A temple of crates in cramped and crated scenery,
what can it prove?
I am tired of breathing this eroded air,
this dryness in which the monument is cracking."

    It is an artifact
60 of wood. Wood holds together better
than sea or cloud or sand could by itself,
much better than real sea or sand or cloud.
It chose that way to grow and not to move.
The monument's an object, yet those decorations,
carelessly nailed, looking like nothing at all,
give it away as having life, and wishing;
wanting to be a monument, to cherish something.
The crudest scroll-work says "commemorate,"
while once each day the light goes around it
70 like a prowling animal,
or the rain falls on it, or the wind blows into it.
It may be solid, may be hollow.
The bones of the artist-prince may be inside
or far away on even drier soil.
But roughly but adequately it can shelter
what is within (which after all
cannot have been intended to be seen).
It is the beginning of a painting,
a piece of sculpture, or poem, or monument,
80 and all of wood. Watch it closely.

                  —*Elizabeth Bishop*

Questions

1. Is this a symbolist poem? What lines or words help you decide?

2. What sorts of symbol can you discover in this poem?

Facing It   (1988)

My black face fades,
hiding inside the black granite.
I said I wouldn't,
dammit: No tears.
I'm stone. I'm flesh.
My clouded reflection eyes me
like a bird of prey, the profile of night
slanted against morning. I turn
this way—the stone lets me go.
10 I turn that way—I'm inside
the Vietnam Veterans Memorial
again, depending on the light
to make a difference.
I go down the 58,022 names,
half-expecting to find
my own in letters like smoke.
I touch the name Andrew Johnson;
I see the booby trap's white flash.
Names shimmer on a woman's blouse
20 but when she walks away
the names stay on the wall.
Brushstrokes flash, a red bird's
wings cutting across my stare.
The sky. A plane in the sky.
A white vet's image floats
closer to me, then his pale eyes
look through mine. I'm a window.
He's lost his right arm
inside the stone. In the black mirror
30 a woman's trying to erase names:
No, she's brushing a boy's hair.
                    —*Yusef Komunyakaa*

Questions

1. This African-American poet fought in Viet Nam. Did you understand as much from the poem? How do we judge true autobiographical anecdote from fiction or even from symbol? Can we be sure?

2. Can we take a real object and turn it into a symbol? Are some real objects created to be symbols? Does this poet turn a symbol into a symbol? How?

The Apparitions   (1940)

Because there is safety in derision
I talked about an apparition,
I took no trouble to convince,
Or seem plausible to a man of sense,

Distrustful of that popular eye
Whether it be bold or sly.
Fifteen apparitions have I seen;
The worst a coat upon a coat-hanger.

I have found nothing half so good
10   As my long-planned half solitude,
Where I can sit up half the night
With some friend that has the wit
Not to allow his looks to tell
When I am unintelligible.
Fifteen apparitions have I seen;
The worst a coat upon a coat-hanger.

When a man grows old his joy
Grows more deep day after day,
His empty heart is full at length,
20   But he has need of all that strength
Because of the increasing Night
That opens her mystery and fright.
Fifteen apparitions have I seen;
The worst a coat upon a coat-hanger.
          —*William Butler Yeats*

Questions

1. Note any use of conventional or traditional symbols.

2. Does the image of *a coat upon a coat-hanger* change its implications as it is repeated?

3. Does the poem make a literary symbol?

The Return   (1912)

See, they return; ah, see the tentative
          Movements, and the slow feet,
          The trouble in the pace and the uncertain
Wavering!

See they return, one, and by one,
With fear, as half-awakened;
As if the snow should hesitate
And murmur in the wind,
          and half turn back;
10   These were the 'Wing'd-with-Awe,'
          Inviolable.

Gods of the wingèd shoe!
With them the silver hounds,
          sniffing the trace of air!

Haie! Haie!

> These were the swift to harry;
These the keen-scented;
These were the souls of blood.

Slow on the leash,
20   pallid the leash-men!

—Ezra Pound

Questions

1. Can you find any allusions in this poem?

2. Can you identify *they* in this poem? If you cannot name a definite identity, can you name a kind of action that *they* embody?

3. If the poem is symbolic, what kind of symbol does it make?

CHAPTER SEVEN

The Sound of Poems

When we explicate a poem, we investigate its sound as well as its symbol, its shape and architecture as well as its paraphrase and implication. Talking about William Carlos Williams's wheelbarrow poem, we looked at the poem as artifact, as made object. This chapter concentrates on the pleasures poems make by their sound.

We derive at least two distinct pleasures from the sound of language in poetry. One is the pleasure of *rhythm,* of words in motion, uncoiling in sentences from poetic line to line. Here is the beginning of *Paradise Lost* by John Milton:

> Of man's first disobedience, and the fruit
> Of that forbidden tree, whose mortal taste
> Brought death into the world, and all our woe,
> With loss of Eden, till one greater Man
> Restore us, and regain the blissful seat,
> Sing, Heavenly Muse . . .

The pleasure of rhythm is like the pleasure of dancing, or of tapping our feet to keep time with music. Rhythm recalls primitive origins of poetry where song and poem and dance happened together. This rhythm-pleasure of poetry's sound connects with our pleasure in bodily motion.

The other pleasure is the delight that we take in adjacent sounds rubbing together, vowels held and savored, consonants clicking together. Here are some lines from "To Autumn" by John Keats:

> Then in a wailful choir the small gnats mourn
> Among the river sallows,° borne aloft   willows
> Or sinking as the light wind lives or dies; . . .

Rhythm and Linebreak

First, let us look at rhythm. The lines of a poem are essential to its signature and its identity. Milton broke some of his lines where the meaning paused, as with

Brought death into the world, and all our woe . . .

When the sense pauses or stops at the end of a line, we call it **end-stopped**. Most of the time, Milton broke his lines in the middle of a phrase, so that the sense of the sentence ran over into the line following, as with

With loss of Eden, till one greater Man
Restore us . . .

When the sense runs over the end of a line, we call the line enjambed, and the practice **enjambment**.

Even when a line is enjambed, it retains its identity as a line of poetry; reading it aloud, we make a slight pause at the end. Or, we show the line-end in another way, by raising our voice perhaps, or by holding on to the last syllable. We do not pause evenly—we pause longer when the line is end-stopped—but we find some means to show with our voice that we have come to the end of a line. If we do not, we might was well be reading prose. One eighteenth-century critic with no ear suggested that we print Milton as prose or that we rebreak his lines according to phrases of sense, which could make the first lines of *Paradise Lost* look like this:

Of man's first disobedience
and the fruit
of that forbidden tree
whose mortal taste
brought death
into the world
and all our woe,
with loss of Eden,
till one greater Man
restore us,
and regain
the blissful seat,
sing
Heavenly Muse . . .

How boring and flat the lines become! There can be little attention to pauses within lines, because the critic would break the line wherever there might be a pause. There is no tension; music and sense become identical, which results in the disappearance of music.

We must develop a sense of the poetic line, if we are to take pleasure in poetry. Here are lines by Louis Simpson:

Caesar Augustus
In his time lay
Dying, and just as
Cold as they,
On the cold morning
Of a cold day.

These lines lose their pleasure, as well as their dance and their power, if we space them according to the phrases of their sense:

> Caesar Augustus
> In his time lay dying
> And just as cold as they
> On the cold morning
> Of a cold day.

As prose, pleasure, dance, and power disappear completely: "Caesar Augustus in his time lay dying and just as cold as they on the cold morning of a cold day." (The complete poem is on page 86–87.)

The examples we have looked at use rhyme and meter, the subjects of the next chapter. With free verse, which lacks any regular beat, the line becomes the major way of organizing sound. Here is a stanza from a free-verse poem by John Haines, "And When the Green Man Comes," revised into phrase-unit lines:

> His eyes are blind with April,
> his breath distilled
> of butterflies and bees,
> and in his beard the maggot sings.

Here it is with lines broken arbitrarily; *not* as the poet broke them in his finished poem:

> His eyes are
> blind with April, his
> breath
> distilled of
> butterflies and
> bees, and in
> his beard the
> maggot sings.

The first version is boring, the second jagged or nervous. Here is the stanza as Haines actually wrote it:

> His eyes are blind
> with April,
> his breath distilled
> of butterflies
> and bees, and in his beard
> the maggot sings.

Notice how the organized rhythm of the last version calls attention to sound; putting *eyes* and *blind* together in a short line, for instance, repeats the long *ai*s. Notice as well the repetition of *l*s, in the last syllable of each of the first four lines.

Sounds can exist for their own sake—and, because they can, sounds organize emphasis. *blind / with April* and *distilled / of butterflies* share a syntactic structure, but, instead of ending at the same place, one of the two clauses continues *of butterflies / and bees.* Syntax and linebreak combine to isolate, in the last line of the stanza, the significant conclusion: *the maggot sings.* My earlier linebreaks, falsifying the poem, obscured or invalidated these possibilities.

Some free-verse poems use a long line in which the linebreak seldom interrupts the sense. They are all end-stopped. Take these lines by Walt Whitman, from "Song of Myself":

> I think I could turn and live with animals, they're so placid and self-contain'd,
> I stand and look at them long and long.
>
> They do not sweat and whine about their condition,
> They do not lie awake in the dark and weep for their sins,
> They do not make me sick discussing their duty to God,
> Not one is dissatisfied, not one is demented with the mania of owning things,
> Not one kneels to another, or to his kind that lived thousands of years ago,
> Not one is respectable or unhappy over the whole earth.

If one printed these lines as prose, in paragraph form, one would lose the slow pace that the long lines give. On the other hand, one could slow the pace into absolute boredom by breaking the lines at the commas, making them shorter:

> I think I could turn and live
> with animals,
> they're so placid
> and self-contain'd.
> I stand and look at them
> long and long.
>
> They do not sweat and whine
> about their condition.
> They do not lie awake in the dark
> and weep for their sins.
> They do not make me sick
> discussing their duty to God.
> Not one is dissatisfied.
> Not one is demented
> with the mania
> of owning things.
> Not one kneels to another
> nor to his kind
> that lived thousands of years ago.
> Not one is respectable
> or unhappy
> over the whole earth.

In this mistreatment, I have reduced the various pauses—commas, shorter pauses between whole phrases, long line-end pauses—into one sort of pause. We should be grateful for Whitman's generous line, which makes a satisfying rhythm within itself—and not only by its motion from line to line. A pause within the line is called a **caesura**, and is shown when we mark it by a pair of vertical lines ‖. Whitman's lines include many pauses or caesuras. In a shorter line like Milton's, we do not have so many, but we can often find an obvious place to pause, sometimes shown by punctuation:

> Of man's first disobedience, ‖ and the fruit

and sometimes not, as in Keats's line:

> Or sinking ‖ as the light wind lives or dies . . .

Poets work with a variety of pauses, at the ends of lines and inside them, and the variety contributes to the rhythm of the poetic line.

Here are some exercises that may be suitable for out-loud performance in the classroom.

Exercises

1. Following is a passage from *Antony and Cleopatra*, done Shakespeare's way (a.) and as two actors with differing interpretations might have done it (b. and c.). Notice which lines are enjambed, which end-stopped, in the first presentation. Discuss the difference the linebreaks make in the three versions.

   a. The barge she sat in, like a burnished throne,
   Burned on the water: the poop was beaten gold;
   Purple the sails, and so perfumèd that
   The winds were love-sick with them; the oars were silver,
   Which to the tune of flutes kept stroke, and made
   The water which they beat to follow faster.

   b. The barge she sat in
   like a burnished throne
   burned on the water.
   The poop was beaten gold,
   purple the sails,
   and so perfumèd
   that the winds
   were love-sick with them.
   The oars were silver,
   which to the flutes kept stroke
   and made the water
   which they beat
   to follow faster.

c. The barge
  she sat in like
  a burnished throne burned on the
  water the poop was
  beaten
  gold purple the
  sails and so perfumèd that the winds
  were love-
  . . .
  sick
  with
  them
  the oars were silver which to the tune of flutes kept stroke and made the water
  which they beat to
  follow
  faster.

2. Here are three versions of a free-verse poem by William Carlos Williams. Which do you think is the poet's? Which is the least pleasing lineation?

  a. As the cat climbed
    over the top of

    the jamcloset first
    the right forefoot

    carefully then the
    hind stepped down

    into the pit of the
    empty flower pot

  b. As the cat
    climbed over
    the top of

    the jamcloset
    first the right
    forefoot

    carefully
    then the hind
    stepped down

    into the pit of
    the empty
    flowerpot

  c. As the cat climbed
    over the top
    of the jamcloset

first the right
forefoot carefully
then the hind
stepped down
into the pit
of the empty
flower pot.

Vowels and Consonants

To enjoy the intimate sounds of poems, we take pleasure in savoring words
and parts of words. This pleasure does not exclude meanings, but it can exist
for its own sake. Sometimes we enjoy tripping along with nonsense sounds,
as when Yeats makes a line of "fol, de rol, de rolly o," or Shakespeare mixes
words and sounds: "With a hey, ho, the wind and the rain."

Alliteration is the repetition of consonant sounds, especially at the beginning of words. When Wallace Stevens writes "In kitchen cups concupiscent
curds," he keeps our tongues flicking at the roofs of our mouths.

Assonance is the repetition of vowel sounds—"beside the white"; "glazed
with rain." We take pleasure in holding onto vowels that remind us of each
other. The last line of Hardy's "During Wind and Rain" shows interlocking
assonance and alliteration:

Down their carved names the rain-drop ploughs.

The two syllables at the beginning and end of the line contain the same *ow*
vowel sound; in the middle of the line, there is the long *a* of *names* and the
long *a* of *rain*. In addition, the line repeats the *n* of *down, names,* and *rain;*
the *r* of *carved, rain,* and *drop;* the *p* of *drop* and *ploughs;* the *d* of *down* and
drop.

Poets typically ascend to assonance, holding long vowels, when their
poems are most exalted, as when Hardy ends his lyric with the line above.
When Keats wrote his odes, he especially delighted in repeating vowels and
consonants—more than in his other poems. This stanza is from "Ode to a
Nightingale":

I cannot see what flowers are at my feet,
   Nor what soft incense hangs upon the boughs,
But, in embalmèd darkness, guess each sweet
   Wherewith the seasonable month endows
The grass, the thicket, and the fruit-tree wild—
White hawthorn, and the pastoral eglantine;
   Fast-fading violets covered up in leaves;
     And mid-May's eldest child,
The coming musk-rose, full of dewy wine,
   The murmurous haunt of flies on summer eves.

10

In the first line, Keats mixes assonance and alliteration. The vowels of *see* and *feet* are identical, while *flowers* and *feet* begin with the same consonant. The consonant sound of *th* repeats softly through lines 4 to 6: *Wherewith, the* (five times), *month, thicket,* and *hawthorn*. Two sets of rhyme words have the same long *ai:* wild, eglantine, child, wine. The identical diphthong (a double vowel, this one composed of *ah* and *ee*) occurs elsewhere in: *White, violets, flies.*

It is not a requirement of great poetry that sounds be so gorgeous. Frost is *never* so ornate, in his alliteration or his assonance, as Keats in the odes. Frost's attention dotes on rhythm, linebreak, and the happy and continuous tension between sentence and line. Here are poems for sound study.

New Year's Day   (1946)

Again and then again . . . the year is born

To ice and death, and it will never do

To skulk behind storm-windows by the stove

To hear the postgirl sounding her French horn

When the thin tidal ice is wearing through.

Here is the understanding not to love

Each other, or tomorrow that will sieve

Our resolutions. While we live, we live

To snuff the smoke of victims. In the snow

10 The kitten heaved its hindlegs, as if fouled,

And died. We bent it in a Christmas box

And scattered blazing weeds to scare the crow

Until the snake-tailed sea-winds coughed and howled

For alms outside the church whose double locks

Wait for St. Peter, the distorted key.

Under St. Peter's bell the parish sea

Swells with its smelt into the burlap shack

Where Joseph plucks his hand-lines like a harp,

And hears the fearful *Puer natus est*[1]

20   Of Circumcision, and relives the wrack

And howls of Jesus whom he holds. How sharp

The burden of the Law before the beast:

Time and the grindstone and the knife of God.

The Child is born in blood, O child of blood.
                                        —*Robert Lowell*

Questions

1. At the end of each line, write either S (for end-stopped) or E (for enjambed).
2. What one consonant is most often repeated at the beginning of words in this poem? Can you discover further alliteration?
3. In the next-to-last line, what vowel sound dominates?

I Wake and Feel the Fell of Dark   (1877)

I wake and feel the fell of dark, not day.

What hours, O what black hours we have spent

This night! what sights you, heart, saw; ways you went!

And more must, in yet longer light's delay.

   With witness I speak this. But where I say

Hours I mean years, mean life. And my lament

Is cries countless, cries like dead letters sent

To dearest him that lives alas! away.

   I am gall, I am heartburn. God's most deep decree

10   Bitter would have me taste: my taste was me;

[1] The Child is born

Bones built in me, flesh filled, blood brimmed the curse.

Selfyeast of spirit a dull dough sours. I see

The lost are like this, and their scourge to be

As I am mine, their sweating selves; but worse.
                                        —*Gerard Manley Hopkins*

Questions

  1. Underline the alliteration in this poem.

  2. Letter each line as end-stopped (S) or enjambed (E).

The Dalliance of the Eagles   (1880)

Skirting the river road, (my forenoon walk, my rest,)

Skyward in air a sudden muffled sound, the dalliance of the eagles,

The rushing amorous contact high in space together,

The clinching interlocking claws, a living, fierce, gyrating wheel,

Four beating wings, two beaks, a swirling mass tight grappling,

In tumbling turning clustering loops, straight downward falling,

Till o'er the river pois'd, the twain yet one, a moment's lull,

A motionless still balance in the air, then parting, talons loosing,

Upward again on slow-firm pinions slanting, their separate diverse flight,

10 She hers, he his, pursuing.
                                        —*Walt Whitman*

Questions

  1. In this poem, mark the pauses within the lines with caesuras (‖).

  2. Note any alliteration or assonance.

Eating Alone   (1985)

I've pulled the last of the year's young onions.
The garden is bare now. The ground is cold,
brown and old. What is left of the day flames
in the maples at the corner of my

eye. I turn, a cardinal vanishes.
By the cellar door, I wash the onions,
then drink from the icy metal spigot.

Once, years back, I walked beside my father
among the windfall pears. I can't recall
10 our words. We may have strolled in silence. But
I still see him bend that way—left hand braced
on knee, creaky—to lift and hold to my
eye a rotten pear. In it, a hornet
spun crazily, glazed in slow, glistening juice.

It was my father I saw this morning
waving to me from the trees. I almost
called to him, until I came close enough
to see the shovel, leaning where I had
left it, in the flickering, deep green shade.

20 White rice steaming, almost done. Sweet green peas
fried in onions. Shrimp braised in sesame
oil and garlic. And my own loneliness.
What more could I, a young man, want.

compare the rhythm if the last line was in another form

                                —*Li-Young Lee*

Questions

1. In the first line, two adjacent words almost rhyme. Find them. How do you describe this phenomenon? Is there anything like it later in the poem?

2. Find assonance. Find alliteration.

3. Find different degrees of enjambment in this poem, and describe its various effects.

4. The last line could end in a question mark but it doesn't. What are the consequences for the sound of the poem?

To Autumn   (1819)

I

Season of mists and mellow fruitfulness,

   Close bosom friend of the maturing sun,

Conspiring with him how to load and bless

   With fruit the vines that round the thatch-eaves run:

To bend with apples the mossed cottage-trees,

   And fill all fruit with ripeness to the core;

To swell the gourd, and plump the hazel shells

With a sweet kernel; to set budding more,

And still more, later flowers for the bees,

10 Until they think warm days will never cease,

For summer has o'er-brimmed their clammy cells.

II

Who hath not seen thee oft amid thy store?

Sometimes whoever seeks abroad may find

Thee sitting careless on a granary floor,

Thy hair soft-lifted by the winnowing wind;

Or on a half-reaped furrow sound asleep,

Drowsed with the fume of poppies, while thy hook

Spares the next swath and all its twinèd flowers;

And sometimes like a gleaner thou dost keep

20   Steady thy laden head across a brook;

Or by a cider-press, with patient look,

Thou watchest the last oozings, hours by hours.

III

Where are the songs of spring? Ay, where are they?

Think not of them, thou hast thy music too—

While barrèd clouds bloom the soft-dying day,

And touch the stubble-plains with rosy hue.

Then in a wailful choir the small gnats mourn

Among the river sallows,° borne aloft   willows

Or sinking as the light wind lives or dies;

30 And full-grown lambs loud bleat from hilly bourn;

Hedge-crickets sing; and now with treble soft

The redbreast whistles from a garden-croft;

And gathering swallows twitter in the skies.
—John Keats

Question

1. Make curved marks over each line of verse, to show the interconnections of alliteration; underneath each line, connect the assonances with horizontal brackets. (See the markings on the line by Thomas Hardy, page 69.)

CHAPTER EIGHT

Meter and Rhyme

meter + rhyme are specialized means toward rhythm — not the only components of it.

Meter and rhyme is examined separately from "The Sound of Poetry" to make a point. From all poems, we demand pleasing sound. All good poems are formal: the poem's words, and their order and arrangement, must seem inevitable and immovable. In some poems, meter and rhyme provide specialized means toward these ends. First we will define meter, distinguishing it from rhythm, and exemplifying its use by poets in the English tradition. Because rhyme is a separate device, and because meter and rhyme can each occur without the other, we will treat rhyme separately, later in the chapter.

Meter

English meter is a count of syllables. Usually, the syllables come in pairs, and one is louder than the other.

Meter is not the same as rhythm. Meter is numbers or counting; rhythm, a vaguer word, implies an approximate recurrence or repetition in the pacing of sound; rhythm, as we saw earlier, is fast or slow, staccato or flowing. Words describing rhythm are imprecise, because rhythm cannot accept precise description. We compare rhythm to a liquid when we call it flowing, or to a broken solid when we call it jagged. The previous chapter devoted space to rhythm in the poetic line, and contrasted the rhythm of Milton's metrical line with the rhythm of the same words broken into different lines; then it made the same contrast with free verse, using poems by John Haines and Walt Whitman (pages 65–67). In each example, the poet's rhythms, deployed in lines, were pleasing to the ear. The same words, broken into other lines, made monotonous or unpleasing rhythms. When we read poems, we invariably perceive rhythm: in a good poem, the rhythm is pleasurable and can even be expressive. In a bad poem, the rhythm tends to be weak, prosaic, boring, and without expressive function. Poems in free verse and poems in meter both have rhythm and, in either type of verse, rhythms may be good or bad.

Meter is numbers, or counting, as we have noted. The word comes from a Greek word, *metron,* which means "measure." In poetry, meter is a count of something we can hear.

In English language poetry, the common meter (known by various names) counts relative loudness and softness of syllables.

Relative Stress

To hear English meter, you must be able to distinguish relative loudness, which is also called *stress* or *accent.* Within a word that has more than one syllable, one syllable is louder than the rest. We speak of proNOUNcing a word, not of PROnouncing or of pronounCING it. In pronouncing the words of our own language, we have memorized a pattern of loudness. When we say conTENT our listeners know we are not speaking of CONtent, because we make two different words, depending on which of the syllables we pronounce more prominently.

Practice your sense of relative loudness. Everyone knows how to pronounce the words that follow; everyone saying them aloud will put the **accent** at the right place. (Accent means prominence; in our language, accent is mostly achieved by relative volume. Sometimes greater length or pitch variation is *added* to volume for the sake of accentuation.) But not everyone can name what is happening when words are pronounced correctly. Pronounce each of these two-syllable words; then decide which of the two syllables is louder.

depict	necktie
hammer	destroy
cowbell	dispatch
rampart	debris
nugget	dental
neglect	

discuss

Try these words of three and more syllables:

memory	implement
rambunctious	implementation
reputation	compliment
dangerous	comprehend

Three-syllable words that take their major accent on the first or the third syllable carry a minor accent on the syllable at the word's other end. In MEM-or-y, *mem* is the accentuated syllable, but the little *-y* at the end is louder, at least, than the *-or-* in the middle. The opposite arrangement works with com-pre-HEND. A word like ar-RANGE-ment, with the accent in the middle, shows no minor accent. (Minor accent is sometimes called secondary stress.) These habits of three-syllable words become important in metrical poems.

Iambic Pentameter: The Foot

For examples, let's start with the English ten-syllable line, arranged as **iambic pentameter**, the most common meter in great English poems. An **iambic foot** in English is a softer syllable followed by a louder one. *Pentameter* translates as "five-measure." Therefore, typical iambic pentameter is five groups of two syllables, the second syllable in each group louder than the first. When we scan—or put marks to indicate the meter of a line—we put bars to separate the feet of the line, making the typical line ˘ ´ | ˘ ´ | ˘ ´ | ˘ ´ | ˘ ´ |. These bars erect a figurative barrier between the feet, to emphasize that stress is relative (and relevant) *only within the foot.*

The ˘ ´ | ˘ ´ | ˘ ´ | ˘ ´ | ˘ ´ | shows the counting that remains constant, which assures that the verse remains metrical. But, while the counting, or **scansion**, stays the same, the rhythm can vary considerably. After all, ˘ ´ | ˘ ´ | ˘ ´ | ˘ ´ | ˘ ´ | could contain ten monosyllables or two polysyllables; it could be fast, it could be slow; it could contain a period, the end of one sentence and the start of another; it could contain many commas, caesuras slowing the line; or it could contain no punctuation at all, and move more quickly. The ˘ ´ | ˘ ´ | ˘ ´ | ˘ ´ | ˘ ´ | tells us very little of what the line will sound like; it shows meter, not rhythm, in five relative hills and five relative valleys. The hills at one point in the line may be lower in elevation than the valleys in another part of the line. "Bang *bang,* bang *bang,* bang *bang,* bang *bang,* bang *bang*" fulfills the pattern. (We can bang this out on the desk top, every even bang louder than every odd one.) But "The University of Michigan" also fulfills the pattern. Say it slowly, exaggerating a little, and you can hear it: "The U-ni-VER-sit-Y of MICH-i-GAN." If you try saying "THE u-NI-ver-SI-ty OF Mich-I-gan," you do not pronounce our language.

The scansion ˘ ´ | ˘ ´ | ˘ ´ | ˘ ´ | ˘ ´ |, common to many lines different in rhythm, describes an expectation the mind develops from reading thousands of lines of poetry. *Iambic pentameter* means, or translates to, "the only thing *all* these lines have in common."

Terms for Feet and for Length of Line

In the examples, we shall continue to concentrate on the iambic foot, most often in the pentameter line. Because we occasionally encounter other meters, it is useful to know terms for the most common feet and lengths of lines.

Some types of feet:
Iambic: a softer syllable followed by a louder: *des*PAIR ˘ ´
Trochaic: a louder syllable followed by a softer: HAPP*y* ´ ˘
Dactylic: a louder syllable followed by two softer ones: CHANGE*able* ´ ˘ ˘
Anapestic: two softer syllables followed by a louder one: *in the* HOUSE ˘ ˘ ´

Some lengths of lines:
Monometer: one foot
Dimeter: two feet
Trimeter: three feet
Tetrameter: four feet
Pentameter: five feet
Hexameter (or the Alexandrine): six feet

Rhythmical Variety within Metrical Regularity

Within absolute metrical regularity, where every line scans as ˘ ´ | ˘ ´ | ˘ ´ | ˘ ´ | ˘ ´ |, iambic pentameter offers all the variety a poet wants or needs. No departure from this scheme is needed for variety's sake. Iambic pentameter finds most of its variety in playing upon the relativity of stress. Seldom in our literature do you find a line as evenly stressed as bang *bang* × 5, or as "The man who stole the bread was making toast." "The University of Michigan," which has only two really loud noises, is more typical of iambic pentameter. Here is the beginning of Keats's "The Eve of St. Agnes":

Sť. Ág | nĕs Ev́e— | Aȟ, bít | tĕr chíll | iť wás . . .

This line scans exactly as our example does, ⌣⌣ | ⌣⌣ | ⌣⌣ | ⌣⌣ | ⌣⌣ |. There is a pause after the fourth syllable, a rhythmical fact the meter does not count. All the even-numbered syllables are louder than all the odd-numbered syllables, and the "louder" sounds are almost equal to each other. The last syllable, *was,* is probably a little softer than the second, fourth, sixth, or eighth syllables—a fact that is part of the rhythm of the line but is irrelevant to its meter. The second line reads:

Tȟe owĺ, | fŏr aĺl | hĭs feáth | eřs, wás | ă-cóld;

which again scans like the pattern. Two caesuras, after the second and the seventh syllables, contribute rhythmical variation. Of the five relatively loud syllables, creating the five feet, three are *quite* loud; two are not so loud as the other three, but still louder than their proximate neighbors *for* and *-ers.* So the variations in true loudness, small as they are, make rhythmical variety, while the sameness of relative loudness makes metrical identity. In the third line,

Tȟe haře | lĭmp'd trémb | lĭng thřough | tȟe fřo | zĕn gráss,

we have another line that scans typically—but this line varies considerably in rhythm from the earlier two. For instance, *through* is louder than the *-ing* of *trembling,* and thus *-ing through* makes a regular foot of relative stress, but *through* is not truly loud at all; its softness—which remains louder than its neighbor—is *metrically* irrelevant, and *rhythmically* pleasing by providing variety. In the first half of this line, the second, third, and fourth syllables are all quite loud. Bang, bang, bang. I do not mean that they are *equally* loud; it would be absurd to suggest that they were each pronounced with an equal number of decibels. But they are all louder than the *through* that takes metrical stress later in the line.

But they cannot be louder than each other. English meter uses *relative stress,* and we can expect that the first loud syllable (the second syllable in the line) is louder than the first soft syllable; the line begins with a regular iamb. Then we have two loud syllables together, *limp'd tremb-,* and in English we would expect that one of the two—the second, if the poem appears iambic—can easily and naturally be spoken more loudly than the first. And so it can.

The order of these four syllables, as a reader says them, may climb four steps of increasing volume, each syllable a little louder than the one before it. If that is so, then *limp'd*—a softer syllable in the meter of the line—would in fact be louder than *hare*—a louder syllable in the meter of the whole line. *Because an invisible foot-separator comes between the two syllables, the relative loudness of* hare *and* limp'd *is metrically irrelevant.*

Keats's fourth line is more like his second line:

Aṅd sí | leṅt wás | tħe flóck | iṅ wóol | lў fóld . . .

Was is not very loud, but it is relatively loud. Nowhere else in the line is there metrical ambiguity or a rhythmical variation.

Thus, English meter, by shrewd use of relativity, can find rhythmical variation without changing the number of syllables in a line, and without changing the order of louder and softer syllables. Once we have read a few thousand lines with a typical swing of louder and softer, we have an expectation in our heads through which we perceive and sort out the syllables on the page. Meter is what lines have in common. If you were asked to scan the single line:

Rocks, caves, lakes, fens, bogs, dens, and shades of death

you would be right to refuse. But if you came upon this line deep in Milton's *Paradise Lost,* when you had learned to step to the tune of iambic pentameter, you would sort it by twos, giving a sharp beat like a foot tap to the even-numbered syllables:

Rocks, *caves,* lakes, *fens,* bogs, *dens,* and *shades* of *death* . . .

You would not sort it (as you could have done if the words had turned up in a prose paragraph) by threes, for instance:

Rocks, caves, *lakes,* bogs, fens, *dens,* and *shades* of *death* . . .

The reading dictated by meter allows large latitude—there can be different heights to these peaks and valleys—but meter imposes limits to its latitude: a peak remains peakish, relative to an adjacent valley.

The Miltonic line gives us an example of iambic pentameter that finds rhythmic variation by adding more volume. It has *more* loud noises in the line than we expect, though it retains only five relative stresses. More commonly, lines like "The University of Michigan" contain *fewer* loud noises than five. Scholars tell us that Shakespeare's pentameter averages about three loud noises a line—and, *not by average but always,* five relative stresses. In *Macbeth*

Tomorrow and tomorrow and tomorrow . . .

makes a typical Shakespearean line. The three *-mor*-s, middles of three *tomorrows,* make three loud noises, each louder than the syllable in front of it, the three *to*s. The two *and*s are not loud, but they are louder than the *-ow*s which come before them, thus adding up to the five iambics of the pentameter.

Metrical Variations

There are several common departures from the ˇˊ | ˇˊ | ˇˊ | ˇˊ | ˇˊ | scheme. These departures are not irregularities; they are variations *within* meter, not outside. We call them metrical variations, and we will talk about them in the order of their frequency. As they are used, they contribute to the variety of metrical verse.

Initial inversion

The most common metrical variation is reversal of the order of louder and softer syllables in one foot. This happens most frequently in the first foot in the line and is called **initial inversion.**

Suppose you have read a hundred lines that share ˇˊ | ˇˊ | ˇˊ | ˇˊ | ˇˊ |. Then you come on a line beginning with a loud syllable—maybe a two-syllable word that can only be pronounced with the louder syllable first, like *studies*. The beginning of this line reverses for one second the order of louder and softer, only to return immediately to the old and expected order. This line with initial inversion scans ˊˇ | ˇˊ | ˇˊ | ˇˊ | ˇˊ |. Look at this sample:

Thĕ Ú | nĭvér | sĭtý | ŏf Mích | ĭgán

Stúdiĕs | thĕ pó | ĕtrý | ŏf Keáts | ănd Fróst.

The little rhythmical turn at the beginning of the second line becomes a familiar dance step in the motion of metrical poetry in English: a little whirl, a sudden tipping-over and recovery, *bang* bang-bang *bang*. This metrical turn resembles the motion of a large inflated toy that is heavily weighted on its rounded bottom surface. When a child pushes it over, the toy immediately rights itself. When Macbeth has said "Tomorrow and tomorrow and tomorrow," he continues,

Creéps ĭn | thĭs pét | tў páce | frŏm dáy | tŏ dáy . . .

and it is clear that *in* is softer than *Creeps*. Although the remainder of this line scans like the pattern, the first foot is inverted—and the expectation that this foot *may* be inverted lurks in the head of the reader. Shakespeare, Milton, Keats, and Frost, all metrical poets, use initial inversion frequently. After Keats wrote "And silent was the flock in woolly fold," his next line made the dance-step of initial inversion:

Numb wĕre | thĕ beáds | măn's fíng | ĕrs, whíle | hĕ tóld . . .

and in the next lines returned to regular motion:

His rosary, and while his frosted breath
Like pious incense from a censor old . . .

Medial inversion

Less frequent than initial inversion is inversion elsewhere in the line, which is called **medial inversion** wherever it comes. Medial inversion makes its own pause, wherever it happens in the line; most medial inversions therefore take place after natural caesuras, often indicated by commas or other marks of punctuation:

> She said to me: open your book and read!

Open your book is that little dance-step of inversion again, now in the middle of the line. In "The Eve of St. Agnes," Keats makes this line:

> Frŏm húr | rў tó | ănd fro. | Soón, ŭp | ălóft . . .

Soon is louder than its neighboring *up*. After the pause for the end of the preceding sentence, Keats has started a new thought with a medial inversion.

Even if the line lacks a natural caesura, medial inversion will make a pause. In Theodore Roethke's "My Papa's Waltz," the poet makes a sudden medial inversion (with an iambic trimeter line; three feet, not five):

> Yŏu béat | tíme ŏn | mў heád . . .

The slight awkwardness of the enforced pause between *beat* and *time* sounds just right for the rhythm of someone beating time on a small boy's head.

Feminine endings

After inversion, the most common metrical variation is the extra syllable. Shakespeare's line

> Tomorrow and tomorrow and tomorrow . . .

is regular iambic. But it has eleven syllables, with an extra syllable at the end of the line. This pattern is called a **feminine ending**. The extra syllable dangles into the pause at the end of the line. It does not feel like a variation, although it varies in fact from the basic scheme. We scan it ˘ ´ | ˘ ´ | ˘ ´ | ˘ ´ | ˘ ´ ˘ | . Robert Frost's blank verse has many feminine endings, as in "The Death of the Hired Man":

> Hĕ búnd | lĕs év | erў fork | fŭl ín | tŏ pláce
>
> Ănd tágs | ănd númb | eřs ít | fŏr fúr | thĕr réferĕnce
>
> Sŏ hé | căn fínd | ănd eás | ĭlý | dĭslódge ĭt.

The last two lines have feminine endings, if you pronounce *reference* with two syllables, as Frost did.

Extra syllables

An extra syllable elsewhere in the line—or in the final foot *before* the last stress—is a palpable metrical variation. The extra syllable, a second softer syllable, makes a foot of three syllables, which scans ⌣⌣ ´. In "The Death of the Hired Man," Frost writes:

> You never see him standing on the hay
> He's trying to lift, straining to lift himself.

Practice scanning these lines. In the second line, the meter begins easily enough with an iambic, *Hĕ's trý-*; the line ends with three feet that start with a medial inversion: *stráining | tŏ líft | hĭmsélf.* In between these two clumps, we have the three syllables of an extra-syllabic foot: *-ĭng tŏ líft.* You may notice that these three syllables are quick to say, occupying no more elapsed time than two syllables elsewhere in the line. Three-syllable feet in an iambic poem tend to be quick to say.

When metrical poetry sounds most conversational and speechlike (in later Shakespeare, in Robert Frost) we find most extra syllables and feminine endings.

Exercises

1. To mark the meter of a line, as we have done in the text, is to *scan;* the result is called *scansion.* Scan the following poems, drawing vertical lines to separate the feet, and showing which syllables are louder, which softer.

from Richard II   (1595)

Let's talk of graves, of worms, and epitaphs,

Make dust our paper, and with rainy eyes

Write sorrow on the bosom of the earth . . .

For God's sake, let us sit upon the ground,

And tell sad stories of the death of kings:

How some have been deposed; some slain in war;

Some haunted by the ghosts they have deposed;

Some poisoned by their wives; some sleeping killed;

All murdered: for within the hollow crown

10 That rounds the mortal temples of a king

Keeps Death his court; and there the antick sits,

Scoffing his state, and grinning at his pomp;

Allowing him a breath, a little scene,

To monarchize, be feared, and kill with looks;

Infusing him with self and vain conceit—

As if this flesh which walls about our life,

Were brass impregnable; and humoured thus,

Comes at the last, and with a little pin

Bores through his castle-wall, and—farewell king!
                    —*William Shakespeare*

To the Western World   (1957)

A siren sang, and Europe turned away

From the high castle and the shepherd's crook.

Three caravels went sailing to Cathay

On the strange ocean, and the captains shook

Their banners out across the Mexique Bay.

And in our early days we did the same.

Remembering our fathers in their wreck

We crossed the sea from Palos where they came

And saw, enormous to the little deck,

10   A shore in silence waiting for a name.

The treasures of Cathay were never found.

In this America, this wilderness

Where the axe echoes with a lonely sound,

The generations labor to possess

And grave by grave we civilize the ground.
                    —*Louis Simpson*

2. The following examples, fabricated for this text, include metrical errors. Assume that they come from poems that have established themselves as iambic pentameter.

> **a.** Ridiculous impoverishments of gold
> Adorn her throat, where jealousy was often told.

> **b.** The dance of death, begun in August air,
> Regales the Autumn and the fair.

> **c.** Harsh moments fail the resplendent flesh of
> Doorjambs heavy, gilt, worn, and repulsive.

Rhyme

Rhyme is a feature common to many metrical poems, not to all. **Blank verse** is iambic pentameter without rhyme; rhyme is what it is blank of. (Do not confuse blank verse with free verse. Free verse, which is free of meters, occasionally has rhyme.) The most common rhyme is the exact repetition, in two or more words, of the final vowel and consonants of a word. *Love,* as we all know, rhymes with *dove.* Here *-ove* is the unity, *l* and *d* the variety.

Direct Rhyme

Look at a rhyming dictionary, and you may be astonished at the variety of rhymes available. Suppose I am writing a rhymed poem and am stuck for a rhyme with the word *decrease.* I could look in *The Complete Rhyming Dictionary and Poet's Craft Book,* edited by Clement Wood, and find under the sound *ees* fifty-nine possible words, beginning: afterpiece/ambergris/battlepiece/Bereneice/Bernice/cantatrice/caprice/cease/surrice/chimneypiece/Clarisse/coulease/crease . . . . If I were rhyming a word like *deletion* on two or more syllables (**feminine rhyme**), I would find another list: accretion/completion/concretion; for a three-syllable rhyme, for *credulous,* for instance, I could find sedulous on another list. These examples are **direct rhyme**.

Indirect Rhyme

Some poets use **indirect rhyme** or **off-rhyme**, almost-but-not-quite directly rhyming. Rhyme/line, for instance, is indirect because the consonants, though similar, are not the same. In rhyme/spice, the vowels rhyme but the consonants differ; this example is also indirect rhyme, but the degree of indirectness is greater. Another poet might rhyme consonants and let the vowels fend for themselves: rhyme/lame/: goat/bleat. Emily Dickinson often used indirect rhyme, sometimes rhyming open vowels that are similar but not the same:

> The Silence condescended—
> Creation stopped—for Me—
> But awed beyond my errand—
> I worshipped—did not "pray"—

If you hold on to the vowel ending of *pray,* its diphthong separates into an *a* and an *e.* The ending *e* rhymes with *Me.* Dickinson also rhymes consonants:

> I cannot live with You—
> It would be Life—
> And Life is over there—
> Behind the Shelf.

Cliché Rhyme

When poets rhyme *love* with *dove,* they make a **cliché rhyme**. Other cliché rhymes include fire/desire, breath/death, and womb/tomb. Occasionally, good poets get away with cliché rhyme, because their syntax or sense makes the second of the cliché rhymes somehow unexpected. Most cliché rhymes are flaws in a poem. Finding cliché rhymes is not an important tool in evaluating poems; rather, it is a way to look at what happens in rhyming. The pairs of rhymes listed above are cliché not only because they have been used so often, but also because the words resemble each other: each of the examples can be a noun, and all but one are monosyllables. Each belongs to the same level of diction. Most important, each recalls its mate by similarity or opposition of meaning. Fire is a symbol of desire. Breath is ended by death. What begins in the womb ends in the tomb. For all these reasons, the first word of each pair leads one to expect the second, and when expectation is exactly fulfilled, the result is boredom. A poem must balance the predictable with the unpredictable, expectation with surprise, unity with variety.

Original Rhyme

In a rhyme, the unity is the repetition of sound; the variety is all the other differences two words can muster. For instance, words can differ in length, and we can rhyme a monosyllable with a polysyllable, like *tracks* with *haversacks.* We can rhyme words spelled differently, like *tracks* with *axe.* We can rhyme different parts of speech, a verb *hacks* with a noun *jacks.* We can rhyme words of different backgrounds, like *egomaniacs* with *humpbacks,* or *kleptomaniacs* with *packs.* We can rhyme combinations of alien words: *Jack's/ hypochondriacs/kayaks/quacks.* In feminine rhyme, we can pair two words with one, rhyming *pluck it* with *Nantucket.*

The further apart the words are, the more original the rhyme. At extremes, rhyme can be witty or comic. In one of his poems, Ogden Nash uses a *boomerang* for hunting in order to cook a *kangaroo meringue.* Witty rhyme would be inappropriate to many poems, in which neither poet nor reader would want rhyme to stand out and be noticeable apart from the poem's other qualities. Highly original rhyme is appropriate in this poem:

Early in the Morning   (1950)

Early in the morning	There's trouble ahead."
The dark Queen said,	Spent with carousing,
"The trumpets are warning	With wine-soaked wits,

Antony drowsing
Whispered, "It's
Too cold a morning
10 To get out of bed."

The army's retreating,
The fleet has fled,
Caesar is beating
His drums through the dead.
"Antony, horses!
We'll get away,
Gather our forces
For another day . . ."

"It's a cold morning,"
20 Antony said.

Caesar Augustus
Cleared his phlegm.
"Corpses disgust us.
Cover them."
Caesar Augustus
In his time lay
Dying, and just as
Cold as they,
On the cold morning
30 Of a cold day.
        —*Louis Simpson*

Line length contributes to the wit of rhyming here; with only two feet to a line, rhyming becomes a stunt. Who would have expected *drowsing* to rhyme with *carousing,* or *Augustus* with *just as* and *disgust us?*

Natural Rhyme

In this poem by Thomas Hardy, rhyme is neither cliché nor witty. Through the skill of the poet, the rhyme appears natural in the poem while it adds its particular music:

The Oxen   (1915)

Christmas Eve, and twelve of the clock.
    "Now they are all on their knees,"
An elder said as we sat in a flock
    By the embers in hearthside ease.

We pictured the meek mild creatures where
    They dwelt in their strawy pen,
Nor did it occur to one of us there
    To doubt they were kneeling then.

So fair a fancy few would weave
10   In these years! Yet, I feel,
If someone said on Christmas Eve,
    "Come; see the oxen kneel

"In the lonely barton° by yonder coomb°   farmyard; a hollow
    Our childhood used to know,"
I should go with him in the gloom,
    Hoping it might be so.
        —*Thomas Hardy*

This rhyme helps fix the poem's form, click the lid of its box; it neither stands out as a stunt of wit nor bores us with the overly predictable.

Rhymed Stanzas

"The Oxen" is written in **stanzas**; a stanza is an arrangement of metrical lines, sometimes different in length, with a repeated order of rhyme, a **rhyme-scheme**. We indicate rhyme-schemes by letters. For "The Oxen," the rhyme-scheme is ABAB, because the first and third lines rhyme, and the second and fourth. Sometimes poets invent stanzas and rhyme schemes of great complexity, varying line length and the arrangements of rhyme.

Tywater (1947)

Death of Sir Nihil, book the *nth,*   a

Upon the charred and clotted sward,   b

Lacking the lily of our Lord,   b

Alases of the hyacinth.   a

Could flicker from behind his ear   c

A whistling silver throwing knife   d

And with a holler punch the life   d

Out of a swallow in the air.   c

Behind the lariat's butterfly   e

10   Shuttled his white and gritted grin,   f

And cuts of sky would roll within   f

The noose-hole, when he spun it high.   e

The violent, neat and practised skill   g

Was all he loved and all he learned;   h

When he was hit, his body turned   h

To clumsy dirt before it fell.   g

And what to say of him, God knows.   i

Such violence. And such repose.   i

                —*Richard Wilbur*

God's Love   (1990)

God loves us all, I'm pleased to say—   *a*

Or those who love him anyway—   *a*

Or those who love him and are good.   *b*

Or so they say. Or so he should.   *b*
                              —*Vikram Seth*

Questions

1. Scan each poem. Mark the rhyme schemes with the appropriate letters.

2. Discriminate between direct and indirect rhymes in the two poems. Find different types of off-rhyme.

3. In these poems, look for examples of cliché rhyme, original rhyme, and natural rhyme. Can you find all of them?

4. To practice scansion, mark the poems double-spaced on pages 70–75. Which poems are free-verse?

CHAPTER NINE

Forms and Types of Poetry

Poetic forms are traditional arrangements of line and rhyme-scheme, like the sonnet. (When we use the word *forms* for these arrangements, we are not calling other poetry—like free verse or blank verse—formless. *Form* is merely a traditional word for this sort of arrangement.)

By types of poetry, we mean distinctions between narrative and dramatic poetry on the one hand and, on the other, subdivisions like the epigram and the prose poem. These forms and types do not exhaust poetry's possibilities; they are exemplary and suggestive.

Poetic Forms

The Limerick

Each form of poetry demands a particular number of lines, of certain length, rhyming in a certain way. In a *limerick,* for instance, two rhyming trimeter lines are followed by two dimeter lines, which also rhyme, and then by a fifth trimeter line, which rhymes with the first two. The rhyme-scheme is AABBA, and the BB lines are often indented. A limerick's feet are usually three syllables long, each an **anapest**: softer, softer, louder, or ⌣⌣ ⌐. (Authors of limericks sometimes substitute iambs for anapests.) Here is an example by a modern master of the form, Edward Gorey (born 1925):

> Each night Father fills me with dread
> When he sits on the foot of my bed;
>   I'd not mind that he speaks
>   In gibbers and squeaks,
> But for seventeen years he's been dead.

These anonymous limericks can provide a refresher course in meter:

> There was a young man of Japan
> Whose verses would never scan.
>   When he was asked why
>   He would reply
> Well, I simply try to get as many syllables into the last line as I possibly can.

There was a young man of China
Whose aesthetic was somewhat fina.
   It was his design
   To make the last line
Short.

So much for limericks, which can serve as an example of many poetic forms using particular line lengths and rhyme schemes.*

The Haiku

Many American students have written haikus in school. When English haiku-writers follow the Japanese syllable count, they use lines of five, seven, and five syllables. The **haiku**, an imagistic poem, usually includes two images, of which the second is a surprise, a leap from the first. At a minimum, the two images conflict. Here is a translation from a sixteenth-century Japanese poet named Moritaki:

A falling petal
drops upward, back to the branch;
it's a butterfly.

Many poets writing haikus in English, aware of differences between English and Japanese, ignore syllable count and concentrate on images.

The Sonnet

The poetic form of the sonnet has remained at the center of English poetry from the sixteenth century onward. English poets from Thomas Wyatt (1503–1542) to the present have found the sonnet a congenial form, mostly for emotional statement. In one of his own sonnets, Wordsworth spoke of the sonnet as the key with which Shakespeare unlocked his heart. Shakespeare wrote a sequence of sonnets, as did many other poets in the sixteenth and seventeenth centuries. Even when it is a part of a sequence, a sonnet is a whole and individual poem, of a certain length, with several possible internal structures whereby a poet can entertain and conclude a whole, small subject. Early sonnets and sonnet sequences were mostly concerned with love. John Donne's "Holy Sonnets" are religious, as are many of Milton's sonnets. More recently, sonnets have extended themselves to all sorts of feelings.

The sonnet is fourteen lines long, and written in iambic pentameter. (We can find poems called sonnets that are exceptions to these rules; the word originally meant "little song" and some poets have interpreted the word broadly.) Sonnets have three main traditional structures and rhyme schemes. One is the **Italian** or **Petrarchan sonnet**, which is divided into two parts. The octave, the first eight lines, uses only two rhymes: ABBAABBA. The sestet in an Italian or Petrarchan sonnet can rhyme in several ways—CDECDE is

---

* Readers interested in the many poetic forms not mentioned here may consult Lewis Turco's *A Book of Forms,* which defines and exemplifies widely among special forms, or look at the pages about poetic forms in Clement Wood's *Complete Rhyming Dictionary.*

common; so is CDCDCD—so long as it does not end in a couplet. Many English poets, notably Milton and Wordsworth, have practiced the Italian sonnet with success.

The English language, however, is noted for the paucity of its rhyme, especially compared to the Italian richness in rhyme-words. The octave of the Italian sonnet can make trouble for the English poet, because it uses only two rhyme-sounds for eight words. The **English sonnet**, more commonly called the **Shakespearean sonnet**, began a little earlier than Shakespeare—it was first used by Henry Howard, Earl of Surrey (1517–1547)—and uses a rhyme scheme more adapted to the English language: ABAB CDCD EFEF GG. Edmund Spenser, finding the Italian sonnet not suited to English but the English sonnet too loose, invented a third rhyme scheme that is a compromise between the two: ABAB BCBC CDCD EE. This arrangement makes the **Spenserian sonnet**.

Rhyme-schemes are probably less important to sonnets than structures of thought, but rhyme-schemes seem to suggest such structures. In the Italian sonnet, the octave and the sestet usually make a two-part structure not further subdivided. Frequently, an octave will set forth a problem, or tell a story, to which the sestet may provide a solution, a counterdirection, a commentary, or a surprise. There are exceptions; some Italian sonnets are indivisible fourteen-line poems.

The English or Shakespearean sonnet, which often breaks down into eight and six, may also break in other places. It may subdivide into four and four, plus four and two; or into four, four, four, and two; or into eight, four, and two. The Shakespearean sonnet, structurally more adaptable, is a less precise form.

Quoted throughout this text are sonnets by Shakespeare (see pages 36 and 39). Here is another:

Let me not to the marriage of true minds   (1609)

Let me not to the marriage of true minds
Admit impediments. Love is not love
Which alters when it alteration finds,
Or bends with the remover to remove.
O no, it is an ever-fixèd mark
That look on tempests and is never shaken;
It is the star to every wand'ring bark,
Whose worth's unknown, although his height be taken.
Love's not Time's fool, though rosy lips and cheeks
10 Within his bending sickle's compass come;
Love alters not with his brief hours and weeks,
But bears it out even to the edge of doom.
    If this be error and upon me proved,
    I never writ, nor no man ever loved.
                    —*William Shakespeare*

Notice the rhyme scheme in this sonnet by John Milton:

On the Late Massacre in Piedmont[1]   (1655)

Avenge, O Lord, thy slaughtered saints, whose bones
Lie scattered on the Alpine mountains cold;
Ev'n them who kept thy truth so pure of old,
When all our fathers worshipped stocks and stones,
Forget not: in thy book record their groans
Who were thy sheep, and in their ancient fold
Slain by the bloody Piedmontese, that rolled
Mother with infant down the rocks. Their moans
The vales redoubled to the hills, and they
10 To heav'n. Their martyred blood and ashes sow
O'er all th' Italian fields, where still doth sway
The triple[2] Tyrant that from these may grow
A hundredfold, who, having learnt thy way,
Early may fly the Babylonian woe.[3]

—John Milton

Italian sonnet

Wordsworth, Keats, Tennyson, Frost—most great poets have turned to the sonnet during their lives. Examples of the sonnet may be found throughout this book. See, for instance, pages 71–72, 153, 221, 318, 322, and 358.

Poetic Types

Ballad

A ballad is almost a form—at least, there are typical stanzas, and even ballads we can call typical—but the word *ballad* does not represent a form as codified as the sonnet. Although ballads tell stories, we separate them from the later category of narrative poetry, because they form a great body of anonymous literature, and from the later, sophisticated imitation of the ballad. Here is an anonymous Scots ballad, with some old Scottish words footnoted:

Edward

"Why dois[1] your brand[2] sae[3] drap[4] wi bluid,[5]
    Edward, Edward,
Why dois your brand sae drap wi bluid,
    And why sae sad gang[6] yee O?"
"O I hae[7] killed my hauke[8] sae guid,[9]
    Mither, mither,
O I hae killed my hauke sae guid,
    And I had nae mair[10] but hee O."

"Your haukis bluid was nevir sae reid,[11]
10   Edward, Edward,

[1] In 1655 the Protestant Waldenses of southern France were suppressed for refusing to adhere to Roman Catholicism.   [2] A reference to the papal crown.   [3] See Revelation 14:1–3,8.

[1] does [2] sword [3] so [4] drip [5] blood [6] go [7] have [8] hawk [9] good [10] more [11] red

Your haukis bluid was nevir sae reid,
    My deir son I tell thee O."
"O I hae killed my reid roan steid,[12]
    Mither, mither,
O I hae killed my reid roan steid,
    That erst [13] was sae fair and free O."

"Your steid was auld,[14] and ye hae gat mair,
    Edward, Edward,
Your steid was auld, and ye hae gat mair,
20   Sum other dule[15] ye drie[16] O."
"O I hae killed my fadir[17] deir,
    Mither, mither,
O I hae killed my fadir deir,
    Alas, and wae[18] is mee O!"

"And whatten penance wul[19] ye drie for that,
    Edward, Edward?
And whatten penance wul ye drie for that?
    My deir son, now tell me O."
"Ile set my feet in yonder boat,
30   Mither, mither,
Ile set me feet in yonder boat,
    And Ile fare ovir the sea O."

"And what wul ye doe wi your towirs and your ha,[20]
    Edward, Edward?
And what wul ye doe wi your towirs and your ha,
    That were sae fair to see O?"
"Ile let thame stand tul they doun fa,
    Mither, mither,
Ile let thame stand tul they doun fa,
40   For here nevir mair maun[21] I bee O."

"And what wul ye leive to your bairns[22] and your wife,
    Edward, Edward?
And what wul ye leive to your bairns and your wife,
    Whan ye gang ovir the sea O?"
"The warldis[23] room, let them beg thrae[24] life,
    Mither, mither,
The warldis room, let them beg thrae life,
    For thame nevir mair wul I see O."

"And what wul ye leive to your ain[25] mither deir?
50   Edward, Edward?
And what wul ye leive to your ain mither dier?
    My deir son, now tell me O."
"The curse of hell frae[26] me sall[27] ye beir,[28]

---

[12] steed   [13] formerly   [14] old   [15] grief   [16] suffer   [17] father   [18] woe   [19] will   [20] hall   [21] mus
[22] children   [23] world's   [24] through   [25] own   [26] from   [27] shall   [28] bear

Mither, mither,
The curse of hell frae me sall ye beir,
   Sic[29] counseils[30] ye gave to me O."

                              —Anonymous

A ballad tells a story. In "Edward," the story is told in dialogue, as if the poem were a tiny play, with the speeches organized into stanzas. In the tight and musical stanzas of this ballad, we hear a son reluctantly telling his mother that he has killed his father, and finally cursing his mother for having urged him to patricide. When a harrowing story is told in rhymed and delicate verses, the tension between form and content, story and music makes a dreadful energy.

Later poets imitated old ballad forms in writing narrative poems. One of the most famous literary ballads in English is by John Keats:

La Belle Dame sans Merci[1]   (1820)

Oh, what can ail thee, knight-at-arms,
   Alone and palely loitering?
The sedge has withered from the lake,
   And no birds sing!

Oh, what can ail thee, knight-at-arms,
   So haggard and so woe-begone?
The squirrel's granary is full,
   And the harvest's done.

I see a lily on thy brow,
10   With anguish moist and fever-dew,
And on thy cheek a fading rose
   Fast withereth too.

I met a lady in the meads
   Full beautiful, a fairy's child.
Her hair was long, her foot was light,
   And her eyes were wild.

I made a garland for her head,
   And bracelets too, and fragrant zone;
She looked at me as she did love,
20   And made sweet moan.

I set her on my pacing steed,
   And nothing else saw all day long;
For sidelong would she bend, and sing
   A fairy's song.

---

[29] such   [30] advice
[1] The beautiful, pitiless woman

She found me roots of relish sweet,
    And honey wild, and manna dew;
And sure in language strange she said,
    "I love thee true."

She took me to her elfin grot,
30   And there she wept, and sighed full sore,
And there I shut her wild wild eyes
    With kisses four.

And there she lullèd me asleep
    And there I dreamed—Ah! woe betide!—
The latest dream I ever dreamed
    On the cold hill side.

I saw pale kings and princes too,
    Pale warriors, death-pale were they all;
The cried—"La belle Dame sans merci
40   Hath thee in thrall!"

I saw their starved lips in the gloam
    With horrid warning gapèd wide,
And I awoke and found me here,
    On the cold hill side.

And this is why I sojourn here,
    Alone and palely loitering,
Though the sedge is withered from the lake,
    And no birds sing.

                —*John Keats*

(On page 114 are examples of Keats's revisions of this poem.) The verse here is smoother and more literary than the old ballads, and the language is closer to our own, but the poem makes its ancestry clear.

Narrative, Epic, Dramatic

Many poems, including ballads, tell stories and are therefore narrative. The earliest surviving poetry is narrative, ancient epics originally chanted or sung to a form of musical accompaniment. *Gilgamesh* is the oldest surviving poem, composed in Sumeria about five thousand years ago; Homer's *Iliad* and *Odyssey* are a mere three thousand years old. These epics were composed orally, before the invention of writing; they were memorized, and changed ("revised") by generations of reciter-poets. (There was no single, innovative, sole-author Homer, though it is possible that one blind bard assembled and organized the *Iliad* and the *Odyssey* more thoroughly than any of his predecessors.)

    Prehistoric Greeks remembered and celebrated their past by memorizing Homer. Epics are historical records of the heroes of the tribe, combining fact and legend. Centuries after these oral epics were composed, professional poets made sophisticated epics in imitation of the old collective style. The Roman Virgil, wishing to write a patriotic poem in service to his emperor Augustus, followed the pattern of Homer when he composed *The Aeneid.*

In the Christian era, Dante's *Divine Comedy* is a sophisticated epic. Its embodiment of Christian theology makes it a vast departure from classical forms, but the ghost who guides Dante through hell to purgatory is Virgil himself. In English, the great epic is *Paradise Lost,* Milton's seventeenth-century account of creation and the war between good and evil.

Many poems are narrative tales, comic or tragic, without being epic. The great narrative poet in English is Geoffrey Chaucer. His language is archaic, and best saved for advanced study, but there is a sample of his poetry on page 203. *The Canterbury Tales* is a lengthy series of different stories told by and about ordinary people—not, like an epic, tales of gods and heroes making history.

After Chaucer, to the present time, many poets have written stories in rhyme and meter (less often in free verse). Some of the stories take dramatic form, most often as monologues by a speaker who reveals himself as he tells his story (see Robert Browning's "My Last Duchess," pages 199–200). One example of modern narrative is a story poem by Robert Frost:

"Out, Out—" (1916)

The buzz saw snarled and rattled in the yard
And made dust and dropped stove-length sticks of wood,
Sweet-scented stuff when the breeze drew across it.
And from there those that lifted eyes could count
Five mountain ranges one behind the other
Under the sunset far into Vermont.
And the saw snarled and rattled, snarled and rattled,
As it ran light, or had to bear a load.
And nothing happened: day was all but done.
10 Call it a day, I wish they might have said
To please the boy by giving him the half hour
That a boy counts so much when saved from work.
His sister stood beside them in her apron
To tell them "Supper." At the word, the saw,
As if to prove saws knew what supper meant,
Leaped out at the boy's hand, or seemed to leap—
He must have given the hand. However it was,
Neither refused the meeting. But the hand!
The boy's first outcry was a rueful laugh,
20 As he swung toward them holding up the hand
Half in appeal, but half as if to keep
The life from spilling. Then the boy saw all—
Since he was old enough to know, big boy
Doing a man's work, though a child at heart—
He saw all spoiled. "Don't let him cut my hand off—
The doctor, when he comes. Don't let him, sister!"

So. But the hand was gone already.
The doctor put him in the dark of ether.
He lay and puffed his lips out with his breath.
30 And then—the watcher at his pulse took fright.
No one believed. They listened at his heart.
Little—less—nothing!—and that ended it.
No more to build on there. And they, since they
Were not the one dead, turned to their affairs.

—Robert Frost

Many younger American poets are returning to poems of narrative and character; their poems might almost be short stories, except that they are written in lines. Here's a story about a Puerto Rican barber in New York, written (we are told in a subtitle) by his daughter remembering her father's talk.

Valentino's Hair   (1987)
1960—my father cannot help but tell

It's been almost thirty-five years.
I can scarcely believe it, niña.
Time trusts no one and so it disappears
before us like the smoke from my
    cigarette.
In 1925 I was young, I was a part
of a world eating at its own edges
without being satisfied.
The Roaring Twenties didn't roar.
10 They swelled with passions.
They danced, and I danced with them.

I had a barber shop in a Manhattan
    hotel.
It is not there anymore.
It burned down during World War II.
But in its time it was elegant, private.
My shop was small, only one chair.
Every comb, every lotion, every towel
    perfect:
20 like the stars which burn in the sky,
everything shined.
The barber chair was gold-leafed
and made of the softest leather.
A man could fall asleep in that chair
with lather still fresh on his face.
There were four large oval mirrors,
two on one wall, two on the opposite
    wall.
They faced each other like distant
30   lovers,
never permitted to kiss,

only permitted to greet each other
with their cool but receptive stares.

The walls had cloth wallpaper.
The wallpaper too had gold leaf
with a blue and brown background of
    leaves
and trees and ocean in the distance.
And it reminded me of my town
40   Aguadilla,
the great stretches of beach,
the lush rain forests of Puerto Rico.
Anyway, fate had been good to me,
and I was owner of the barber shop
in the hotel, and I made good money,
and the times looked good,
and I lost a lot of money
before the Twenties were gone.
But that's not why I'm telling you this.

50 One day in 1926, early afternoon, 1:00
    P.M.,
things were slow, and I was reading
    the paper,
studying the horse racing sheet.
Mangual had come by, picked up a
    couple of bets
from me and got a haircut.
He had hair in those days.
It was just after he had left,
60 and I remember thinking what a hot
    summer

we were having, and I was tipped back
in my barber chair,
almost sleeping, almost dreaming.
You know how it is when you're
    between
sleep and dream and a slight push
can send you into one world or the
    other.
70 Well, suddenly the wall phone rang.
I thought for sure it was Mangual.
Sometimes he'd call and try to get me
to change my bets. He'd tell me
I was wasting my money,
and he had a tip on a horse
so fast you'd think it had six legs.

The phone rang a second time.
I did not hurry. I don't quite know why,
but I waited until the fourth ring
80 and snapped forward in the chair
and lifted the phone receiver off the
    hook.
The front desk at the hotel was calling.
A guest wanted a haircut and shave.
I had no customers in the shop, except
maybe a fly seeking decay in summer
    heat.
I said I was available, asked for the
    room number.
90 That was that. Just another customer,
I remember thinking. Possibly a
    stockbroker,
a businessman, maybe Mafia.
I'd given them haircuts and shaves too.

I took my best tools.
I had recently purchased them
and had a special black leather box
    made.
Like a doctor.
100 In a way I was a kind of doctor.
What I did helped people ride a stream
to slow recovery, to arrive on the shore
of something new, something hidden.
A secret place. A secret person.
Well, so I went. I closed my shop,
putting a note on the door saying
I'd be back in an hour, and then I
    strutted down
the wine-red carpeted hallway into the
110   lobby,

past the front desk and into the elevator.
I pressed the button for the eighth floor
and rode up alone to my destiny.

There was a small mirror on the
    elevator wall,
just above the button panel.
It was there for the ladies and
    gentlemen,
on their way to parties,
120 to look one last time at the present.
And so I did. I stared into the face
of a twenty-seven-year-old man
who knew little about the ways of this
    world.
And for that moment I thought I saw
    someone else.
Someone who was walking towards me
from another place we held in common.
The elevator door opened
130 to wake me from my daydream.

Room 808 was my customer,
and I found myself at the door
tapping lightly on its face.
The rooms were spacious,
and the windows faced Central Park.
I could hear the sound of an electric
    fan
as the door opened, and I was greeted
by a fair-haired, frail-looking man.
140 He was in a dark suit,
and he was smoking a cigarette in a
    holder.
Quite a dandy. He greeted me warmly,
thanked me for being so prompt.
His employer was absolutely desperate
to be ready for an evening engagement
and had little time or desire to walk
the busy streets looking for a barber
    shop,
150 and if he did walk the streets,
he probably would be mobbed by
    admirers,
and he would definitely make my time
    worthwhile,
and I had come highly recommended.

Well, all these things came quickly
out of this amiable, high-strung
    American

as he led me to a room where the light
160   was good
and which had been prepared
with a chair, table, and large mirror.
The sink was to the left of the table.
I began setting the tools on the table
and emptying my satchel of hair and
    skin products,
which I had also brought with me.
As I did, I looked up at the mirror,
more so to see if it was clean than
170   anything else.
When I did, I saw the reflection,
a dark-haired man in the mirror
standing in the doorway behind me.
It was the ladykiller.
It was Rudolph Valentino.
He looked drawn and tired.
He had obviously not shaved
for his face was already darkening with
    whiskers.
180   He was wearing a very white
    undershirt
and a pair of dark pants.
By his side was a very slim, exotic
    looking woman.
They were arguing, but very quietly,
in whispers like lovers separated
by a thin wall from their neighbors.
The woman kept insisting on
    something,
190   and she called him Rudy.
He finally looked at me staring at him
in the mirror and smiled slightly,
    stopping the woman
in her sentence by simply saying,
    "Enough!"
He closed the door behind him,
    walked towards me,
his hand out to shake my hand.

And to my surprise he said my name.
200   "I'm glad to meet you, Señor Sapia."
The look of amazement must have
    been on my face.
I suddenly began to feel flushed.
In the mirror I could see how red my
    cheeks were.
And then he apologized and told me
his secretary had a bad habit

of never informing people who their
    customer was.
210   One time in California
he needed a manicure and a pedicure.
The hotel sent up an elderly lady
to give him what he requested.
But she was never told who her client
    was.
When Valentino walked out to greet
    her,
his pants leg rolled up, barefoot,
the woman drew in a long hard look
220   and fainted on the royal blue rug,
her silver hair perfectly in place.
Valentino tried to revive her
and members of his party called
for the house doctor and all was panic.
And the strange thing was
they couldn't revive her.
They declared the woman dead,
Valentino concluded, remorse in his
    voice.
230   The hotel cooperated,
reported the woman died of a heart
    attack
in the hallway, not Valentino's room.
He had enough of scandal.
This would have been too cruel,
too bizarre, he confessed.
I was struck by Valentino's story.
Why should he tell me,
Facundo Sapia, a simple barber?

240   My girl, I was suddenly caught
between laughing and crying.
The poor man had a power
he couldn't control,
and here I was absolving him
of his sin, listening to his confession
like a priest in my white smock.
And now he was to do penance,
he was to give something up to me.
I would raise my chalice of shaving
250   cream
and lift my silver razor to the light.

"Sapia means wisdom, doesn't it?" he
    asked.
"Yes," I told him. "My mother's name
    was Inocencia."

"Ah," he said. "What a beautiful name,
  Innocent Wisdom."
And he sat down in the chair,
looked into the mirror, and asked me
260 to help him with this man in the mirror,
meaning, of course, himself.
I covered him with the white apron.
And I began to apply the shaving cream
to his face while his eyes stared directly
into the eyes of the pitiful man
he thought he saw in the mirror.
I began to lather and disguise
that perfect face, slowly, with
  compliance,
270 like an accomplice to the development
of the belief in one god.
Perhaps her god was what
the elderly lady thought she saw
before she fainted into death.

As I shaved Rudolph Valentino,
he remained silent, and I remained
  silent.
My hands had to be steady,
for they guided the instrument
280 and I simply followed.
Valentino noticed my hands.
They looked like his father's hands,
the way the fingers naturally curved
when the hand relaxed.
I began to cut his hair;
he trained his eyes on my hands.
"You do not realize it," he said,
"but you are cutting away at my life too,
time leaving me like moments
290 falling to the floor."

Suddenly, I was afraid of a man
I could easily destroy
with one swerve of my razor,
with one jolt of my scissors.
A man who was a great lover,
not philosopher.
I didn't want to hear philosophy.
I wanted to know about the desert at
  night,
300 the ride of the four horsemen,
the posture of the tango.
But he was speaking about death,
his own death.

And he was implicating me.
But most frightening of all,
I had this disturbing feeling he was
  right.
He was dying. I was dying.
We were all dying at this moment,
310 in this place, where his hair fell calmly
to the floor like our simple desires.

Somehow I gathered my courage
and told him he had something
all men wished they had.
It was not his money or his appearance.
He immediately turned directly to me,
causing my scissor to glance
slightly off of his left ear.
He just stared at me.
320 Didn't say one word.
He just looked and looked into my face.
I felt like a broken fish under the eye
  of God;
he was waiting for the answer.
What he had was a way with women.
I told him about the woman I was in
  love with
but who did not even care if I lived or
  died.
330 She did not even know I existed.
Oh, she was a friend of a friend,
and we talked, but I could sense
she had no fascination for me.
It was odd to tell this to Rudolph
  Valentino,
a man never scorned by a woman,
a man who had probably made love
to every woman he touched.

Well, we continued in silence.
340 I trimming his hair,
which was in need of a haircut,
and he turned toward the mirror,
staring into his own eyes,
then once or twice stealing
a quick, deliberate glance at me.
The silence in the room
made everything else around us so
  loud.

My scissors clipping steadily.
350 The car horns from down on the street.

Suddenly I could hear the young man
and the exotic looking woman
in the next room arguing,
at first with quick exchanges and long
    pauses.
Then their voices grew more intense,
    more hateful,
until finally I heard a crash or a fall,
I really wasn't sure which.
360 But I could hear someone crying and
    gasping
and trying to talk, trying to defend.
It was the young man's voice.
I think she had hit him with something.
Valentino's eyes changed.
"Damn it, damn it," he started saying.
"Yes, I'm lucky," he said to me,
"and I'll probably be lucky in hell too."

He suddenly laughed, as if he realized
370 something ridiculous
far beyond his reach,
distant as his past.
By then I had begun putting talcum
    powder
around his neck, ready to remove
the white apron covered with his hair.
His image in the mirror was the image
I had seen in the dark theatre.
Valentino gave the mirror his famous
380   profile,
the delicate ears, the high forehead,
    the angular nose.

"Señor Sapia," he said, very
    conclusively,
"your reputation is not exaggerated."
With that, he gave me a one hundred
    dollar bill
from a money clip he had in his
    pocket,
390 and he walked ceremoniously out the
    door.

Something happened to me, mi
    muchacha.
Something seized my senses.
He had said it himself:
"You are cutting away at my life too."
We all take something from each other.
It was then I got down on my knees,
began gathering with these hands his
400   hair,
hurrying like a mad man,
afraid someone would open the door,
    catch me,
afraid someone would see my
    uncontrollable frenzy.
One month later he died and I
    discovered
the magical power of the hair.
It was then when I used that power.
410 I used it to seduce a woman I loved.
The woman who didn't love me.
                —*Yvonne Sapia*

Here's a poem more of character than of narrative. David Dooley takes on the voice of an old writer submitting to an interview:

How I Wrote It   (1988)

What the goddamn hell are you talking about, boy,
I never did one thing in my life on account of a theory—
look here: do you breathe theory? do you piss theory? do you fuck theory?
When I was living in Paris with Olga, if you've read me
you know about Olga, Polish whore and a damn good one,
claimed to be a Russian countess, that was her theory,
but she forgot she was a countess, even forgot she was a whore,
she liked it so much you see, opened her legs, dark thick hair,
rich-cunted—one point I will make for your tape recorder,
10 you can't be an artist without a sense of smell,
    nights when I'd stagger home to Olga, I'd stop in the alley

and get a whiff of the beer, the piss, rotting vegetables,
some nights vomit, before I hauled upstairs and put it to her,
a woman who made use of a man's efforts,
not like that Oriental whore, she's in one of the books too,
who started chewing an apple when I was ready to explode.
So I'd give her the kind of fucking she was meant for
and afterwards sometimes I'd go to the typewriter buck naked
and start writing till she bitched about the noise
20 though more than once she fell asleep and honked like a flight of geese
but she'd bitch so I'd open a notebook and while she slept,
on summer nights the windows open and she lay there naked asleep
the covers tangled down at her knees till I wouldn't know
if I were writing with my pen or my cock, I'd use
whatever tool I needed. There were no answers
because there were never any questions. If you write,
you don't need answers. That's where you fellows go wrong.
You need books and paper and food and cunt and drink
and that's it. By daybreak there'd be pages of Olga in the typewriter,
30 pages of Olga in the notebook, and squirming in the bed
she'd be rubbing the yellow muck out of her big cow eyes.
Pages of Olga, and growing up in Baltimore,
the train ride to Marseille in the dead of winter,
Kontarsky and the pimples on his ass, the baptistery doors in Florence.
And I bought this great roll of wrapping paper
from a butcher shop, and on it I wrote plans, ideas, images.
Then I hung these scrolls of wrapping paper on the walls,
all around me were the books I was going to write.
Olga would have preferred pictures of milkmaids,
40 things she could sell for whiskey when times were bad.
The novel, how to write the novel, I heard that guff
in *caves,* bars, cafés, from writers who drank when
they should have been writing, and some, as Prescott said,
who wrote when they should have been drinking.
Art, Prescott went on and on about art, significant form,
he and his nancy-boy friends over from Oxford.
You mean writing, I said? Writing means getting your hands dirty,
writing means getting filthy all over. Holy men like dirt.
A holy man told me that once. Gurudev, surely you've heard the name.
50 Gurudev told me that in my room, Anneke's room actually,
I was living with Anneke then, she had a razor scar that long
across her left cheek where a crazy pimp cut her,
and the damnedest thing was, it made her sexier than before.
Every writer in Paris wanted to bang her, and a lot of them did.
One evening Gurudev was sitting cross-legged on the floor
so I decided to try it too, turned out I was a natural at it,
and Anneke got mad and pitched one of her crazy fits,
she could throw fits the way sows piss, so she was raving about men,
what pigs they were, how life was *merde* and God was a wad of snot.
60 Before I could swear at her, Gurudev leaned toward her, grinned,
and said, "I couldn't agree more!" Even Anneke had to laugh at that,
although she had absolutely no sense of humor and was drunk,

if he hadn't been a holy man she'd have ripped off his cotton pajamas,
damn near did it anyway—if a vixen in heat trapped in quicksand
could laugh, that was how she barked and howled with laughter.
Then she calmed down, tried to sit cross-legged and fell over backwards.
Gurudev taught us some of his chanting, and I was inspired to sing
"Don't Sit Under the Apple Tree with Anyone Else but Me,"
which Anneke thought was funny, and clapped her hands like a baby,
70   then I sang "I'll Take You Home Again, Kathleen" like an Irish tenor,
which sounds like when you began to sing, someone grabbed your balls
and twisted. Gurudev giggled. Indian holy men have fine giggles.
That night I explained to Gurudev how to be a writer. What was it
you said to me earlier, something about the form of the novel having failed
so that only the not-novel could be the novel? Horseshit!
Horseshit! It's the volcano inside you that has to erupt.
The lava doesn't care where it burns. If the book is bleeding chunks,
so is life. The blood lets you recognize the source.
What became of Anneke? What happened when she was with me
80   is in the books. After that, who knows? Now Prescott,
Prescott jumped into the Seine and hit his head on a piling.
He was in a coma for months and two of the nuns
fell in love with him. Then he recovered. Young man,
could your generation satisfy a whore? I doubt it.
I knew how to live with the grime, you see.
The grime on a tenement is as beautiful as the sunrise.

—*David Dooley*

Lyric and Song

We have come to use lyric to mean a short poem, usually emotional or descriptive. The term is perhaps too general to be useful. Originally derived from the word for lyre (a musical instrument) the word indicated a poem composed for singing. Many old poems were originally written as songs. Here is one of Shakespeare's songs, from *Love's Labour's Lost:*

Winter   (1595)

When icicles hang by the wall,
    And Dick the shepherd blows his nail,
And Tom bears logs into the hall,
    And milk comes frozen home in pail,
When blood is nipp'd, and ways be foul,
Then nightly sings the staring owl,
                    Tu-who;

Tu-whit, tu-who—a merry note,
While greasy Joan doth keel the pot.

10   When all aloud the wind doth blow,
    And coughing drowns the parson's saw,
And birds sit brooding in the snow,
    And Marian's nose looks red and raw,
When roasted crabs hiss in the bowl,
Then nightly sings the staring owl,
                    Tu-who;

Tu-whit, tu-who—a merry note,
While greasy Joan doth keel the pot.
                    —*William Shakespeare*

Epigrams

An epigram is short, pithy, witty, and conclusive. Here is one by Thomas Hardy:

Epitaph on a Pessimist   (1925)

I'm Smith of Stoke, aged sixty-odd,
   I've lived without a dame
From youth-time on; and would to God
   My Dad had done the same.
                    —*Thomas Hardy*

(An **epitaph** is an inscription for a gravestone; some epitaphs are also epigrams. Note that there is a third word sometimes confused with epigram and
epitaph; an **epigraph** is a quotation an author places at the start of a work.)
Walter Savage Landor wrote many epigrams, among them this one:

I strove with none, for none was worth my strife.
   Nature I loved and, next to Nature, Art:
I warmed both hands before the fire of life;
   It sinks, and I am ready to depart.
                    —*Walter Savage Landon*

Countee Cullen, a leader of the Harlem renaissance in the 1920s, wrote
this epigram:

For a Lady I Know   (1925)

She even thinks that up in heaven
Her class lies late and snores,
While poor black cherubs rise at seven
To do celestial chores.
                    —*Countee Cullen*

J. V. Cunningham wrote most of his work in epigrammatic form, some of it
funny:

(1950)

Naked I came, naked I leave the scene,
And naked was my pastime in between.

some not:

(1950)

On a cold night I came through the cold rain
And false snow to the wind shrill on your pane
With no hope and no anger and no fear:
Who are you? and with whom do you sleep here?
                    —*J. V. Cunningham*

Most epigrams rhyme. We call a short free-verse poem an epigram only when brevity combines with wit:

The Bath Tub   (1916)

As a bathtub lined with white porcelain,
When the hot water gives out or goes tepid,
So is the slow cooling of our chivalrous passion,
O my much praised but-not-altogether-satisfactory lady.

—Ezra Pound

Visual Poetry

While most poetry appeals to the ear, some poetry arranges itself for the pleasure of the eye. Early in the seventeenth century, George Herbert wrote:

Easter Wings   (1633)

Lord, who createdst man in wealth and store,
Though foolishly he lost the same,
Decaying more and more
Till he became
Most poor:
With thee
O let me rise
As larks, harmoniously,
And sing this day thy victories:
10 Then shall the fall further the flight in me.

My tender age in sorrow did begin;
And still with sicknesses and shame
Thou didst so punish sin,
That I became
Most thin.
With thee
Let me combine,
And feel this day thy victory;
For, if I imp my wing on thine,
20 Affliction shall advance the flight in me.

—George Herbert

This poem is a pleasure both to ear and to eye. If you heard the poem read aloud, you would be aware of lines becoming shorter, then longer again—a closing in, an opening up—but you would not be aware that the poem created on the page the visual shape of an angel's wings. Reading and seeing the poem are separate pleasures. Herbert's "Easter Wings" is a **concrete poem** because a portion of its creation is visual.

Modern poems sometimes exist to the eye and not to the ear. When E. E. Cummings makes

(1958)

l(a
le
af
fa
ll
s)
one
l
iness

there is no way to pronounce the poem except by spelling it and indicating marks of punctuation. (Even then, the voicing will detract from the poem; the voice will have to decide whether the first character is *ell* or *one*. (It is *ell*, in terms of the words *loneliness* and *a leaf falls*, but the meaning of the poem is underscored by the visual pun on *ell* and *one*.) The poem exists, not to the eye and ear together, nor to both eye and ear separately, but to the eye alone.

Concrete poetry is a blend of poetry and painting, or visual art. Ian Hamilton Finlay is a contemporary leader among concretists. Here is his "Homage to Malevich"—the painter who tilted a white square on a white background in "White on White":

(1971)

lackblockblackb
lockblackblockb
lackblockblackb
lockblackblockb
lackblockblackb
lockblackblockb
lackblockblackb
lockblackblockb

lackblockblackb   lackblockblackb   lackblockblackb
lockblackblockb   lockblackblockb   lockblackblockb
lackblockblackb   lackblockblackb   lackblockblackb
lockblackblockb   lockblackblockb   lockblackblockb
lackblockblackb   lackblockblackb   lackblockblackb
lockblackblockb   lockblackblockb   lockblackblockb
lackblockblackb   lackblockblackb   lackblockblackb
lockblackblockb   lockblackblockb   lockblackblockb

lackblockblackb
lockblackblockb
lackblockblackb
lockblackblockb
lackblockblackb
lockblackblockb
lackblockblackb
lockblackblockb

—*Ian Hamilton Finlay*

Some poems assembled as concrete are less like pictures and more like collections of letters for the mind to dwell on—like the French movement *lettrism*. Aram Saroyan has composed poems of a single word like *oxygen,* or a single nonword like *blod* (immortalized by the *Guinness Book of Records* as the world's shortest poem). These poems are not so interesting in their own sensuous shape as they are in the thoughts they lead to. They resemble conceptual sculpture, like Yoko Ono's row of empty flowerpots titled *Imagining Flowers.*

Prose Poems

Poems written in paragraphs have been a part of literature for more than a hundred years. Usually, a prose poem shares most of the qualities we associate with poetry—images, metaphor, figures, controlled rhythm, and fantasy—except for lines and linebreaks. Most poets who make prose poems write lined poems also. Robert Bly's lined poems appear on pages 57 and 196.

The Dead Seal near McClure's Beach   (1975)

1

Walking north toward the point, I came on a dead seal. From a few feet away, he looks like a brown log. The body is on its back, dead only a few hours. I stand and look at him. There's a quiver in the dead flesh. My God he is still alive. A shock goes through me, as if a wall of my room had fallen away.

His head is arched back, the small eyes closed, the whiskers sometimes rise and fall. He is dying. This is the oil. Here on its back is the oil that heats our houses so efficiently. Wind blows fine sand back toward the ocean. The flipper near me lies folded over the stomach, looking like an unfinished arm, lightly glazed with sand at the edges. The other flipper lies half underneath. The seal's skin looks like an old overcoat, scratched here and there, by sharp mussel-shells maybe. . . .

I reach out and touch him. Suddenly he rears up, turns over, gives three cries, Awaark! Awaark! Awaark!—like the cries from Christmas toys. He lunges toward me. I am terrified and leap back, although I know there can be no teeth in that jaw. He starts flopping toward the sea. But he falls over, on his face. He does not want to go back to the sea. He looks up at the sky, and he looks like an old lady who has lost her hair.

He puts his chin back on the sand, rearranges his flippers, and waits for me to go. I go.

2

Today I go back to say goodbye: he's dead now. But he's not—he's a quarter mile farther up the shore. Today he is thinner, squatting on his stomach, head out. The ribs show more—each vertebra on the back under the coat is now visible, shiny. He breathes in and out.

He raises himself up, and tucks his flippers under, as if to keep them warm. A wave comes in, touches his nose. He turns and looks at me—the eyes slanted, the crown of his head is like a black leather jacket. He is taking a long time to die. The whiskers white as porcupine quills, the forehead slopes . . . goodbye brother, die in the sound of waves, forgive us if we have killed you, long live your race, your inner-tube race, so uncomfortable on land, so comfortable in the ocean. Be comfortable in death then, where the sand will be out of your nostrils, and you can swim in long loops through the pure death, ducking under as assassinations break above you. You don't want to be touched by me. I climb the cliff and go home the other way.

Notice how, in the form of prose, Bly uses the details of the world and yet (as in a poem) leaps across spaces of thought to see inside things.

Russell Edson is a contemporary American who writes prose poems. He writes tiny narratives—which might be called fables, or novels-to-read-through-a-microscope—that other people call prose poems. When it becomes difficult to decide whether a piece of writing is a story, a poem, a play, or an essay, then the task is useless. Here is a prose poem—I'll call it—by Russell Edson:

Bringing a Dead Man Back into Life   (1976)

The dead man is introduced back into life. They take him to a country fair, to a French restaurant, a round of late night parties . . . He's beginning to smell.
They give him a few days off in bed.

He's taken to a country fair again; a second engagement at the French restaurant; another round of late night parties . . . No response . . . They brush the maggots away . . . That terrible smell! . . . No use . . .
What's wrong with you?
. . . No use . . .
They slap his face. His cheek comes off; bone underneath, jaws and teeth . . .

Another round of late night parties . . . Dropping his fingers . . . An ear falls off . . . Loses a foot in a taxi . . . No use . . . The smell . . . Maggots everywhere!

Another round of late night parties. His head comes off, rolls on the floor. A woman stumbles on it, an eye rolls out. She screams.
No use . . . Under his jacket nothing but maggots and ribs . . . No use . . .

—*Russell Edson*

CHAPTER TEN

Versions of the Same

This chapter gathers different versions of the same texts: poets' revisions of their own work, variant translations of one original, and a pedagogic paraphrase. Saying that different words express the same content, we beg questions; when two texts differ in their wording, by definition nothing is truly the same. Still, revisions and variant translations can give us multiple examples of phrases that resemble each other and are *not* the same, thus providing opportunity to examine differences of diction, rhythm, image, metaphor, sound, and (often) meter. By noticing these differences, we can review the study of poetry and sharpen our ability to tell better from good, best from better.

Poets' Revisions

William Butler Yeats revised his poems many times. He published his first volume in 1885, and by 1895 he had revised some of these poems in a new collection of his work. When he was in his sixties, he rewrote some poems he had written in his twenties. When people objected, he answered:

> The friends that have it I do wrong
> Whenever I remake a song,
> Should know what issue is at stake:
> It is myself that I remake.

With his early revisions, he remade style, not self. He changed:

> In three days' time he stood up with a moan
> And he went down to the long sands alone.

to:

> In three days' time, Cuchulain[1] with a moan
> Stood up, and came to the long sands alone.

[1] *Cuchulain* is pronounced cuh-HULL-an.

In this revision, a proper name replaces a pronoun, and a boring rhythm becomes varied and expressive: *Stood up,* with a pause after it, then eight syllables of walking, seems to imitate in its rhythm the action it describes.

In 1892, in the first version of a famous poem called "When You Are Old," Yeats wrote the couplet:

> Murmur, a little sad, "From us fled Love.
> He paced upon the mountains far above . . ."

The adjective *sad* goes strangely with the verb *murmur,* and the normal word order at the end of the first line would have been *Love fled from us.* Dissatisfied six years later, Yeats rewrote the lines to read:

> Murmur, a little sadly, how Love fled
> And paced upon the mountains overhead . . .

Now this line approaches natural speech, without affectation or awkwardness.

Four versions of the last stanza of "Cradle Song" show Yeats growing in simplicity and directness:

1889

> My darling I kiss you,
>   With arms round my own.
> Ah, how I shall miss you
>   When heavy and grown.

1892

> I kiss you and kiss you
>   With arms round my own.
> Ah, how I shall miss you
>   When, dear, you have grown.

1901

> I kiss you and kiss you
> My pigeon, my own.
> Ah, how I shall miss you,
> When you have grown.

1925

> I sigh that kiss you
> For I must own
> That I shall miss you
> When you have grown.

In the 1889 stanza, the first line lacks the energy it picked up when Yeats paced the line with two verbs. In the last line, the word *heavy* is unfortunate— the kind of error any writer can make, where a word brings in an irrelevant association the writer is blind to. *Heavy* for Yeats probably implied ponderous and slow-moving, an end to youth; unfortunately, it is a euphemism for obesity. In 1892, he improved the first line and in the fourth line got rid of *heavy* but substituted the rhythmically awkward *dear,* chopping the line up with commas. In 1901, he repaired the fourth line—finally—but left behind the decorative *pigeon* and the decorative *Ah.* By 1925, he was all for spareness. In judging among these "versions of the same," there is room for difference of opinion, but I like the last version best. This 1925 change comes close to remaking the self, like these two versions of "The Lamentation of the Old Pensioner" (original title "The Old Pensioner"):

1890

I had a chair at every hearth,
When no one turned to see
With "Look at that old fellow there;
And who may he be?"
And therefore do I wander on,
And the fret is on me.

The road-side trees keep murmuring—
Ah, wherefore murmur ye
As in the old days long gone by,
10 Green oak and poplar tree!
The well-known faces are all gone,
And the fret is on me.

1939

Although I shelter from the rain
Under a broken tree
My chair was nearest to the fire
In every company
That talked of love or politics,
Ere Time transfigured me.

Though lads are making pikes again
For some conspiracy,
And crazy rascals rage their fill
10 At human tyranny,
My contemplations are of Time
That has transfigured me.

There's not a woman turns her face
Upon a broken tree,
And yet the beauties that I loved
Are in my memory;
I spit into the face of Time
That has transfigured me.

Questions

1. The two poems use a different sort of sound, for different effect. Pick out the characteristic sounds of each poem.

2. It is often said that Yeats's poems became more speechlike as he matured. Could you use these poems to support this assertion?

Here are more examples of Yeats's revisions. Those labeled A are the earlier versions; the B versions came later. See whether you can decide why Yeats changed the lines.

A

"My father," made he smiling answer then,
"Still treads the world amid his armed men."

B

"My father dwells among the sea-worn bands,
And breaks the ridge of battle with his hands."

A

The oldest hound with mournful din
    Lifts slow his wintery head:—
The servants bear the body in—
    The hounds keen for the dead.

B

The blind hound with a mournful din
    Lifts slow his wintery head;—
The servants bear the body in—
    The hounds wail for the dead.

Yeats was not the only great poet to revise his work. William Blake in "London" (page 53), originally wrote:

But most the midnight Harlot's curse
From every dismal street I hear,
Weaves around the Marriage hearse
And blasts the new born Infant's tear.

A year later, he revised these lines into:

But most thro' midnight streets I hear
How the youthful Harlot's curse
Blasts the new-born Infant's tear
And blights with plagues the Marriage hearse.

Notice that the elements of the first stanza—midnight, harlot's curse, street, marriage hearse, blasts, infant, tear—turn up again in the later stanza. We lose *dismal* and we gain another adjective, *youthful*. We lose the pretty word *weave*—to weave is to create, to turn thread into cloth; in this context the pretty word is oddly used for destructive purpose—and we have in return the far more powerful *blights with plagues,* combining diseases of plants and animals. Although the first stanza was powerful, the revision increases the poem's power, intensity, and density, adding a new area of meaning in the metaphor of diseases. Before, death entered with *hearse,* but we lacked the cause of death. The order of things is changed in the second version, and the order itself makes the poetry more powerful. It moves from the innocent streets to the prostitute and her oath, to the damnation of the infant's weeping, and finally to the disease and death of the institution of marriage.

Exercise

In "La Belle Dame sans Merci," Keats originally wrote the stanza:

> She took me to her elfin grot,
>> And there she wept, and sighed full sore,
> And there I shut her wild wild eyes
>> With kisses four.

He changed these lines—three out of four—into:

> She took me to her elfin grot,
>> And there she gazed and sighèd deep,
> And there I shut her wild sad eyes—
>> So kissed to sleep.

Many critics feel that Keats's revision is inferior to the original. What do you think, and why?

Robert Frost kept most of his variant versions from the public. He liked to give the impression that he revised little. Still, he published a number of poems in an early version, tinkered with them, and published them in revised form. His most remarkable printed revision is that of "Design," one of his greatest poems. In 1912 he included in a letter this poem:

In White   (1912)

A dented spider like a snowdrop white
On a white Heal-all,[1] holding up a moth
Like a white piece of lifeless satin cloth—
Saw ever curious eye so strange a sight?
Portent in little, assorted death and blight
Like the ingredients of a witches' broth?
The beady spider, the flower like a froth,
And the moth carried like a paper kite.

What had that flower to do with being white,
10 The blue Brunella,[2] every child's delight?
What brought the kindred spider to that height?

---

[1] A flower, normally blue, reported to have healing qualities   [2] Another name for the heal-all

(Make we no thesis of the miller's° plight.)   moth
What but design of darkness and of night?
Design, design! Do I use the word aright?
                                        —*Robert Frost*

Not until 1922 did "In White" turn up again, retitled:

Design   (1922)

I found a dimpled spider, fat and white,
On a white heal-all, holding up a moth
Like a white piece of rigid satin cloth—
Assorted characters of death and blight
Mixed ready to begin the morning right,
Like the ingredients of a witches' broth—
A snow-drop spider, a flower like a froth,
And dead wings carried like a paper kite.

What had that flower to do with being white,
10 The wayside blue and innocent heal-all?
What brought the kindred spider to that height,
Then steered the white moth thither in the night?
What but design of darkness to appall?—
If design govern in a thing so small.
                                        —*Robert Frost*

It is useful with this poem, or these two poems, to compare them line by line.
Here "In White" is in roman type, "Design" in italic:

1. A dented spider like a snowdrop white
   1. I found a dimpled spider, fat and white,

2. On a white Heal-all, holding up a moth
   2. On a white heal-all, holding up a moth

3. Like a white piece of lifeless satin cloth—
   3. Like a white piece of rigid satin cloth—

4. Saw ever curious eye so strange a sight?
   4. Assorted characters of death and blight

5. Portent in little, assorted death and blight
   5. Mixed ready to begin the morning right,

6. Like the ingredients of a witches' broth?
   6. Like the ingredients of a witches' broth—

7. The beady spider, the flower like a froth,
   7. A snow-drop spider, a flower like a froth,

8. And the moth carried like a paper kite.
   8. And dead wings carried like a paper kite.

9. What had that flower to do with being white,
   9. What had that flower to do with being white,

10. The blue Brunella every child's delight?
    10. The wayside blue and innocent heal-all?

11. What brought the kindred spider to that height?
    11. What brought the kindred spider to that height,

12. (Make we no thesis of the miller's plight.)
    12. Then steered the white moth thither in the night?

13. What but design of darkness and of night?
    13. What but design of darkness to appall?—

14. Design, design! Do I use the word aright?
    14. If design govern in a thing so small.

Exercises

1. In 1/*1*, compare *dented* with *dimpled*. What kind of object do you associate with *dented?* What kind with *dimpled?* Is either association preferable to the other in the context of the whole poem?

2. In 3/*3*, could you defend *lifeless* against *rigid?* Is either of these adjectives more specific than the other? More physical?

3. Paraphrase 3/4. How does the sentence work? Does *3/4* say something similar? Different? Does the grammar help in the later version?

4. In 7/*7*, compare *beady* and *snow-drop.*

5. In 8/*8*, compare the rhythms of the two lines at the beginning. What are the changes? Do you like them? Can you say why?

6. The second stanzas or sestets of these two versions differ in a number of ways. List all the differences you can see. Decide whether you approve of the changes made. Imagine why Robert Frost might have wanted to make them. Look up the history of *appall* and decide how it is used in this poem. Which of the two poems is clearer? Which of the two poems is better? Why?

Different Translations

Different translations of the same poem can offer us an opportunity to compare style, rhythm, and diction—even when we do not know the original. We can turn translations to our purposes by deciding which version we prefer, and why. We can sharpen our wits by defining our choices. Here is the Twenty-third Psalm, translated from the Hebrew of the Old Testament, in the seventeenth-century King James version:

> The Lord is my shepherd;
> I shall not want.
> He maketh me to lie down in green pastures: he leadeth me beside the still
>   waters.
>   He restoreth my soul: he leadeth me in the paths of righteousness for his
>   name's sake.

Yea, though I walk through the valley of the shadow of death, I will fear no evil:
    for thou art with me; thy rod and thy staff they comfort me.
    Thou preparest a table before me in the presence of mine enemies:
10   Thou annointest my head with oil; my cup runneth over.
    Surely goodness and mercy shall follow me all the days of my life:
And I will dwell in the house of the Lord forever.

Here is the Revised Standard Version, which came out first in 1952—very close, but not the same:

The Lord is my shepherd, I shall not want;
    he makes me lie down in green pastures.
He leads me beside still waters;
    he restores my soul.
He leads me in paths of righteousness
    for his name's sake.

Even though I walk through the valley of the shadow of death,
    I fear no evil; for thou art with me;
    thy rod and thy staff,
10   they comfort me.
Thou preparest a table before me
in the presence of my enemies;
thou anointest my head with oil,
    my cup overflows.
Surely goodness and mercy shall follow me
    all the days of my life;
and I shall dwell in the house of the LORD
    for ever.

Here is the same Psalm in a version from *The Book of Psalms* copyrighted by the American Bible Society in 1976:

The LORD is my shepherd;
    I have everything I need.
He lets me rest in fields of green grass
    and leads me to quiet pools of fresh water.
He gives me new strength.
He guides me in the right paths,
    as he has promised.
Even if I go through deepest darkness,
    I will not be afraid, LORD,
10   for you are with me.
Your shepherd's rod and staff protect me.

You prepare a banquet for me,
    where all my enemies can see me;
You welcome me as an honored guest
    and fill my cup to the brim.
I know that your goodness and love
    will be with me all my life;
    and your house will be my home as long as I live.

Finally, here is a version by David Rosenberg, an American poet who is translating the Bible, book by book, in his "A Poet's Bible." This modern version is taken from *Blues of the Sky,* Rosenberg's selection from the Psalms:

The Lord is my shepherd
and keeps me from wanting
what I can't have

lush green grass is set
around me and crystal water
to graze by

there I revive with my soul
find the way that love makes
for his name

10 and though I pass through cities of pain, through death's living shadow
I'm not afraid to touch
to know what I am

your shepherd's staff is always there
to keep me calm
in my body

you set a table before me
in the presence of my enemies
you give me grace to speak

to quiet them
20 to be full with humanness
to be warm in my soul's lightness

to feel contact every day
in my hand and in my belly
love coming down to me

in the air of your name, Lord
in your house
in my life

Here is a poem in Pablo Neruda's Spanish, followed by four American translations:

Entierro en el Este   (1974)

Yo trabajo de noche, rodeado de ciudad,
de pescadores, de alfareros, de difuntos quemados
con azafrán y frutas, envueltos en muselina escarlata:
bajo mi balcón esos muertos terribles

pasan sonando cadenas y flautas de cobre,
estridentes y finas y lúgubres silban
entre el color de las pesadas flores envenenadas
y el grito de los cenicientos danzarines
y el creciente monótono de los tamtam
10 y el humo de las maderas que arden y huelen.

Porque una vez doblado el camino, junto al turbio río,
sus corazones, detenidos o iniciando un mayor movimiento,
rodarán quemados, con la pierna y el pie hechos fuego,
y la trémula ceniza caerá sobre el agua,
flotará como ramo de flores calcinadas
o como extinto fuego dejado por tan poderosos viajeros
que hicieron arder algo sobre las negras aguas, y devoraron
un aliento desaparecido y un licor extremo.

Burial in the East

I work nights, in the ring of the city,
among fisherfolk, potters, cadavers, cremations
of saffron and fruits shrouded into red muslin.
Under my balcony pass the terrible dead
sounding their coppery flutes and their chains,
strident and mournful and delicate—they hiss
in a blazon of poisoned and ponderous flowers,
through the cries of the smoldering dancers,
the tom-tom's augmented monotony,
10 in the crackle and fume of the woodsmoke.

One turn in the road, by the ooze of the river,
and their hearts, clogging up or preparing some monstrous exertion,
will whirl away burning, their legs and their feet incandescent;
the tremulous ash will descend on the water
and float like a branching of carbonized flowers—
a bonfire put out by the might of some wayfarer
who lighted the black of the water and devoured some part
of a vanished subsistence, a consummate libation.
                                        —*Ben Bellitt*

Burial in the East

I work at night, surrounded by city,
by fishermen, by potters, by the dead burned
with saffron and fruits, wrapped in red muslin:
under my balcony these terrible corpses
go past playing chains and copper flutes,
strident and thin and lugubrious they whistle
amidst the colour of the heavy poisoned flowers
and the cry of the holy fire-dancers

and the growing monotony of the tom-toms
10 and the smoke of the different woods burning and giving off odours.

Because once around the corner, by the muddy river,
their hearts, held in check or beginning a major motion,
will roll, burning, their legs and feet will be fire
and the tremulous ash will fall over the water,
will float like a branch of calcined flowers
or like an extinct fire left by such mighty voyagers
as forced to burn something over the black waters, and devoured
a vanished breath and an extreme liquor.

— W. S. Merwin

Burial in the East

I work at night, surrounded by city,
by fishermen, by potters, by corpses burned
with saffron and fruit, wrapped in scarlet muslin:
underneath my balcony those terrible dead
go by, sounding their chains and copper flutes,
strident and clear and lugubrious they pipe
amid the colour of heavy poisoned flowers
and the cry of the ash-coloured dancers
and the mounting monotony of the drums
10 and smoke from logs that burn and smell.

For, once they reach the turn in the road, near the turbid river,
their hearts unmoving, or in greater movement,
they will roll burning, leg and foot made flame,
and the tremulous ashes will fall upon the water,
will float like a cluster of calcined flowers
or a quenched fire left by travelers so powerful
that they burned something over the black waters, and devoured
a vanished food, an utter liquor.

—Angel Flores

Funeral in the East

I work at night, the city all around me,
fishermen, and potters, and corpses that are burned
with saffron and fruit, rolled in scarlet muslin:
those terrifying corpses go past under my balcony,
making their chains and copper flutes give off noise,
whistling sounds, harsh and pure and mournful,
among the brightness of the flowers heavy and poisoned,
and the cries of the dancers covered with ashes,
and the constantly rising monotony of the drum,
10 and the smoke from the logs scented and burning.

For once around the corner, near the muddy river,
their hearts, either stopping or starting off at a greater speed,
will roll over, burned, the leg and the foot turned to fire,
and the fluttering ashes will settle down on the water
and float like a branch of chalky flowers,
or like an extinct fire left by travellers with such great powers
they made something blaze up on the black waters, and bolted down
a food no longer found, and one finishing drink.

—Robert Bly

Shakespeare in Paraphrase

Let us end with a gross example of paraphrase. Recently, a publisher issued
four Shakespearean tragedies with the original lines on the left-hand page and
line-by-line paraphrases on the right. The editors—or translators—intended
to provide pedagogical help for contemporary students, changing archaic
words into modern synonyms. At the same time, they often turned Shakespeare's metaphors into plain speech. At the beginning of *Hamlet,* when the
guards, Francisco and Bernardo, challenge each other, Francisco says "Stand
and unfold yourself." In the paraphrase, the sentence reads "Stand still and tell
me who you are."

When we remove metaphor in favor of plain speech, we remove images—
and those images often carry feelings on their backs. When Francisco asked
Bernardo "Stand and unfold yourself," he thought of Bernardo physically like
a butterfly expanding vulnerable wings or perhaps like a flag unfurling. But
when Francisco asks Bernardo in the paraphrase "Stand still and tell me who
you are," we have a mere request for identification. We have no picture, no
image, no sense of something vulnerable or formerly closed in on itself, now
opening up.

Here is a well-known speech, with Shakespeare's text in roman type. In
italic, after each Shakespearean line, is the modern paraphrase. You can read
each speech as a whole or read one line at a time, first the original and then
the paraphrase.

1. To be, or not to be: that is the question:
   1. To be, or not to be: that is what really matters.

2. Whether 'tis nobler in the mind to suffer
   2. Is it nobler to accept passively

3. The slings and arrows of outrageous fortune,
   3. the trials and tribulations that unjust fate sends.

4. Or to take arms against a sea of troubles,
   4. or to resist an ocean of troubles,

5. And by opposing end them. To die, to sleep—
   5. and, by our own effort, defeat them? To die, to fall asleep—

6. No more—and by a sleep to say we end
   6. perhaps that's all there is to it—and by that sleep suppose we put an end to

7. The heartache, and the thousand natural shocks
   7. the heartache and the thousands of pains and worries

8. That flesh is heir to! 'Tis a consummation
   8. that are a part of being human! That's an end

9. Devoutly to be wished. To die, to sleep—
   9. we could all look forward to. To die, to sleep—

10. To sleep—perchance to dream: ay, there's the rub,
    10. to sleep—maybe to dream: yes, that's the catch.

11. For in that sleep of death what dreams may come
    11. For in that sleep of death the nightmares that may come

12. When we have shuffled off this mortal coil,
    12. when we have freed ourselves from the turmoil of this mortal life

13. Must give us pause. There's the respect
    13. must make us hesitate. There's the thought

14. That makes calamity of so long life:
    14. that makes a disaster out of living to a ripe old age.

15. For who would bear the whips and scorns of time,
    15. After all, who wants to put up with the lashes and insults of this world,

16. Th' oppressor's wrong, the proud man's contumely,
    16. the tyrant's injustice and contempt of arrogant men,

17. The pangs of despised love, the law's delay,
    17. the pains of rejected love, the law's frustrating slowness,

18. The insolence of office, and the spurns
    18. insults from our superiors, and the snubs

19. That patient merit of th' unworthy takes,
    19. that deserving and hopeful people have to take from powerful inferiors,

20. When he himself might his quietus make
    20. when he could end the whole process by killing himself

21. With a bare bodkin? . . .
    21. with a bare dagger? . . .

In Shakespeare's first line, Hamlet speaks of *the question,* which, as he thinks out loud, becomes a true, unanswerable question—not a question in the abstracted sense of problem, like "the Middle East question." Instead of using *question,* the paraphraser speaks of *what really matters,* which is empty language. The difference is small, because Shakespeare's *question* is not a word of great importance in Hamlet's speech. Yet, the difference in the two words is typical: *question* is concrete, in the form of a real question; *what really matters* has neither "reality" nor "matter" in its syllabic bones.

When the paraphraser substitutes *to accept passively* for *in the mind to suffer,* one wants to argue. Shakespeare distinguishes between inaction, which includes mental suffering, and external action against huge forces. The paraphraser includes the notion of passivity but excludes mental suffering; Shakespeare seems mistranslated. In *trials and tribulations* we find a cliché to substitute for an image of weapons. Although the *slings and arrows* may be abstracted into *trials and tribulations* in our minds—almost like calling them "nuisances and annoyances"—the cliché is pale; we lose the implication of pain and death carried in *slings and arrows.* Paraphrasing *outrageous* as *unjust* is another diminishment. *Outrageous* retains in modern speech most of its old character, especially when we denounce something with the noun *outrage. Unjust* is less emotional, more intellectual. We begin to see that the paraphrase, by draining the language of particularity in metaphor and image, drains the poetry of feeling.

So much for the first five lines. The rest of this speech can bear more attention.

Exercises

1. In 7/7, discuss the removal of *natural.* Is anything missing that Shakespeare may have felt essential?

2. In 8/8, what is the first metaphor removed? Does the missing metaphor have any general relevance to this play?

3. In 9/9, is *devoutly* paraphrased?

4. 12/12. Using a large dictionary (the *Oxford English Dictionary,* usually in a college library, would be the best) consider the metaphor of *shuffle . . . coil.* Does *the turmoil of this mortal life* paraphrase parts of Shakespeare's line? Does it paraphrase the whole?

5. In 14/14, find a new metaphor added by the paraphraser. Is it good poetry?

6. 15/15, are the substitute words examples of the occasional usefulness of paraphrases in reading older authors? Do you find other good examples of paraphrase in this passage from *Hamlet?*

CHAPTER ELEVEN

Five Poets

We have been studying elements of poetry, with examples as brief as a line and as long as a single poem. It will be useful to concentrate next on a group of poems by a single poet. This chapter has selections from the work of one English and four American poets, each represented by characteristic poems. The Englishman was born in 1795; when he died at the age of twenty-five, he had written several of the best poems of the language. The Americans are two women and two men, born in 1830, 1874, 1908, and 1929: an Easterner who lived most of her life in one town, a Californian who became the great poet of New England, a Michigander who emigrated to the Northwest, and a woman from the East who now lives in California.

John Keats

John Keats (1795–1821) trained to become a physician, then gave up his medical studies to devote himself to poetry. Among his friends were the critic William Hazlitt and the older poet Liegh Hunt. Keats published his first book of poems in 1817. In the nineteenth century, literary criticism was frequently affected by political beliefs or associations, and Keats's poems were attacked viciously because of his associations with the liberal thinkers of his day. He developed tuberculosis early. In the space of a few months he wrote his best work, his poems on a Grecian Urn, to a Nightingale, to Autumn. He went to Italy for his health in September 1820 but died on February 23 of the next year. Carved on his tomb at his request were the words "Here lies one whose name was writ in water." Keats's letters contain superb speculations on the nature of poetry. See also pages 73–75 and 95–96.

On First Looking into Chapman's Homer   (1816)

Much have I travelled in the realms of gold,
   And many goodly states and kingdoms seen;

Round many western islands have I been
Which bards in fealty to Apollo hold.
Oft of one wide expanse had I been told
    That deep-browed Homer ruled as his demesne;
    Yet did I never breathe its pure serene
Till I heard Chapman speak out loud and bold.
Then felt I like some watcher of the skies
10   When a new planet swims into his ken;
Or like stout Cortez when with eagle eyes
    He stared at the Pacific, and all his men
Looked at each other with a wild surmise—
    Silent, upon a peak in Darien.

Italian

When I have fears that I may cease to be   (1818)

When I have fears that I may cease to be
    Before my pen has gleaned my teeming brain,
Before high-pilèd books, in charactery,
    Hold like rich garners the full ripened grain;
When I behold, upon the night's starred face,
    Huge cloudy symbols of a high romance,
And think that I may never live to trace
    Their shadows with the magic hand of chance;
And when I feel, fair creature of an hour,
10   That I shall never look upon thee more,
Never have relish in the fairy power
    Of unreflecting love; then on the shore
Of the wide world I stand alone and think
Till love and fame to nothingness do sink.

English

The Eve of St. Agnes   (1820)

I

St. Agnes' Eve—ah, bitter chill it was!
The owl, for all his feathers, was a-cold;
The hare limped trembling through the frozen grass,
And silent was the flock in woolly fold.
Numb were the Beadsman's fingers, while he told
His rosary, and while his frosted breath,
Like pious incense from a censer old,
Seemed taking flight for heaven, without a death,
Past the sweet Virgin's picture, while his prayer he saith.

II

10   His prayer he saith, this patient, holy man;
Then takes his lamp, and riseth from his knees,
And back returneth, meagre, barefoot, wan,
Along the chapel aisle by slow degrees.
The sculptured dead, on each side, seem to freeze,

Emprisoned in black, purgatorial rails.
Knights, ladies, praying in dumb orat'ries,
He passeth by; and his weak spirit fails
To think how they may ache in icy hoods and mails.

III

Northward he turneth through a little door,
20   And scarce three steps, ere music's golden tongue
Flattered to tears this agèd man and poor;
But no—already had his deathbell rung,
The joys of all his life were said and sung;
His was harsh penance on St. Agnes' Eve.
Another way he went, and soon among
Rough ashes sat he for his soul's reprieve,
And all night kept awake for sinners' sake to grieve.

IV

That ancient Beadsman heard the prelude soft,
And so it chanced for many a door was wide
30   From hurry to and fro. Soon, up aloft,
The silver, snarling trumpets 'gan to chide;
The level chambers, ready with their pride,
Were glowing to receive a thousand guests;
The carvèd angels, ever eager-eyed,
Stared, where upon their heads the cornice rests,
With hair blown back, and wings put cross-wise on their breasts.

V

At length burst in the argent revelry,
With plume, tiara, and all rich array,
Numerous as shadows haunting fairily
40   The brain, new-stuffed in youth, with triumphs gay
Of old romance. These let us wish away,
And turn, sole-thoughted, to one Lady there,
Whose heart had brooded, all that wintry day,
On love, and winged St. Agnes' saintly care,
As she had heard old dames full many times declare.

VI

They told her how, upon St. Agnes' Eve,
Young virgins might have visions of delight,
And soft adorings from their loves receive
Upon the honeyed middle of the night,
50   If ceremonies due they did aright;
As, supperless to bed they must retire,
And couch supine their beauties, lily white,
Nor look behind, nor sideways, but require
Of Heaven with upward eyes for all that they desire.

VII

Full o' this whim was thoughtful Madeline.
The music, yearning like a God in pain,
She scarcely heard; her maiden eyes divine,
Fixed on the floor, saw many a sweeping train
Pass by—she heeded not at all; in vain
60   Came many a tiptoe, amorous cavalier,
And back retired—not cooled by high disdain,
But she saw not; her heart was otherwhere.
She sighed for Agnes' dreams, the sweetest of the year.

VIII

She danced along with vague, regardless eyes,
Anxious her lips, her breathing quick and short.
The hallowed hour was near at hand. She sighs
Amid the timbrels and the thronged resort
Of whisperers in anger, or in sport;
'Mid looks of love, defiance, hate, and scorn,
70   Hoodwinked with fairy fancy—all amort,
Save to St. Agnes and her lambs unshorn,
And all the bliss to be before to-morrow morn.

IX

So, purposing each moment to retire,
She lingered still. Meantime, across the moors,
Had come young Porphyro, with heart on fire
For Madeline. Beside the portal doors,
Buttressed from moonlight, stands he and implores
All saints to give him sight of Madeline
But for one moment in the tedious hours,
80   That he might gaze and worship all unseen;
Perchance speak, kneel, touch, kiss—in sooth such things have been.

X

He ventures in—let no buzzed whisper tell,
All eyes be muffled, or a hundred swords
Will storm his heart, love's feverous citadel.
For him, those chambers held barbarian hordes,
Hyena foemen, and hot-blooded lords,
Whose very dogs would execrations howl
Against his lineage; not one breast affords
Him any mercy, in that mansion foul,
90   Save one old beldame, weak in body and in soul.

XI

Ah, happy chance! The agèd creature came,
Shuffling along with ivory-headed wand,
To where he stood, hid from the torch's flame,

Behind a broad hall-pillar, far beyond
The sound of merriment and chorus bland.
He startled her; but soon she knew his face,
And grasped his fingers in her palsied hand,
Saying, 'Mercy, Porphyro! Hie thee from this place;
They are all here to-night, the whole blood-thirsty race!

XII

100   'Get hence! get hence! there's dwarfish Hildebrand—
He had a fever late, and in the fit
He cursèd thee and thine, both house and land;
Then there's that old Lord Maurice, not a whit
More tame for his gray hairs. Alas me! Flit,
Flit like a ghost away!' 'Ah, Gossip dear,
We're safe enough; here in this arm-chair sit,
And tell me how—' 'Good saints! Not here, not here;
Follow me, child, or else these stones will be thy bier.'

XIII

He followed through a lowly archèd way,
110   Brushing the cobwebs with his lofty plume,
And as she muttered 'Well-a—well-a-day!'
He found him in a little moonlight room,
Pale, latticed, chill, and silent as a tomb.
'Now tell me where is Madeline,' said he,
'Oh, tell me, Angela, by the holy loom
Which none but secret sisterhood may see,
When they St. Agnes' wool are weaving piously.'

XIV

'St. Agnes? Ah! It is St. Agnes' Eve—
Yet men will murder upon holy days:
120   Thou must hold water in a witch's sieve,
And be liege-lord of all the elves and fays,
To venture so; it fills me with amaze
To see thee, Porphyro!—St. Agnes' Eve!
God's help! My lady fair the conjuror plays
This very night. Good angels her deceive!
But let me laugh awhile, I've mickle time to grieve.'

XV

Feebly she laugheth in the languid moon,
While Porphyro upon her face doth look,
Like puzzled urchin on an agèd crone
130   Who keepeth closed a wondrous riddle-book,
As spectacled she sits in chimney nook.
But soon his eyes grew brilliant, when she told
His lady's purpose, and he scarce could brook
Tears at the thought of those enchantments cold,
And Madeline asleep in lap of legends old.

XVI

Sudden a thought came like a full-blown rose,
Flushing his brow, and in his painèd heart
Made purple riot; then doth he propose
A stratagem that makes the beldame start:
140   'A cruel man and impious thou art—
Sweet lady, let her pray, and sleep, and dream
Alone with her good angels, far apart
From wicked men like thee. Go, go! I deem
Thou canst not surely be the same that thou didst seem.'

XVII

'I will not harm her, by all saints I swear,'
Quoth Porphyro: 'Oh, may I ne'er find grace
When my weak voice shall whisper its last prayer,
If one of her soft ringlets I displace,
Or look with ruffian passion in her face—
150   Good Angela, believe me by these tears,
Or I will, even in a moment's space,
Awake with horrid shout my foemen's ears,
And beard them, though they be more fanged than wolves and bears.'

XVIII

'Ah! why wilt thou affright a feeble soul?
A poor, weak, palsy-stricken, churchyard thing,
Whose passing-bell may ere the midnight toll!
Whose prayers for thee, each morn and evening,
Were never missed.' Thus plaining doth she bring
A gentler speech from burning Porphyro,
160   So woeful, and of such deep sorrowing,
That Angela gives promise she will do
Whatever he shall wish, betide her weal or woe.

XIX

Which was, to lead him, in close secrecy,
Even to Madeline's chamber, and there hide
Him in a closet, of such privacy
That he might see her beauty unespied,
And win perhaps that night a peerless bride,
While legioned fairies paced the coverlet
And pale enchantment held her sleepy-eyed.
170   Never on such a night have lovers met
Since Merlin paid his Demon all the monstrous debt.

XX

'It shall be as thou wishest,' said the Dame,
'All cates and dainties shall be storèd there
Quickly on this feast-night; by the tambour frame
Her own lute thou wilt see. No time to spare,

For I am slow and feeble, and scarce dare
On such a catering trust my dizzy head.
Wait here, my child, with patience; kneel in prayer
The while. Ah! Thou must needs the lady wed,
180 Or may I never leave my grave among the dead.'

XXI

So saying she hobbled off with busy fear.
The lover's endless minutes slowly passed;
The dame returned, and whispered in his ear
To follow her; with agèd eyes aghast
From fright of dim espial. Safe at last,
Through many a dusky gallery, they gain
The maiden's chamber, silken, hushed, and chaste,
Where Porphyro took covert, pleased amain.
His poor guide hurried back with agues in her brain.

XXII

190 Her faltering hand upon the balustrade,
Old Angela was feeling for the stair,
When Madeline, St. Agnes' charmèd maid,
Rose, like a missioned spirit, unaware.
With silver taper's light, and pious care,
She turned and down the agèd gossip led
To a safe level matting. Now prepare,
Young Porphyro, for gazing on that bed—
She comes, she comes again, like ring-dove frayed and fled.

XXIII

Out went the taper as she hurried in;
200 Its little smoke, in pallid moonshine, died.
She closed the door, she panted, all akin
To spirits of the air, and visions wide—
No uttered syllable, or woe betide!
But to her heart, her heart was voluble,
Paining with eloquence her balmy side,
As though a tongueless nightingale should swell
Her throat in vain, and die, heart-stifled, in her dell.

XXIV

A casement high and triple-arched there was,
All garlanded with carven imageries,
210 Of fruits, and flowers, and bunches of knot-grass,
And diamonded with panes of quaint device
Innumerable of stains and splendid dyes,
As are the tiger-moth's deep-damasked wings;
And in the midst, 'mong thousand heraldries,
And twilight saints, and dim emblazonings,
A shielded scutcheon blushed with blood of queens and kings.

XXV

Full on this casement shone the wintry moon,
And threw warm gules on Madeline's fair breast
As down she knelt for Heaven's grace and boon;
220   Rose-bloom fell on her hands, together pressed,
And on her silver cross soft amethyst,
And on her hair a glory, like a saint.
She seemed a splendid angel, newly dressed,
Save wings, for heaven. Porphyro grew faint;
She knelt, so pure a thing, so free from mortal taint.

XXVI

Anon his heart revives; her vespers done,
Of all its wreathèd pearls her hair she frees;
Unclasps her warmèd jewels one by one;
Loosens her fragrant bodice; by degrees
230   Her rich attire creeps rustling to her knees.
Half-hidden, like a mermaid in sea-weed,
Pensive awhile she dreams awake, and sees,
In fancy, fair St. Agnes in her bed,
But dares not look behind, or all the charm is fled.

XXVII

Soon, trembling in her soft and chilly nest,
In sort of wakeful swoon, perplexed she lay,
Until the poppied warmth of sleep oppressed
Her soothèd limbs, and soul fatigued—away
Flown, like a thought, until the morrow-day;
240   Blissfully havened both from joy and pain;
Clasped like a missal where swart Paynims pray;
Blinded alike from sunshine and from rain,
As though a rose should shut, and be a bud again.

XXVIII

Stol'n to this paradise, and so entranced,
Porphyro gazed upon her empty dress,
And listened to her breathing, if it chanced
To wake into a slumbrous tenderness;
Which when he heard, that minute did he bless,
And breathed himself, then from the closet crept,
250   Noiseless as fear in a wide wilderness—
And over the hushed carpet, silent, stepped,
And 'tween the curtains peeped, where, lo!—how fast she slept.

XXIX

Then by the bed-side, where the faded moon
Made a dim, silver twilight, soft he set
A table and, half anguished, threw thereon
A cloth of woven crimson, gold, and jet.

Oh, for some drowsy Morphean amulet!
The boisterous, midnight, festive clarion,
The kettle-drum, and far-heard clarionet,
260   Affray his ears, though but in dying tone;
The hall door shuts again, and all the noise is gone.

XXX

And still she slept an azure-lidded sleep,
In blanchèd linen, smooth, and lavendered,
While he from forth the closet brought a heap
Of candied apple, quince, and plum, and gourd,
With jellies soother than the creamy curd,
And lucent syrops, tinct with cinnamon;
Manna and dates, in argosy transferred
From Fez, and spicèd dainties, every one,
270 From silken Samarcand to cedared Lebanon.

XXXI

These delicates he heaped with glowing hand
On golden dishes and in baskets bright
Of wreathèd silver; sumptuous they stand
In the retired quiet of the night,
Filling the chilly room with perfume light.
'And now, my love, my seraph fair, awake!
Thou art my heaven, and I thine eremite.
Open thine eyes, for meek St. Agnes' sake,
Or I shall drowse beside thee, so my soul doth ache.'

XXXII

280   Thus whispering, his warm, unnervèd arm
Sank in her pillow. Shaded was her dream
By the dusk curtains: 'twas a midnight charm
Impossible to melt as icèd stream.
The lustrous salvers in the moonlight gleam,
Broad golden fringe upon the carpet lies.
It seemed he never, never could redeem
From such a steadfast spell his lady's eyes;
So mused awhile, entoiled in woofèd phantasies.

XXXIII

Awakening up, he took her hollow lute,
290   Tumultuous, and, in chords that tenderest be,
He played an ancient ditty, long since mute,
In Provence called, 'La belle dame sans mercy,'
Close to her ear touching the melody—
Wherewith disturbed, she uttered a soft moan.
He ceased—she panted quick—and suddenly
Her blue affrayèd eyes wide open shone;
Upon his knees he sank, pale as smooth-sculptured stone.

XXXIV

Her eyes were open, but she still beheld,
Now wide awake, the vision of her sleep—
300   There was a painful change, that nigh expelled
The blisses of her dream so pure and deep.
At which fair Madeline began to weep,
And moan forth witless words with many a sigh,
While still her gaze on Porphyro would keep;
Who knelt, with joinèd hands and piteous eye,
Fearing to move or speak, she looked so dreamingly.

XXXV

'Ah, Porphyro!' said she, 'but even now
Thy voice was at sweet tremble in mine ear,
Made tuneable with every sweetest vow,
310   And those sad eyes were spiritual and clear.
How changed thou art! How pallid, chill, and drear!
Give me that voice again, my Porphyro,
Those looks immortal, those complainings dear!
Oh, leave me not in this eternal woe,
For if thou diest, my love, I know not where to go.'

XXXVI

Beyond a mortal man impassioned far
At these voluptuous accents, he arose,
Ethereal, flushed, and like a throbbing star
Seen mid the sapphire heaven's deep repose;
320   Into her dream he melted, as the rose
Blendeth its odour with the violet,
Solution sweet—meantime the frost-wind blows
Like Love's alarum, pattering the sharp sleet
Against the window-panes; St. Agnes' moon hath set.

XXXVII

'Tis dark: quick pattereth the flaw-blown sleet.
'This is no dream, my bride, my Madeline!'
'Tis dark; the icèd gusts still rave and beat.
'No dream, alas! alas! and woe is mine!
Porphyro will leave me here to fade and pine.
330   Cruel! What traitor could thee hither bring?
I curse not, for my heart is lost in thine,
Though thou forsakest a deceivèd thing—
A dove forlorn and lost with sick, unprunèd wing.'

XXXVIII

'My Madeline! Sweet dreamer! Lovely bride!
Say, may I be for ay thy vassal blest?
Thy beauty's shield, heart-shaped and vermeil dyed?
Ah, silver shrine, here will I take my rest

After so many hours of toil and quest,
A famished pilgrim—saved by miracle.
340   Though I have found, I will not rob thy nest
Saving of thy sweet self; if thou think'st well
To trust, fair Madeline, to no rude infidel.

XXXIX

'Hark! 'Tis an elfin-storm from fairy land,
Of haggard seeming, but a boon indeed.
Arise—arise! The morning is at hand;
The bloated wassaillers will never heed.
Let us away, my love, with happy speed—
There are no ears to hear, or eyes to see,
Drowned all in Rhenish and the sleepy mead.
350   Awake! Arise, my love, and fearless be!
For o'er the southern moors I have a home for thee.'

XL

She hurried at his words, beset with fears,
For there were sleeping dragons all around,
At glaring watch, perhaps, with ready spears;
Down the wide stairs a darkling way they found.
In all the house was heard no human sound;
A chain-drooped lamp was flickering by each door;
The arras, rich with horseman, hawk, and hound,
Fluttered in the besieging wind's uproar;
360 And the long carpets rose along the gusty floor.

XLI

They glide, like phantoms, into the wide hall;
Like phantoms, to the iron porch they glide;
Where lay the Porter, in uneasy sprawl,
With a huge empty flagon by his side.
The wakeful bloodhound rose and shook his hide,
But his sagacious eye an inmate owns.
By one, and one, the bolts full easy slide;
The chains lie silent on the footworn stones;
The key turns, and the door upon its hinges groans.

XLII

370 And they are gone—aye, ages long ago
These lovers fled away into the storm.
That night the Baron dreamt of many a woe,
And all his warrior-guests, with shade and form
Of witch, and demon, and large coffin-worm,
Were long be-nightmared. Angela the old
Died palsy-twitched, with meagre face deform;
The Beadsman, after thousand aves told,
For ay unsought for slept among his ashes cold.

Ode to a Nightingale   (1819)

I

My heart aches, and a drowsy numbness pains
   My sense, as though of hemlock[1] I had drunk,
Or emptied some dull opiate to the drains
   One minute past, and Lethe-wards[2] had sunk.
'Tis not through envy of thy happy lot,
   But being too happy in thine happiness,—
     That thou, light-wingèd Dryad° of the trees,   nymph
       In some melodious plot
Of beechen green, and shadows numberless,
10   Singest of summer in full-throated ease.

II

O for a draught of vintage that hath been
   Cooled a long age in the deep-delvèd earth,
Tasting of Flora[3] and the country green,
   Dance, and Provençal song,[4] and sunburnt mirth!
O for a beaker full of the warm South,
   Full of the true, the blushful Hippocrene,[5]
     With beaded bubbles winking at the brim,
       And purple-stainèd mouth,
That I might drink, and leave the world unseen,
20   And with thee fade away into the forest dim.

III

Fade far away, dissolve, and quite forget
   What thou among the leaves hast never known,
The weariness, the fever, and the fret
   Here, where men sit and hear each other groan;
Where palsy shakes a few, sad, last gray hairs,
   Where youth grows pale, and spectre-thin, and dies;
     Where but to think is to be full of sorrow
       And leaden-eyed despairs;
Where Beauty cannot keep her lustrous eyes,
30   Or new Love pine at them beyond to-morrow.

IV

Away! away! for I will fly to thee,
   Not charioted by Bacchus and his pards,[6]
But on the viewless° wings of Poesy,   invisible

---

[1] Poison hemlock, a lethally poisonous herb of the carrot family, was used in ancient Greece to execute criminals.   [2] In Greek mythology, Lethe was the river in the underworld from which the shades of the dead drank to obtain forgetfulness of the past.   [3] Roman goddess of flowers and spring   [4] Provence, the South of France, was famous for the songs of love and adventure constructed or repeated by its medieval troubadors.   [5] The "Fountain of the Horse" on Mount Helicon, sacred to the Muses   [6] Bacchus, the Roman god of wine, was sometimes portrayed riding in a chariot drawn by leopards.

Though the dull brain perplexes and retards.
Already with thee! tender is the night,
    And haply the Queen-Moon is on her throne,
        Clustered around by all her starry fays;°   fairies
           But here there is no light,
Save what from heaven is with the breezes blown
40   Through verdurous glooms and winding mossy ways.

V

I cannot see what flowers are at my feet,
    Nor what soft incense hangs upon the boughs,
But, in embalmèd° darkness, guess each sweet   fragrant
    Wherewith the seasonable month endows
The grass, the thicket, and the fruit-tree wild—
    White hawthorn, and the pastoral eglantine;
        Fast-fading violets covered up in leaves;
           And mid-May's eldest child,
The coming musk-rose, full of dewy wine,
50   The murmurous haunt of flies on summer eves.

VI

Darkling° I listen, and for many a time   In darkness
    I have been half in love with easeful Death,
Called him soft names in many a musèd rhyme,
    To take into the air my quiet breath;
Now more than ever seems it rich to die,
    To cease upon the midnight with no pain,
        While thou art pouring forth thy soul abroad
           In such an ecstasy.
Still wouldst thou sing, and I have ears in vain—
60   To thy high requiem become a sod.

VII

Thou wast not born for death, immortal bird!
    No hungry generations tread thee down;
The voice I hear this passing night was heard
    In ancient days by emperor and clown:
Perhaps the self-same song that found a path
    Through the sad heart of Ruth,[7] when, sick for home,
        She stood in tears amid the alien corn;°   wheat
        The same that oft-times hath
Charmed magic casements, opening on the foam
70   Of perilous seas, in faery lands forlorn.

VIII

Forlorn! the very word is like a bell
    To toll me back from thee to my sole self!

---

[7] A reference to the Moabite widow whose story is told in the Old Testament book of Ruth

Adieu! the fancy cannot cheat so well
　　As she is famed to do, deceiving elf.
Adieu! adieu! thy plaintive anthem fades
　　　Past the near meadows, over the still stream,
　　　　Up the hill-side; and now 'tis buried deep
　　　　　In the next valley-glades:
Was it a vision, or a waking dream?
80　　Fled is that music . . . Do I wake or sleep?

Ode on a Grecian Urn　(1819)

I

Thou still unravished bride of quietness,
　　Thou foster-child of silence and slow time,
Sylvan historian, who canst thus express
　　A flowery tale more sweetly than our rhyme!
What leaf-fringed legend haunts about thy shape
　　Of deities or mortals, or of both,
　　　In Tempe or the dales of Arcady?[1]
What men or gods are these? What maidens loth?
　　What mad pursuit? What struggle to escape?
10　　　What pipes and timbrels? What wild ecstasy?

II

Heard melodies are sweet, but those unheard
　　Are sweeter; therefore, ye soft pipes, play on;
Not to the sensual° ear, but, more endeared,　　　　　　　　　sensuous
　　Pipe to the spirit ditties of no tone.
Fair youth beneath the trees, thou canst not leave
　　Thy song, nor ever can those trees be bare;
　　　Bold lover, never, never canst thou kiss,
Though winning near the goal—yet do not grieve:
　　She cannot fade, though thou hast not thy bliss,
20　　　For ever wilt thou love, and she be fair!

III

Ah, happy, happy boughs, that cannot shed
　　Your leaves, nor ever bid the spring adieu;
And, happy melodist, unwearièd,
　　For ever piping songs for ever new!
More happy love, more happy, happy love!
　　For ever warm and still to be enjoyed,
　　　For ever panting, and for ever young—
All breathing human passion far above,
　　That leaves a heart high-sorrowful and cloyed,
30　　　A burning forehead, and a parching tongue.

---

[1] Tempe and the glens of Arcady are landscapes of legendary beauty.

IV

Who are these coming to the sacrifice?
   To what green altar, O mysterious priest,
Lead'st thou that heifer lowing at the skies,
   And all her silken flanks with garlands drest?
What little town by river or sea shore,
   Or mountain built with peaceful citadel,
     Is emptied of this folk, this pious morn?
And, little town, thy streets for evermore
   Will silent be; and not a soul to tell
40   Why thou art desolate can e'er return.

V

O Attic² shape! Fair attitude! With brede°   pattern, design
   Of marble men and maidens overwrought,
With forest branches and the trodden weed—
   Thou, silent form, dost tease us out of thought
As doth eternity. Cold pastoral!
   When old age shall this generation waste,
     Thou shalt remain, in midst of other woe
Than ours, a friend to man, to whom thou say'st,
   "Beauty is truth, truth beauty"—that is all
50   Ye know on earth, and all ye need to know.

This Living Hand   (1820)

This living hand, now warm and capable
Of earnest grasping, would, if it were cold
And in the icy silence of the tomb,
So haunt thy days and chill thy dreaming nights
That thou would wish thine own heart dry of blood
So in my veins red life might stream again,
And thou be conscience-calmed. See here it is—
I hold it towards you.

---

² Attic equals Athenian and therefore classic grace and simplicity.

Emily Dickinson

Emily Dickinson (1830–1886) grew up in Amherst, Massachusetts, where her family was associated with Amherst College. She attended school with other young women but, as she grew older, became reclusive, until she rarely left her own room. When she was young, she made attempts to print her poems and she placed a few in obscure publications. Then she apparently renounced this notion of fame and wrote, so far as we know, for herself. Her eccentricities of punctuation, not to mention the strangeness of her metaphors and rhymes, may derive from her sense that she was her own and only audience. Yet power and insight accumulated in her isolation. She is probably the greatest female poet of our language, and every year her audience grows wider.

He put the Belt around my life   (1861)

He put the Belt around my life—
I heard the Buckle snap—
And turned away, imperial,
My Lifetime folding up—
Deliberate, as a Duke would do
A Kingdom's Title Deed—
Henceforth, a Dedicated sort—
A Member of the Cloud.

10 Yet not too far to come at call—
And do the little Toils
That make the Circuit of the Rest—
And deal occasional smiles
To lives that stoop to notice mine—
And kindly ask it in—
Whose invitation, know you not
For Whom I must decline?

slant rhyme + substitutions

He fumbles at your Soul   (1862)

He fumbles at your Soul
As Players at the Keys
Before they drop full Music on—
He stuns you by degrees—
Prepares your brittle Nature
For the Ethereal Blow
By fainter Hammers—further heard—
Then nearer—Then so slow

10 Your Breath has time to straighten—
Your Brain—to bubble Cool—
Deals—One—imperial—Thunderbolt—
That scalps your naked Soul—

When Winds take Forests in their
Paws— The Universe—is still—

After great pain, a formal feeling comes—   (1862)

After great pain, a formal feeling
    comes—
The Nerves sit ceremonious, like
    Tombs—
The stiff Heart questions was it He,
    that bore,
And Yesterday, or Centuries before?

The Feet, mechanical, go round—
Of Ground, or Air, or Ought—

10 A Wooden way
Regardless grown,
A Quartz contentment, like a stone—

This is the Hour of Lead—
Remembered, if outlived,
As Freezing persons, recollect the
    Snow—
First—Chill—then Stupor—then the
    letting go—

The first Day's Night had come—   (1862)

The first Day's Night had come—
And grateful that a thing
So terrible—had been endured—
I told my Soul to sing—

She said her Strings were snapt—
Her Bow—to Atoms blown—
And so to mend her—gave me work
Until another Morn—

And then—a Day as huge
10   As Yesterdays in pairs,

Unrolled its horror in my face—
Until it blocked my eyes—

My Brain—begun to laugh—
I mumbled—like a fool—
And tho' 'tis Years ago—that Day—
My Brain keeps giggling—still.

And Something's odd—within—
That person that I was—
And this One—do not feel the same—
20   Could it be Madness—this?

Much Madness is divinest Sense—   (1862)

Much Madness is divinest Sense—
To a discerning Eye—
Much Sense—the starkest Madness—
'Tis the Majority

In this, as All, prevail—
Assent—and you are sane—
Demur—you're straightway dangerous—
And handled with a Chain—

I heard a Fly buzz—when I died—   (1862)

I heard a Fly buzz—when I died—
The Stillness in the Room
Was like the Stillness in the Air—
Between the Heaves of Storm—

The Eyes around—had wrung them
    dry—
And Breaths were gathering firm
For that last Onset—when the King
Be witnessed—in the Room—

10   I willed my Keepsakes—Signed away
What portion of me be
Assignable—and then it was
There interposed a Fly—

With Blue—uncertain stumbling
    Buzz—
Between the light—and me—
And then the Windows failed—and then
I could not see to see—

I would not paint—a picture—   (1862)

I would not paint—a picture—
I'd rather be the One
Its bright impossibility
To dwell—delicious—on—
And wonder how the fingers feel
Whose rare—celestial—stir—
Evokes so sweet a Torment—
Such sumptuous—Despair—

I would not talk, like Cornets—
10   I'd rather be the One
Raised softly to the Ceilings—
And out, and easy on—

Through Villages of Ether—
Myself endued Balloon
By but a lip of Metal—
The pier to my Pontoon—

Nor would I be a Poet—
It's finer—own the Ear—
Enamored—impotent—content—
20   The License to revere,
A privilege so awful
What would the Dower be,
Had I the Art to stun myself
With Bolts of Melody!

I'm ceded—I've stopped being Theirs— (1862)

I'm ceded—I've stopped being
    Theirs—
The name They dropped upon my face
With water, in the country church
Is finished using, now,
And They can put it with my Dolls,
My childhood, and the string of spools,
I've finished threading—too—

Baptized, before, without the choice,
10 But this time, consciously, of Grace—
Unto supremest name—

Called to my Full—The Crescent
    dropped—
Existence's whole Arc, filled up,
With one small Diadem.

My second Rank—too small the first—
Crowned—Crowing—on my Father's
    breast—
A half unconscious Queen—
20 But this time—Adequate—Erect,
With Will to choose, or to reject,
And I choose, just a Crown—

The Soul has Bandaged moments— (1862)

The Soul has Bandaged moments—
When too appalled to stir—
She feels some ghastly Fright come up
And stop to look at her—

Salute her—with long fingers—
Caress her freezing hair—
Sip, Goblin, from the very lips
The Lover—hovered—o'er—
Unworthy, that a thought so mean
10 Accost a Theme—so—fair—

The soul has moments of Escape—
When bursting all the doors—

She dances like a Bomb, abroad,
And swings upon the Hours,

As do the Bee—delirious borne—
Long Dungeoned from his Rose—
Touch Liberty—then know no more,
But Noon, and Paradise—
The Soul's retaken moments—
20 When, Felon led along,
With shackles on the plumed feet,
And staples, in the Song,

The Horror welcomes her, again,
These, are not brayed of Tongue—

The Province of the Saved (1862)

The Province of the Saved
Should be the Art—To save—
Through Skill obtained in Themselves—
The Science of the Grave

No Man can understand
But He that hath endured

The Dissolution—in Himself—
That Man—be qualified

To qualify Despair
10 To Those who failing new—
Mistake Defeat for Death—Each time—
Till acclimated—to—

A still—Volcano—Life— (1862)

A still—Volcano—Life—
That flickered in the night—
When it was dark enough to do
Without erasing sight—

A quiet—Earthquake Style—
Too subtle to suspect

By natures this side Naples—
The North cannot detect

The Solemn—Torrid—Symbol—
10 The lips that never lie—
Whose hissing Corals part—and shut—
And Cities—ooze away—

I cannot live with You— (1862)

I cannot live with You—
It would be Life—
And Life is over there—
Behind the Shelf

The Sexton keeps the Key to—
Putting up
Our Life—His Porcelain—
Like a Cup—

Discarded of the Housewife—
10 Quaint—or Broke—
A newer Sevres pleases—
Old Ones crack—

I could not die—with You—
For One must wait
To shut the Other's Gaze down—
You—could not—

And I—Could I stand by
And see You—freeze—
Without my Right of Frost—
20 Death's privilege?

Nor could I rise—with You—
Because Your Face
Would put out Jesus'—
That New Grace

Glow plain—and foreign

On my homesick Eye—
Except that You than He
Shone closer by—

They'd judge Us—How—
30 For You—served Heaven—You know,
Or sought to—
I could not—

Because You saturated Sight—
And I had no more Eyes
For sordid excellence
As Paradise

And were You lost, I would be—
Though My Name
Rang loudest
40 On the Heavenly fame—

And were You—saved—
And I—condemned to be
Where You were not—
That self—were Hell to Me—

So We must meet apart—
You there—I—here—
With just the Door ajar
That Oceans are—and Prayer—
And that White Sustenance—
50 Despair—

Me from Myself—to banish— (1862)

Me from Myself—to banish—
Had I Art—
Impregnable my Fortress
Unto All Heart—

But since Myself—assault Me—
How have I peace

Except by subjugating
Consciousness?

And since We're mutual Monarch
10 How this be
Except by Abdication—
Me—of Me?

Because I could not stop for Death— (1863)

Because I could not stop for Death—
He kindly stopped for me—
The Carriage held but just Ourselves—
And Immortality.

We slowly drove—He knew no haste
And I had put away
My labor and my leisure too,
For His Civility—

We passed the School, where Children
10   strove
At Recess—in the Ring—
We passed the Fields of Gazing Grain—
We passed the Setting Sun—

Or rather—He passed Us—
The Dews drew quivering and chill—
For only Gossamer, my Gown—
My Tippet—only Tulle—

We paused before a House that seemed
A Swelling of the Ground—
20 The Roof was scarcely visible—
The Cornice—in the Ground—

Since then—'tis Centuries—and yet
Feels shorter than the Day
I first surmised the Horse's Heads
Were toward Eternity—

My Life had stood—a Loaded Gun—   (1863)

My Life had stood—a Loaded Gun—
In Corners—till a Day
The Owner passed—identified—
And carried Me away—

And now We roam in Sovereign
      Woods—
And now We hunt the Doe—
And every time I speak for Him—
The Mountains straight reply—

10 And do I smile, such cordial light
Upon the Valley glow—
It is as a Vesuvian face
Had let its pleasure through—

And when at Night—Our good Day
      done—
I guard My Master's Head—
'Tis better than the Eider-Duck's
Deep Pillow—to have shared—

To foe of His—I'm deadly foe—
20 None stir the second time—
On whom I lay a Yellow Eye—
Or an emphatic Thumb—

Though I than He— may longer live
He longer must—than I—
For I have but the power to kill,
Without—the power to die—

Severer Service of myself   (1863)

Severer Service of myself
I—hastened to demand
To fill the awful Vacuum
Your life had left behind—

I worried Nature with my Wheels
When Hers had ceased to run—
When she had put away Her Work
My own had just begun.

I strove to weary Brain and Bone—
10 To harass to fatigue
The glittering Retinue of nerves—
Vitality to clog

To some dull comfort Those obtain
Who put a Head away
They knew the Hair to—
And forget the color of the Day—

Affliction would not be appeased—
The Darkness braced as firm
As all my stratagem had been
20 The Midnight to confirm—

No Drug for Consciousness—can be—
Alternative to die
Is Nature's only Pharmacy
For Being's Malady—

I felt a Cleaving in my Mind—   (1864)

I felt a Cleaving in my Mind—
As if my Brain had split—
I tried to match it—Seam by Seam—
But could not make them fit.

The thought behind, I strove to join
Unto the thought before—
But Sequence ravelled out of Sound
Like Balls—upon a Floor.

A narrow Fellow in the Grass   (1865)

A narrow Fellow in the Grass
Occasionally rides—
You may have met Him—did you not
His notice sudden is—

The Grass divides as with a Comb—
A spotted shaft is seen—
And then it closes at your feet
And opens further on—

He likes a Boggy Acre
10 A Floor too cool for Corn—
Yet when a Boy, and Barefoot—
I more than once at Noon

Have passed, I thought, a Whip lash
Unbraiding in the Sun
When stooping to secure it
It wrinkled, and was gone—

Several of Nature's People
I know, and they know me—
I feel for them a transport
20 Of cordiality—

But never met this Fellow
Attended, or alone
Without a tighter breathing
And Zero at the Bone—

Robert Frost

Robert Frost (1874–1963) was born in California and died in New England at the age of eighty-eight. The New England countryside, its people, and their speech take center stage in his poems. Frost's father died when he was ten, and his mother took him back East. He attended high school in Massachusetts, went to Dartmouth briefly, worked in mills, and, after marriage, spent two years at Harvard without taking a degree. He tried his hand at farming while he wrote poems, but his poems did not win acceptance from American editors. In 1912, he took his family to England, where a London publisher recognized the quality of the work; *A Boy's Will* appeared in 1913. When Frost returned to the United States in 1915, he found America ready for him. He won the Pulitzer Prize four times. Two years before he died, he read a poem at the inauguration of President John F. Kennedy. Other poems by Robert Frost appear on pages 1, 20–21, 50–51, 57, 97–98, and 114–115.

The Pasture   (1913)

I'm going out to clean the pasture spring;
I'll only stop to rake the leaves away
(And wait to watch the water clear, I may)
I sha'n't be gone long.—You come too.

I'm going out to fetch the little calf
That's standing by the mother. It's so young
It totters when she licks it with her tongue.
I sha'n't be gone long.—You come too.

Mowing   (1913)

There was never a sound beside the wood but one,
And that was my long scythe whispering to the ground.
What was it it whispered? I knew not well myself;
Perhaps it was something about the heat of the sun,
Something, perhaps, about the lack of sound—
And that was why it whispered and did not speak.
It was no dream of the gift of idle hours,
Or easy gold at the hand of fay or elf:
Anything more than the truth would have seemed too weak
10 To the earnest love that laid the swale in rows,
Not without feeble-pointed spikes of flowers
(Pale orchises), and scared a bright green snake.
The fact is the sweetest dream that labor knows.
My long scythe whispered and left the hay to make.

Home Burial   (1914)

He saw her from the bottom of the stairs
Before she saw him. She was starting down,
Looking back over her shoulder at some fear.
She took a doubtful step and then undid it
To raise herself and look again. He spoke
Advancing toward her: 'What is it you see
From up there always—for I want to know.'
She turned and sank upon her skirts at that,
And her face changed from terrified to dull.
10 He said to gain time: 'What is it you see,'
Mounting until she cowered under him.
'I will find out now—you must tell me, dear.'
She, in her place, refused him any help
With the least stiffening of her neck and silence.
She let him look, sure that he wouldn't see,
Blind creature; and awhile he didn't see.
But at last he murmured, 'Oh,' and again, 'Oh.'

'What is it—what?' she said.

                              'Just that I see.'

20 'You don't,' she challenged. 'Tell me what it is.'

'The wonder is I didn't see at once.
I never noticed it from here before.
I must be wonted to it—that's the reason.

The little graveyard where my people are!
So small the window frames the whole of it.
Not so much larger than a bedroom, is it?
There are three stones of slate and one of marble,
Broad-shouldered little slabs there in the sunlight
On the sidehill. We haven't to mind *those*.
30   But I understand: it is not the stones,
But the child's mound—'

                    'Don't, don't, don't, don't,' she cried.

She withdrew shrinking from beneath his arm
That rested on the bannister, and slid downstairs;
And turned on him with such a daunting look,
He said twice over before he knew himself:
'Can't a man speak of his own child he's lost?'

'Not you! Oh, where's my hat? Oh, I don't need it!
I must get out of here. I must get air.
40   I don't know rightly whether any man can.'

'Amy! Don't go to someone else this time.
Listen to me. I won't come down the stairs.'
He sat and fixed his chin between his fists.
'There's something I should like to ask you, dear.'

'You don't know how to ask it.'

                        'Help me, then.'

Her fingers moved the latch for all reply.

'My words are nearly always an offense.
I don't know how to speak of anything
50   So as to please you. But I might be taught
I should suppose. I can't say I see how.
A man must partly give up being a man
With women-folk. We could have some arrangement
By which I'd bind myself to keep hands off
Anything special you're a-mind to name.
Though I don't like such things 'twixt those that love.
Two that don't love can't live together without them.
But two that do can't live together with them.'
She moved the latch a little. 'Don't—don't go.
60   Don't carry it to someone else this time.
Tell me about it if it's something human.
Let me into your grief. I'm not so much
Unlike other folks as your standing there
Apart would make me out. Give me my chance.
I do think, though, you overdo it a little.
What was it brought you up to think it the thing

To take your mother-loss of a first child
So inconsolably—in the face of love.
You'd think his memory might be satisfied—'

70　'There you go sneering now!'

'I'm not, I'm not!

You make me angry. I'll come down to you.
God, what a woman! And it's come to this,
A man can't speak of his own child that's dead.'

'You can't because you don't know how to speak.
If you had any feelings, you that dug
With your own hand—how could you?—his little grave;
I saw you from that very window there,
Making the gravel leap and leap in air,
80　Leap up, like that, like that, and land so lightly
And roll back down the mound beside the hole.
I thought, Who is that man? I didn't know you.
And I crept down the stairs and up the stairs
To look again, and still your spade kept lifting.
Then you came in. I heard your rumbling voice
Out in the kitchen, and I don't know why,
But I went near to see with my own eyes.
You could sit there with the stains on your shoes
Of the fresh earth from your own baby's grave
90　And talk about your everyday concerns.
You had stood the spade up against the wall
Outside there in the entry, for I saw it.'

'I shall laugh the worst laugh I ever laughed.
I'm cursed. God, if I don't believe I'm cursed.'

'I can repeat the very words you were saying.
"Three foggy mornings and one rainy day
Will rot the best birch fence a man can build."
Think of it, talk like that at such a time!
What had how long it takes a birch to rot
100　To do with what was in the darkened parlor.
You *couldn't* care! The nearest friends can go
With anyone to death, comes so far short
They might as well not try to go at all.
No, from the time when one is sick to death,
One is alone, and he dies more alone.
Friends make pretense of following to the grave,
But before one is in it, their minds are turned
And making the best of their way back to life
And living people, and things they understand.
110　But the world's evil. I won't have grief so
If I can change it. Oh, I won't, I won't!'

'There, you have said it all and you feel better.
You won't go now. You're crying. Close the door.
The heart's gone out of it: why keep it up.
Amy! There's someone coming down the road!'

'*You*—oh, you think the talk is all. I must go—
Somewhere out of this house. How can I make you—'

'If—you—do!' She was opening the door wider.
'Where do you mean to go? First tell me that.
120   I'll follow and bring you back by force. I *will!*—'

After Apple-Picking   (1914)

My long two-pointed ladder's sticking through a tree
Toward heaven still,
And there's a barrel that I didn't fill
Beside it, and there may be two or three
Apples I didn't pick upon some bough.
But I am done with apple-picking now.
Essence of winter sleep is on the night,
The scent of apples: I am drowsing off.
I cannot rub the strangeness from my sight
10   I got from looking through a pane of glass
I skimmed this morning from the drinking trough
And held against the world of hoary grass.
It melted, and I let it fall and break.
But I was well
Upon my way to sleep before it fell,
And I could tell
What form my dreaming was about to take.
Magnified apples appear and disappear,
Stem end and blossom end,
20   And every fleck of russet showing clear.
My instep arch not only keeps the ache,
It keeps the pressure of a ladder round.
I feel the ladder sway as the boughs bend.
And I keep hearing from the cellar bin
The rumbling sound
Of load on load of apples coming in.
For I have had too much
Of apple-picking: I am overtired
Of the great harvest I myself desired.
30   There were ten thousand thousand fruit to touch,
Cherish in hand, lift down, and not let fall.
For all
That struck the earth,
No matter if not bruised or spiked with stubble,
Went surely to the cider-apple heap
As of no worth.

One can see what will trouble
This sleep of mine, whatever sleep it is.
Were he not gone,
40 The woodchuck could say whether it's like his
Long sleep, as I describe its coming on,
Or just some human sleep.

The Road Not Taken   (1916)

Two roads diverged in a yellow wood,
And sorry I could not travel both
And be one traveler, long I stood
And looked down one as far as I could
To where it bent in the undergrowth;

Then took the other, as just as fair,
And having perhaps the better claim,
Because it was grassy and wanted wear;
Though as for that the passing there
10 Had worn them really about the same,

And both that morning equally lay
In leaves no step had trodden black.
Oh, I kept the first for another day!
Yet knowing how way leads on to way,
I doubted if I should ever come back.

I shall be telling this with a sigh
Somewhere ages and ages hence:
Two roads diverged in a wood, and I—
I took the one less traveled by,
20 And that has made all the difference.

Birches   (1915)

When I see birches bend to left and right
Across the lines of straighter darker trees,
I like to think some boy's been swinging them.
But swinging doesn't bend them down to stay
As ice-storms do. Often you must have seen them
Loaded with ice a sunny winter morning
After a rain. They click upon themselves
As the breeze rises, and turn many-colored
As the stir cracks and crazes their enamel.
10 Soon the sun's warmth makes them shed crystal shells
Shattering and avalanching on the snow-crust—
Such heaps of broken glass to sweep away
You'd think the inner dome of heaven had fallen.
They are dragged to the withered bracken by the load,
And they seem not to break; though once they are bowed
So low for long, they never right themselves:
You may see their trunks arching in the woods
Years afterwards, trailing their leaves on the ground
Like girls on hands and knees that throw their hair
20 Before them over their heads to dry in the sun.
But I was going to say when Truth broke in
With all her matter-of-fact about the ice-storm
I should prefer to have some boy bend them
As he went out and in to fetch the cows—
Some boy too far from town to learn baseball,
Whose only play was what he found himself,

Summer or winter, and could play alone.
One by one he subdued his father's trees
By riding them down over and over again
30 Until he took the stiffness out of them,
And not one but hung limp, not one was left
For him to conquer. He learned all there was
To learn about not launching out too soon
And so not carrying the tree away
Clear to the ground. He always kept his poise
To the top branches, climbing carefully
With the same pains you use to fill a cup
Up to the brim, and even above the brim.
Then he flung outward, feet first, with a swish,
40 Kicking his way down through the air to the ground.
So was I once myself a swinger of birches.
And so I dream of going back to be.
It's when I'm weary of considerations,
And life is too much like a pathless wood
Where your face burns and tickles with the cobwebs
Broken across it, and one eye is weeping
From a twig's having lashed across it open.
I'd like to get away from earth awhile
And then come back to it and begin over.
50 May no fate willfully misunderstand me
And half grant what I wish and snatch me away
Not to return. Earth's the right place for love:
I don't know where it's likely to go better.
I'd like to go by climbing a birch tree,
And climb black branches up a snow-white trunk
Toward heaven, till the tree could bear no more,
But dipped its top and set me down again.
That would be good both going and coming back.
One could do worse than be a swinger of birches.

To Earthward (1923)

Love at the lips was touch
As sweet as I could bear;
And once that seemed too much;
I lived on air

That crossed me from sweet things
The flow of—was it musk
From hidden grapevine springs
Down hill at dusk?

I had the swirl and ache
10 From sprays of honeysuckle
That when they're gathered shake
Dew on the knuckle.

I craved strong sweets, but those
Seemed strong when I was young;
The petal of the rose
It was that stung.

Now no joy but lacks salt
That is not dashed with pain
And weariness and fault;
20 I crave the stain

Of tears, the aftermark
Of almost too much love,
The sweet of bitter bark
And burning clove.

When stiff and sore and scarred
I take away my hand
From leaning on it hard
In grass and sand,

30 The hurt is not enough:
I long for weight and strength
To feel the earth as rough
To all my length.

The Need of Being Versed in Country Things   (1920)

The house had gone to bring again
To the midnight sky a sunset glow.
Now the chimney was all of the house that stood,
Like a pistil after the petals go.

The barn opposed across the way,
That would have joined the house in flame
Had it been the will of the wind, was left
To bear forsaken the place's name.

No more it opened with all one end
10 For teams that came by the stony road
To drum on the floor with scurrying hoofs
And brush the mow with the summer load.

The birds that came to it through the air
At broken windows flew out and in,
Their murmur more like the sigh we sigh
From too much dwelling on what has been.

Yet for them the lilac renewed its leaf,
And the aged elm, though touched with fire;
And the dry pump flung up an awkward arm;
20 And the fence post carried a strand of wire.

For them there was really nothing sad.
But though they rejoiced in the nest they kept,
One had to be versed in country things
Not to believe the phoebes wept.

Once by the Pacific   (1926)

The shattered water made a misty din.
Great waves looked over others coming in,
And thought of doing something to the shore
That water never did to land before.
The clouds were low and hairy in the skies,
Like locks blown forward in the gleam of eyes.
You could not tell, and yet it looked as if
The shore was lucky in being backed by cliff,
The cliff in being backed by continent;
10 It looked as if a night of dark intent

Was coming, and not only a night, an age.
Someone had better be prepared for rage.
There would be more than ocean-water broken
Before God's last *Put out the Light* was spoken.

Acquainted with the Night   (1928)

I have been one acquainted with the night.
I have walked out in rain—and back in rain.
I have outwalked the furthest city light.

I have looked down the saddest city lane.
I have passed by the watchman on his beat
And dropped my eyes, unwilling to explain.

I have stood still and stopped the sound of feet
When far away an interrupted cry
Came over houses from another street,

10   But not to call me back or say good-by;
And further still at an unearthly height,
One luminary clock against the sky

Proclaimed the time was neither wrong nor right.
I have been one acquainted with the night.

Desert Places   (1934)

Snow falling and night falling fast, oh, fast
In a field I looked into going past,
And the ground almost covered smooth in snow,
But a few weeds and stubble showing last.

The woods around it have it—it is theirs.
All animals are smothered in their lairs.
I am too absent-spirited to count;
The loneliness includes me unawares.

And lonely as it is that loneliness
10   Will be more lonely ere it will be less—
A blanker whiteness of benighted snow
With no expression, nothing to express.

They cannot scare me with their empty spaces
Between stars—on stars where no human race is.
I have it in me so much nearer home
To scare myself with my own desert places.

Neither Out Far Nor In Deep   (1934)

The people along the sand
All turn and look one way.
They turn their back on the land.
They look at the sea all day.

As long as it takes to pass
A ship keeps raising its hull;
The wetter ground like glass
Reflects a standing gull.

10 The land may vary more;
But wherever the truth may be—
The water comes ashore,
And the people look at the sea.

They cannot look out far.
They cannot look in deep.
But when was that ever a bar
To any watch they keep?

The Silken Tent   (1939)

She is as in a field a silken tent
At midday when a sunny summer breeze
Has dried the dew and all its ropes relent,
So that in guys it gently sways at ease,
And its supporting central cedar pole,
That is its pinnacle to heavenward
And signifies the sureness of the soul,
Seems to owe naught to any single cord,
But strictly held by none, is loosely bound
10 By countless silken ties of love and thought
To everything on earth the compass round,
And only by one's going slightly taut
In the capriciousness of summer air
Is of the slightest bondage made aware.

Come In   (1941)

As I came to the edge of the woods,
Thrush music—hark!
Now if it was dusk outside,
Inside it was dark.

Too dark in the woods for a bird
By sleight of wing
To better its perch for the night,
Though it still could sing.

The last of the light of the sun
10 That had died in the west

Still lived for one song more
In a thrush's breast.

Far in the pillared dark
Thrush music went—
Almost like a call to come in
To the dark and lament.

But no, I was out for stars:
I would not come in.
I meant not even if asked,
20 And I hadn't been.

The Most of It   (1942)

He thought he kept the universe alone;
For all the voice in answer he could wake
Was but the mocking echo of his own
From some tree-hidden cliff across the lake.
Some morning from the boulder-broken beach
He would cry out on life, that what it wants
Is not its own love back in copy speech,
But counter-love, original response.
And nothing ever came of what he cried
10 Unless it was the embodiment that crashed
In the cliff's talus on the other side,
And then in the far distant water splashed.
But after a time allowed for it to swim,
Instead of proving human when it neared
And someone else additional to him,
As a great buck it powerfully appeared,
Pushing the crumpled water up ahead,
And landed pouring like a waterfall,
And stumbled through the rocks with horny tread,
20 And forced the underbrush—and that was all.

Theodore Roethke

Theodore Roethke (1908–1963) was born in Saginaw, Michigan, where his father kept the greenhouse that figures so prominently in his poems. He attended the University of Michigan and spent his last sixteen years in Seattle, where he was a professor at the University of Washington. He began by writing tight, formal stanzas and later broadened his repertoire to include a wide variety of tones and manners. Possibly no other major poet has traveled so widely in the realms of style. When he died, he had recently written his best work, notably "The Rose." See also page 39.

Cuttings   (1948)
(later)

This urge, wrestle, resurrection of dry sticks,
Cut stems struggling to put down feet,
What saint strained so much,
Rose on such lopped limbs to a new life?

I can hear, underground, that sucking and sobbing,
In my veins, in my bones I feel it,—
The small waters seeping upward,
The tight grains parting at last.
When sprouts break out,
10 Slippery as fish,
I quail, lean to beginnings, sheath-wet.

Big Wind   (1947)

Where were the greenhouses going,
Lunging into the lashing
Wind driving water
So far down the river
All the faucets stopped?—
So we drained the manure-machine
For the steam plant,
Pumping the stale mixture
Into the rusty boilers,
10 Watching the pressure gauge
Waver over to red,
As the seams hissed
And the live steam
Drove to the far
End of the rose-house,
Where the worst wind was,
Creaking the cypress window-frames,
Cracking so much thin glass
We stayed all night,
20 Stuffing the holes with burlap;
But she rode it out,
That old rose-house,
She hove into the teeth of it,
The core and pith of that ugly storm,
Ploughing with her stiff prow,
Bucking into the wind-waves
That broke over the whole of her,
Flailing her sides with spray,
Flinging long strings of wet across the roof-top,
30 Finally veering, wearing themselves out, merely
Whistling thinly under the wind-vents;
She sailed until the calm morning,
Carrying her full cargo of roses.

Dolor   (1943)

I have known the inexorable sadness of pencils,
Neat in their boxes, dolor of pad and paper-weight,
All the misery of manilla folders and mucilage,
Desolation in immaculate public places,

Lonely reception room, lavatory, switchboard,
The unalterable pathos of basin and pitcher,
Ritual of multigraph, paper-clip, comma,
Endless duplication of lives and objects.
And I have seen dust from the walls of institutions,
10 Finer than flour, alive, more dangerous than silica,
Sift, almost invisible, through long afternoons of tedium,
Dropping a fine film on nails and delicate eyebrows,
Glazing the pale hair, the duplicate grey standard faces.

My Papa's Waltz (1948)

The whiskey on your breath
Could make a small boy dizzy;
But I hung on like death:
Such waltzing was not easy.

We romped until the pans
Slid from the kitchen shelf;
My mother's countenance
Could not unfrown itself.

10 The hand that held my wrist
Was battered on one knuckle;
At every step you missed
My right ear scraped a buckle.

You beat time on my head
With a palm caked hard by dirt,
Then waltzed me off to bed
Still clinging to your shirt.

The Lost Son (1947)

1. The Flight

At Woodlawn I heard the dead cry:
I was lulled by the slamming of iron,
A slow drip over stones,
Toads brooding wells.
All the leaves stuck out their tongues;
I shook the softening chalk of my bones,
Saying,
Snail, snail, glister me forward,
Bird, soft-sigh me home,
10 Worm, be with me.
This is my hard time.

Fished in an old wound,
The soft pond of repose;
Nothing nibbled my line,
Not even the minnows came.

Sat in an empty house
Watching shadows crawl,
Scratching.
There was one fly.

20 Voice, come out of the silence.
Say something.

Appear in the form of a spider
Or a moth beating the curtain.

Tell me:
Which is the way I take;
Out of what door do I go,
Where and to whom?

Dark hollows said, lee to the wind,
The moon said, back of an eel,
30   The salt said, look by the sea,
Your tears are not enough praise,
You will find no comfort here,
In the kingdom of bang and blab.

Running lightly over spongy ground,
Past the pasture of flat stones,
The three elms,
The sheep strewn on a field,
Over a rickety bridge
Toward the quick-water, wrinkling and rippling.

40   Hunting along the river,
Down among the rubbish, the bug-riddled foliage,
By the muddy pond-edge, by the bog-holes,
By the shrunken lake, hunting, in the heat of summer.

The shape of a rat?
    It's bigger than that.
    It's less than a leg
    And more than a nose,
    Just under the water
    It usually goes.

50   Is it soft like a mouse?
Can it wrinkle its nose?
Could it come in the house
On the tips of its toes?

Take the skin of a cat
And the back of an eel,
Then roll them in grease,—
That's the way it would feel.

It's sleek as an otter
With wide webby toes
60   Just under the water
It usually goes.

2. The Pit

Where do the roots go?
   Look down under the leaves.
Who put the moss there?
   These stones have been here too long.
Who stunned the dirt into noise?
   Ask the mole, he knows.
I feel the slime of a wet nest.
   Beware Mother Mildew.
70 Nibble again, fish nerves.

3. The Gibber

At the wood's mouth,
By the cave's door,
I listened to something
I had heard before.

Dogs of the groin
Barked and howled,
The sun was against me,
The moon would not have me.

The weeds whined,
80 The snakes cried,
The cows and briars
Said to me: Die.

What a small song. What slow clouds. What dark water.
Hath the rain a father? All the caves are ice. Only the snow's here.
I'm cold. I'm cold all over. Rub me in father and mother.
Fear was my father, Father Fear.
His look drained the stones.

     What gliding shape
     Beckoning through halls,
90   Stood poised on the stair,
     Fell dreamily down?

     From the mouths of jugs
     Perched on many shelves,
     I saw substance flowing
     That cold morning.

     Like a slither of eels
     That watery cheek
     As my own tongue kissed
     My lips awake.

100 Is this the storm's heart? The ground is unstilling itself.
   My veins are running nowhere. Do the bones cast out their fire?

Is the seed leaving the old bed? These buds are live as birds.
Where, where are the tears of the world?
Let the kisses resound, flat like a butcher's palm;
Let the gestures freeze; our doom is already decided.
All the windows are burning! What's left of my life?
I want the old rage, the lash of primordial milk!
Goodbye, goodbye, old stones, the time-order is going,
I have married my hands to perpetual agitation,
110 I run, I run to the whistle of money.

    Money money money
    Water water water

    How cool the grass is.
    Has the bird left?
    The stalk still sways.
    Has the worm a shadow?
    What do the clouds say?

These sweeps of light undo me.
Look, look, the ditch is running white!
120 I've more veins than a tree!
Kiss me, ashes, I'm falling through a dark swirl.

4. The Return

    The way to the boiler was dark,
    Dark all the way,
    Over slippery cinders
    Through the long greenhouse.

    The roses kept breathing in the dark.
    They had many mouths to breathe with.
    My knees made little winds underneath
    Where the weeds slept.

130   There was always a single light
    Swinging by the fire-pit,
    Where the fireman pulled out roses,
    The big roses, the big bloody clinkers.

    Once I stayed all night.
    The light in the morning came slowly over the white
    Snow.
    There were many kinds of cool
    Air.
    Then came steam.

140   Pipe-knock.

Scurry of warm over small plants.
Ordnung! ordnung!
Papa is coming!

A fine haze moved off the leaves;
Frost melted on far panes;
The rose, the chrysanthemum turned toward the light.
Even the hushed forms, the bent yellowy weeds
Moved in a slow up-sway.

5. "It was beginning winter"

It was beginning winter,
150 An in-between time,
The landscape still partly brown:
The bones of weeds kept swinging in the wind,
Above the blue snow.

It was beginning winter,
The light moved slowly over the frozen field,
Over the dry seed-crowns,
The beautiful surviving bones
Swinging in the wind.

Light traveled over the wide field;
160 Stayed.
The weeds stopped swinging.
The mind moved, not alone,
Through the clear air, in the silence.

Was it light?
Was it light within?
Was it light within light?
Stillness becoming alive,
Yet still?

A lively understandable spirit
170 Once entertained you.
It will come again.
Be still.
Wait.

Elegy for Jane   (1950)
My Student, Thrown by a Horse

I remember the neckcurls, limp and damp as tendrils;
And her quick look, a sidelong pickerel smile;
And how, once startled into talk, the light syllables leaped for her,
And she balanced in the delight of her thought,
A wren, happy, tail into the wind,
Her song trembling the twigs and small branches.
The shade sang with her;
The leaves, their whispers turned to kissing;
And the mold sang in the bleached valleys under the rose.

10 Oh, when she was sad, she cast herself down into such a pure depth,
Even a father could not find her:
Scraping her cheek against straw;
Stirring the clearest water.

My sparrow, you are not here,
Waiting like a fern, making a spiny shadow.
The sides of wet stones cannot console me,
Nor the moss, wound with the last light.

If only I could nudge you from this sleep,
My maimed darling, my skittery pigeon.
20 Over this damp grave I speak the words of my love:
I, with no rights in this matter,
Neither father nor lover.

The Sloth   (1950)

In moving-slow he has no Peer.
You ask him something in his Ear,
He thinks about it for a Year;

And, then, before he says a Word
There, upside down (unlike a Bird),
He will assume that you have Heard—

A most Ex-as-per-at-ing Lug.
But should you call his manner Smug,
He'll sigh and give his Branch a Hug;

10 Then off again to Sleep he goes,
Still swaying gently by his Toes,
And you just *know* he knows he knows.

I Knew a Woman   (1954)

I knew a woman, lovely in her bones,
When small birds sighed, she would sigh back at them;
Ah, when she moved, she moved more ways than one:
The shapes a bright container can contain!
Of her choice virtues only gods should speak,
Or English poets who grew up on Greek
(I'd have them sing in chorus, cheek to cheek).

How well her wishes went! She stroked my chin,
She taught me Turn, and Counter-turn, and Stand;
10 She taught me Touch, that undulant white skin;
I nibbled meekly from her proffered hand;
She was the sickle; I, poor I, the rake,

Coming behind her for her pretty sake
(But what prodigious mowing we did make).

Love likes a gander, and adores a goose:
Her full lips pursed, the errant note to seize;
She played it quick, she played it light and loose;
My eyes, they dazzled at her flowing knees;
Her several parts could keep a pure repose,
20 Or one hip quiver with a mobile nose
(She moved in circles, and those circles moved).

Let seed be grass, and grass turn into hay:
I'm martyr to a motion not my own;
What's freedom for? To know eternity.
I swear she cast a shadow white as stone.
But who would count eternity in days?
These old bones live to learn her wanton ways:
(I measure time by how a body sways).

The Visitant   (1950)

1

A cloud moved close. The bulk of the wind shifted.
A tree swayed over water.
A voice said:
Stay. Stay by the slip-ooze. Stay.

Dearest tree, I said, may I rest here?
A ripple made a soft reply.
I waited, alert as a dog.
The leech clinging to a stone waited;
And the crab, the quiet breather.

2

10 Slow, slow as a fish she came,
Slow as a fish coming forward,
Swaying in a long wave;
Her skirts not touching a leaf,
Her white arms reaching towards me.

She came without sound,
Without brushing the wet stones;

In the soft dark of early evening,
She came,
The wind in her hair,
20 The moon beginning.

3

I woke in the first of morning.
Staring at a tree, I felt the pulse of a stone.
Where's she now, I kept saying.
Where's she now, the mountain's downy girl?
But the bright day had no answer.
A wind stirred in a web of appleworms;
The tree, the close willow, swayed.

Journey to the Interior   (1961)

1

In the long journey out of the self,
There are many detours, washed-out interrupted raw places
Where the shale slides dangerously
And the back wheels hang almost over the edge
At the sudden veering, the moment of turning.
Better to hug close, wary of rubble and falling stones.
The arroyo cracking the road, the wind-bitten buttes, the canyons,
Creeks swollen in midsummer from the flash-flood roaring into the narrow valley.
Reeds beaten flat by wind and rain,
10 Grey from the long winter, burnt at the base in late summer.
—Or the path narrowing,
Winding upward toward the stream with its sharp stones,
The upland of alder and birchtrees,
Through the swamp alive with quicksand,
The way blocked at last by a fallen fir-tree,
The thickets darkening,
The ravines ugly.

2

I remember how it was to drive in gravel,
Watching for dangerous down-hill places, where the wheels whined beyond
      eighty—
20 When you hit the deep pit at the bottom of the swale,
The trick was to throw the car sideways and charge over the hill, full of the throttle.
Grinding up and over the narrow road, spitting and roaring.
A chance? Perhaps. But the road was part of me, and its ditches,
And the dust lay thick on my eyelids,—Who ever wore goggles?—
Always a sharp turn to the left past a barn close to the roadside,
To a scurry of small dogs and a shriek of children,
The highway ribboning out in a straight thrust to the North,
To the sand dunes and fish flies, hanging, thicker than moths,
Dying brightly under the street lights sunk in coarse concrete,
30 The towns with their high pitted road-crowns and deep gutters,
Their wooden stores of silvery pine and weather-beaten red courthouses,

An old bridge below with a buckled iron railing, broken by some idiot plunger;
Underneath, the sluggish water running between weeds, broken wheels, tires,
    stones.
And all flows past—
The cemetery with two scrubby trees in the middle of the prairie,
The dead snakes and muskrats, the turtles gasping in the rubble,
The spikey purple bushes in the winding dry creek bed—
The floating hawks, the jackrabbits, the grazing cattle—
I am not moving but they are,
40 And the sun comes out of a blue cloud over the Tetons,
While, farther away, the heat-lightning flashes.
I rise and fall in the slow sea of a grassy plain,
The wind veering the car slightly to the right,
Whipping the line of white laundry, bending the cottonwoods apart,
The scraggly wind-break of a dusty ranch-house.
I rise and fall, and time folds
Into a long moment;
And I hear the lichen speak,
And the ivy advance with its white lizard feet—
50 On the shimmering road,
On the dusty detour.

3

I see the flower of all water, above and below me, the never receding,
Moving, unmoving in a parched land, white in the moonlight:
The soul at a still-stand,
At ease after rocking the flesh to sleep,
Petals and reflections of petals mixed on the surface of a glassy pool,
And the waves flattening out when the fishermen drag their nets over the stones.

In the moment of time when the small drop forms, but does not fall,
I have known the heart of the sun,—
60 In the dark and light of a dry place,
In a flicker of fire brisked by a dusty wind.
I have heard, in a drip of leaves,
A slight song,
After the midnight cries.
I rehearse myself for this:
The stand at the stretch in the face of death,
Delighting in surface change, the glitter of light on waves,
And I roam elsewhere, my body thinking,
Turning toward the other side of light,
70 In a tower of wind, a tree idling in air,
Beyond my own echo,
Neither forward nor backward,
Unperplexed, in a place leading nowhere.

As a blind man, lifting a curtain, knows it is morning,
I know this change:
On one side of silence there is no smile;

But when I breathe with the birds,
The spirit of wrath becomes the spirit of blessing,
And the dead begin from their dark to sing in my sleep.

The Rose   (1963)

1

There are those to whom place is unimportant,
But this place, where sea and fresh water meet,
Is important—
Where the hawks sway out into the wind,
Without a single wingbeat,
And the eagles sail low over the fir trees,
And the gulls cry against the crows
In the curved harbors,
And the tide rises up against the grass
10 Nibbled by sheep and rabbits.

A time for watching the tide,
For the heron's hieratic fishing,
For the sleepy cries of the towhee,
The morning birds gone, the twittering finches,
But still the flash of the kingfisher, the wingbeat of the scoter,
The sun a ball of fire coming down over the water,
The last geese crossing against the reflected afterlight,
The moon retreating into a vague cloud-shape
To the cries of the owl, the eerie whooper.
20 The old log subsides with the lessening waves,
And there is silence.

I sway outside myself
Into the darkening currents,
Into the small spillage of driftwood,
The waters swirling past the tiny headlands.
Was it here I wore a crown of birds for a moment
While on a far point of the rocks
The light heightened,
And below, in a mist out of nowhere,
30 The first rain gathered?

2

As when a ship sails with a light wind—
The waves less than the ripples made by rising fish,
The lacelike wrinkles of the wake widening, thinning out,
Sliding away from the traveler's eye,
The prow pitching easily up and down,
The whole ship rolling slightly sideways,
The stern high, dipping like a child's boat in a pond—
Our motion continues.

But this rose, this rose in the sea-wind,
40 Stays,
Stays in its true place,
Flowering out of the dark,
Widening at high noon, face upward,
A single wild rose, struggling out of the white embrace of the morning-glory,
Out of the briary hedge, the tangle of matted underbrush,
Beyond the clover, the ragged hay,
Beyond the sea pine, the oak, the wind-tipped madrona,
Moving with the waves, the undulating driftwood,
Where the slow creek winds down to the black sand of the shore
50 With its thick grassy scum and crabs scuttling back into their glistening craters.

And I think of roses, roses,
White and red, in the wide six-hundred-foot greenhouses,
And my father standing astride the cement benches,
Lifting me high over the four-foot stems, the Mrs. Russells, and his own elaborate
    hybrids.
And how those flowerheads seemed to flow toward me, to beckon me, only a child,
    out of myself.

What need for heaven, then,
With that man, and those roses?

3

60 What do they tell us, sound and silence?
I think of American sounds in this silence:
On the banks of the Tombstone, the wind-harps having their say,
The thrush singing alone, that easy bird,
The killdeer whistling away from me,
The mimetic chortling of the catbird
Down in the corner of the garden, among the raggedy lilacs,
The bobolink skirring from a broken fencepost,
The bluebird, lover of holes in old wood, lilting its light song,
And that thin cry, like a needle piercing the ear, the insistent cicada,
70 And the ticking of snow around oil drums in the Dakotas,
The thin whine of telephone wires in the wind of a Michigan winter,
The shriek of nails as old shingles are ripped from the top of a roof,
The bulldozer backing away, the hiss of the sandblaster,
And the deep chorus of horns coming up from the streets in early morning.
I return to the twittering of swallows above water,
And that sound, that single sound,
When the mind remembers all,
And gently the light enters the sleeping soul,
A sound so thin it could not woo a bird,

80 Beautiful my desire, and the place of my desire.

I think of the rock singing, and light making its own silence,
At the edge of a ripening meadow, in early summer,
The moon lolling in the close elm, a shimmer of silver,
Or that lonely time before the breaking of morning

When the slow freight winds along the edge of the ravaged hillside,
And the wind tries the shape of a tree,
While the moon lingers,
And a drop of rain water hangs at the tip of a leaf
Shifting in the wakening sunlight
90 Like the eye of a new-caught fish.

4

I live with the rocks, their weeds,
Their filmy fringes of green, their harsh
Edges, their holes
Cut by the sea-slime, far from the crash
Of the long swell,
The oily, tar-laden walls
Of the toppling waves,
Where the salmon ease their way into the kelp beds,
And the sea rearranges itself among the small islands.

100 Near this rose, in this grove of sun-parched, wind-warped madronas,
Among the half-dead trees, I came upon the true ease of myself,
As if another man appeared out of the depths of my being,
And I stood outside myself,
Beyond becoming and perishing,
A something wholly other,
As if I swayed out on the wildest wave alive,
And yet was still.
And I rejoiced in being what I was:
In the lilac change, the white reptilian calm,
110 In the bird beyond the bough, the single one
With all the air to greet him as he flies,
The dolphin rising from the darkening waves;

And in this rose, this rose in the sea-wind,
Rooted in stone, keeping the whole of light,
Gathering to itself sound and silence—
Mine and the sea-wind's.

The Meadow Mouse   (1963)

1

In a shoe box stuffed in an old nylon stocking
Sleeps the baby mouse I found in the meadow,
Where he trembled and shook beneath a stick
Till I caught him up by the tail and brought him in,
Cradled in my hand,
A little quaker, the whole body of him trembling,
His absurd whiskers sticking out like a cartoon-mouse,
His feet like small leaves,
Little lizard-feet,
10 Whitish and spread wide when he tried to struggle away,
Wriggling like a miniscule puppy.

Now he's eaten his three kinds of cheese and drunk from his bottle-cap
    watering-trough—
So much he just lies in one corner,
His tail curled under him, his belly big
As his head: his bat-like ears
Twitching, tilting toward the least sound.

Do I imagine he no longer trembles
When I come close to him?
20 He seems no longer to tremble.

2

But this morning the shoe-box house on the back porch is empty.
Where has he gone, my meadow mouse,
My thumb of a child that nuzzled in my palm?—
To run under the hawk's wing,
Under the eye of the great owl watching from the elm-tree,
To live by courtesy of the shrike, the snake, the tom-cat.

I think of the nestling fallen into the deep grass,
The turtle gasping in the dusty rubble of the highway,
The paralytic stunned in the tub, and the water rising,—
30 All things innocent, hapless, forsaken.

Adrienne Rich

Adrienne Rich (1929–   ) grew up in Baltimore and attended Radcliffe College. She published her first book, *A Change of World,* as Yale Younger Poet in her senior year at college, and two years later received a Guggenheim Fellowship. Her second volume, *The Diamond Cutters* (1955), was followed by a gap of some years, during which she had three sons in quick succession. Over the years, her work has changed considerably, diminishing in decorativeness, becoming starker, tighter, tougher, and more emotional. Her prose book, *Of Woman Born* (1977), is a monument of the feminist movement. Most of the poems reproduced here come from *The Fact of a Doorframe,* which selects among her poems from 1950 to 1984. Long a resident of the northeast—Massachusetts, New York, Vermont—Rich now lives in California.

Aunt Jennifer's Tigers   (1951)

Aunt Jennifer's tigers prance across a screen,
Bright topaz denizens of a world of green.
They do not fear the men beneath the tree;
They pace in sleek chivalric certainty.

Aunt Jennifer's fingers fluttering through her wool
Find even the ivory needle hard to pull.
The massive weight of Uncle's wedding band
Sits heavily upon Aunt Jennifer's hand.

When Aunt is dead, her terrified hands will lie
10 Still ringed with ordeals she was mastered by.
The tigers in the panel that she made
Will go on prancing, proud and unafraid.

A Marriage in the 'Sixties   (1961)

As solid-seeming as antiquity,
you frown above
the *New York Sunday Times*
where Castro, like a walk-on out of *Carmen,*
mutters into a bearded henchman's ear.

They say the second's getting shorter—
I knew it in my bones—
and pieces of the universe are missing.
I feel the gears of this late afternoon
10 slip, cog by cog, even as I read.
"I'm old," we both complain,
half-laughing, oftener now.

Time serves you well. That face—
part Roman emperor, part Raimu—
nothing this side of Absence can undo.
Bliss, revulsion, your rare angers can
only carry through what's well begun.

When
I read your letters long ago
20 in that half-defunct
hotel in Magdalen Street
every word primed my nerves.
A geographical misery
composed of oceans, fogbound planes
and misdelivered cablegrams
lay round me, a Nova Zembla
only your live breath could unfreeze.
Today we stalk
in the raging desert of our thought
30 whose single drop of mercy is
each knows the other there.
Two strangers, thrust for life upon a rock,
may have at last the perfect hour of talk
that language aches for; still—
two minds, two messages.

Your brows knit into flourishes. Some piece
of mere time has you tangled there.
Some mote of history has flown into your eye.
Will nothing ever be the same,
40   even our quarrels take a different key,
our dreams exhume new metaphors?
The world breathes underneath our bed.
Don't look. We're at each other's mercy too.

Dear fellow-particle, electric dust
I'm blown with—ancestor
to what euphoric cluster—
see how particularity dissolves
in all that hints of chaos. Let one finger
hover toward you from There
50   and see this furious grain
suspend its dance to hang
beside you like your twin.

Women   (1968)
  —for C.R.G.

My three sisters are sitting
on rocks of black obsidian.
For the first time, in this light, I can see who they are.

My first sister is sewing her costume for the procession.
She is going as the Transparent Lady
and all her nerves will be visible.

My second sister is also sewing,
at the seam over her heart which has never healed entirely.
At last, she hopes, this tightness in her chest will ease.

10   My third sister is gazing
at a dark-red crust spreading westward far out on the sea.
Her stockings are torn but she is beautiful.

After Twenty Years   (1971)
  —for A.P.C.

Two women sit at a table by a window. Light breaks
unevenly on both of them.
Their talk is a striking of sparks
which passers-by in the street observe
as a glitter in the glass of that window.
Two women in the prime of life.
Their babies are old enough to have babies.
Loneliness has been part of their story for twenty years,

the dark edge of the clever tongue,
10 the obscure underside of the imagination.
It is snow and thunder in the street.
While they speak the lightning flashes purple.
It is strange to be so many women,
eating and drinking at the same table,
those who bathed their children in the same basin
who kept their secrets from each other
walked the floors of their lives in separate rooms
and flow into history now as the woman of their time
living in the prime of life
20 as in a city where nothing is forbidden
and nothing permanent.

From an Old House in America   (1974)

1.

Deliberately, long ago
the carcasses

of old bugs crumbled
into the rut of the window

and we started sleeping here
Fresh June bugs batter this June's

screens, June-lightning batters
the spiderweb

10 I sweep the wood-dust
from the wood-box

the snout of the vacuum cleaner
sucks the past away

2.

Other lives were lived here:
mostly un-articulate

yet someone left her creamy signature
in the trail of rusticated

narcissus straggling up
20 through meadowgrass and vetch

Families breathed close
boxed-in from the cold

hard times, short growing season
the old rainwater cistern

hulks in the cellar

3.

Like turning through the contents of a
            drawer:
these rusted screws, this empty vial

30 useless, this box of watercolor paints
dried to insolubility—

but this—
this pack of cards with no card missing

still playable
and three good fuses

and this toy: a little truck
scarred red, yet all its wheels still turn

The humble tenacity of things
waiting for people, waiting for months,
40   for years

4.

*Often rebuked, yet always back
      returning*
I place my hand on the hand

of the dead, invisible palm-print
on the doorframe

spiked with daylilies, green leaves
catching in the screen door

or I read the backs of old postcards
50 curling from thumbtacks, winter and
            summer

fading through cobweb-tinted panes—
white church in Norway

Dutch hyacinths bleeding azure
red beach on Corsica

set-pieces of the world
stuck to this house of plank

I flash on wife and husband
embattled, in the years

60 that dried, dim ink was wet
those signatures

5.

If they call me man-hater, you
would have known it for a lie

but the *you* I want to speak to
has become your death

If I dream of you these days
I know my dreams are mine and not of
    you

70 yet something hangs between us
older and stranger than ourselves

like a translucent curtain, a sheet of
    water
a dusty window

the irreducible, incomplete connection
between the dead and living

or between man and woman in this
savagely fathered and unmothered
    world

80 ### 6.

The other side of a translucent
curtain, a sheet of water

a dusty window, Non-being
utters its flat tones

the speech of an actor learning his lines
phonetically

the final autistic statement
of the self-destroyer

All my energy reaches out tonight
90 to comprehend a miracle beyond

raising the dead: the undead to watch
back on the road of birth

7.

I am an American woman:
I turn that over

like a leaf pressed in a book
I stop and look up from

into the coals of the stove
or the black square of the window

100 Foot-slogging through the Bering Strait
jumping from the *Arbella* to my death

chained to the corpse beside me
I feel my pains begin

I am washed up on this continent
shipped here to be fruitful

my body a hollow ship
bearing sons to the wilderness

sons who ride away
on horseback, daughters

110 whose juices drain like mine
into the *arroyo* of stillbirths, massacres

Hanged as witches, sold as
    breeding-wenches
my sisters leave me

I am not the wheatfield
nor the virgin forest

I never chose this place
yet I am of it now

In my decent collar, in the
120   daguerrotype
I pierce its legend with my look

my hands wring the necks of prairie
    chickens
I am used to blood

When the men hit the hobo track
I stay on with the children

my power is brief and local
but I know my power

I have lived in isolation
130 from other women, so much

in the mining camps, the first cities
the Great Plains winters

Most of the time, in my sex, I was
    alone

8.

Tonight in this northeast kingdom
striated iris stand in a jar with daisies

the porcupine gnaws in the shed
fireflies beat and simmer

140 caterpillars begin again
their long, innocent climb

the length of leaves of burdock
or webbing of a garden chair

plain and ordinary things
speak softly

the light square on old wallpaper
where a poster has fallen down

Robert Indiana's LOVE
leftover of a decade

150 ## 9.

I do not want to simplify
Or: I would simplify

by naming the complexity
It was made over-simple all along

the separation of powers
the allotment of sufferings

her spine cracking in labor
his plow driving across the Indian
    graves

160 her hand unconscious on the cradle,
    her mind
with the wild geese

his mother-hatred driving him
into exile from the earth

the refugee couple with their
    cardboard luggage
standing on the ramshackle
    landing-stage

he with fingers frozen around his Law
170 she with her down quilt sewn through
    iron nights

—the weight of the old world, plucked
drags after them, a random feather-bed

10.

Her children dead of diphtheria, she
set herself on fire with kerosene

(O Lord I was unworthy
Thou didst find me out)

she left the kitchen scrubbed
180 down to the marrow of its boards

"The penalty for barrenness
is emptiness

my punishment is my crime
what I have failed to do, is me . . ."

—Another month without a show
and this the seventh year

O Father let this thing pass out of me
I swear to You

I will live for the others, asking nothing
190 *I will ask nothing, ever, for myself*

11.

Out back of this old house
datura tangles with a gentler weed

its spiked pods smelling
of bad dreams and death

I reach through the dark, groping
past spines of nightmare

to brush the leaves of sensuality
A dream of tenderness

200 wrestles with all I know of history
I cannot now lie down

with a man who fears my power
or reaches for me as for death

or with a lover who imagines
we are not in danger

12.

If it was lust that had defined us—
their lust and fear of our deep places

we have done our time
210 as faceless torsos licked by fire

we are in thf open, on our way—
our counterparts

the pinyon jay, the small
gilt-winged insect

the Cessna throbbing level
the raven floating in the gorge

the rose and violet vulva of the earth
filling with darkness

yet deep within a single sparkle
220 of red, a human fire

and near and yet above the western
          planet
calmly biding her time

13.

They were the distractions, lust and fear
but are

themselves a key
Everything that can be used, will be:

the fathers in their ceremonies
230 the genital contests

the cleansing of blood from pubic hair
the placenta buried and guarded

their terror of blinding
by the look of her who bore them

If you do not believe
that fear and hatred

read the lesson again
in the old dialect

14.

240 *But can't you see me as a human being*
he said

What is a human being
she said

I try to understand
he said

what will you undertake
she said

will you punish me for history
he said

250 *what will you undertake*
she said

do you believe in collective guilt
he said

let me look in your eyes
she said

15.

Who is here. The Erinyes.
One to sit in judgment.

One to speak tenderness.
260 One to inscribe the verdict on the
          canyon wall.

If you have not confessed
the damage

if you have not recognized
the Mother of reparations

if you have not come to terms
with the women in the mirror

if you have not come to terms
with the inscription

270   the terms of the ordeal
the discipline   the verdict

if still you are on your way
still She awaits your coming

16.

"Such women are dangerous
to the order of things"

and yes, we will be dangerous
to ourselves

groping through spines of nightmare
280   (*datura* tangling with a simpler herb)

because the line dividing
lucidity from darkness

is yet to be marked out

Isolation, the dream
of the frontier woman

leveling her rifle along
the homestead fence

still snares our pride
—a suicidal leaf

290   laid under the burning-glass
in the sun's eye

Any woman's death diminishes me

from Twenty-One Love Poems   (1976)

II

I wake up in your bed. I know I have been dreaming.
Much earlier, the alarm broke us from each other,
you've been at your desk for hours. I know what I dreamed:
our friend the poet comes into my room
where I've been writing for days,
drafts, carbons, poems are scattered everywhere,
and I want to show her one poem
which is the poem of my life. But I hesitate,
and wake. You've kissed my hair
10   to wake me. *I dreamed you were a poem,*
I say, *a poem I wanted to show someone* . . .
and I laugh and fall dreaming again
of the desire to show you to everyone I love,
to move openly together
in the pull of gravity, which is not simple,
which carries the feathered grass a long way down the upbreathing air.

VI

Your small hands, precisely equal to my own—
only the thumb is larger, longer—in these hands
I could trust the world, or in many hands like these,
20   handling power-tools or steering-wheel
or touching a human face. . . . Such hands could turn

the unborn child rightways in the birth canal
or pilot the exploratory rescue-ship
through icebergs, or piece together
the fine, needle-like sherds of a great krater-cup
bearing on its sides
figures of esctatic women striding
to the sibyl's den or the Eleusinian cave—
such hands might carry out an unavoidable violence
30 with such restraint, with such a grasp
of the range and limits of violence
that violence ever after would be obsolete.

XII

Sleeping, turning in turn like planets
rotating in their midnight meadow:
a touch is enough to let us know
40 we're not alone in the universe, even in sleep:
the dream-ghosts of two worlds
walking their ghost-towns, almost address each other.
I've wakened to your muttered words
spoken light- or dark-years away
as if my own voice had spoken.
But we have different voices, even in sleep,
and our bodies, so alike, are yet so different
and the past echoing through our bloodstreams
is freighted with different language, different meanings—
50 though in any chronicle of the world we share
it could be written with new meaning
we were two lovers of one gender,
we were two women of one generation.

Living Memory   (1988)

Open the book of tales you knew by heart,
begin driving the old roads again,
repeating the old sentences, which have changed
minutely from the wordings you remembered.
A full moon on the first of May
drags silver film on the Winooski River.
The villages are shut
for the night, the woods are open
and soon you arrive at a crossroads
10 where late, late in time you recognize
part of yourself is buried.   Call it Danville,
village of water-witches.

From here on instinct is uncompromised and clear:
the tales come crowding like the Kalevala
longing to burst from the tongue.   Under the trees
of the backroad you rumor the dark

with houses, sheds, the long barn
moored like a barge on the hillside.
Chapter and verse.   A mailbox.   A dooryard.
20 A drink of springwater from the kitchen tap.
An old bed, old wallpaper.   Falling asleep like a child
in the heart of the story.

Reopen the book.   A light mist soaks the page,
blunt naked buds tip the wild lilac scribbled
at the margin of the road, no one knows when.
Broken stones of drywall mark the onset
of familiar paragraphs slanting up and away
each with its own version, nothing ever
has looked the same from anywhere.
30 We came like others to a country of farmers—
Puritans, Catholics, Scotch Irish, Québecois:
bought a failed Yankee's empty house and barn
from a prospering Yankee,
Jews following Yankee footprints,
prey to many myths but most of all
that Nature makes us free.   That the land can save us.
Pioneer, indigenous; we were neither.

You whose stories these farms secrete,
you whose absence these fields publish,
40 all you whose lifelong travail
took as given this place and weather
who did what you could with the means you had—
it was pick and shovel work
done with a pair of horses, a stone boat
a strong back, and an iron bar: clearing pasture—
Your memories crouched, foreshortened in our text.
Pages torn.   New words crowding the old.

I knew a woman whose clavicle was smashed
inside a white clapboard house with an apple tree
50 and a row of tulips by the door.   I had a friend
with six children and a tumor like a seventh
who drove me to my driver's test and in exchange
wanted to see Goddard College, in Plainfield.   She'd heard
women without diplomas could study there.
I knew a woman who walked
straight across cut stubble in her bare feet away,
women who said, *He's a good man, never*
laid a hand to me as living proof.
A man they said fought death
60 to keep fire for his wife for one more winter, leave
a woodpile to outlast him.
I was left the legacy of a pile of stovewood
split by a man in the mute chains of rage.
The land he loved as landscape

could not unchain him.   There are many,
Gentile and Jew, it has not saved.   Many hearts have burst
over these rocks, in the shacks
on the failure sides of these hills.   Many guns
turned on brains already splitting
70 in silence.   Where are those versions?
Written-across like nineteenth-century letters
or secrets penned in vinegar, invisible
till the page is held over flame.

I was left the legacy of three sons
—as if in an old legend of three brothers
where one changes into a rufous hawk
one into a snowy owl
one into a whistling swan
and each flies to the mother's side
80 as she travels, bringing something she has lost,
and she sees their eyes are the eyes of her children
and speaks their names and they become her sons.
But there is no one legend and one legend only.

This month the land still leafless, out from snow
opens in all directions, the transparent woods
with sugar-house, pond, cellar-hole unscreened.
Winter and summer cover the closed roads
but for a few weeks they lie exposed,
the old nervous-system of the land.   It's the time
90 when history speaks in a row of crazy fence-poles
a blackened chimney, houseless, a spring
soon to be choked in second growth
a stack of rusting buckets, a rotting sledge.
It's the time when your own living
laid open between seasons
ponders clues like the *One Way* sign defaced
to *Bone Way,* the stones
of a graveyard in Vermont, a Jewish cemetery
in Birmingham, Alabama.
100 How you have needed these places,
as a tall gaunt woman used to need to sit
at the knees of bronze-hooded *Grief*
by Clover Adams' grave.
But you will end somewhere else, a sift of ashes
awkwardly flung by hands you have held and loved
or, nothing so individual, bones reduced
with, among, other bones, anonymous,
or wherever the Jewish dead
have to be sought in the wild grass overwhelming
110 the cracked stones.   Hebrew spelled in wilderness.

All we can read is life.   Death is invisible.
A yahrzeit candle belongs

to life.   The sugar skulls
eaten on graves for the Day of the Dead
belong to life.   To the living.   The Kaddish is to the living,
the Day of the Dead, for the living.   Only the living
invent these plumes, tombs, mounds, funeral ships,
living hands turn the mirrors to the walls,
tear the boughs of yew to lay on the casket,
120   rip the clothes of mourning.   Only the living
decide death's color: is it white or black?
The granite bulkhead
incised with names, the quilt of names, were made
by the living, for the living.
                                      I have watched
films from a Pathé camera, a picnic
in sepia, I have seen my mother
tossing an acorn into the air;
my grandfather, alone in the heart of his family;
my father, young, dark, theatrical;
130   myself, a six-month child.
Watching the dead we see them living
their moments, they were at play, nobody thought
they would be watched so.
                                      When Selma threw
her husband's ashes into the Hudson
and they blew back on her and on us, her friends,
it was life.   Our blood raced in that gritty wind.

Such details get bunched, packed, stored
in these cellar-holes of memory
140   so little is needed
to call on the power, though you can't name its name:
It has its ways of coming back:
a truck going into gear on the crown of the road
the white-throat sparrow's notes
the moon in her fullness standing
right over the concrete steps the way
she stood the night they landed there.
                                      From here
nothing has changed, and everything.

150   The scratched and treasured photograph Richard showed me
taken in '29, the year I was born:
it's the same road I saw
strewn with the Perseids one August night,
looking older, steeper than now
and rougher, yet I knew it.   Time's
power, the only just power—would you
give it away?

A Gathering of Poems

A. R. Ammons

Archie Randolph Ammons (1926–   ) worked in business for many years before he became a professor of English. He teaches at Cornell.

Working with Tools   (1971)

I make a simple assertion
like a nice piece of stone
and you
alert to presence and entrance
man your pick and hammer

and by chip and deflection
distract simplicity
and cut my assertion
back to mangles, little heaps:

10 well, baby, that's the way
you get along: it's all right,
I understand such
ways of being afraid:
sometimes you want my come-on

hard, something to
take in and be around:
sometimes you want
a vaguer touch: I understand
and won't give assertion up.

Anonymous

Adam Lay I-Bowndyn

Adam lay i-bowndyn,
    Bowndyn in a bond—
Fowre thousand wynter
    Thoght he not too long;
And al was for an appil,
    An appil that he tok,
As clerkes° fynden,   scholars
    Writen in here° book.   their

Ne hadde the appil takë ben,[1]
10   The appil taken ben,
Ne haddë never our lady
    A ben° hevenë quene.   have been
Blyssid be the tyme
    That appil takë was,
Ther fore we mown° syngyn   must
    Deo Gracias.[2]

Lord Randal

"O where hae° ye been, Lord Randal, my son?   have
O where hae ye been, my handsome young man?"
"I hae been to the wild wood; mother, make my bed soon,
For I'm weary wi hunting, and fain wald° lie down."   would

"Where gat ye your dinner, Lord Randal, my son?
Where gat ye your dinner, my handsome young man?"
"I din'd wi my true-love; mother, make my bed soon,
For I'm weary wi hunting, and fain wald lie down."

"What gat ye to your dinner, Lord Randal, my son?
10 What gat ye to your dinner, my handsome young man?"
"I gat eels boiled in broo;° mother, make my bed soon,   broth
For I'm weary wi hunting, and fain wald lie down."

"What became of your bloodhounds, Lord Randal, my son?
What became of your bloodhounds, my handsome young man?"
"O they swelld and they died; mother, make my bed soon,
For I'm weary wi hunting, and fain wald lie down."

"O I fear ye are poisond, Lord Randal, my son!
O I fear ye are poisond, my handsome young man!"
"O yes! I am poisond; mother, make my bed soon,
20 For I'm sick at the heart, and I fain wald lie down."

[1] If the apple had not been taken   [2] Thanks be to God

Matthew Arnold

Matthew Arnold (1822–1888) comes after Tennyson and Browning as a poet of the Victorian age; as a man of letters, he comes after no one. His father was headmaster of Rugby, and Arnold was educated at Rugby, at Winchester, and at Oxford, where he won the Newdigate Prize for Poetry. For many years, he inspected schools for the government. He lectured on poetry at Oxford. He wrote his poems mostly in early life; as he grew older, he concentrated on the essay.

Dover Beach (1851)

The sea is calm tonight,
The tide is full, the moon lies fair
Upon the straits;—on the French coast the light
Gleams and is gone; the cliffs of England stand,
Glimmering and vast, out in the tranquil bay.
Come to the window, sweet is the night-air!
Only, from the long line of spray
Where the sea meets the moon-blanched land,
Listen! you hear the grating roar
10 Of pebbles which the waves draw back, and fling,
At their return, up the high strand,
Begin and cease, and then again begin,
With tremulous cadence slow, and bring
The eternal note of sadness in.

Sophocles long ago
Heard it on the Aegean, and it brought
Into his mind the turbid ebb and flow
Of human misery; we
Find also in the sound a thought,
20 Hearing it by this distant northern sea.

The Sea of Faith
Was once, too, at the full, and round earth's shore
Lay like the folds of a bright girdle furled.
But now I only hear
Its melancholy, long, withdrawing roar,
Retreating, to the breath
Of the night-wind, down the vast edges drear
And naked shingles of the world.

Ah, love, let us be true
30 To one another! for the world, which seems
To lie before us like a land of dreams,
So various, so beautiful, so new,
Hath really neither joy, nor love, nor light,
Nor certitude, nor peace, nor help for pain;
And we are here as on a darkling plain
Swept with confused alarms of struggle and flight,
Where ignorant armies clash by night.

(See also "The Dover Bitch," page 249.)

John Ashbery

John Ashbery (1927–   ) attended Harvard, overlapping with Robert Creeley,
Robert Bly, Adrienne Rich, and Frank O'Hara. He spent ten years in Paris, writing
for an American newspaper there, and later worked for *Art News* in New York. For
many years, his poetry attracted a small but enthusiastic group of readers. In
1975, he won the Pulitzer Prize, the National Book Award, and the award of the
National Book Critics Circle. His *Selected Poems* appeared in 1985.

Rivers and Mountains   (1962)

On the secret map the assassins
Cloistered, the Moon River was marked
Near the eighteen peaks and the city
Of humiliation and defeat—wan ending
Of the trail among dry, papery leaves
Gray-brown quills like thoughts
In the melodious but vast mass of today's
Writing through fields and swamps
Marked, on the map, with little bunches of weeds.
10 Certainly squirrels lived in the woods
But devastation and dull sleep still
Hung over the land, quelled
The rioters turned out of sleep in the peace of prisons
Singing on marble factory walls
Deaf consolation of minor tunes that pack
The air with heavy invisible rods
Pent in some sand valley from
Which only quiet walking ever instructs.
The bird flew over and
20 Sat—there was nothing else to do.
Do not mistake its silence for pride or strength
Or the waterfall for a harbor
Full of light boats that is there
Performing for thousands of people
In clothes some with places to go
Or games. Sometimes over the pillar
Of square stones its impact
Makes a light print.
So going around cities
30 To get to other places you found
It all on paper but the land
Was made of paper processed
To look like ferns, mud or other
Whose sea unrolled its magic
Distances and then rolled them up
Its secret was only a pocket
After all but some corners are darker
Than these moonless nights spent as on a raft
In the seclusion of a melody heard
40 As though through trees

And you can never ignite their touch
Long but there were homes
Flung far out near the asperities
Of a sharp, rocky pinnacle
And other collective places
Shadows of vineyards whose wine
Tasted of the forest floor
Fisheries and oyster beds
Tides under the pole
50 Seminaries of instruction, public
Places for electric light
And the major tax assessment area
Wrinkled on the plan
Of election to public office
Sixty-two years old bath and breakfast
The formal traffic, shadows
To make it not worth joining
After the ox had pulled away the cart.

Your plan was to separate the enemy into two groups
60 With the razor-edged mountains between.
It worked well on paper
But their camp had grown
To be the mountains and the map
Carefully peeled away and not torn
Was the light, a tender but tough bark
On everything. Fortunately the war was solved
In another way by isolating the two sections
Of the enemy's navy so that the mainland
Warded away the big floating ships.
70 Light bounced off the ends
Of the small gray waves to tell
Them in the observatory
About the great drama that was being won
To turn off the machinery
And quietly move among the rustic landscape
Scooping snow off the mountains rinsing
The coarser ones that love had
Slowly risen in the night to overflow
Wetting pillow and petal
80 Determined to place the letter
On the unassassinated president's desk
So that a stamp could reproduce all this
In detail, down to the last autumn leaf
And the affliction of June ride
Slowly out into the sun-blackened landscape.

Margaret Atwood

Margaret Atwood (1939–   ) was born in Ottawa, grew up largely in northern Ontario and Quebec, and now lives in Toronto with her husband and daughter. She is novelist, poet, short story writer, and critic. She has published nine books of poems, including *Selected Poems* in 1976, followed by *Two-Headed Poems* (1978) and *True Stories* (1981).

You Are Happy   (1974)

The water turns
a long way down over the raw stone,
ice crusts around it

We walk separately
along the hill to the open
beach, unused
picnic tables, wind
shoving the brown waves, erosion,
    gravel
10 rasping on gravel.

In the ditch a deer
carcass, no head. Bird
running across the glaring
road against the low pink sun.

When you are this
cold you can think about
nothing but the cold, the images

hitting into your eyes
like needles, crystals, you are happy.

W. H. Auden

Wystan Hugh Auden (1907–1973) began to publish at the end of the 1920s and, in the next decade, became the spokesman of a generation. Marxist and psychological, he wrote a poetry of ideas; then his ideas changed. Just before the Second World War he emigrated to America and lived in New York for most of the remainder of his life, becoming an Anglo-Catholic and altering his old political concepts.

Musée des Beaux Arts[1]   (1938)

About suffering they were never wrong,
The Old Masters: how well they understood
Its human position; how it takes place
While someone else is eating or opening a window or just walking dully along;
How, when the aged are reverently, passionately waiting
For the miraculous birth, there always must be
Children who did not specially want it to happen, skating
On a pond at the edge of the wood:
They never forgot
10 That even the dreadful martyrdom must run its course
Anyhow in a corner, some untidy spot
Where the dogs go on with their doggy life and the torturer's horse
Scratches its innocent behind on a tree.

[1] Museum of Fine Arts

In Brueghel's *Icarus,*[2] for instance: how everything turns away
Quite leisurely from the disaster; the ploughman may
Have heard the splash, the forsaken cry,
But for him it was not an important failure; the sun shone
As it had to on the white legs disappearing into the green
Water; and the expensive delicate ship that must have seen
20 Something amazing, a boy falling out of the sky,
Had somewhere to get to and sailed calmly on.

In Memory of W. B. Yeats   (1939)
(d. Jan. 1939)

1

He disappeared in the dead of winter:
The brooks were frozen, the airports almost deserted,
And snow disfigured the public statues;
The mercury sank in the mouth of the dying day.
O all the instruments agree
The day of his death was a dark cold day.

Far from his illness
The wolves ran on through the evergreen forests,
The peasant river was untempted by the fashionable quays;
10 By mourning tongues
The death of the poet was kept from his poems.

But for him it was his last afternoon as himself,
An afternoon of nurses and rumors;
The provinces of his body revolted,
The squares of his mind were empty,
Silence invaded the suburbs,
The current of his feeling failed: he became his admirers.

Now he is scattered among a hundred cities
And wholly given over to unfamiliar affections;
20 To find his happiness in another kind of wood
And be punished under a foreign code of conscience.
The words of a dead man
Are modified in the guts of the living.

But in the importance and noise of tomorrow
When the brokers are roaring like beasts on the floor of the Bourse,
And the poor have the sufferings to which they are fairly accustomed,
And each in the cell of himself is almost convinced of his freedom;
A few thousand will think of this day
As one thinks of a day when one did something slightly unusual.

[2] Pieter Brueghel the Elder (1520?–1569) was a major sixteenth-century Flemish painter. His *The Fall of Icarus,* to which Auden alludes here, is in the Musée des Beaux Arts in Brussels.

30 O all the instruments agree
The day of his death was a dark cold day.

2

You were silly like us; your gift survived it all;
The parish of rich women, physical decay,
Yourself; mad Ireland hurt you into poetry.
Now Ireland has her madness and her weather still,
For poetry makes nothing happen: it survives
In the valley of its saying where executives
Would never want to tamper; it flows south
From ranches of isolation and the busy griefs,
40 Raw towns that we believe and die in; it survives,
A way of happening, a mouth.

3

Earth, receive an honored guest;
William Yeats is laid to rest:
Let the Irish vessel lie
Emptied of its poetry.

Time that is intolerant
Of the brave and innocent,
And indifferent in a week
To a beautiful physique,

50 Worships language and forgives
Everyone by whom it lives;
Pardons cowardice, conceit,
Lays its honors at their feet.

Time that with this strange excuse
Pardoned Kipling[1] and his views,
And will pardon Paul Claudel,[2]
Pardons him for writing well.

In the nightmare of the dark
All the dogs of Europe bark,
60 And the living nations wait,
Each sequestered in its hate;

Intellectual disgrace
Stares from every human face,
And the seas of pity lie
Locked and frozen in each eye.

---

[1] Rudyard Kipling (1865–1936), British writer born in Bombay and author of the *Jungle Books, Kim,* novels, short stories, and many poems, wrote much about the British Empire. [2] Paul Claudel (1868–1955), French dramatist, poet, and diplomat, produced works that were highly mystical and often symbolist.

Follow, poet, follow right
To the bottom of the night,
With your unconstraining voice
Still persuade us to rejoice;

70 With the farming of a verse
Make a vineyard of the curse,
Sing of human unsuccess
In a rapture of distress;

In the deserts of the heart
Let the healing fountain start,
In the prison of his days
Teach the free man how to praise.

The Unknown Citizen   (1939)
To JS/07/M/378
This Marble Monument is Erected by the State

He was found by the Bureau of Statistics to be
One against whom there was no official complaint,
And all the reports on his conduct agree
That, in the modern sense of an old-fashioned word, he was a saint,

For in everything he did he served the Greater Community.
Except for the War till the day he retired
He worked in a factory and never got fired,
But satisfied his employers, Fudge Motors Inc.
Yet he wasn't a scab or odd in his views,
10 For his Union reports that he paid his dues,
(Our report on his Union shows it was sound)
And our Social Psychology workers found
That he was popular with his mates and liked a drink.
The Press are convinced that he bought a paper every day
And that his reactions to advertisements were normal in every way.

Policies taken out in his name prove that he was fully insured,
And his Health-card shows he was once in hospital but left it cured.

Both Producers Research and High-Grade Living declare
He was fully sensible to the advantages of the Installment Plan
20 And had everything necessary to the Modern Man,
A gramophone, a radio, a car and a frigidaire.
Our researchers into Public Opinion are content
That he held the proper opinions for the time of year;
When there was peace, he was for peace; when there was war, he went.

He was married and added five children to the population.
Which our Eugenist says was the right number for a parent of his generation.

And our teachers report that he never interfered with their education.

Was he free? Was he happy? The question is absurd:
Had anything been wrong, we should certainly have heard.

Jimmy Santiago Baca

Jimmy Santiago Baca (1952–   ) is author of *Martin and Meditations on the South Valley* (1987), which won the American Book Award of the Before Columbus Foundation, and *Black Mesa Poems* (1990), among other works.

Perfecto Flores   (1989)
for Perfecto

We banter
back and forth
the price
for laying brick.
"You people only pay
the rich, those who
already have money.
I have a whole yard of bricks
collected over thirty years
10 working as a mason.
I offer you a good price,
load them on the truck,
bring sand and gravel,
do the work almost for nothing,
and you won't pay me
half what Hunter charges."
He was right, I relented,
paid him seventy cents a block.
The next day
20 he brought them,
towing cement mixer
behind his old truck.
He rounded the weeping willow
trunk with blocks
left over from apartments
he worked on
six years ago,
then poured cement
and troweled it smooth.
30 After he was done, he asked,
"Can I have that roll of wire back there?"
He lives by scraps, built three houses
for his daughter with construction site
scraps.

In English
his name is Perfect Flower.
Brawny man with bull shoulders,
who forty years ago came from
Mexico,
tired of the mines, the somnolent
40 spirit of Mexicans. ". . . I was the first
one
to say I wouldn't ride the old bus.
It was falling apart. I refused, and
the rest followed, and soon a new bus
was brought up the mountain."
I gave him our old Falcon
for pouring cement floor
in the guest cottage,
jar of blessed black-purple
Acoma corn kernels
50 for helping me uproot a tree,
gave him seven rabbits
and a box of chickens
for helping me cut adobe arches.
We curse and laugh as we work.
He proudly hefts a wheelbarrow
brimmed with cement. "Ah! Sixty-two,
cabrón!
And you, naa! You would break your
back!"
He ribs me, proud of his strength.
He has nothing that glows his face
60 so much as stories of his working
years,
feats of courage in the mines
when he was called upon to defuse
dynamite

that didn't explode. Short, stocky
gray-haired man, always in his yard
scattering chicken seed, nailing, sawing,
always in jean overalls.
Chews a ground weed,
carries a stub pencil and grimy wad
of paper
for figuring, and
70 always turns to me when I drive
or walk into his yard
with a roguish grin,

his love of telling stories
competing with mine.
He growls with laughter
at the blisters on my hands,
takes his gloves off,
spreads his palms up—
a gallery owner who strips black cloth
80 off his prized Van Gogh painting,
"Look! You could sharpen a file
on these hands," he grins proudly.

Imamu Amiri Baraka

Imamu Amiri Baraka (LeRoi Jones) (1934–   ) is a leading black playwright
and poet. He has also published short stories and polemical prose. He began
publishing as an integrated black writer and edited a magazine in collaboration
with white editors. In later years his politics have moved from black separatism
to Marxism-Leninism.

Careers   (1979)

What is the life
of the old lady
standing
on the stair
print flowered
housedress
gray and orange
hair
bent
10 on a rail
eyes open for
jr.
bobby
jb, somebody
to come, and carry her
wish
slow
cripple woman, still does
white folks work
20 in the mornings she get up
creeps into a cadillac
up into the florient lilac titty valleys
of blind ugliness, you think the woman loves
the younger white woman
the woman she ladles soup for
the radio she turns on when the white lady nods
she carries them in her bowed back hunched face

my grandmother workd the same
but stole things for jesus' sake
30 we wore boss rags in grammar school
straight off the backs of straight up americans
used but groovy and my grandmother when she returned at night
with mason jars and hat boxes full of goods
probably asked for forgiveness on the bus
i think the lady across from me must do the same
though she comes back in a cab, so times, it seems,
have changed.

Wendell Berry

Wendell Berry (1934–   ) was born in Kentucky, lived in New York briefly,
and returned to his home state, where he taught at the University of Kentucky.
Increasingly, Berry has turned to farming his own land and to writing about
"culture and agriculture." He has written novels and books of essays as well as
poems. With Gary Snyder, he is a poet whose work and life serve to preserve
the planet.

The Wild Geese   (1971)

Horseback on Sunday morning,
harvest over, we taste persimmon
and wild grape, sharp sweet
of summer's end. In time's maze
over the fall fields, we name names
that went west from here, names
that rest on graves. We open
a persimmon seed to find the tree
that stands in promise,
10 pale, in the seed's marrow.

Geese appear high over us,
pass, and the sky closes. Abandon,
as in love or sleep, holds
them to their way, clear,
in the ancient faith: what we need
is here. And we pray, not
for new earth or heaven, but to be
quiet in heart, and in eye
clear. What we need is here.

John Berryman

John Berryman (1914–1972) wrote with great ambition and intensity (fiction and
essays as well as poetry) and is best known for *Homage to Mistress Bradstreet*
(1954) and *The Dream Songs* (1969).

from The Dream Songs   (1964)

14

Life, friends, is boring. We must not say so.
After all, the sky flashes, the great sea yearns,
we ourselves flash and yearn,

and moreover my mother told me as a boy
(repeatingly) 'Ever to confess you're bored
means you have no

Inner Resources.' I conclude now I have no
inner resources, because I am heavy bored.
Peoples bore me,
10 literature bores me, especially great literature,
Henry bores me, with his plights & gripes
as bad as achilles,

who loves people and valiant art, which bores me.
And the tranquil hills, & gin, look like a drag
and somehow a dog
has taken itself & its tail considerably away
into mountains or sea or sky, leaving
behind: me, wag.

16

Henry's pelt was put on sundry walls
20 where it did much resemble Henry and
them persons was delighted.
Especially his long & glowing tail
by all them was admired, and visitors.
They whistled: This is *it!*

Golden, whilst your frozen daiquiris
whir at midnight, gleams on you his fur
& silky & black.
Mission accomplished, pal.
My molten yellow & moonless bag,
30 drained, hangs at rest.

Collect in the cold depths barracuda. Ay,
In Sealdah Station some possessionless
children survive to die.
The Chinese communes hum. Two daiquiris
withdrew into a corner of the gorgeous room
and one told the other a lie.

312

I have moved to Dublin to have it out with you,
majestic Shade,[1] You whom I read so well
so many years ago,
40 did I read your lesson right? did I see through
your phases to the real? your heaven, your hell

---

[1] A reference to William Butler Yeats

did I enquire properly into?
For years then I forgot you, I put you down,
ingratitude is the necessary curse
of making things new:
I brought my family to see me through,
I brought my homage & my soft remorse,
I brought a book or two

only, including in the end your last
50 strange poems made under the shadow of death
Your high figures float
again across my mind and all your past
fills my walled garden with your honey breath
wherein I move, a mote.

Elizabeth Bishop

Elizabeth Bishop (1911–1979) was born in Massachusetts, attended Vassar, and
lived for many years in Brazil. Critics noticed the influence of Marianne Moore
on her first book of poems, *North and South* (1946). She won a Pulitzer Prize in
1956 for *Poems,* and later published *Questions of Travel* (1965) and *Geography III*
(1977). *The Complete Poems 1927–1979* appeared in 1983. See also page 58–59.

The Fish   (1939)

I caught a tremendous fish
and held him beside the boat
half out of water, with my hook
fast in a corner of his mouth.
He didn't fight.
He hadn't fought at all.
He hung a grunting weight,
battered and venerable
and homely. Here and there
10 his brown skin hung in strips
like ancient wallpaper,
and its pattern of darker brown
was like wallpaper:
shapes like full-blown roses
stained and lost through age.
He was speckled with barnacles,
fine rosettes of lime,
and infested
with tiny white sea-lice,
20 and underneath two or three
rags of green weed hung down.
While his gills were breathing in

the terrible oxygen
—the frightening gills,
fresh and crisp with blood,
that can cut so badly—
I thought of the coarse white flesh
packed in like feathers,
the big bones and the little bones,
30 the dramatic reds and blacks
of his shiny entrails,
and the pink swim-bladder
like a big peony.
I looked into his eyes
which were far larger than mine
but shallower, and yellowed,
the irises backed and packed
with tarnished tinfoil
seen through the lenses
40 of old scratched isinglass.
They shifted a little, but not
to return my stare.
—It was more like the tipping
of an object toward the light.

I admired his sullen face,
the mechanism of his jaw,
and then I saw
that from his lower lip
—if you could call it a lip—
50 grim, wet, and weaponlike,
hung five old pieces of fish-line,
or four and a wire leader
with the swivel still attached,
with all their five big hooks
grown firmly in his mouth.
A green line, frayed at the end
where he broke it, two heavier lines,
and a fine black thread
still crimped from the strain and snap
60 when it broke and he got away.

Like medals with their ribbons
frayed and wavering,
a five-haired beard of wisdom
trailing from his aching jaw.
I stared and stared
and victory filled up
the little rented boat,
from the pool of bilge
where oil had spread a rainbow
70 around the rusted engine
to the bailer rusted orange,
the sun-cracked thwarts,
the oarlocks on their strings,
the gunnels—until everything
was rainbow, rainbow, rainbow!
And I let the fish go.

William Blake

William Blake (1757–1827) called his first major work *Songs of Innocence and Experience*. This sequence included many pairings of poems, the one viewed under the aspect of innocence and the other under the aspect of experience. Some of Blake's paired poems have the same names; in another pairing, we have the lamb and the tiger. His later work is obscure, difficult—and superbly rewarding. He was an engraver by trade, and executed his own etchings and engravings. Like Campion, Blake was master of two arts. He was a mystic, and told how some of his poems were dictated to him by voices. See also pages 53 and 113.

The Lamb   (1789)

Little Lamb, who made thee?
  Dost thou know who made thee;
Gave thee life and bid thee feed
By the stream and o'er the mead;
Gave thee clothing of delight,
Softest clothing, woolly, bright;
Gave thee such a tender voice
Making all the vales rejoice?
  Little Lamb, who made thee?
10   Dost thou know who made thee?

Little Lamb, I'll tell thee,
  Little Lamb, I'll tell thee:
He is callèd by thy name,
For He calls Himself a Lamb.
He is meek and He is mild:
He became a little child.
I a child and thou a lamb,
We are callèd by His name.
  Little Lamb, God bless thee.
20   Little Lamb, God bless thee.

The Tyger   (1794)

Tyger! Tyger! burning bright
In the forests of the night,
What immortal hand or eye
Could frame thy fearful symmetry?

In what distant deeps or skies
Burnt the fire of thine eyes?
On what wings dare he aspire?
What the hand dare seize the fire?

And what shoulder, and what art,
10 Could twist the sinews of thy heart?
And when thy heart began to beat,
What dread hand? and what dread feet?

What the hammer? what the chain?
In what furnace was thy brain?
What the anvil? what dread grasp
Dare its deadly terrors clasp?

When the stars threw down their spears
And watered heaven with their tears,
Did he smile his work to see?
20 Did he who made the Lamb make thee?

Tyger! Tyger! burning bright
In the forests of the night,
What immortal hand or eye
Dare frame thy fearful symmetry?

The Garden of Love   (1794)

I went to the Garden of Love,
And saw what I never had seen:
A Chapel was built in the midst,
Where I used to play on the green.

And the gates of this Chapel were shut,
And "Thou shalt not" writ over the
        door;
So I turned to the Garden of Love

That so many sweet flowers bore;

10 And I saw it was filled with graves,
And tomb-stones where flowers should
        be,
And Priests in black gowns were
        walking their rounds,
And binding with briars my joys and
        desires.

London   (1794)

I wander thro' each chartered street,
Near where the chartered Thames
        does flow,
And mark in every face I meet
Marks of weakness, marks of woe.

In every cry of every Man,
In every Infant's cry of fear,
In every voice, in every ban,
The mind-forged manacles I hear.

10 How the Chimney-sweeper's cry
Every black'ning Church appalls;
And the hapless Soldier's sigh
Runs in blood down Palace walls.

But most thro' midnight streets I hear
How the youthful Harlot's curse
Blasts the new-born Infant's tear,
And blights with plagues the Marriage
        hearse.

Robert Bly

Robert Bly (1926–   ) comes from a farm in western Minnesota. After some time in the Navy, he attended Harvard, from which he graduated in 1950. Editor of an influential literary magazine—variously called *The Fifties, The Sixties,* and *The Seventies*—he has championed modernist poets of other literatures and has extended great influence on a younger generation of American poets. His own poems have been collected in *Silence in the Snowy Fields* (1962), *The Light Around the Body* (1967)—which won a National Book Award—and in many other collections, including a *Selected Poems* in 1986. See also pages 31–33, 57, and 108–109.

Hunting Pheasants in a Cornfield   (1960)

I

What is so strange about a tree alone in an open field?
It is a willow tree. I walk around and around it.
The body is strangely torn, and cannot leave it.
At last I sit down beneath it.

II

It is a willow tree alone in acres of dry corn.
Its leaves are scattered around its trunk, and around me,
Brown now, and speckled with delicate black.
Only the cornstalks now can make a noise.

III

The sun is cold, burning through the frosty distances of space.
10 The weeds are frozen to death long ago.
Why then do I love to watch
The sun moving on the chill skin of the branches?

IV

The mind has shed leaves alone for years.
It stands apart with small creatures near its roots.
I am happy in this ancient place,
A spot easily caught sight of above the corn,
If I were a young animal ready to turn home at dusk.

Louise Bogan

Louise Bogan (1897–1970) was born in Maine and lived most of her life in New York City. She was an excellent critic. Her letters and journals were extraordinary, and her poems were few, spare, and perfect. See also page 55.

Cartography   (1941)

As you lay in sleep
I saw the chart
Of artery and vein
Running from your heart,

Plain as the strength
Marked upon the leaf
Along the length,
Mortal and brief,

Of your gaunt hand.
10 I saw it clear:
The wiry brand
Of the life we bear

Mapped like the great
Rivers that rise
Beyond our fate
And distant from our eyes.

Emily Brontë

Emily Brontë (1818–1848) was sister of Charlotte and Anne; all were novelists and poets in their youth. Emily wrote *Wuthering Heights.*

No Coward Soul Is Mine   (1846)

No coward soul is mine,
No trembler in the world's storm-troubled sphere:
I see Heaven's glories shine,
And faith shines equal, arming me from fear.

O God within my breast,
Almighty, ever-present Deity!
Life, that in me hast rest
As I, undying life, have power in Thee!

Vain are the thousand creeds
10 That move men's hearts; unutterably vain;
Worthless as withered weeds,
Or idlest froth amid the boundless main,

To waken doubt in one
Holding so fast by Thy infinity,
So surely anchored on
The steadfast rock of immortality.

With wide embracing love
Thy spirit animates eternal years,
    Pervades and broods above,
20 Changes, sustains, dissolves, creates, and rears.

    Though earth and moon were gone,
And suns and universes cease to be,
    And Thou wert left alone,
Every existence would exist in Thee.

    There is not room for death,
Nor atom that his might could render void:
    Since Thou art Being and Breath
And what Thou art may never be destroyed.

Gwendolyn Brooks

Gwendolyn Brooks (1917–   ) is a leading black American poet, born in
Kansas and long resident of Chicago, who began publishing with *A Street in
Bronzeville* in 1945. *Annie Allen,* published in 1949, received a Pulitzer Prize.
Brooks took a new life from the vitality of the black movement of the 1960s.

The Bean Eaters   (1959)

They eat beans mostly, this old yellow pair.
Dinner is a casual affair.
Plain chipware on a plain and creaking wood,
Tin flatware.

Two who are Mostly Good.
Two who have lived their day,
But keep on putting on their clothes
And putting things away.

And remembering . . .
10 Remembering, with twinklings and twinges,
As they lean over the beans in their rented back room that is full of beads and
        receipts and dolls and cloths, tobacco crumbs, vases and fringes.

We Real Cool   (1959)
The Pool Players.
Seven at the Golden Shovel.

We real cool. We
Left school. We

Lurk late. We
Strike straight. We

Sing sin. We
Thin gin. We

Jazz June. We
Die soon.

Robert Browning

Robert Browning (1812–1889) was three years younger than Tennyson and
shared with him first rank among Victorian poets. In 1846, he and Elizabeth
Barrett were married. They wrote poems together for fifteen years, until she died
in 1861. He is most celebrated for his dramatic monologues. He is buried in
Westminster Abbey.

My Last Duchess   (1842)
FERRARA

That's my last Duchess painted on the wall,
Looking as if she were alive. I call
That piece a wonder, now: Frà Pandolf's hands
Worked busily a day, and there she stands.
Will't please you sit and look at her? I said
"Frà Pandolf" by design, for never read
Strangers like you that pictured countenance,
The depth and passion of its earnest glance,
But to myself they turned (since none puts by
10   The curtain I have drawn for you, but I)
And seemed as they would ask me, if they durst,
How such a glance came there; so, not the first
Are you to turn and ask thus. Sir, 'twas not
Her husband's presence only, called that spot
Of joy into the Duchess' cheek: perhaps
Frà Pandolf chanced to say, "Her mantle laps
Over my lady's wrist too much," or "Paint
Must never hope to reproduce the faint
Half-flush that dies along her throat." Such stuff
20   Was courtesy, she thought, and cause enough
For calling up that spot of joy. She had
A heart—how shall I say?—too soon made glad,
Too easily impressed; she liked whate'er
She looked on, and her looks went everywhere.
Sir, 'twas all one! My favour at her breast,
The dropping of the daylight in the West,
The bough of cherries some officious fool
Broke in the orchard for her, the white mule
She rode with round the terrace—all and each
30   Would draw from her alike the approving speech,
Or blush, at least. She thanked men,—good! but thanked
Somehow—I know not how—as if she ranked
My gift of a nine-hundred-years-old name
With anybody's gift. Who'd stoop to blame
This sort of trifling? Even had you skill
In speech—(which I have not)—to make your will
Quite clear to such an one, and say, "Just this
"Or that in you disgusts me; here you miss,
"Or there exceed the mark"—and if she let

40 Herself be lessoned so, nor plainly set
   Her wits to yours, forsooth, and made excuse,
   —E'en then would be some stooping; and I choose
   Never to stoop. Oh sir, she smiled, no doubt,
   Whene'er I passed her; but who passed without
   Much the same smile? This grew; I gave commands;
   Then all smiles stopped together. There she stands
   As if alive. Will't please you rise? We'll meet
   The company below, then. I repeat,
   The Count your master's known munificence
50 Is ample warrant that no just pretense
   Of mine for dowry will be disallowed;
   Though his fair daughter's self, as I avowed
   At starting, is my object. Nay, we'll go
   Together down, sir. Notice Neptune, though,
   Taming a sea-horse, thought a rarity,
   Which Claus of Innsbruck cast in bronze for me!

David Budbill

David Budbill (1940–   ) lives in Vermont and has published four books of poems, books for young adults, and plays that have been produced in San Francisco and Princeton, New Jersey. In 1991 he published his *Collected Poems.*

Robert Burns

Robert Burns (1759–1796), after the medieval poets, is the great poet of Scotland. He is one of the few British poets to arise from the working classes, having begun life as a farm laborer. Much of his work derives from a folk tradition and from anonymous Scots songs.

John Anderson My Jo   (1790)

John Anderson my jo,° John,   darling
   When we were first acquent,
Your locks were like the raven,
   Your bonnie brow was brent;°   straight, steep
But now your brow is beld,° John,   bald
   Your locks are like the snaw,
But blessings on your frosty pow,°   head
   John Anderson, my jo.

John Anderson my jo, John,
10   We clamb° the hill thegither,   climbed

And monie a cantie° day, John,   merry
   We've had wi' ane anither:
Now we maun° totter down, John,   must
   And hand in hand we'll go,
And sleep thegither at the foot,
   John Anderson my jo.

George Gordon, Lord Byron

George Gordon, Lord Byron (1788–1824) in his life was the stereotype of the
romantic poet—handsome, promiscuous, daring. His most romantic poems,
valuing emotion above all things, were not his best work, which was satirical and
comic and shared attitudes, though not form or diction, with the poets of the
eighteenth century. In 1823 Byron joined a Greek revolutionary movement striving
to establish freedom for the Greek people; he died of a fever at Missolonghi in
April 1824.

Stanzas   (1820)
(When a man hath no freedom to fight for at home)

When a man hath no freedom to fight for at home,
   Let him combat for that of his neighbors;
Let him think of the glories of Greece and of Rome,
   And get knocked on the head for his labors.

To do good to mankind is the chivalrous plan,
   And is always as nobly requited;
Then battle for freedom wherever you can,
   And, if not shot or hanged, you'll get knighted.

Thomas Campion

Thomas Campion (1567–1620) composed music for his lyrics, one of the few
artists to become master of two arts. Although he could rhyme well enough when
he wanted to, he despised English rhyming as vulgar, and argued for the
establishment of Greek and Roman meters in English verse.

Rose-Cheeked Laura   (1610)

Rose-cheeked Laura, come,
Sing thou smoothly with thy beauty's
Silent music, either other
   Sweetly gracing.

Lovely forms do flow
From concent° divinely framèd;   sounds in harmony
Heaven is music, and thy beauty's
    Birth is heavenly.

These dull notes we sing
10 Discords need for helps to grace them;
Only beauty purely loving
    Knows no discord,

But still moves delight,
Like clear springs renewed by flowing,
Ever perfect, ever in them-
    Selves eternal.

Lewis Carroll

Lewis Carroll was the pen name of Charles Lutwidge Dodgson (1832–1898), a
distinguished mathematician, when he wrote *Alice's Adventures in Wonderland*
and other works of fantasy and nonsense. On the faculty at Oxford, amateur
photographer as well as writer, Carroll made up numerous words when he
composed "Jabberwocky"; some of them have taken their place in the language.

Jabberwocky   (1871)

'Twas brillig, and the slithy toves
    Did gyre and gimble in the wabe:
All mimsy were the borogoves,
    And the mome raths outgrabe.

"Beware the Jabberwock, my son!
    The jaws that bite, the claws that catch!
Beware the Jubjub bird, and shun
    The frumious Bandersnatch!"

He took his vorpal sword in hand;
10   Long time the manxome foe he sought—
So rested he by the Tumtum tree,
    And stood awhile in thought.

And, as in uffish thought he stood,
    The Jabberwock, with eyes of flame,
Came whiffling through the tulgey wood,
    And burbled as it came!

One, two! One, two! And through and through
    The vorpal blade went snicker-snack!

He left it dead, and with its head
20   He went galumphing back.

"And hast thou slain the Jabberwock?
     Come to my arms, my beamish boy!
O frabjous day! Callooh, Callay!"
     He chortled in his joy.

'Twas brillig, and the slithy toves
     Did gyre and gimble in the wabe:
All mimsy were the borogoves,
     And the mome raths outgrabe.

Geoffrey Chaucer

Geoffrey Chaucer (1340?–1400) grew up in London, son of a man who made
wine. He fought for England in France, and later worked for his king as a
diplomat on foreign service. During his busy public life, he wrote poems, most
notably *The Canterbury Tales,* a loose assemblage of stories told by pilgrims
traveling to the shrine in Kent. He is the first great poet of England, and remains
the funniest. Because the Middle English that was his language requires special
study, this selection is small—only a hint of the sound that Chaucer makes.

from the Prologue to *The Canterbury Tales*   (1387)

Whan that Aprill with his shoures soote[1]
The droghte[2] of March hath perced[3] to the roote,
And bathed every veyne[4] in swich licour,[5]
Of which vertu[6] engendred is the flour;[7]
When Zephyrus eek[8] with his sweete breeth
Inspired hath in every holt and heeth
The tendre croppes,[9] and the yonge sonne
Hath in the Ram his halfe cours yronne,
And smale foweles[10] maken melodye
10   That slepen al the nyght with open yë[11]—
So priketh hem Nature in hir corages[12]—
Thanne longen folk to goon on pilgrimages,
And palmeres for to seken staunge strondes[13]
To ferne halwes,[14] kouthe[15] in sondry londes;
And specially from every shires ende
Of Engelond to Caunterbury[16] they wende,
The holy blisful martir for to seke
That hem[17] hath holpen[18] whan that they were seeke.[19]

---

[1] sweet showers   [2] drought   [3] pierced   [4] vein   [5] such liquid   [6] power   [7] flower   [8] also
[9] shoots   [10] birds   [11] eye   [12] hearts   [13] shores   [14] distant shrines   [15] known   [16] shrine of
Thomas à Becket (1118?–1170), English martyr   [17] them   [18] helped   [19] sick

John Clare

John Clare (1793–1864) was an agricultural laborer who went insane in 1837 but
continued to write poems in the asylum.

I Am   (1848)

I am: yet what I am none cares or knows,
    My friends forsake me like a memory lost;
I am the self-consumer of my woes,
    They rise and vanish in oblivious host,
Like shades in love and death's oblivion lost;
And yet I am, and live with shadows tost

Into the nothingness of scorn and noise,
    Into the living sea of waking dreams,
Where there is neither sense of life nor joys,
10   But the vast shipwreck of my life's esteems;
And e'en the dearest—that I loved the best—
Are strange—nay, rather stranger than the rest.

I long for scenes where man has never trod,
    A place where woman never smiled or wept;
There to abide with my Creator, God,
    And sleep as I in childhood sweetly slept:
Untroubling and untroubled where I lie,
The grass below—above the vaulted sky.

Tom Clark

Tom Clark (1941–   ) was born in Illinois, attended the University of Michigan,
and studied at Cambridge University in England. He writes books on baseball:
Champagne and Baloney about Charles Finley, *No Big Deal* about Mark Fidrych.

Poem   (1969)

Like musical instruments
Abandoned in a field
The parts of your feelings

Are starting to know a quiet
The pure conversion of your
Life into art seems destined

Never to occur
You don't mind
You feel spiritual and alert

10   As the air must feel
Turning into sky aloft and blue
You feel like

You'll never feel like touching
    anything or anyone
Again
And then you do

Lucille Clifton

Lucille Clifton (1936–   ) grew up in New York State and now teaches at the University of California at Santa Cruz. She has published six books of poems, beginning with *Good Times* in 1969. More recently, *Good Woman: Poems and a Memoir 1969–1980,* and *Next* appeared, both in 1987. Clifton has also written works for children. See also page 19.

my dream about the cows   (1987)

and then i see the cattle of my own town,
rustled already,
prodded by pale cowboys with a foreign smell
into dark pens built to hold them forever,
and then i see a few of them
rib thin and weeping low over
sparse fields and milkless lives but
standing somehow standing,
and then i see how all despair is
10   thin and weak and personal and
then i see it's only
the dream about the cows.

my dream about the poet   (1987)

a man.
i think it is a man.
sits down with wood.
i think he's holding wood.
he carves.
he is making a world
he says
as his fingers cut citizens
trees and things
10   which he perceives to be a world
but someone says that is
only a poem.
he laughs.
i think he is laughing.

Samuel Taylor Coleridge

Samuel Taylor Coleridge (1772–1834), thinker, talker, and preacher as well as poet, was a man of enormous promise. His failure to live up to the extent of his promise has obscured his real accomplishment. After he collaborated with Wordsworth on *Lyrical Ballads,* the volume of his poetry declined considerably, though the quality of an occasional poem remained high. His literary autobiography, called *Biographia Literaria,* adds to the valuable critical work English poets have contributed to the language.

Kubla Khan   (1797)

In Xanadu did Kubla Khan
A stately pleasure-dome decree:
Where Alph, the sacred river, ran
Through caverns measureless to man
    Down to a sunless sea.
So twice five miles of fertile ground
With walls and towers were girdled round:
And there were gardens bright with sinuous rills,
Where blossomed many an incense-bearing tree;
10 And here were forests ancient as the hills,
Enfolding sunny spots of greenery.

But oh! that deep romantic chasm which slanted
Down the green hill athwart a cedarn cover!
A savage place! as holy and enchanted
As e'er beneath a waning moon was haunted
By woman wailing for her demon-lover!
And from this chasm, with ceaseless turmoil seething,
As if this earth in fast thick pants were breathing,
A mighty fountain momently was forced:
20 Amid whose swift half-intermitted burst
Huge fragments vaulted like rebounding hail,
Or chaffy grain beneath the thresher's flail:
And 'mid these dancing rocks at once and ever
It flung up momently the sacred river
Five miles meandering with a mazy motion
Through wood and dale the sacred river ran,
Then reached the caverns measureless to man,
And sank in tumult to a lifeless ocean:
And 'mid this tumult Kubla heard from far
30 Ancestral voices prophesying war!
    The shadow of the dome of pleasure
    Floated midway on the waves;
    Where was heard the mingled measure
    From the fountain and the caves.
It was a miracle of rare device,
A sunny pleasure-dome with caves of ice!

A damsel with a dulcimer
In a vision once I saw:
It was an Abyssinian maid,
40   And on her dulcimer she played,
Singing on Mount Abora.
Could I revive within me
Her symphony and song,
To such a deep delight 'twould win me,
That with music loud and long,
I would build that dome in air,
That sunny dome! those caves of ice!
And all who heard should see them there,
And all should cry, Beware! Beware!
50 His flashing eyes, his floating hair!
Weave a circle round him thrice,
And close your eyes with holy dread,
For he on honey-dew hath fed,
And drunk the milk of Paradise.

Gregory Corso

Gregory Corso (1930–   ), born in New York, has worked as a manual laborer,
a merchant seaman, and a teacher. Two of his early books were published by City
Lights Books in San Francisco, where he belonged to the Beat Generation.

Marriage   (1960)

Should I get married? Should I be good?
Astound the girl next door with my velvet suit and faustus hood?
Don't take her to movies but to cemeteries
tell all about werewolf bathtubs and forked clarinets
then desire her and kiss her and all the preliminaries
and she going just so far and I understanding why
not getting angry saying You must feel! It's beautiful to feel!
Instead take her in my arms lean against an old crooked tombstone
and woo her the entire night the constellations in the sky—

10 When she introduces me to her parents
back straightened, hair finally combed, strangled by a tie,
should I sit knees together on their 3rd degree sofa
and not ask Where's the bathroom?
How else to feel other than I am,
often thinking Flash Gordon soap—
O how terrible it must be for a young man
seated before a family and the family thinking
We never saw him before! He wants our Mary Lou!

After tea and homemade cookies they ask What do you do for a living?
20 Should I tell them? Would they like me then?
Say All right get married, we're losing a daughter
but we're gaining a son—
And should I then ask Where's the bathroom?

O God, and the wedding! All her family and her friends
and only a handful of mine all scroungy and bearded
just wait to get at the drinks and food—
And the priest! he looking at me as if I masturbated
asking me Do you take this woman for your lawful wedded wife?
And I trembling what to say say Pie Glue!
30 I kiss the bride all those corny men slapping me on the back
She's all yours, boy! Ha-ha-ha!
And in their eyes you could see some obscene honeymoon going on—
Then all that absurd rice and clanky cans and shoes
Niagara Falls! Hordes of us! Husbands! Wives! Flowers! Chocolates!
All streaming into cozy hotels
All going to do the same thing tonight
The indifferent clerk he knowing what was going to happen
The lobby zombies they knowing what
The whistling elevator man he knowing
40 The winking bellboy knowing
Everybody knowing! I'd be almost inclined not to do anything!
Stay up all night! Stare that hotel clerk in the eye!
Screaming: I deny honeymoon! I deny honeymoon!
running rampant into those almost climactic suites
yelling Radio belly! Cat shovel!
O I'd live in Niagara forever! in a dark cave beneath the Falls
I'd sit there the Mad Honeymooner
devising ways to break marriages, a scourge of bigamy
a saint of divorce—

50 But I should get married I should be good
How nice it'd be to come home to her
and sit by the fireplace and she in the kitchen
aproned young and lovely wanting my baby
and so happy about me she burns the roast beef
and comes crying to me and I get up from my big papa chair
saying Christmas teeth! Radiant brains! Apple deaf!
God what a husband I'd make! Yes, I should get married!
So much to do! like sneaking into Mr Jones' house late at night
and cover his golf clubs with 1920 Norwegian books
60 Like hanging a picture of Rimbaud on the lawnmower
like pasting Tannu Tuva postage stamps all over the picket fence
like when Mrs Kindhead comes to collect for the Community Chest
grab her and tell her There are unfavorable omens in the sky!
And when the mayor comes to get my vote tell him
When are you going to stop people killing whales!
And when the milkman comes leave him a note in the bottle
Penguin dust, bring me penguin dust, I want penguin dust—

Yet if I should get married and it's Connecticut and snow
and she gives birth to a child and I am sleepless, worn,
70 up for nights, head bowed against a quiet window, the past behind me,
finding myself in the most common of situations a trembling man
knowledged with responsibility not twig-smear nor Roman coin soup—
O what would that be like!
Surely I'd give it for a nipple a rubber Tacitus
For a rattle a bag of broken Bach records
Tack Della Francesca all over its crib
Sew the Greek alphabet on its bib
And build for its playpen a roofless Parthenon

No, I doubt I'd be that kind of father
80 not rural not snow no quiet window
but hot smelly tight New York City
seven flights up, roaches and rats in the walls
a fat Reichian wife screeching over potatoes Get a job!
And five nose running brats in love with Batman
And the neighbors all toothless and dry haired
like those hag masses of the 18th century
all wanting to come in and watch TV
The landlord wants his rent
Grocery store Blue Cross & Electric Knights of Columbus
90 Impossible to lie back and dream Telephone snow, ghost parking—
No! I should not get married I should never get married!
But—imagine If I were married to a beautiful sophisticated woman
tall and pale wearing an elegant black dress and long black gloves
holding a cigarette holder in one hand and a highball in the other
and we lived high up in a penthouse with a huge window
from which we could see all of New York and ever farther on clearer days
No, can't imagine myself married to that pleasant prison dream—

O but what about love? I forget love
not that I am incapable of love
100 it's just that I see love as odd as wearing shoes—
I never wanted to marry a girl who was like my mother
And Ingrid Bergman was always impossible
And there's maybe a girl now but she's already married
And I don't like men and—
but there's got to be somebody!
Because what if I'm 60 years old and not married,
all alone in a furnished room with pee stains on my underwear
and everybody else is married! All the universe married but me!

Ah, yet well I know that were a woman possible as I am possible
110 then marriage would be possible—
Like SHE in her lonely alien gaud waiting her Egyptian lover
so I wait—bereft of 2,000 years and the bath of life.

Sam Cornish

Sam Cornish (1935–   ) teaches literature at Emerson College in Boston, and is the author of *1935* (1991) and *Songs of Jubilee* (1986).

Brother of the Streets   (1990)

children
this is the blood
the other men named Uncle Remus
and sometimes Boy
and always brother
men of
mysterious deaths
sudden deaths
brothers of the streets
10 the poetry
and high-five
like old gods
from the mother
country
strange and unknown country
of common history
origin
and many languages
and strange tongues
20 men who sacrificed
the Fifties
the Korean War
Detroit Riot
Harlem Riot
Scottsboro
the Mississippi River
who found the soul of Africa in zoot suits
the songs hip from the Fifties the street
corners of the Forties
30 the dusk in the voice of Billie Holiday song
for these brothers

William Cowper

William Cowper (1731–1800) suffered from fits of depression and was suicidal. His temporary insanity was influenced, in its particular shape, by his Calvinism, whereby he was convinced that he was one of the damned. His metaphor for damnation is "The Castaway." If Elizabethan poets suffered from a malady of executions, many eighteenth-century poets seem to have specialized in insanity.

The Castaway   (1799)

Obscurest night involved the sky,
   The Atlantic billows roared,
When such a destined wretch as I,
   Washed headlong from on board,
Of friends, of hope, of all bereft,
His floating home forever left.

No braver chief could Albion° boast   England
   Than he with whom he went,[1]
Nor ever ship left Albion's coast,
10   With warmer wishes sent.
He loved them both, but both in vain.
Nor him beheld, nor her again.

Not long beneath the whelming brine,
   Expert to swim, he lay;
Nor soon he felt his strength decline,
   Or courage die away;
But waged with death a lasting strife,
Supported by despair of life.

He shouted; nor his friends had failed
20   To check the vessel's course,
But so the furious blast prevailed,
   That, pitiless perforce,
They left their outcast mate behind,
And scudded still before the wind.

Some succor yet they could afford;
   And, such as storms allow,
The cask, the coop, the floated cord,
   Delayed not to bestow.
But he (they knew) nor ship, nor shore,
30 Whate'er they gave, should visit more.

Nor, cruel as it seemed, could he
   Their haste himself condemn,

[1] "He" is George, Lord Anson (1697–1762), from whose *Voyage Round the World* Cowper took this story.

Aware that flight, in such a sea,
    Alone could rescue them;
Yet bitter felt it still to die
Deserted, and his friends so nigh.

He long survives, who lives an hour
    In ocean, self-upheld;
And so long he, with unspent power,
40   His destiny repelled;
And ever, as the minutes flew,
Entreated help, or cried, "Adieu!"

At length, his transient respite past,
    His comrades, who before
Had heard his voice in every blast,
    Could catch the sound no more.
For then, by toil subdued, he drank
The stifling wave, and then he sank.

No poet wept him; but the page
50   Of narrative sincere,
That tells his name, his worth, his age,
    Is wet with Anson's tear.
And tears by bards or heroes shed
Alike immortalize the dead.

I therefore purpose not, or dream,
    Descanting on his fate,
To give the melancholy theme
    A more enduring date:
But misery still delights to trace
60 Its semblance in another's case.

No voice divine the storm allayed,
    No light propitious shone,
When, snatched from all effectual aid,
    We perished, each alone;
But I beneath a rougher sea,
And whelmed in deeper gulfs than he.

Hart Crane

Hart Crane (1899–1932) published his first book of poems, *White Buildings,* in 1926. *The Bridge* (1930), a long poem centering on the Brooklyn Bridge, was an attempt to provide a myth of America. Alcoholic and homosexual, prone to binges and fights, Crane lived a short and turbulent life, ended by suicide when he jumped from a ship taking him from Mexico back to New York in 1932.

from The Bridge   (1930)
To Brooklyn Bridge

How many dawns, chill from his rippling rest
The seagull's wings shall dip and pivot him,
Shedding white rings of tumult, building high
Over the chained bay waters Liberty—

Then, with inviolate curve, forsake our eyes
As apparitional as sails that cross
Some page of figures to be filed away;
—Till elevators drop us from our day . . .

I think of cinemas, panoramic sleights
10 With multitudes bent toward some flashing scene
Never disclosed, but hastened to again,
Foretold to other eyes on the same screen;

And Thee, across the harbor, silver-paced
As though the sun took step of thee, yet left
Some motion ever unspent in thy stride,—
Implicitly thy freedom staying thee!

Out of some subway scuttle, cell or loft
A bedlamite speeds to thy parapets,
Tilting there momently, shrill shirt ballooning,
20 A jest falls from the speechless caravan.

Down Wall, from girder into street noon leaks,
A rip-tooth of the sky's acetylene;
All afternoon the cloud-flown derricks turn . . .
Thy cables breathe the North Atlantic still.

And obscure as that heaven of the Jews,
Thy guerdon . . . Accolade thou dost bestow
Of anonymity time cannot raise:
Vibrant reprieve and pardon thou dost show.

O harp and altar, of the fury fused,
30 (How could mere toil align thy choiring strings!)
Terrific threshold of the prophet's pledge,
Prayer of pariah, and the lover's cry,—

Again the traffic lights that skim thy swift
Unfractioned idiom, immaculate sigh of stars,
Beading thy path—condense eternity:
And we have seen night lifted in thine arms.

Under thy shadow by the piers I waited;
Only in darkness is thy shadow clear.
The City's fiery parcels all undone,
40 Already snow submerges an iron year . . .

O Sleepless as the river under thee,
Vaulting the sea, the prairies' dreaming sod,
Unto us lowliest sometime sweep, descend
And of the curveship lend a myth to God.

from Voyages   (1926)

II

And yet this great wink of eternity,
Of rimless floods, unfettered leewardings,
Samite sheeted and processioned where
Her undinal vast belly moonward bends,
Laughing the wrapt inflections of our love;

Take this Sea, whose diapason knells
On scrolls of silver snowy sentences,
The sceptred terror of whose sessions rends
As her demeanors motion well or ill,
10 All but the pieties of lovers' hands.

And onward, as bells off San Salvador
Salute the crocus lustres of the stars,
In these poinsettia meadows of her tides,—
Adagios of islands, O my Prodigal,
Complete the dark confessions her veins spell.

Mark how her turning shoulders wind the hours,
And hasten while her penniless rich palms
Pass superscription of bent foam and wave,—
Hasten, while they are true,—sleep, death, desire,
20 Close round one instant in one floating flower.

Bind us in time, O Seasons clear, and awe.
O minstrel galleons of Carib fire,
Bequeath us to no earthly shore until
Is answered in the vortex of our grave
The seal's wide spindrift gaze toward paradise.

Robert Creeley

Robert Creeley (1926–   ) grew up in New England, and attended Harvard, after which he tried chicken farming in New Hampshire, then lived on the Spanish island of Majorca. Most recently, he has alternated between Waldoboro, Maine, and the University of Buffalo, in New York. Creeley taught at Black Mountain College and edited the *Black Mountain Review,* contributing to the formation of the Black Mountain school of poetry. His *Collected Poems* appeared in 1982. See also page 40.

The Rain (1962)

All night the sound had
come back again,
and again falls
this quiet, persistent rain.

What am I to myself
that must be remembered,
insisted upon
so often? Is it

10 that never the ease,
even the hardness,
of rain falling
will have for me

something other than this,
something not so insistent—
am I to be locked in this
final uneasiness.

Love, if you love me,
lie next to me.
Be for me, like rain,
20 the getting out

of the tiredness, the fatuousness, the
   semi-
lust of intentional indifference.
Be wet
with a decent happiness.

For My Mother: Genevieve Jules Creeley (1976)
(April 8, 1887–October 7, 1972)

Tender, semi-
articulate flickers
of your

presence, all
those years
past

now, eighty-
five, impossible to
count them

10 one by one, like
addition, sub-
traction, missing

not one. The last
curled up, in
on yourself,

position you take
in the bed, hair
wisped up

on your head, a
20 top knot, body
skeletal, eyes

closed against,
it must be,
further disturbance—

breathing a skim
of time, lightly
kicks the intervals—

days, days and
years of it,
30 work, changes,

sweet flesh caught
at the edges,
dignity's faded

dilemma. It
is *your* life, oh
no one's

forgotten anything
ever. They want
to make you

40 happy when
they remember. Walk
a little, get

up, now, die
safely,
easily, into

singleness, too
tired with it
to keep

on and on.
50 Waves break at
the darkness

under the road, sounds
in the faint
night's softness. Look

at them, catching
the light, white
edge as they turn—

always again
and again. Dead
60 one, two,

three hours—
all these minutes
pass. Is it,

was it, ever
you alone
again, how

long you kept
at it, your
pride, your

70 lovely, confusing
discretion. Mother, I
love you—for

whatever that
means,
meant—more

than I know, body
gave me my
own, generous,

inexorable place
80 of you. I feel
the mouth's sluggish-

ness, slips on
turns of things
said, to you,

too soon, too late,
wants to
go back to beginning,

smells of the hospital
room, the doctor
90 she responds

to now, the
order—get me
there. "Death's

let you out—"
comes true,
this, that,

endlessly circular
life, and we
came back

100 to see you one
last
time, this

time? Your head
shuddered
it seemed, your

eyes wanted,
I thought,
to see

who it was.
110 I am here,
and will follow.

Countee Cullen

Countee Cullen (1903–1946) was a leader in the Harlem renaissance of the 1920s. He wrote many books of poems, and edited a black magazine called *Opportunity* as well as an influential anthology called *Caroling Dusk* (1927). Anchor Books has published his collected works in paperback.

E. E. Cummings

Edward Estlin Cummings (1894–1962) grew up in Cambridge, Massachusetts, and attended Harvard before becoming a volunteer ambulance driver in the First World War. He wrote a prose book about this experience, *The Enormous Room,* and began to publish books of poems in 1923. His typographical innovations tended to conceal a diction which, much of the time, was traditional and romantic. The bitter humor of his satires proved his best work in poetry. See also pages 42–43 and 107.

Poem, or Beauty Hurts Mr. Vinal   (1926)

take it from me kiddo
believe me
my country, 'tis of

you, land of the Cluett
Shirt Boston Garter and Spearmint
Girl With The Wrigley Eyes(of you
land of the Arrow Ide
and Earl &
Wilson
10 Collars) of you i
sing: land of Abraham Lincoln and Lydia E. Pinkham,
land above all of Just Add Hot Water And Serve—
from every B.V.D.

let freedom ring

amen. i do however protest, anent the un
-spontaneous and otherwise scented merde which
greets one (Everywhere Why) as divine poesy per
that and this radically defunct periodical. i would
suggest that certain ideas gestures
20 rhymes, like Gillette Razor Blades
having been used and reused
to the mystical moment of dullness emphatically are
Not To Be Resharpened. (Case in point

if we are to believe these gently O sweetly
melancholy trillers amid the thrillers
these crepuscular violinists among my and your
skyscrapers—Helen & Cleopatra were Just Too Lovely,

The Snail's On The Thorn enter Morn and God's
In His andsoforth

30 do you get me?)according
to such supposedly indigenous
throstles Art is O World O Life
a formula: example, Turn Your Shirttails Into
Drawers and If It Isn't An Eastman It Isn't A
Kodak therefore my friends let
us now sing each and all fortissimo A-
mer
i
ca, I
40 love,
You. And there're a
hun-dred-mil-lion-oth-ers, like
all of you successfully if
delicately gelded(or spaded)
gentlemen(and ladies)—pretty

littleliverpill-
hearted-Nujolneeding-There's-A-Reason
americans(who tensetendoned and with
upward vacant eyes, painfully
50 perpetually crouched, quivering, upon the
sternly allotted sandpile
—how silently
emit a tiny violetflavored nuisance:Odor?

ono.
comes out like a ribbon lies flat on the brush

J. V. Cunningham

J. V. Cunningham (1911–1985) was a Professor of English at Brandeis University, a scholar and critic as well as a poet. His *Collected Poems and Epigrams* came out in 1971.

James Dickey

James Dickey (1923–   ) was an All-Southern halfback and then a fighter pilot during the Second World War and the Korean War. He tried teaching and advertising and, after publishing volumes of poetry, returned to teaching again. His *Buckdancer's Choice* won the National Book Award in 1966. His novel *Deliverance* became a successful motion picture.

The Heaven of Animals   (1961)

Here they are. The soft eyes open.
If they have lived in a wood
It is a wood.

If they have lived on plains
It is grass rolling
Under their feet forever.

Having no souls, they have come,
Anyway, beyond their knowing.
Their instincts wholly bloom
10 And they rise.
The soft eyes open.

To match them, the landscape flowers,
Outdoing, desperately
Outdoing what is required:
The richest wood,
The deepest field.

For some of these,
It could not be the place
It is, without blood.
20 These hunt, as they have done,
But with claws and teeth grown perfect,

More deadly than they can believe.
They stalk more silently,
And crouch on the limbs of trees,

And their descent
Upon the bright backs of their prey

May take years
In a sovereign floating of joy.
And those that are hunted
30 Know this as their life,
Their reward: to walk

Under such trees in full knowledge
Of what is in glory above them,
And to feel no fear,
But acceptance, compliance.
Fulfilling themselves without pain

At the cycle's center,
They tremble, they walk
Under the tree,
40 They fall, they are torn,
They rise, they walk again.

Emily Dickinson   *(1830–1886)*

See pages 139–144.

John Donne

John Donne (1572–1631) was chief of the "Metaphysical Poets." It was his wit, and that of other metaphysicals, to speak of one thing in terms of another far removed, as when the parting of husband and wife is compared to the two feet of a geometric compass. In his youth, he wrote playful and complex erotic poetry; after he became an Anglican priest in 1615, his poetry became increasingly religious, thus providing literary observers with a division into two poets, Jack Donne and Dr. Donne. His devotional prose, including his sermons, ranks among the best English prose of the seventeenth century. From 1621 until he died, he was Dean of St. Paul's in London. He preached his final sermon wearing a shroud.

The Canonization   (1633)

For Godsake hold your tongue, and let me love,
  Or chide my palsy, or my gout,
My five grey hairs, or ruined fortune flout;
  With wealth your state, your mind with arts improve,

Take you a course, get you a place,
Observe his Honor, or his Grace;
Or the king's real, or his stampèd face[1]
Contemplate; what you will, approve,
So you will let me love.

10 Alas, alas, who's injured by my love?
What merchant's ships have my sighs drowned?
Who says my tears have overflowed his ground?
When did my colds a forward spring remove?
When did the heats which my veins fill
Add one more to the plaguy bill?[2]
Soldiers find wars, and lawyers find out still
Litigious men, which quarrels move,
Though she and I do love.

Call us what you will, we are made such by love;
20 Call her one, me another fly,
We're tapers too, and at our own cost die,
And we in us find the eagle and the dove.
The phoenix riddle hath more wit
By us; we two being one are it.
So to one neutral thing both sexes fit,
We die and rise the same, and prove
Mysterious by this love.

We can die by it, if not live by love,
And if unfit for tombs and hearse
30 Our legend be, it will be fit for verse;
And if no piece of chronicle we prove,
We'll build in sonnets pretty rooms;
As well a well-wrought urn becomes
The greatest ashes, as half-acre tombs,
And by these hymns all shall approve
Us canonized for love:

And thus invoke us; You, whom reverend love
Made one another's hermitage;
You, to whom love was peace, that now is rage;
40 Who did the whole world's soul contract, and drove
Into the glasses of your eyes—
So made such mirrors, and such spies,
That they did all to you epitomize,
Countries, towns, courts: beg from above
A pattern of your love!

[1] On coins   [2] List of those dead of plague

Death, Be Not Proud (1610)

Death, be not proud, though some have callèd thee
Mighty and dreadful, for thou are not so;
For those whom thou think'st thou dost overthrow
Die not, poor Death; nor yet canst thou kill me.
From rest and sleep, which but thy pictures be,
Much pleasure; then from thee much more must flow;
And soonest our best men with thee do go—
Rest of their bones and souls' delivery!
Thou'rt slave to fate, chance, kings, and desperate men,
10 And dost with poison, war, and sickness dwell;
And poppy or charms can make us sleep as well
And better than thy stroke. Why swell'st thou then?
One short sleep past, we wake eternally,
And Death shall be no more: Death, thou shalt die.

David Dooley

David Dooley (1947–   ) grew up in Tennessee and took his B.A. at Johns
Hopkins University. He works as a legal assistant in San Antonio, Texas, and has
published a book of poems, *The Volcano Inside* (1988).

Edward Dorn

Edward Dorn (1929–   ) attended Black Mountain College and studied with
Robert Creeley and Charles Olson. One of Olson's didactic pamphlets is a
bibliography addressed to Ed Dorn. Perhaps his best work is the long poem
originally called *Gunslinger,* now shortened to *Slinger.*

On the Debt My Mother Owed to Sears Roebuck (1964)

Summer was dry, dry the garden
our beating hearts, on that farm, dry
with the rows of corn the grasshoppers
came happily to strip, in hordes, the first
thing I knew about locust was they came
dry under the foot like the breaking of
a mechanical bare heart which collapses
from an unkind an incessant word whispered
in the house of the major farmer
10 and the catalogue company,
from no fault of anyone

my father coming home tired
and grinning down the road, turning in
is the tank full? thinking of the horse
and my lazy arms thinking of the water
so far below the well platform.

On the debt my mother owed to sears roebuck
we brooded, she in the house, a little heavy
from too much corn meal, she
20   a little melancholy from the dust of the fields
in her eye, the only title she ever had to lands—
and man's ways winged their way to her through the mail
saying so much per month
so many months, this is yours, take it
take it, take it, take it
and in the corncrib, like her lives in that house
the mouse nibbled away at the cob's yellow grain
until six o'clock when her sorrows grew less
and my father came home

30   On the debt my mother owed to sears roebuck?
I have nothing to say, it gave me clothes to
wear to school,
and my mother brooded
in the rooms of the house, the kitchen, waiting
for the men she knew, her husband, her son
from work, from school, from the air of locusts
and dust masking the hedges of fields she knew
in her eye as a vague land where she lived,
boundaries, whose tractors chugged pulling harrows
40   pulling discs, pulling great yields from the earth
pulse for the armies in two hemispheres, 1943
and she was part of that *stay at home army* to keep
things going, owing that debt.

Rita Dove

Rita Dove (1952–   ) won the Pulitzer Prize in 1987 for *Thomas and Beulah*,
her third book of poems. This lyric comes from her fourth collection, *Grace
Notes* (1989). She teaches at the University of Virginia. See also pages 24–25.

Horse and Tree   (1989)

Everybody who's anybody longs to be a tree—
or ride one, hair blown to froth.
That's why horses were invented, and saddles
tooled with singular stars.

This is why we braid their harsh manes
as if they were children, why children
might fear a carousel at first for the way
it insists that life is round. No,

we reply, there is music and then it stops;
10 the beautiful is always rising and falling.
We call and the children sing back *one more time.*
In the tree the luminous sap ascends.

John Dryden

John Dryden (1631–1700) was a prolific writer, a great literary man, Milton's
successor, and Pope's predecessor—without being quite so great a poet as either
of them. He wrote many of his plays in rhymed couplets. The heroic couplet is
Dryden's particular measure: pairs of end-stopped pentameter lines, rhymed
directly, usually forming a complete two-line unit of thought or narrative; Dryden
codified the form. Chaucer had written in couplets, as had Ben Jonson. Dryden
made the form more rigid while retaining great vigor and force. Pope, with
unprecedented dexterity and skill, carried it even further, but some feel that
Dryden's verse is more vigorous than Pope's. Most of his best work is in long
poems—philosophical or satirical, allusive, and difficult to read without study of
the age. This short poem shows Dryden's finish and his energy.

To the Memory of Mr. Oldham   (1684)

Farewell, too little and too lately known,
Whom I began to think and call my own;
For sure our souls were near allied, and thine
Cast in the same poetic mold with mine.
One common note on either lyre did strike,
And knaves and fools we both abhorred alike.
To the same goal did both our studies drive:
The last set out the soonest did arrive.
Thus Nisus[1] fell upon the slippery place,
10 Whilst his young friend performed and won the race.
O early ripe! to thy abundant store
What could advancing age have added more?
It might (what nature never gives the young)
Have taught the numbers° of thy native tongue.   poetic meters
But satire needs not those, and wit will shine
Through the harsh cadence of a rugged line.
A noble error, and but seldom made,
When poets are by too much force betrayed.

---

[1] In Vergil's *Aeneid* Nisus is beaten in a race by a younger friend.

Thy gen'rous fruits, though gathered ere their prime,
20 Still shewed a quickness; and maturing time
But mellows what we write to the dull sweets of rhyme.
Once more, hail, and farewell! farewell, thou young,
But ah! too short, Marcellus[2] of our tongue!
Thy brows with ivy and with laurels bound;
But fate and gloomy night encompass thee around.

Alan Dugan

Alan Dugan (1923–   ) was Yale Younger Poet in 1961, with *Poems,* his first book, which won both the Pulitzer Prize and the National Book Award. His *New and Collected Poems (1961–1983)* appeared in 1983. He was born in Brooklyn, attended Queens College, spent World War II in the Air Force, and lives in Provincetown, Massachusetts.

On Hurricane Jackson   (1961)

Now his nose's bridge is broken, one
    eye
will not focus and the other is a stray;
trainers whisper in his mouth while
    one ear
listens to itself, clenched like a fish;
generally shadowboxing in a smoky
    room,

10 his mind hides like the aching boys
who lost a contest in the Panhellenic
    games
and had to take the back roads home,
but someone else, his perfect youth,
laureled in newsprint and dollar bills,
triumphs forever on the great white way
to the statistical Sparta of the champs.

Robert Duncan

Robert Duncan (1919–1990) born in Oakland, was a San Francisco poet for most of his life, associated with the Black Mountain group of poets. Erudite and prolific, Duncan was a source of energy for other poets, especially in the Bay Area, in ideas and example.

Poetry, a Natural Thing   (1960)

Neither our vices nor our virtues
further the poem. "They came up
    and died

---

[2] Marcus Claudius Marcellus, nephew and adopted son of Augustus Caesar, died at twenty and is lamented by Vergil in the sixth book of the *Aeneid.*

just like they do every year
    on the rocks."
    The poem
feeds upon thought, feeling, impulse,
    to breed itself,
a spiritual urgency at the dark ladders leaping.

10 This beauty is an inner persistence
    toward the source
striving against (within) down-rushet of the river,
    a call we heard and answer
in the lateness of the world
    primordial bellowings
from which the youngest world might spring,

salmon not in the well where the
    hazelnut falls
but at the falls battling, inarticulate,
20   blindly making it.

This is one picture apt for the mind.

A second: a moose painted by Stubbs,[1]
where last year's extravagant antlers
    lie on the ground.
The forlorn moosey-faced poem wears
    new antler-buds,
    the same,

"a little heavy, a little contrived,"

his only beauty to be
30   all moose.

Richard Eberhart

Richard Eberhart (1904–   ) attended Dartmouth College in New Hampshire and went from there to Cambridge University in England, where he first published. He taught at a preparatory school, served in the Navy (some of his poems of the Second World War are deservedly famous), and for many years taught at Dartmouth.

The Groundhog   (1932)

In June, amid the golden fields,
I saw a groundhog lying dead.

Dead lay he; my senses shook,
And mind outshot our naked frailty.

---

[1] George Stubbs (1724–1806), an English artist, is best known for his animal paintings.

There lowly in the vigorous summer
His form began its senseless change,
And made my senses waver dim
Seeing nature ferocious in him.
Inspecting close his maggots' might
10 And seething cauldron of his being,
Half with loathing, half with a strange
    love,
I poked him with an angry stick.
The fever arose, became a flame
And Vigour circumscribed the skies,
Immense energy in the sun,
And through my frame a sunless
    trembling.
My stick had done nor good nor harm.
20 Then stood I silent in the day
Watching the object, as before;
And kept my reverence for knowledge
Trying for control, to be still,
To quell the passion of the blood;
Until I had bent down on my knees
Praying for joy in the sight of decay.
And so I left; and I returned

In Autumn strict of eye, to see
The sap gone out of the groundhog,
30 But the bony sodden hulk remained.
But the year had lost its meaning,
And in intellectual chains
I lost both love and loathing,
Mured up in the wall of wisdom.
Another summer took the fields again
Massive and burning, full of life,
But when I chanced upon the spot
There was only a little hair left,
And bones bleaching in the sunlight
40 Beautiful as architecture;
I watched them like a geometer,
And cut a walking stick from a birch.
It has been three years, now.
There is no sign of the groundhog.
I stood there in the whirling summer,
My hand capped a withered heart,
And thought of China and of Greece,
Of Alexander in his tent;
Of Montaigne in his tower,
50 Of Saint Theresa in her wild lament.

T. S. Eliot

Thomas Stearns Eliot (1888–1965) was born in St. Louis, Missouri, into a family
two generations removed from Boston that had created its own small Boston in
St. Louis. Eliot went to prep school in Massachusetts, to Harvard, and then abroad.
After some time in Europe on fellowships (he expected to finish a doctorate in
philosophy at Harvard), he married an Englishwoman and settled in England,
dedicating himself to the life of a poet. For a time, he taught school; for a longer
time, he worked in a bank, and finally he became a publisher, overseer of the best
poetry list in England, at Faber & Faber. His early work, derived largely from
French sources, was notable for its irony and for the desolation of its landscape.
This work culminated in the great modernist poem *The Waste Land,* in 1922.
Toward the end of the 1920s, Eliot converted to Anglo-Catholicism, and most of
the rest of his poetry was dedicated to exploring the implications of conversion.
"Journey of the Magi" is one record. *Four Quartets* is the last of his great work in
poetry, though he wrote verse plays for the West End and Broadway afterward, with
success more commercial than poetical. He was awarded the Nobel Prize in 1948,
was widely celebrated as a critic, and was the leading literary figure of the
English-speaking world during the first half of the twentieth century.

The Love Song of J. Alfred Prufrock   (1911)

S'io credesse che mia resposta fosse
A persona che mai tornasse al mondo,
Questa fiamma staria senza piu scosse.

Ma perciocche giammai di questo fondo
Non torno vivo alcun, s'i'odo il vero,
Senza tema d'infamia ti rispondo.[1]

Let us go then, you and I,
When the evening is spread out against the sky
Like a patient etherized upon a table;
Let us go, through certain half-deserted streets,
The muttering retreats
Of restless nights in one-night cheap hotels
And sawdust restaurants with oyster-shells:
Streets that follow like a tedious argument
Of insidious intent
10 To lead you to an overwhelming question . . .
Oh, do not ask, "What is it?"
Let us go and make our visit.

In the room the women come and go
Talking of Michelangelo.

The yellow fog that rubs its back upon the window-panes,
The yellow smoke that rubs its muzzle on the window-panes
Licked its tongue into the corners of the evening,
Lingered upon the pools that stand in drains,
Let fall upon its back the soot that falls from chimneys,
20 Slipped by the terrace, made a sudden leap,
And seeing that it was a soft October night,
Curled once about the house, and fell asleep.

And indeed there will be time
For the yellow smoke that slides along the street,
Rubbing its back upon the window-panes;
There will be time, there will be time
To prepare a face to meet the faces that you meet;
There will be time to murder and create,
And time for all the works and days of hands
30 That lift and drop a question on your plate;
Time for you and time for me,
And time yet for a hundred indecisions,
And for a hundred visions and revisions,
Before the taking of a toast and tea.

In the room the women come and go
Talking of Michelangelo.

---

[1] The Italian epigraph, from Dante's *Inferno,* is the speech of one who is dead and damned, whose punishment is to be wrapped in a constantly burning flame. He believes his hearer also will remain in Hell and thus says: "If I thought my reply were to someone who could ever return to the world, this flame would waver no more [i.e., I would speak no more]. But since, I'm told, nobody ever escapes from this pit, I'll tell you without fear of ill fame."

And indeed there will be time
To wonder, "Do I dare?" and, "Do I dare?"
Time to turn back and descend the stair,
40 With a bald spot in the middle of my hair—
[They will say: "How his hair is growing thin!"]
My morning coat, my collar mounting firmly to the chin,
My necktie rich and modest, but asserted by a simple pin—
[They will say: "But how his arms and legs are thin!"]
Do I dare
Disturb the universe?
In a minute there is time
For decisions and revisions which a minute will reverse.

For I have known them all already, known them all:—
50 Have known the evenings, mornings, afternoons,
I have measured out my life with coffee spoons;
I know the voices dying with a dying fall
Beneath the music from a farther room.
    So how should I presume?

And I have known the eyes already, known them all—
The eyes that fix you in a formulated phrase,
And when I am formulated, sprawling on a pin,
When I am pinned and wriggling on the wall,
Then how should I begin
60 To spit out all the butt-ends of my days and ways?
    And how should I presume?

And I have known the arms already, known them all—
Arms that are braceleted and white and bare
[But in the lamplight, downed with light brown hair!]
Is it perfume from a dress
That makes me so digress?
Arms that lie along a table, or wrap about a shawl.
    And should I then presume?
    And how should I begin?
                    . . . .

70 Shall I say, I have gone at dusk through narrow streets
And watched the smoke that rises from the pipes
Of lonely men in shirt-sleeves, leaning out of windows? . . .

    I should have been a pair of ragged claws
Scuttling across the floors of silent seas.
                    . . . .

And the afternoon, the evening, sleeps so peacefully!
Smoothed by long fingers,
Asleep . . . tired . . . or it malingers,
Stretched on the floor, here beside you and me.
Should I, after tea and cakes and ices,
80 Have the strength to force the moment to its crisis?

But though I have wept and fasted, wept and prayed,
Though I have seen my head [grown slightly bald] brought in upon a platter,
I am no prophet—and here's no great matter;
I have seen the moment of my greatness flicker,
And I have seen the eternal Footman hold my coat, and snicker,
And in short, I was afraid.

    And would it have been worth it, after all,
After the cups, the marmalade, the tea,
Among the porcelain, among some talk of you and me,
90 Would it have been worth while,
To have bitten off the matter with a smile,
To have squeezed the universe into a ball
To roll it toward some overwhelming question,
To say: "I am Lazarus, come from the dead,
Come back to tell you all, I shall tell you all"—
If one, settling a pillow by her head,
    Should say: "That is not what I meant at all.
    That is not it, at all."

    And would it have been worth it, after all,
100 Would it have been worth while,
After the sunsets and the dooryards and the sprinkled streets,
After the novels, after the teacups, after the skirts that trail along the floor—
And this, and so much more?—
It is impossible to say just what I mean!
But as if a magic lantern threw the nerves in patterns on a screen:
Would it have been worth while
If one, settling a pillow or throwing off a shawl,
And turning toward the window, should say:
    "That is not it at all,
110   That is not what I meant, at all."

        . . . .

No! I am not Prince Hamlet, nor was meant to be;
Am an attendant lord, one that will do
To swell a progress, start a scene or two,
Advise the prince; no doubt, an easy tool,
Deferential, glad to be of use,
Politic, cautious, and meticulous;
Full of high sentence, but a bit obtuse;
At times, indeed, almost ridiculous—
Almost, at times, the Fool.

120   I grow old . . . I grow old . . .
I shall wear the bottoms of my trousers rolled.

    Shall I part my hair behind? Do I dare to eat a peach?
I shall wear white flannel trousers, and walk upon the beach.
I have heard the mermaids singing, each to each.

    I do not think that they will sing to me.

I have seen them riding seaward on the waves
Combing the white hair of the waves blown back
When the wind blows the water white and black.

We have lingered in the chambers of the sea
130 By sea-girls wreathed with seaweed red and brown
Till human voices wake us, and we drown.

Journey of the Magi   (1927)

'A cold coming we had of it,
Just the worst time of the year
For a journey, and such a long journey:
The ways deep and the weather sharp,
The very dead of winter.'
And the camels galled, sore-footed, refractory,
Lying down in the melting snow.
There were times we regretted
The summer palaces on slopes, the terraces,
10 And the silken girls bringing sherbet.
Then the camel men cursing and grumbling
And running away, and wanting their liquor and women,
And the night-fires going out, and the lack of shelters,
And the cities hostile and the towns unfriendly
And the villages dirty and charging high prices:
A hard time we had of it.
At the end we preferred to travel all night,
Sleeping in snatches,
With the voices singing in our ears, saying
20 That this was all folly.

Then at dawn we came down to a temperate valley,
Wet, below the snow line, smelling of vegetation;
With a running stream and a water-mill beating the darkness,
And three trees on the low sky,
And an old white horse galloped away in the meadow.
Then we came to a tavern with vine-leaves over the lintel,
Six hands at an open door dicing for pieces of silver,
And feet kicking the empty wine-skins.
But there was no information, and so we continued
30 And arrived at evening, not a moment too soon
Finding the place; it was (you may say) satisfactory.

All this was a long time ago, I remember,
And I would do it again, but set down
This set down
This: were we led all that way for
Birth or Death? There was a Birth, certainly,
We had evidence and no doubt. I had seen birth and death,
But had thought they were different; this Birth was

Hard and bitter agony for us, like Death, our death.
40 We returned to our places, these Kingdoms,
But no longer at ease here, in the old dispensation,
With an alien people clutching their gods.
I should be glad of another death.

William Empson

William Empson (1906–   ) is known for his criticism, especially *Seven Types of Ambiguity* (1930), and for his ambiguous poems. He taught in China for many years, now lives and teaches in Sheffield, England.

Villanelle   (1949)

It is the pain, it is the pain, endures.
Your chemic beauty burned my muscles through.
Poise of my hands reminded me of yours.

What later purge from this deep toxin cures?
What kindness now could the old salve renew?
It is the pain, it is the pain, endures.

The infection slept (custom or change inures)
And when pain's secondary phase was due
Poise of my hands reminded me of yours.

10 How safe I felt, whom memory assures,
Rich that your grace safely by heart I knew.
It is the pain, it is the pain, endures.

My stare drank deep beauty that still allures.
My heart pumps yet the poison draught of you.
Poise of my hands reminded me of yours.

You are still kind whom the same shape immures.
Kind and beyond adieu. We miss our cue.
It is the pain, it is the pain, endures.
Poise of my hands reminded me of yours.

Louise Erdrich

Louise Erdrich (1954–   ) grew up in North Dakota and graduated from
Dartmouth College. Her first novel was *Love Medicine* (1984), which won a
National Book Award. *Beet Queen* followed in 1986 and *Tracks* in 1988. She has
also published two books of poems, *Jacklight* in 1984 and *Baptism of Desire* in
1989. Her heritage is partly German-American and partly Turtle Mountain
Chippewa.

Owls   (1989)

The barred owls scream in the black pines,
searching for mates. Each night
the noise wakes me, a death
rattle, everything in sex that wounds.
There is nothing in the sound but raw need
of one feathered body for another.
Yet, even when they find one another,
there is no peace.

In Ojibwa, the owl is Kokoko, and not
10   even the smallest child loves the gentle sound
of the word. Because the hairball
of bones and vole teeth can be hidden
under snow, to kill the man who walks over it.
Because the owl looks behind itself to see you coming,
the vane of the feather does not disturb
air, and the barb is ominously soft.

Have you ever seen, at dusk,
an owl take flight from the throat of a dead tree?
Mist, troubled spirit.
20   You will notice only after
its great silver body has turned to bark.
The flight was soundless.

That is how we make love,
when there are people in the halls around us,
clashing dishes, filling their mouths
with air, with debris, pulling
switches and filters as the whole machinery
of life goes on, eliminating and eliminating
until there are just the two bodies
30   fiercely attached, the feathers
floating down and cleaving to their shapes.

Martín Espada

Martín Espada (1957–   ), who was born in Brooklyn, has become a leader among Latino poets in the United States. He lives in Boston and works as a tenant lawyer and supervisor of a legal services program called Su Clinica. Most recently, he has published three collections: *The Immigrant Iceboy's Bolero* (1982), *Trumpets from the Islands of Their Eviction* (1987), and *Rebellion is the Circle of a Lover's Hands* (1990) from which we reprint these poems. See also page 27.

The Savior is Abducted in Puerto Rico   (1990)
Adjuntas, Puerto Rico, 1985

At a place in the mountains,
where the road skids
into tangled trees
and stacks of rock,
a single white cross leans.

The name has dissolved,
obscured in a century of storms
that asphyxiated shacks
with mud, yanking
10 the stone vertebrae
from bridges.

On the cross,
the dark absence of Christ
spreads and hangs,
a crucified shadow
where thieves
tore the brass body down,
leaving amputated feet and hands
still nailed,
20 and the accidental dead
without a guide
on the mountain roads
of the underworld.

Edward Fitzgerald

Edward Fitzgerald (1809–1883) first translated the *Rubáiyát* of Omar Khayyám in 1859 and continued to revise it the rest of his life. His other poems and translations have attracted little attention, but this translation—more adaptation than translation—has endured like no other foreign poem done into English.

from The Rubáiyát of Omar Khayyám   (tr. 1859)

1

Wake! for the Sun, who scattered into flight
The Stars before him from the Field of Night,
    Drives Night along with them from Heav'n, and strikes
The Sultán's Turret with a Shaft of Light.

7

Come, fill the Cup, and in the fire of Spring
Your Winter-garment of Repentance fling:
    The Bird of Time has but a little way
To flutter—and the Bird is on the Wing.

12

A Book of Verses underneath the Bough,
A jug of Wine, a Loaf of Bread—and Thou
    Beside me singing in the Wilderness—
Oh, Wilderness were Paradise enow!

13

Some for the Glories of This World; and some
Sigh for the Prophet's Paradise to come;
    Ah, take the Cash, and let the Credit go,
Nor heed the rumble of a distant Drum!

19

I sometimes think that never blows so red
The Rose as where some buried Caesar bled;
    That every Hyacinth the Garden wears
Dropt in her Lap from some once lovely Head.

22

For some we loved, the loveliest and the best
That from his Vintage rolling Time hath prest,
    Have drunk their Cup a Round or two before,
And one by one crept silently to rest.

27

Myself when young did eagerly frequent
Doctor and Saint, and heard great argument
    About it and about: but evermore
Came out by the same door where in I went.

71

The Moving Finger writes; and, having writ,
Moves on: nor all your Piety nor Wit
    Shall lure it back to cancel half a Line,
Nor all your Tears wash out a Word of it.

100

Yon rising Moon that looks for us again—
How oft hereafter will she wax and wane;
    How oft hereafter rising look for us
Through this same Garden—and for *one* in vain!

101

And when like her, oh Sákí, you shall pass
Among the Guests Star-scatter'd on the Grass,
    And in your joyous errand reach the spot
Where I made One—turn down an empty Glass!

Robert Francis

Robert Francis (1901–1987) lived most of his life in Massachusetts, mostly in a house called Fort Juniper in the countryside outside Amherst. He wrote an autobiography, some fiction, and some satirical prose. A poet of reticence and quiet, he lived without much attention from critics and prizegivers, writing his finished poems one at a time. See also page 17.

Three Woodchoppers   (1944)

Three woodchoppers walk up the
   road.
Day after day it is the same.
The short man always takes the lead
Limping like one a trifle lame.

And number two leans as he goes
And number three walks very straight.
I do not time them but I know
They're never early, never late.

10 So I have seen them for a week,
Have seen them but have heard no
   sound.
I never saw one turn to speak.
I never saw one look around.

Out of a window to the south
I watch them come against the light.
I cross the room and to the north
I watch till they are out of sight.

Robert Frost   *(1874–1963)*

See pages 144–154.

Allen Ginsberg

Allen Ginsberg (1926–   ) was born in New Jersey and attended Columbia University in New York City, but became known as a San Francisco poet with the publication of *Howl* in 1956. At the forefront of the Beat Generation (he appears in several novels by Jack Kerouac, under different names), Ginsberg has been a leader, spiritual and political as well as poetic. See also pages 23–24.

America   (1956)

America I've given you all and now I'm nothing.
America two dollars and twentyseven cents January 17, 1956.
I can't stand my own mind.
America when will we end the human war?
Go fuck yourself with your atom bomb.
I don't feel good don't bother me.
I won't write my poem till I'm in my right mind.

America when will you be angelic?
When will you take off your clothes?
10 When will you look at yourself through the grave?
When will you be worthy of your million Trotskyites?
America why are your libraries full of tears?
America when will you send your eggs to India?
I'm sick of your insane demands.
When can I go into the supermarket and buy what I need with my good looks?
America after all it is you and I who are perfect not the next world.
Your machinery is too much for me.
You made me want to be a saint.
There must be some other way to settle this argument.
20 Burroughs is in Tangiers I don't think he'll come back it's sinister.
Are you being sinister or is this some form of practical joke?
I'm trying to come to the point.
I refuse to give up my obsession.
America stop pushing I know what I'm doing.
America the plum blossoms are falling.
I haven't read the newspapers for months, everyday somebody goes on trial for
    murder.
America I feel sentimental about the Wobblies.
America I used to be a communist when I was a kid I'm not sorry.
30 I smoke marijuana every chance I get.
I sit in my house for days on end and stare at the roses in the closet.
When I go to Chinatown I get drunk and never get laid.
My mind is made up there's going to be trouble.
You should have seen me reading Marx.
My psychoanalyst thinks I'm perfectly right.
I won't say the Lord's Prayer.
I have mystical visions and cosmic vibrations.
America I still haven't told you what you did to Uncle Max after he came over from
    Russia.

40 I'm addressing you.
Are you going to let your emotional life be run by Time Magazine?
I'm obsessed by Time Magazine.
I read it every week.
Its cover stares at me every time I slink past the corner candystore.
I read it in the basement of the Berkeley Public Library.
It's always telling me about responsibility. Businessmen are serious.
    Movie producers are serious. Everybody's serious but me.
It occurs to me that I am America.
I am talking to myself again.

50 Asia is rising against me.
I haven't got a chinaman's chance.
I'd better consider my national resources.
My national resources consist of two joints of marijuana millions of genitals
    an unpublishable private literature that goes 1400 miles an hour and
    twentyfive-thousand mental institutions.

I say nothing about my prisons nor the millions of underprivileged who live in
   my flowerpots under the light of five hundred suns.
I have abolished the whorehouses of France, Tangiers is the next to go.
My ambition is to be President despite the fact that I'm a Catholic.

60 America how can I write a holy litany in your silly mood?
I will continue like Henry Ford my strophes are as individual as his automobiles
      more so they're all different sexes.
America I will sell you strophes $2500 apiece $500 down on your old strophe
America free Tom Mooney
America save the Spanish Loyalists
America Sacco & Vanzetti must not die
America I am the Scottsboro boys.
America when I was seven momma took me to Communist Cell meetings
      they sold us garbanzos a handful per ticket a ticket costs a nickel and the
70   speeches were free everybody was angelic and sentimental about the
      workers it was all so sincere you have no idea what a good thing the
      party was in 1835 Scott Nearing was a grand old man a real mensch
      Mother Bloor made me cry I once saw Israel Amter plain. Everybody
      must have been a spy.
America you don't really want to go to war.
America it's them bad Russians.
Them Russians them Russians and them Chinamen. And them Russians.
The Russia wants to eat us alive. The Russia's power mad. She wants to take
      our cars from out our garages.
80 Her wants to grab Chicago. Her needs a Red Readers' Digest. Her wants our
      auto plants in Siberia. Him big bureaucracy running our fillingstations.
That no good. Ugh. Him make Indians learn read. Him need big black niggers.
      Hah. Her make us all work sixteen hours a day. Help.
America this is quite serious.
America this is the impression I get from looking in the television set.
America is this correct?
I'd better get right down to the job.
It's true I don't want to join the Army or turn lathes in precision parts factories,
      I'm nearsighted and psychopathic anyway.
90 America I'm putting my queer shoulder to the wheel.

Louise Glück

Louise Glück (1943–   ) lives in Vermont and has published five collections of
her poems; the latest is *Ararat* (1990).

Gratitude   (1975)

Do not think I am not grateful for your small
kindness to me.
I like small kindnesses.

In fact I actually prefer them to the more
substantial kindness, that is always eying you,
like a large animal on a rug,
until your whole life reduces
to nothing but waking up morning after morning
cramped, and the bright sun shining on its tusks.

Robert Graves

Robert Graves (1895–1986) fought in the First World War directly upon
graduation from English public school. He was one of the survivors, and later
wrote, in his autobiographical *Good-Bye to All That,* one of the great accounts of
that war. He wrote many novels, including *I, Claudius,* and collections of essays
and humor, but he was first and foremost a poet throughout a long and prolific
career. His mythic system, concerned with the muse of poetry, was described in
The White Goddess, and he remained faithful to his Muse through many poems,
revised many times, in the many volumes of his *Collected Poems.*

In Broken Images (1947)

He is quick, thinking in clear images;
I am slow, thinking in broken images.

He becomes dull, trusting to his clear images;
I become sharp, mistrusting my broken images.

Trusting his images, he assumes their relevance;
Mistrusting my images, I question their relevance.

Assuming their relevance, he assumes the fact;
Questioning their relevance, I question the fact.

When the fact fails him, he questions his senses;
10 When the fact fails me, I approve my senses.

He continues quick and dull in his clear images;
I continue slow and sharp in my broken images.

He in a new confusion of his understanding;
I in a new understanding of my confusion.

Thom Gunn

Thom Gunn (1929–   ) grew up in England, son of a successful journalist, attended Cambridge, and came to California in 1954. He lives in San Francisco, where he has spent most of the time since leaving England.

On the Move   (1957)

'Man, you gotta Go.'

The blue jay scuffling in the bushes follows
Some hidden purpose, and the gust of birds
That spurts across the field, the wheeling swallows,
Have nested in the trees and undergrowth.
Seeking their instinct, or their poise, or both,
One moves with an uncertain violence
Under the dust thrown by a baffled sense
Or the dull thunder of approximate words.

On motorcycles, up the road, they come:
10 Small, black, as flies hanging in heat, the Boys,
Until the distance throws them forth, their hum
Bulges to thunder held by calf and thigh.
In goggles, donned impersonality,
In gleaming jackets trophied with the dust,
They strap in doubt—by hiding it, robust—
And almost hear a meaning in their noise.

Exact conclusion of their hardiness
Has no shape yet, but from known whereabouts
They ride, direction where the tires press.
20 They scare a flight of birds across the field:
Much that is natural, to the will must yield.
Men manufacture both machine and soul,
And use what they imperfectly control
To dare a future from the taken routes.

It is a part solution, after all.
One is not necessarily discord
On earth; or damned because, half animal,
One lacks direct instinct, because one wakes
Afloat on movement that divides and breaks.
30 One joins the movement in a valueless world,
Choosing it, till, both hurler and the hurled,
One moves as well, always toward, toward.

A minute holds them, who have come to go:
The self-defined, astride the created will
They burst away; the towns they travel through
Are home for neither bird nor holiness,
For birds and saints complete their purposes.

At worst, one is in motion; and at best,
Reaching no absolute, in which to rest,
40 One is always nearer by not keeping still.

H.D. (Hilda Doolittle)

Hilda Doolittle (1886–1961) attended Bryn Mawr College and knew William Carlos Williams and Ezra Pound when all three poets were young. (It was at Pound's suggestion that she began signing her poems with her initials only.) She began as an imagist poet; later in life she wrote long philosophic poems. See also page 22.

Sea Rose   (1916)

Rose, harsh rose,
marred and with stint of petals,
meagre flower, thin,
sparse of leaf,

more precious
than a wet rose,
single on a stem—
you are caught in the drift.

Stunted, with small leaf,
10 you are flung on the sand,
you are lifted
in the crisp sand
that drives in the wind.

Can the spice-rose
drip such acrid fragrance
hardened in a leaf?

John Haines

John Haines (1924–   ) was a homesteader in Alaska for fifteen years and now divides his time between Alaska and the continental United States.

To Turn Back   (1964)

The grass people bow
their heads before the wind.

How would it be
to stand among them, bending
our heads like that . . . ?

Yes . . . and no . . . perhaps . . .
lifting our dusty faces
as if we were waiting for
the rain . . . ?

10 The grass people stand
all year, patient and obedient—

to be among them
is to have only simple
and friendly thoughts,

and not be afraid.

Donald Hall

Donald Hall (1928–   ) edited this anthology. See the author biography on the
back cover.

My Son My Executioner   (1954)

My son, my executioner,
   I take you in my arms,
Quiet and small and just astir
   And whom my body warms.

Sweet death, small son, our instrument
   Of immortality,
Your cries and hungers document
   Our bodily decay.

We twenty-five and twenty-two,
10   Who seemed to live forever,
Observe enduring life in you
   And start to die together.

Names of Horses   (1978)

All winter your brute shoulders strained against collars, padding
and steerhide over the ash hames, to haul
sledges of cordwood for drying through spring and summer,
for the Glenwood stove next winter, and for the simmering range.

In April you pulled cartloads of manure to spread on the fields,
dark manure of Holsteins, and knobs of your own clustered with oats.
All summer you mowed the grass in meadow and hayfield, the mowing machine
clacketing beside you, while the sun walked high in the morning;

and after noon's heat, you pulled a clawed rake through the same acres,
10 gathering stacks, and dragged the wagon from stack to stack,
and the built hayrack back, up hill to the chaffy barn,
three loads of hay a day, hanging wide from the hayrack.

Sundays you trotted the two miles to church with the light load
of a leather quartertop buggy, and grazed in the sound of hymns.
Generation on generation, your neck rubbed the window sill
of the stall, smoothing the wood as the sea smooths glass.

When you were old and lame, when your shoulders hurt bending to graze,
one October the man who fed you and kept you, and harnessed you every morning,
led you through corn stubble to sandy ground above Eagle Pond,
20 and dug a hole beside you where you stood shuddering in your skin,

and lay the shotgun's muzzle in the boneless hollow behind your ear,
and fired the slug into your brain, and felled you into your grave,
shoveling sand to cover you, setting goldenrod upright above you,
where by next summer a dent in the ground made your monument.

For a hundred and fifty years, in the pasture of dead horses,
roots of pine trees pushed through the pale curves of your ribs,
yellow blossoms flourished above you in autumn, and in winter
frost heaved your bones in the ground—old toilers, soil makers:

O Roger, Mackerel, Riley, Ned, Nellie, Chester, Lady Ghost.

Thomas Hardy

Thomas Hardy (1840–1928) is better known as a novelist than as a poet, but
many devoted readers find the poetry even better than the fiction. He began life
as an architect and published his first novel when he was thirty-two. For many
years Hardy wrote few poems and concentrated on novels, of which the best
known are *The Return of the Native, The Mayor of Casterbridge, Tess of the
D'Urbervilles,* and *Jude the Obscure. Jude* appeared in 1896, and was denounced
as obscene. Perhaps using that denunciation as an excuse, Hardy renounced
fiction, and—now freed by the success of his fiction from the necessity to make
money—devoted himself to poetry, as he had always wanted to do. He was
almost sixty when his first book of poems appeared. Between 1898 and his death
at eighty-eight in 1928 he published the fifteen hundred poems that appear in his
Collected Poems. He is a poet admired by other poets. See also pages 18, 45–46,
87, and 105.

The Ruined Maid   (1866)

"O' Melia, my dear, this does everything crown!
Who could have supposed I should meet you in Town?
And whence such fair garments, such prosperi·ty?"—
"O didn't you know I'd been ruined?" said she.

—"You left us in tatters, without shoes or socks,
Tired of digging potatoes, and spudding up docks;°   digging weeds
And now you've gay bracelets and bright feathers three!"—
"Yes: that's how we dress when we're ruined," said she.

—"At home in the barton° you said 'thee' and 'thou,'   farmyard
10   And 'thik oon,' and 'theäs oon,' and 't'other'; but now
Your talking quite fits 'ee for high compa·ny!"—
"Some polish is gained with one's ruin," said she.

—"Your hands were like paws then, your face blue and bleak
But now I'm bewitched by your delicate cheek.
And your little gloves fit as on any la-dy!"—
"We never do work when we're ruined," said she.

—"You used to call home-life a hag-ridden dream,
And you'd sigh, and you'd sock; but at present you seem
To know not of megrims° or melancho-ly!"—   depressions
20 "True. One's pretty lively when ruined," said she.

—"I wish I had feathers, a fine sweeping gown,
And a delicate face, and could strut about Town!"—
"My dear—a raw country girl, such as you be,
Cannot quite expect that. You ain't ruined," said she.

Robert Hayden

Robert Hayden (1913–1980) grew up in Detroit, where he attended Wayne State
University, later studying at the University of Michigan. He taught at Fisk in
Nashville for many years, and then returned to teach at Michigan. In 1976 he
went to Washington as Poetry Consultant at the Library of Congress. His poems
explored areas of the black American experience, and in a time of militancy
Hayden avoided militancy. He became an adherent of the Bahá'i faith when he
was a young man and remained true to it.

Middle Passage   (1970)

I

Jesús, Estrella, Esperanza, Mercy:

> Sails flashing to the wind like weapons,
> sharks following the moans the fever and the dying;
> horror the corposant and compass rose.

Middle Passage:
>   voyage through death
>   to life upon these shores.

> "10 April 1800—
> Blacks rebellious. Crew uneasy. Our linguist says
10   their moaning is a prayer for death,
> ours and their own. Some try to starve themselves.
> Lost three this morning leaped with crazy laughter
> to the waiting sharks, sang as they went under."

Desire, Adventure, Tartar, Ann:

> Standing to America, bringing home
> black gold, black ivory, black seed.
>> *Deep in the festering hold thy father lies,*
>> *of his bones New England pews are made,*
>> *those are altar lights that were his eyes.*

20 Jesus   Saviour   Pilot   Me
Over   Life's   Tempestuous   Sea
We pray that Thou wilt grant, O Lord,
safe passage to our vessels bringing
heathen souls unto Thy chastening.

Jesus Saviour
>> "8 bells. I cannot sleep, for I am sick
>> with fear, but writing eases fear a little
>> since still my eyes can see these words take shape
>> upon the page & so I write, as one
30 >> would turn to exorcism. 4 days scudding,
>> but now the sea is calm again. Misfortune
>> follows in our wake like sharks (our grinning
>> tutelary gods). Which one of us
>> has killed an albatross? A plague among
>> our blacks—Ophthalmia: blindness—& we
>> have jettisoned the blind to no avail.
>> It spreads, the terrifying sickness spreads.
>> Its claws have scratched sight from the Capt.'s eyes
>> & there is blindness in the fo'c'sle
40 >> & we must sail 3 weeks before we come
>> to port."

>> *What port awaits us, Davy Jones'*
>> *or home? I've heard of slavers drifting, drifting,*
>> *playthings of wind and storm and chance, their crews*
>> *gone blind, the jungle hatred*
>> *crawling up on deck.*

Thou   Who   Walked   On   Galilee

>> "Deponent further sayeth *The Bella J*
>> left the Guinea Coast
50 >> with cargo of five hundred blacks and odd
>> for the barracoons of Florida:

>> "That there was hardly room 'tween-decks for half
>> the sweltering cattle stowed spoon-fashion there;
>> that some went mad of thirst and tore their flesh
>> and sucked the blood:

"That Crew and Captain lusted with the comeliest
of the savage girls kept naked in the cabins;
that there was one they called The Guinea Rose
and they cast lots and fought to lie with her:

60   "That when the Bo's'n piped all hands, the flames
spreading from starboard already were beyond
control, the negroes howling and their chains
entangled with the flames:

"That the burning blacks could not be reached,
that the Crew abandoned ship,
leaving their shrieking negresses behind,
that the Captain perished drunken with the wenches:

"Further Deponent sayeth not."

Pilot   Oh   Pilot   Me

II

70 Aye, lad, and I have seen those factories,
Gambia, Rio Pongo, Calabar;
have watched the artful mongos baiting traps
of war wherein the victor and the vanquished

Were caught as prizes for our barracoons.
Have seen the nigger kings whose vanity
and greed turned wild black hides of Fellatah,
Mandingo, Ibo, Kru to gold for us.

And there was one—King Anthracite we named him—
fetish face beneath French parasols
80 of brass and orange velvet, impudent mouth
whose cups were carven skulls of enemies:

He'd honor us with drum and feast and conjo
and palm-oil-glistening wenches deft in love,
and for tin crowns that shone with paste,
red calico and German-silver trinkets

Would have the drums talk war and send
his warriors to burn the sleeping villages
and kill the sick and old and lead the young
in coffles to our factories.

90 Twenty years a trader, twenty years,
for there was wealth aplenty to be harvested
from those black fields, and I'd be trading still
but for the fevers melting down my bones.

III

Shuttles in the rocking loom of history,
the dark ships move, the dark ships move,
their bright ironical names
like jests of kindness on a murderer's mouth;
plough through thrashing glister toward
fata morgana's lucent melting shore,
100 weave toward New World littorals that are
mirage and myth and actual shore.
Voyage through death,
                              voyage whose chartings are unlove.

A charnel stench, effluvium of living death
spreads outward from the hold,
where the living and the dead, the horribly dying,
lie interlocked, lie foul with blood and excrement.

>   *Deep in the festering hold thy father lies,*
>   *the corpse of mercy rots with him,*
> 110   *rats eat love's rotten gelid eyes.*

>   *But, oh, the living look at you*
>   *with human eyes whose suffering accuses you,*
>   *whose hatred reaches through the swill of dark*
>   *to strike you like a leper's claw.*

>   *You cannot stare that hatred down*
>   *or chain the fear that stalks the watches*
>   *and breathes on you its fetid scorching breath;*
>   *cannot kill the deep immortal human wish,*
>   *the timeless will.*

120   "But for the storm that flung up barriers
          of wind and wave, *The Amistad,* señores,
          would have reached the port of Príncipe in two,
          three days at most; but for the storm we should
          have been prepared for what befell.
          Swift as the puma's leap it came. There was
          that interval of moonless calm filled only
          with the water's and the rigging's usual sounds,
          then sudden movement, blows and snarling cries
          and they had fallen on us with machete
130   and marlinspike. It was as though the very
          air, the night itself were striking us.
          Exhausted by the rigors of the storm,
          we were no match for them. Our men went down
          before the murderous Africans. Our loyal
          Celestino ran from below with gun
          and lantern and I saw, before the cane-
          knife's wounding flash, Cinquez,

that surly brute who calls himself a prince,
directing, urging on the ghastly work.
140   He hacked the poor mulatto down, and then
he turned on me. The decks were slippery
when daylight finally came. It sickens me
to think of what I saw, of how these apes
threw overboard the butchered bodies of
our men, true Christians all, like so much jetsam.
Enough, enough. The rest is quickly told:
Cinquez was forced to spare the two of us
You see to steer the ship to Africa,
and we like phantoms doomed to rove the sea
150   voyaged east by day and west by night,
deceiving them, hoping for rescue,
prisoners on our own vessel, till
at length we drifted to the shores of this
your land, America, where we were freed
from our unspeakable misery. Now we
demand, good sirs, the extradition of
Cinquez and his accomplices to La
Havana. And it distresses us to know
there are so many here who seem inclined
160   to justify the mutiny of these blacks.
We find it paradoxical indeed
that you whose wealth, whose tree of liberty
are rooted in the labor of your slaves
should suffer the august John Quincy Adams
to speak with so much passion of the right
of chattel slaves to kill their lawful masters
and with his Roman rhetoric weave a hero's
garland for Cinquez. I tell you that
we are determined to return to Cuba
170   with our slaves and there see justice done. Cinquez—
or let us say 'the Prince'—Cinquez shall die."

The deep immortal human wish,
the timeless will:

Cinquez its deathless primaveral image,
life that transfigures many lives.

Voyage through death

                   to life upon these shores.

Seamus Heaney

Seamus Heaney (1939–   ) was born in County Derry in Northern Ireland, and now lives in Dublin with his wife and three children. He has visited the United States on many occasions and currently teaches one term a year at Harvard University. *Field Work* (1979) was his fourth book of poems. In 1980 he published *Preoccupations: Selected Prose* and reissued his first three books as *Poems 1965–1975. Station Island* appeared in 1984. In 1990 he published a *Selected Poems.*

A Drink of Water   (1976)

She came every morning to draw water
Like an old bat staggering up the field:
The pump's whooping cough, the bucket's clatter
And slow diminuendo as it filled,
Announced her. I recall
Her grey apron, the pocked white enamel
Of the brimming bucket, and the treble
Creak of her voice like the pump's handle.
Nights when a full moon lifted past her gable
10 It fell back through her window and would lie
Into the water set out on the table.
Where I have dipped to drink again, to be
Faithful to the admonishment on her cup,
Remember the Giver fading off the lip.

Song   (1979)

A rowan like a lipsticked girl.
Between the by-road and the main road
Alder trees at a wet and dripping distance
Stand off among the rushes.

There are the mud-flowers of dialect
And the immortelles of perfect pitch
And that moment when the bird sings very close
To the music of what happens.

Iron Spike   (1985)

So like a harrow pin
I hear harness creaks and the click
of stones in a ploughed-up field.
But it was the age of steam

at Eagle Pond, New Hampshire,
when this rusted spike I found there

was aimed and driven in
to fix a cog on the line.

What guarantees things keeping
10 if a railway can be lifted
like a long briar out of ditch growth?
I felt I had come on myself

in the grassy silent path
where I drew the iron like a thorn
or a word I had thought my own
out of a stranger's mouth.

And the sledge-head that sank it
with a last opaque report

20 deep into the creosoted
sleeper, where is that?

And the sweat-cured haft?
Ask the ones on the buggy,
inaudible and upright
and sped along without shadows.

Anthony Hecht

Anthony Hecht (1923–   ) fought in the infantry in the Second World War and
has taught at American universities for most of his life. He is not prolific, finishes
few poems, and finishes them with an extraordinarily high gloss. In 1990 he
published *Collected Earlier Poems* together with a new collection called *The
Transparent Man*.

The Dover Bitch: A Criticism of Life   (1967)
(for Andrews Wanning)

So there stood Matthew Arnold and this girl
With the cliffs of England crumbling away behind them,
And he said to her, "Try to be true to me,
And I'll do the same for you, for things are bad
All over, etc., etc."
Well now, I knew this girl. It's true she had read
Sophocles in a fairly good translation
And caught that bitter allusion to the sea,
But all the time he was talking she had in mind
10 The notion of what his whiskers would feel like
On the back of her neck. She told me later on
That after a while she got to looking out
At the lights across the channel, and really felt sad,
Thinking of all the wine and enormous beds
And blandishments in French and the perfumes.
And then she got really angry. To have been brought
All the way down from London, and then be addressed
As a sort of mournful cosmic last resort
Is really tough on a girl, and she was pretty.
20 Anyway, she watched him pace the room
And finger his watch-chain and seem to sweat a bit,
And then she said one or two unprintable things.
But you mustn't judge her by that. What I mean to say is,
She's really all right. I still see her once in a while
And she always treats me right. We have a drink
And I give her a good time, and perhaps it's a year
Before I see her again, but there she is,
Running to fat, but dependable as they come.
And sometimes I bring her a bottle of *Nuit d'Amour.*

George Herbert

George Herbert (1593–1633) was an English priest and author of great religious poetry. He attended Cambridge University and died as a country parson. See also page 106.

Church Monuments   (1633)

While that my soul repairs to her devotion,
Here I intomb my flesh, that it betimes
May take acquaintance of this heap of dust;
To which the blast of death's incessant motion,
Fed with the exhalation of our crimes,
Drives all at last. Therefore I gladly trust

My body to this school, that it may learn
To spell his elements, and find his birth
Written in dusty heraldry and lines;
10 Which dissolution sure doth best discern,
Comparing dust with dust, and earth with earth.
These laugh at jet and marble, put for signs,

To sever the good fellowship of dust,
And spoil the meeting. What shall point out them
When they shall bow, and kneel, and fall down flat
To kiss those heaps, which now they have in trust?
Dear flesh, while I do pray, learn here thy stem
And true descent, that when thou shalt grow fat,

And wanton in thy cravings, thou mayst know,
20 That flesh is but the glass which holds the dust
That measures all our time; which also shall
Be crumbled into dust. Mark here below
How tame these ashes are, how free from lust—
That thou mayst fit thyself against thy fall.

Robert Herrick

Robert Herrick (1591–1674) is among the most playful of English poets. An admirer of Ben Jonson, he wrote short poems, sacred and profane, in a variety of forms. See also page 23.

Delight in Disorder   (1648)

A sweet disorder in the dress
Kindles in clothes a wantonness:
A lawn° about the shoulders thrown   a thin fabric

Into a fine distraction;
An erring lace, which here and there
Enthralls the crimson stomacher,°   decorative garment, often embroidered
A cuff neglectful, and thereby
Ribands to flow confusedly;
A winning wave, deserving note,
10 In the tempestuous petticoat;
A careless shoe-string, in whose tie
I see a wild civility,—
Do more bewitch me, than when art
Is too precise in every part.

Geoffrey Hill

Geoffrey Hill (1932–   ) grew up in a small town in the English Midlands, where his father was the policeman. He attended Oxford, and, after earning his degree, went to Leeds University, where he lectured and taught. After several years of teaching at Cambridge University, he moved to the United States in 1988 and is now at Boston University. In 1985, he brought out his *Collected Poems.*

Merlin   (1959)

I will consider the outnumbering dead:
For they are the husks of what was rich seed.
Now, should they come together to be fed,
They would outstrip the locusts' covering tide.

Arthur, Elaine, Mordred; they are all gone
Among the raftered galleries of bone.
By the long barrows of Logres they are made one,
And over their city stands the pinnacled corn.

Orpheus and Eurydice   (1959)

Though there are wild dogs
    Infesting the roads
We have recitals, catalogues
    Of protected birds;

And the rare pale sun
    To water our days.
Men turn to savagery now or turn
    To the laws'

Immutable black and red.
10   To be judged for his song,
Traversing the still-moist dead,
    The newly-stung,

Love goes, carrying compassion
    To the rawly-difficult;
His countenance, his hands' motion,
    Serene even to a fault.

Linda Hogan

Linda Hogan (1947–   ) is a Chickasaw Native American who has written many books of poetry, short stories, and essays. She has taught at the University of Minnesota and received fellowships from the National Endowment for the Arts as well as fellowships from Colorado and Minnesota. Some of her books include *The New Native American Novel* (1986) and *Savings* (1988).

The Rainy Season   (1985)

The women are walking to town
beneath black umbrellas
and the roofs are leaking.
Oh, let them be,
let the buckled wood give way this once
and the mildew rot the plaster,
the way it happens with age
when a single thought of loneliness
is enough to bring collapse.

10 See, here they come,
the witches are downstairs
undermining the foundations.
The skeletal clothes hanger
has unwound from its life at last,
hidden in a dark coat
thrown over its shoulders.

Nothing is concealed,
not silver moths
falling out the empty sleeves
20 or the old cat with shining fur
covering his bony spine,
that string of knots
for keeping track of this mouse
and that.

Even the mice have their days of woe.
In the field and in the world
there are unknown sorrows.
Every day collapses
despite the women
30 walking to town with black umbrellas
holding up the sky.

Garrett Hongo

Garrett Hongo (1951–   ) was born in Volcano, Hawaii, and grew up mostly in California. After graduating from Pomona College, he attended the University of Michigan, where he won a Hopwood Award. He has published two books of his poems, *Yellow Light* (1982) and *The River of Heaven* (1988). He teaches at the University of Oregon.

The Legend   (1988)

In Chicago, it is snowing softly
and a man has just done his wash for the week.
He steps into the twilight of early evening,
carrying a wrinkled shopping bag
full of neatly folded clothes,
and, for a moment, enjoys
the feel of warm laundry and crinkled paper,
flannellike against his gloveless hands.
There's a Rembrandt glow on his face,

10 a triangle of orange in the hollow of his cheek
   as a last flash of sunset
   blazes the storefronts and lit windows of the street.

   He is Asian, Thai or Vietnamese,
   and very skinny, dressed as one of the poor
   in rumpled suit pants and a plaid mackinaw,
   dingy and too large.
   He negotiates the slick of ice
   on the sidewalk by his car,
   opens the Fairlane's back door,
20 leans to place the laundry in,
   and turns, for an instant,
   toward the flurry of footsteps
   and cries of pedestrians
   as a boy—that's all he was—
   backs from the corner package store
   shooting a pistol, firing it,
   once, at the dumbfounded man
   who falls forward,
   grabbing at his chest.

30 A few sounds escape from his mouth,
   a babbling no one understands
   as people surround him
   bewildered at his speech.
   The noises he makes are nothing to them.
   The boy has gone, lost
   in the light array of foot traffic
   dappling the snow with fresh prints.
   Tonight, I read about Descartes'
   grand courage to doubt everything
40 except his own miraculous existence
   and I feel so distinct
   from the wounded man lying on the concrete
   I am ashamed.

   Let the night sky cover him as he dies.
   Let the weaver girl cross the bridge of heaven
   and take up his cold hands.

            IN MEMORY OF JAY KASHIWAMURA

Gerard Manley Hopkins

Gerard Manley Hopkins (1844–1889) attended Oxford. In his early twenties, he converted to Roman Catholicism, becoming a Jesuit in 1868. He corresponded with Robert Bridges and Coventry Patmore and devoted himself considerably to his poetry insofar as such devotion was consistent with his calling. But he did not publish, and he was not known until Robert Bridges collected his poems after Hopkins's death and edited and published them. He has been a major influence on modern poets. See also pages 71–72.

Spring and Fall   (1877)
To a Young Child

Márgarét, are you grîeving
Over Goldengrove unleaving?
Leáves, lîke the things of man, you
With your fresh thoughts care for, can you?
Áh! ás the heart grows older
It will come to such sights colder
By and by, nor spare a sigh
Though worlds of wanwood leafmeal lie;
And yet you wíll weep and know why.
10   Now no matter, child, the name:
Sórrow's spríngs áre the same.
Nor mouth had, no nor mind, expressed
What heart heard of, ghost guessed:
Is ís the blight man was born for,
It is Margaret you mourn for.

The Windhover   (1877)
To Christ Our Lord

I caught this morning morning's minion, king-
    dom of daylight's dauphin, dapple-dawn-drawn Falcon, in his riding
    Of the rolling level underneath him steady air, and striding
High there, how he rung upon the rein of a wimpling wing
In his ecstacy! then off, off forth on swing,
    As a skate's heel sweeps smooth on a bow-bend; the hurl and gliding
    Rebuffed the big wind. My heart in hiding
Stirred for a bird,—the achieve of, the mastery of the thing!

Brute beauty and valor and act, oh, air, pride, plume, here
10   Buckle! AND the fire that breaks from thee then, a billion
Times told lovelier, more dangerous, O my chevalier!

    No wonder of it: shéer plód makes plough down sillion
Shine, and blue-bleak embers, ah my dear,
    Fall, gall themselves, and gash gold-vermilion.

A. E. Housman

Alfred Edward Housman (1859–1936) was a classical scholar and professor of Latin at Cambridge University. He wrote little poetry, notably *A Shropshire Lad* in 1896 and *Last Poems* in 1922, but what he wrote was extraordinarily fine and finished, if lacking in range and depth.

To an Athlete Dying Young   (1896)

The time you won your town the race
We chaired you through the
   marketplace;
Man and boy stood cheering by,
And home we brought you
   shoulder-high.

To-day, the road all runners come,
Shoulder-high we bring you home,
And set you at your threshold down,
10 Townsman of a stiller town.

Smart lad, to slip betimes away
From fields where glory does not stay
And early though the laurel grows
It withers quicker than the rose.

Eyes the shady night has shut
Cannot see the record cut,

And silence sounds no worse than
   cheers
After earth has stopped the ears:

20 Now you will not swell the rout
Of lads that wore their honors out,
Runners whom renown outran
And the name died before the man.

So set, before its echoes fade,
The fleet foot on the sill of shade,
And hold to the low lintel up
The still-defended challenge-cup.

And round that early-laurelled head
Will flock to gaze the strengthless
30   dead,
And find unwithered on its curls
The garland briefer than a girl's.

Langston Hughes

Langston Hughes (1902–1967), a leader of the Harlem renaissance of black American literature, often used folk sources in his poetry, especially the forms, diction, and rhythm of blues. He also wrote fiction, essays, and drama.

Hope   (1942)

Sometimes when I'm lonely,
Don't know why,
Keep thinkin' I won't be lonely
By and by.

Bad Luck Card   (1927)

Cause you don't love me
Is awful, awful hard.
Gypsy done showed me
My bad luck card.

There ain't no good left
In this world for me.

Gypsy done tole me—
Unlucky as can be.

I don't know what
10 Po' weary me can do.
Gypsy says I'd kill my self
If I was you.

Homecoming   (1959)

I went back in the alley
And I opened up my door.
All her clothes was gone:
She wasn't home no more.

I pulled back the covers,
I made down the bed.
A *whole* lot of room
Was the only thing I had.

Ted Hughes

Ted Hughes (1930–   ) attended Cambridge University, where he met and married Sylvia Plath. His poems have been continually difficult, obdurate, and violent, often about animals—real or mythical. He is concerned to discover and explore instinctual life. In 1984, he became Poet Laureate of England.

Thrushes   (1959)

Terrifying are the attent sleek thrushes on the lawn,
More coiled steel than living—a poised
Dark deadly eye, those delicate legs
Triggered to stirrings beyond sense—with a start, a bounce, a stab
Overtake the instant and drag out some writhing thing.
No indolent procrastinations and no yawning stares,
No sighs or head-scratchings. Nothing but bounce and stab
And a ravening second.

Is it their single-mind-sized skulls, or a trained
10 Body, or genius, or a nestful of brats
Gives their days this bullet and automatic
Purpose? Mozart's brain had it, and the shark's mouth
That hungers down the blood-smell even to a leak of its own
Side and devouring of itself: efficiency which
Strikes too streamlined for any doubt to pluck at it
Or obstruction deflect.

With a man it is otherwise. Heroisms on horseback,
Outstripping his desk-diary at a broad desk,

Carving at a tiny ivory ornament
20 For years: his act worships itself—while for him,
Though he bends to be blent in the prayer, how loud and above what
Furious spaces of fire do the distracting devils
Orgy and hosannah, under what wilderness
Of black silent waters weep.

Richard Hugo

Richard Hugo (1923–1982) was born in Seattle and lived much of his adult life in Montana. The Northwest and the Rocky Mountains form the background of much of his poetry. After his first collection, *A Run of Jacks* (1961), he published eight more books of poems before he died, and his posthumous *Collected Poems* is widely available. *The Triggering Town* (1979) collects essays and lectures on poetry. He also wrote a detective story called *Death and the Good Life* (1981).

Degrees of Gray in Philipsburg   (1973)

You might come here Sunday on a whim.
Say your life broke down. The last good kiss
you had was years ago. You walk these streets
laid out by the insane, past hotels
that didn't last, bars that did, the tortured try
of local drivers to accelerate their lives.
Only churches are kept up. The jail
turned 70 this year. The only prisoner
is always in, not knowing what he's done.

10 The principal supporting business now
is rage. Hatred of the various grays
the mountain sends, hatred of the mill,
The Silver Bill repeal, the best liked girls
who leave each year for Butte. One good
restaurant and bars can't wipe the boredom out.
The 1907 boom, eight going silver mines,
a dance floor built on springs—
all memory resolves itself in gaze,
in panoramic green you know the cattle eat
20 or two stacks high above the town,
two dead kilns, the huge mill in collapse
for fifty years that won't fall finally down.

Isn't this your life? That ancient kiss
still burning out your eyes? Isn't this defeat
so accurate, the church bell simply seems
a pure announcement: ring and no one comes?
Don't empty houses ring? Are magnesium

and scorn sufficient to support a town,
not just Philipsburg, but towns
30 of towering blondes, good jazz and booze
the world will never let you have
until the town you came from dies inside?

Say no to yourself. The old man, twenty
when the jail was built, still laughs
although his lips collapse. Someday soon,
he says, I'll go to sleep and not wake up.
You tell him no. You're talking to yourself.
The car that brought you here still runs.
The money you buy lunch with,
40 no matter where it's mined, is silver
and the girl who serves your food
is slender and her red hair lights the wall.

Randall Jarrell

Randall Jarrell (1914–1965) was born in Tennessee and studied at Vanderbilt. He taught at Kenyon College as a young man, along with John Crowe Ransom. Robert Lowell and Peter Taylor were students there, and from this concentration of talent emerged much American literature. Jarrell served in World War II and wrote about it. In the last decades of his life, he lived in North Carolina, where he taught, and he wrote criticism that was possibly better known during his lifetime than his poetry.

Eighth Air Force[1]   (1947)

If, in an odd angle of the hutment,
A puppy laps the water from a can
Of flowers, and the drunk sergeant shaving
Whistles *O Paradiso!*[2]—shall I say that man
Is not as men have said: a wolf to man?

The other murderers troop in yawning;
Three of them play Pitch, one sleeps, and one
Lies counting missions, lies there sweating
Till even his heart beats: One; One; One.
10 *O murderers!* . . . Still, this is how it's done:

This is war. . . . But since these play, before they die,
Like puppies with their puppy; since, a man,
I did as these have done, but did not die—

---

[1] In World War II, the U.S. Eighth Air Force bombed Germany and occupied Europe from bases in England.   [2] An aria from Meyerbeer's *L'Africaine*

I will content the people as I can
And give up these to them: Behold the man![3]

I have suffered, in a dream, because of him,
Many things;[4] for this last saviour, man,
I have lied as I lie now. But what is lying?
Men wash their hands, in blood, as best they can:
20   I find no fault in this just man.

Robinson Jeffers

Robinson Jeffers (1887–1962) settled with his family in California when he was sixteen years old. His third book, *Tamar and Other Poems* (1924), brought him to readers' attention. As he grew older, he became progressively more misanthropic, with a passionate and romantic love for the natural world. He found man pathetic and inadequate in comparison to natural grandeurs. He built his own house out of stone in Carmel.

Hurt Hawks   (1928)

I

The broken pillar of the wing jags from the clotted shoulder,
The wing trails like a banner in defeat,
No more to use the sky forever but live with famine
And pain a few days: cat nor coyote
Will shorten the week of waiting for death, there is game without talons.
He stands under the oak-bush and waits
The lame feet of salvation; at night he remembers freedom
And flies in a dream, the dawns ruin it.
He is strong and pain is worse to the strong, incapacity is worse.
10   The curs of the day come and torment him
At distance, no one but death the redeemer will humble that head,
The intrepid readiness, the terrible eyes.
The wild God of the world is sometimes merciful to those
That ask mercy, not often to the arrogant,
You do not know him, you communal people, or you have forgotten him;
Intemperate and savage, the hawk remembers him;
Beautiful and wild, the hawks, and men that are dying, remember him.

II

I'd sooner, except the penalties, kill a man than a hawk; but the great redtail[1]
Had nothing left but unable misery
20   From the bone too shattered for mending, the wing that trailed under his talons
        when he moved.

---

[3] John 19:4–5   [4] Matthew 27:19
[1] Red-tailed hawk

We had fed him six weeks, I gave him freedom,
He wandered over the foreland hill and returned in the evening, asking for death,
Not like a beggar, still eyed with the old
Implacable arrogance. I gave him the lead gift in the twilight. What fell was relaxed,
Owl-downy, soft feminine feathers; but what
Soared: the fierce rush: the night-herons by the flooded river cried fear at its rising
Before it was quite unsheathed from reality.

Ben Jonson

Ben Jonson (1572–1637) was actor as well as playwright, and his great plays rank
second only to Shakespeare's. In 1598, he killed another actor in a duel but
avoided execution by pleading benefit of clergy—at least he spoke Latin. Although
his plays remain at the center of his work, he mastered the art of poetry in all
forms, and his works are voluminous and superb in range and in accomplishment.
See also page 21.

To Heaven   (1616)

Good and great God! can I not think of Thee,
    But it must straight my melancholy be?
Is it interpreted in me disease,
    That, laden with my sins, I seek for ease?
O be Thou witness, that the reins dost know
    And hearts of all, if I be sad for show;
And judge me after, if I dare pretend
    To aught but grace, or aim at other end.
As Thou art all, so be Thou all to me,
10   First, midst, and last, converted One and Three!
My faith, my hope, my love; and, in this state,
    My judge, my witness, and my advocate!
Where have I been this while exiled from Thee,
    And whither rapt, now Thou but stoop'st to me?
Dwell, dwell here still! O, being everywhere,
    How can I doubt to find Thee ever here?
I know my state, both full of shame and scorn,
    Conceived in sin, and unto labor born,
Standing with fear, and must with horror fall,
20   And destined unto judgment, after all.
I feel my griefs too, and there scarce is ground
    Upon my flesh t'inflict another wound;
Yet dare I not complain or wish for death
    With holy Paul, lest it be thought the breath
Of discontent; or that these prayers be
    For weariness of life, not love of Thee.

Donald Justice

Donald Justice (1925–   ) grew up in Florida and attended the Writers
Workshop at Iowa, where he taught for some years before returning to his home
state and the University of Florida. His *Selected Poems* appeared in 1979.

Counting the Mad   (1957)

This one was put in a jacket,
This one was sent home,
This one was given bread and meat
But would eat none,
And this one cried No No No No
All day long.

This one looked at the window
As though it were a wall,
This one saw things that were not
10   there,

This one things that were,
And this one cried No No No No
All day long.

This one thought himself a bird,
This one a dog,
And this one thought himself a man,
An ordinary man,
And cried and cried No No No No
All day long.

John Keats   (1795–1821)

See pages 124–138.

X. J. Kennedy

X. J. Kennedy (1929–   ) was named Joseph Kennedy, but he felt that there
had been enough Joseph Kennedys in the news. He is the author of poems for
children, successful textbooks, and many collections of poems.

In a Prominent Bar in Secaucus One Day   (1961)
(To the tune of 'The Old Orange Flute' or the tune of 'Sweet Betsy from Pike')

In a prominent bar in Secaucus one day
Rose a lady in skunk with a topheavy sway,
Raised a knobby red finger—all turned from their beer—
While with eyes bright as snowcrust she sang high and clear:

'Now who of you'd think from an eyeload of me
That I once was a lady as proud as could be?
Oh I'd never sit down by a tumbledown drunk
If it wasn't, my dears, for the high cost of junk.

'All the gents used to swear that the white of my calf
10 Beat the down of the swan by a length and a half.
In the kerchief of linen I caught to my nose
Ah, there never fell snot, but a little gold rose.

'I had seven gold teeth and a toothpick of gold,
My Virginia cheroot was a leaf of it rolled
And I'd light it each time with a thousand in cash—
Why the bums used to fight if I flicked them an ash.

'Once the toast of the Biltmore, the belle of the Taft,
I would drink bottle beer at the Drake, never draught,
And dine at the Astor on Salisbury steak
20 With a clean tablecloth for each bite I did take.

'In a car like the Roxy I'd roll to the track,
A steel-guitar trio, a bar in the back,
And the wheels made no noise, they turned over so fast,
Still it took you ten minutes to see me go past.

'When the horses bowed down to me that I might choose,
I bet on them all, for I hated to lose.
Now I'm saddled each night for my butter and eggs
And the broken threads race down the backs of my legs.

'Let you hold in mind, girls, that your beauty must pass
30 Like a lovely white clover that rusts with its grass.
Keep your bottoms off bar stools and marry you young
Or be left—an old barrel with many a bung.

'For when time takes you out for a spin in his car
You'll be hard-pressed to stop him from going too far
And be left by the roadside, for all your good deeds,
Two toadstools for tits and a face full of weeds.'

All the house raised a cheer, but the man at the bar
Made a phonecall and up pulled a red patrol car
And she blew us a kiss as they copped her away
40 From that prominent bar in Secaucus, N.J.

Galway Kinnell

Galway Kinnell (1927–   ) grew up in Rhode Island and attended Princeton
University. For many years, he supported himself by teaching correspondence
courses. He spent a year teaching in Iran and an occasional term at an American
university while he devoted himself to literary work. He has published one novel,
and translations of Villon and the contemporary French poet Yves Bonnefoy. The
Book of Nightmares, probably his best-known book of poems, appeared in 1971.
His *Selected Poems* appeared in 1982 and won the Pulitzer Prize. In 1985, he
published *The Past,* and in 1990 *When One Has Lived a Long Time Alone.*

The Bear   (1967)

1

In late winter
I sometimes glimpse bits of steam
coming up from
some fault in the old snow
and bend close and see it is lung-colored
and put down my nose
and know
the chilly, enduring odor of bear.

2

I take a wolf's rib and whittle
10 it sharp at both ends
and coil it up
and freeze it in blubber and place it out
on the fairway of the bears.

And when it has vanished
I move out on the bear tracks,
roaming in circles
until I come to the first, tentative, dark
splash on the earth.

And I set out
20 running, following the splashes
of blood wandering over the world.
At the cut, gashed resting places
I stop and rest,
at the crawl-marks
where he lay out on his belly
to overpass some stretch of bauchy ice
I lie out
dragging myself forward with bear-knives in my fists.

3

On the third day I begin to starve,
30   at nightfall I bend down as I knew I would
at a turd sopped in blood,
and hesitate, and pick it up,
and thrust it in my mouth, and gnash it down,
and rise
and go on running.

4

On the seventh day,
living by now on bear blood alone,
I can see his upturned carcass far out ahead, a scraggled,
steamy hulk,
40   the heavy fur riffling in the wind.

I come up to him
and stare at the narrow-spaced, petty eyes,
the dismayed
face laid back on the shoulder, the nostrils
flared, catching
perhaps the first taint of me as he
died.

I hack
a ravine in his thigh, and eat and drink,
50   and tear him down his whole length
and open him and climb in
and close him up after me, against the wind
and sleep.

5

And dream
of lumbering flatfooted
over the tundra,
stabbed twice from within,
splattering a trail behind me,
splattering it out no matter which way I lurch,
60   no matter which parabola of bear-transcendence,
which dance of solitude I attempt,
which gravity-clutched leap,
which trudge, which groan.

6

Until one day I totter and fall—
fall on this
stomach that has tried so hard to keep up,
to digest the blood as it leaked in,

to break up
and digest the bone itself: and now the breeze
70 blows over me, blows off
the hideous belches of ill-digested bear blood
and rotted stomach
and the ordinary, wretched odor of bear,

blows across
my sore, lolled tongue a song
or screech, until I think I must rise up
and dance. And I lie still.

7

I awaken I think. Marshlights
reappear, geese
80 come trailing again up the flyway.
In her ravine under old snow the dam-bear
lies, licking
lumps of smeared fur
and drizzly eyes into shapes

with her tongue. And one
hairy-soled trudge stuck out before me,
the next groaned out,
the next,
the next,
90 the rest of my days I spend
wandering: wondering
what, anyway,
was that sticky infusion, that rank flavor of blood, that poetry, by which I lived?

Etheridge Knight

Etheridge Knight (1933–1991) fought in the Korean War and later became
addicted to heroin. He supported his habit by stealing, which landed him in the
Indiana State Prison. He began to write poems in prison, where Gwendolyn
Brooks visited and encouraged him. His first volume was called *Poems from
Prison*. After his release, he taught poetry at various colleges and conducted
workshops all over the United States.

Hard Rock Returns to Prison from the Hospital for the Criminal Insane (1968)

Hard Rock was "known not to take no shit
From nobody," and he had the scars to prove it:
Split purple lips, lumped ears, welts above

His yellow eyes, and one long scar that cut
Across his temple and plowed through a thick
Canopy of kinky hair.

The WORD was that Hard Rock wasn't a mean nigger
Anymore, that the doctors had bored a hole in his head,
Cut out part of his brain, and shot electricity
10 Through the rest. When they brought Hard Rock back,
Handcuffed and chained, he was turned loose,
Like a freshly gelded stallion, to try his new status.
And we all waited and watched, like indians at a corral,
To see if the WORD was true.

As we waited we wrapped ourselves in the cloak
Of his exploits: "Man, the last time, it took eight
Screws to put him in the Hole." "Yeah, remember when he
Smacked the captain with his dinner tray?" "He set
The record for time in the Hole—67 straight days!"
20 "Ol Hard Rock! man, that's one crazy nigger."
And then the jewel of a myth that Hard Rock had once bit
A screw on the thumb and poisoned him with syphilitic spit.

The testing came, to see if Hard Rock was really tame.
A hillbilly called him a black son of a bitch
And didn't lose his teeth, a screw who knew Hard Rock
From before shook him down and barked in his face.
And Hard Rock did *nothing.* Just grinned and looked silly,
His eyes empty like knot holes in a fence.

And even after we discovered that it took Hard Rock
30 Exactly 3 minutes to tell you his first name,
We told ourselves that he had just wised up,
Was being cool; but we could not fool ourselves for long,
And we turned away, our eyes on the ground. Crushed.
He had been our Destroyer, the doer of things
We dreamed of doing but could not bring ourselves to do,
The fears of years, like a biting whip,
Had cut grooves too deeply across our backs.

Yusef Komunyakaa

Yusef Komunyakaa (1947–   ) has written three books of poems—*Copasetic* (1984), *I Apologize for the Eyes in My Head* (1986), and *Dien Cai Dau* (1989). At Indiana University he teaches both Afro-American studies and creative writing. He served in 1969 and 1970 with the Army in Vietnam.

Walter Savage Landor

Walter Savage Landor (1775–1864) wrote short poems over a long life. He was famous for his violent temper; according to one often-repeated anecdote, he took out his anger on a servant by throwing her through a window onto a garden. He was best at the epigram and short, pointed verse. See also page 105.

I Strove with None   (1849)

I strove with none, for none was worth my strife.
　　Nature I loved and, next to Nature, Art:
I warmed both hands before the fire of life;
　　It sinks, and I am ready to depart.

Philip Larkin

Philip Larkin (1922–1985) attended Oxford, wrote two early novels, and chose the life of a professional librarian. He wrote little, but his work was finished and fine. In the eyes of most observers, he was the best English poet of his time. He was librarian of the University at Hull. His volumes are *The Less Deceived* (1955), *The Whitsun Weddings* (1964), and *High Windows* (1974). His *Collected Poems* was issued in the United States in 1989.

Mr. Bleaney   (1964)

'This was Mr. Bleaney's room. He stayed
The whole time he was at the Bodies, till
They moved him.' Flowered curtains, thin and frayed,
Fall to within five inches of the sill,

Whose window shows a strip of building land,
Tussocky, littered. 'Mr. Bleaney took
My bit of garden properly in hand.'
Bed, upright chair, sixty-watt bulb, no hook

Behind the door, no room for books or bags—
10 'I'll take it.' So it happens that I lie
Where Mr. Bleaney lay, and stub my fags
On the same saucer-souvenir, and try

Stuffing my ears with cotton-wool, to drown
The jabbering set he egged her on to buy.
I know his habits—what time he came down,
His preference for sauce to gravy, why

He kept on plugging at the four aways[1]—
Likewise their yearly frame: the Frinton folk
Who put him up for summer holidays,
20 And Christmas at his sister's house in Stoke.

But if he stood and watched the frigid wind
Tousling the clouds, lay on the fusty bed
Telling himself that this was home, and grinned,
And shivered, without shaking off the dread

That how we live measures our own nature,
And at his age having no more to show
Than one hired box should make him pretty sure
He warranted no better, I don't know.

Aubade   (1978)

I work all day, and get half drunk at night.
Waking at four to soundless dark, I stare.
In time the curtain-edges will grow light.
Till then I see what's really always there:
Unresting death, a whole day nearer now,
Making all thought impossible but how
And where and when I shall myself die.
Arid interrogation: yet the dread
Of dying, and being dead,
10 Flashes afresh to hold and horrify.

The mind blanks at the glare. Not in remorse
—The good not done, the love not given, time
Torn off unused—nor wretchedly because
An only life can take so long to climb
Clear of its wrong beginnings, and may never;
But at the total emptiness for ever,
The sure extinction that we travel to
And shall be lost in always. Not to be here,
Not to be anywhere,
20 And soon; nothing more terrible, nothing more true.

This is a special way of being afraid
No trick dispels. Religion used to try,
That vast moth-eaten musical brocade
Created to pretend we never die,
And specious stuff that says *No rational being
Can fear a thing it will not feel,* not seeing
That this is what we fear—no sight, no sound,
No touch or taste or smell, nothing to think with,

---

[1] A form of betting on English professional soccer games

Nothing to love or link with,
30 The anaesthetic from which none come round.

And so it stays just on the edge of vision,
A small unfocused blur, a standing chill
That slows each impulse down to indecision.
Most things may never happen: this one will,
And realisation of it rages out
In furnace-fear when we are caught without
People or drink. Courage is no good:
It means not scaring others. Being brave
Lets no one off the grave.
40 Death is no different whined at than withstood.

Slowly light strengthens, and the room takes shape.
It stands plain as a wardrobe, what we know,
Have always known, know that we can't escape,
Yet can't accept. One side will have to go.
Meanwhile telephones crouch, getting ready to ring
In locked-up offices, and all the uncaring
Intricate rented world begins to rouse.
The sky is white as clay, with no sun.
Work has to be done.
50 Postmen like doctors go from house to house.

D. H. Lawrence

David Herbert Lawrence (1885–1930) was the son of a coalminer, born in a working-class district of England. He wrote from an early age, and with the aid of scholarships wrested himself away from his background to become a writer. Best known as a novelist, especially for *The Rainbow, Women in Love,* and *Lady Chatterley's Lover,* he was a great essayist, literary critic, writer of travel books, letter-writer—and to some critics best of all as a poet. He died of tuberculosis, having accomplished an enormous volume of work, before he turned forty-five.

The Song of a Man Who Has Come Through   (1914)

Not I, not I, but the wind that blows through me!
A fine wind is blowing the new direction of Time.
If only I let it bear me, carry me, if only it carry me!
If only I am sensitive, subtle, oh, delicate, a winged gift!
If only, most lovely of all, I yield myself and am borrowed
By the fine, fine wind that takes its course through the chaos of the world
Like a fine, an exquisite chisel, a wedge-blade inserted;
If only I am keen and hard like the sheer tip of a wedge

Driven by invisible blows,
10 The rock will split, we shall come at the wonder, we shall find the Hesperides.[1]

Oh, for the wonder that bubbles into my soul,
I would be a good fountain, a good well-head,
Would blur no whisper, spoil no expression.

What is the knocking?
What is the knocking at the door in the night?
It is somebody wants to do us harm.

No, no, it is the three strange angels.
Admit them, admit them.

Bavarian Gentians   (1929)

Not every man has gentians in his house
In soft September, at slow, sad Michaelmas.

Bavarian gentians, tall and dark, but dark
darkening the daytime torch-like with the smoking blueness of Pluto's gloom,
ribbed hellish flowers erect, with their blaze of darkness spread blue,
blown flat into points, by the heavy white draught of the day.

Torch-flowers of the blue-smoking darkness, Pluto's dark-blue blaze
black lamps from the halls of Dis,[1] smoking dark blue
giving off darkness, blue darkness, upon Demeter's yellow-pale day
10 whom have you come for, here in the white-cast day?
Reach me a gentian, give me a torch!
let me guide myself with the blue, forked torch of a flower
down the darker and darker stairs, where blue is darkened on blueness
down the way Persephone goes, just now, in first-frosted September
to the sightless realm where darkness is married to dark
and Persephone herself is but a voice, as a bride,
a gloom invisible enfolded in the deeper dark
of the arms of Pluto as he ravishes her once again
and pierces her once more with his passion of the utter dark
20 among the splendour of black-blue torches, shedding fathomless darkness on the
    nuptials.

Give me a flower on a tall stem, and three dark flames,
for I will go to the wedding, and be wedding-guest
at the marriage of the living dark.

---

[1] In Greek mythology, sisters who protected a garden in which grew a tree bearing golden apples

[1] Dis, Dispater, the Roman name for a deity who was the same as the Greek Pluto, god of the underworld

Piano (1918)

Softly, in the dusk, a woman is singing to me;
Taking me back down the vista of years, till I see
A child sitting under the piano, in the boom of the tingling strings
And pressing the small, poised feet of a mother who smiles as she sings.

In spite of myself, the insidious mastery of song
Betrays me back, till the heart of me weeps to belong
To the old Sunday evenings at home, with winter outside
And hymns in the cozy parlour, the tinkling piano our guide.

So now it is vain for the singer to burst into clamour
10 With the great black piano appassionato. The glamour
Of childish days is upon me, my manhood is cast
Down in the flood of remembrance, I weep like a child for the past.

Li-Young Lee

Li-Young Lee (1957–   ) was born of Chinese parents in Indonesia, where
his father was a political prisoner. Escaping from Indonesia in 1959, the family
wandered among Hong Kong, Macau, and Japan and finally arrived in the
United States in 1964. With his wife and children, Li-Young Lee lives in
Chicago, where he works as a commercial artist. He has published two
collections of his poetry: *Rose* (1986) and *The City in Which I Love You* (1990).
See also pages 72–73.

From Blossoms (1986)

From blossoms comes
this brown paper bag of peaches
we bought from the boy
at the bend in the road where we turned toward
signs painted *Peaches.*

From laden boughs, from hands,
from sweet fellowship in the bins,
comes nectar at the roadside, succulent
peaches we devour, dusty skin and all,
10 comes the familiar dust of summer, dust we eat.

O, to take what we love inside,
to carry within us an orchard, to eat
not only the skin, but the shade,
not only the sugar, but the days, to hold
the fruit in our hands, adore it, then bite into
the round jubilance of peach.

There are days we live
as if death were nowhere

in the background; from joy
20 to joy to joy, from wing to wing,
from blossom to blossom to
impossible blossom, to sweet impossible blossom.

Between Seasons   (1986)

Today I bring you cold chrysanthemums,
white as absence, long-stemmed as my grief.
I stand before your grave, a few unfallen
leaves overhead, the sucking mud beneath.

What survives best are chrysanthemums
in a month which arrives austere as grief.
The hearty blossoms persevere, unfallen.
Suffering even snow, they flourish beneath.

You walked in mornings among chrysanthemums,
10 and bowed to them as if to hear their grief.
Your sleeves grew damp from brushing unfallen
dew. A drop lay by your eye, and one beneath.

Truest to your nature were chrysanthemums,
brilliant while first snows descended like grief.
You watched them from your bed, your heart unfallen,
steadfast through winter, and then you slipped beneath.

What is it they told you, once, the chrysanthemums?
It made you sigh, *Ah, Grief!*
Who savors you more than us, the unfallen,
20 *long after we've forgotten the fallen beneath?*

Denise Levertov

Denise Levertov (1923–   ), who was born in England, came to the United
States when she married an American soldier. Her early poems were collected in
England. After her move to the United States, she became affiliated with the
Black Mountain group of poets and her style changed considerably. She was a
leader in the antiwar movement during the Vietnam years. See also page 26.

October   (1961)

Certain branches cut
certain leaves fallen
the grapes
          cooked and put up
for winter

mountains without one
shrug of cloud

no feint of blurred
wind-willow leaf-light

10 their chins up
in blue of the eastern sky
their red cloaks
wrapped tight to the bone

Philip Levine

Philip Levine (1928–   ) grew up in Detroit and attended the Writers Workshop at Iowa. His work was formal at the beginning, restrained and delicate, and has acquired strength and vitality as he has grown older. His volumes include a *Selected Poems* (1984).

Salami   (1972)

Stomach of goat, crushed
sheep balls, soft full
pearls of pig eyes,
snout gristle, fresh earth,
worn iron of trotter, slate
of Zaragoza, dried cat heart,
cock claws. She grinds
them with one hand and
with the other fists
10 mountain thyme, basil,
paprika, and knobs of garlic.
And if a tooth of stink thistle
pulls blood from the round
blue marbled hand
all the better for
this ruby of Pamplona,
this bright jewel of Vich,
this stained crown
of Solsona, this
20 salami.
            The daughter
of mismatched eyes,
36 year old infant smelling
of milk. Mama, she cries, mama,
but mama is gone,
and the old stone cutter
must wipe the drool
from her jumper. His puffed fingers
unbutton and point her
30 to toilet. Ten, twelve hours
a day, as long as the winter sun
holds up he rebuilds
the unvisited church
of San Martin. Cheep cheep
of the hammer high above
the town, sparrow cries
lost in the wind or lost
in the mind. At dusk he leans
to the coal dull wooden Virgin
40 and asks for blessings on

the slow one and peace
on his grizzled head, asks
finally and each night
for the forbidden, for
the knowledge of every
mysterious stone, and
the words go out on
the overwhelming incense
of salami.
50   A single crow
passed high over the house,
I wakened out of nightmare.
The winds had changed,
the Tremontana was tearing
out of the Holy Mountains
to meet the sea winds
in my yard, burning and
scaring the young pines.
The single poplar wailed
60 in terror. With salt,
with guilt, with the need
to die, the vestments
of my life flared, I
was on fire, a stranger
staggering through my house
butting walls and falling
over furniture, looking
for a way out. In the last room
where moonlight slanted
70 through a broken shutter
I found my smallest son
asleep or dead, floating
on a bed of colorless light.
When I leaned closer
I could smell the small breaths
going and coming, and each
bore its prayer for me,
the true and earthy prayer
of salami.

Vachel Lindsay

Vachel Lindsay (1879–1931) is best known for the long poems—like "General William Booth Enters into Heaven" and "The Congo"—which he recited on platforms with energy, showmanship, and pizzaz. His readings were popular, his poetry successful for many years. Toward the end of his life, during the Great Depression, he found it difficult to make a living. He had perhaps published too much, too uncritically.

The Flower-Fed Buffaloes   (1926)

The flower-fed buffaloes of the spring
In the days of long ago,
Ranged where the locomotives sing
And the prairie flowers lie low:—
The tossing, blooming, perfumed
    grass
Is swept away by the wheat,
Wheels and wheels and wheels spin by
In the spring that still is sweet.

10 But the flower-fed buffaloes of the
    spring
Left us, long ago.
They gore no more, they bellow no
    more,
They trundle around the hills no more:—
With the Blackfeet, lying low,
With the Pawnees, lying low,
Lying low.

John Logan

John Logan (1923–1987) was born in Red Oak, Iowa, and went to school in the Midwest. In more recent years, he lived in California, in upstate New York, and in Hawaii, writing his poems and editing *Choice*.

The Picnic   (1960)

It is the picnic with Ruth in the spring.
Ruth was third on my list of seven girls
But the first two were gone (Betty) or else
Had someone (Ellen has accepted Doug).
Indian Gully the last day of school;
Girls make the lunches for the boys too.
I wrote a note to Ruth in algebra class
Day before the test. She smiled, and nodded.
We left the cars and walked through the young corn
10 The shoots green as paint and the leaves like tongues
Trembling. Beyond the fence where we stood
Some wild strawberry flowered by an elm tree
And Jack-in-the-pulpit was olive ripe.
A blackbird fled as I crossed, and showed
A spot of gold or red under its quick wing.
I held the wire for Ruth and watched the whip
Of her long, striped skirt as she followed.
Three freckles blossomed on her thin, white back

Underneath the loop where the blouse buttoned.
20 We went for our lunch away from the rest,
    Stretched in the new grass, our heads close
    Over unknown things wrapped up in wax papers.
    Ruth tried for the same, I forget what it was,
    And our hands were together. She laughed,
    And a breeze caught the edge of her little
    Collar and the edge of her brown, loose hair
    That touched my cheek. I turned my face in-
    to the gentle fall. I saw how sweet it smelled.
    She didn't move her head or take her hand.
30 I felt a soft caving in my stomach
    As at the top of the highest slide
    When I had been a child, but was not afraid,
    And did not know why my eyes moved with wet
    As I brushed her cheek with my lips and brushed
    Her lips with my own lips. She said to me
    Jack, Jack, different than I had ever heard,
    Because she wasn't calling me, I think,
    Or telling me. She used my name to
    Talk in another way I wanted to know.
40 She laughed again and then she took her hand;
    I gave her what we both had touched—can't
    Remember what it was, and we ate the lunch.
    Afterward we walked in the small, cool creek
    Our shoes off, her skirt hitched, and she smiling,
    My pants rolled, and then we climbed up the high
    Side of Indian Gully and looked
    Where we had been, our hands together again.
    It was then some bright thing came in my eyes,
    Starting at the back of them and flowing
50 Suddenly through my head and down my arms
    And stomach and my bare legs that seemed not
    To stop in feet, not to feel the red earth
    Of the Gully, as though we hung in a
    Touch of birds. There was a word in my throat
    With the feeling and I knew the first time
    What it meant and I said, it's beautiful.
    Yes, she said, and I felt the sound and word
    In my hand join the sound and word in hers
    As in one name said, or in one cupped hand.
60 We put back on our shoes and socks and we
    Sat in the grass awhile, crosslegged, under
    A blowing tree, not saying anything.
    And Ruth played with shells she found in the creek,
    As I watched. Her small wrist which was so sweet
    To me turned by her breast and the shells dropped
    Green, white, blue, easily into her lap,
    Passing light through themselves. She gave the pale
    Shells to me, and got up and touched her hips
    With her light hands, and we walked down slowly
70 To play the school games with the others.

Audre Lorde

Audre Lorde (1934–   ) was born in New York City. She has edited magazines, written books of poems, and received a grant from the National Endowment for the Arts. She now teaches at New York's Hunter College.

Hanging Fire   (1978)

I am fourteen
and my skin has betrayed me
the boy I cannot live without
still sucks his thumb
in secret
how come my knees are
always so ashy
what if I die
before morning
10 and momma's in the bedroom
with the door closed.

I have to learn how to dance
in time for the next party
my room is too small for me
suppose I die before graduation
they will sing sad melodies
but finally
tell the truth about me

There is nothing I want to do
20 and too much
that has to be done
and momma's in the bedroom
with the door closed.

Nobody even stops to think
about my side of it
I should have been on Math Team
my marks were better than his
why do I have to be
the one
30 wearing braces
I have nothing to wear tomorrow
will I live long enough
to grow up
and momma's in the bedroom
with the door closed.

Robert Lowell

Robert Lowell (1917–1977) was born in Massachusetts into the eminent literary and academic family of the Lowells, related to the poets Amy and James Russell Lowell and to a president of Harvard. After attending Harvard for several terms, he transferred to Kenyon College in Ohio, where he studied with John Crowe Ransom and made the acquaintance of Allen Tate and Randall Jarrell. His first book, *Land of Unlikeness,* published in a small edition in 1944, was followed by *Lord Weary's Castle* in 1947, which won the Pulitzer Prize. With *Life Studies* in 1959, his work took an abrupt turn away from the formal stanzas and couplets of his early poetry into the painful confessional verse that came to characterize him. In his last years, he wrote with a prolixity he had lacked as a young man and perhaps with less success. He published nine volumes in the last twelve years of his life, before he died of a heart attack at the age of sixty. See also pages 70–71.

After the Surprising Conversions   (1946)

September twenty-second, Sir: today
I answer. In the latter part of May,
Hard on our Lord's Ascension, it began

To be more sensible. A gentleman
Of more than common understanding, strict
In morals, pious in behavior, kicked
Against our goad. A man of some renown,
An useful, honored person in the town,
He came of melancholy parents; prone
10 To secret spells, for years they kept alone—
His uncle, I believe, was killed of it:
Good people, but of too much or little wit.
I preached one Sabbath on a text from Kings;
He showed concernment for his soul. Some things
In his experience were hopeful. He
Would sit and watch the wind knocking a tree
And praise this countryside our Lord has made.
Once when a poor man's heifer died, he laid
A shilling on the doorsill; though a thirst
20 For loving shook him like a snake, he durst
Not entertain much hope of his estate
In heaven. Once we saw him sitting late
Behind his attic window by a light
That guttered on his Bible; through that night
He meditated terror, and he seemed
Beyond advice or reason, for he dreamed
That he was called to trumpet Judgment Day
To Concord. In the latter part of May
He cut his throat. And though the coroner
30 Judged him delirious, soon a noisome stir
Palsied our village. At Jehovah's nod
Satan seemed more let loose amongst us: God
Abandoned us to Satan, and he pressed
Us hard, until we thought we could not rest
Till we had done with life. Content was gone.
All the good work was quashed. We were undone.
The breath of God had carried out a planned
And sensible withdrawal from this land;
The multitude, once unconcerned with doubt,
40 Once neither callous, curious nor devout,
Jumped at broad noon, as though some peddler groaned
At it in its familiar twang: "My friend,
Cut your own throat. Cut your own throat. Now! Now!"
September twenty-second, Sir, the bough
Cracks with the unpicked apples, and at dawn
The small-mouth bass breaks water, gorged with spawn.

Skunk Hour   (1957)
(For Elizabeth Bishop)

Nautilus Island's hermit
heiress still lives through winter in her Spartan cottage;
her sheep still graze above the sea.

Her son's a bishop. Her farmer
is first selectman in our village;
she's in her dotage.

Thirsting for
the hierarchic privacy
of Queen Victoria's century,
10 she buys up all
the eyesores facing her shore,
and lets them fall.

The season's ill—
we've lost our summer millionaire,
who seemed to leap from an L. L. Bean[1]
catalogue. His nine-knot yawl
was auctioned off to lobstermen.
A red fox stain covers Blue Hill.

And now our fairy
20 decorator brightens his shop for fall;
his fishnet's filled with orange cork,
orange, his cobbler's bench and awl;
there is no money in his work,
he'd rather marry.

One dark night,
my Tudor Ford climbed the hill's skull;
I watched for love-cars. Lights turned down,
they lay together, hull to hull,
where the graveyard shelves on the town. . . .
30 My mind's not right.

A car radio bleats,
"Love, O careless Love. . . ." I hear
my ill-spirit sob in each blood cell,
as if my hand were at its throat. . . .
I myself am hell;
nobody's here—

only skunks, that search
in the moonlight for a bite to eat.
They march on their soles up Main Street:
40 white stripes, moonstruck eyes' red fire
under the chalk-dry and spar spire
of the Trinitarian Church.

I stand on top
of our back steps and breathe the rich air—

---

[1] A Maine store that specializes in outdoor gear and country clothing; its label is popular
among affluent city people who summer in the country.

a mother skunk with her column of kittens swills the garbage pail.
She jabs her wedge-head in a cup
of sour cream, drops her ostrich tail,
and will not scare.

For the Union Dead   (1960)

"Relinquunt Omnia Servare Rem Publicam."[1]

The old South Boston Aquarium stands
in a Sahara of snow now. Its broken windows are boarded.
The bronze weathervane cod has lost half its scales.
The airy tanks are dry.

Once my nose crawled like a snail on the glass;
my hand tingled
to burst the bubbles
drifting from the noses of the cowed, compliant fish.

My hand draws back. I often sigh still
10 for the dark downward and vegetating kingdom
of the fish and reptile. One morning last March,
I pressed against the new barbed and galvanized

fence on the Boston Common. Behind their cage,
yellow dinosaur steamshovels were grunting
as they cropped up tons of mush and grass
to gouge their underworld garage.

Parking spaces luxuriate like civic
sandpiles in the heart of Boston.
A girdle of orange, Puritan-pumpkin colored girders
20 braces the tingling Statehouse,

shaking over the excavations, as it faces Colonel Shaw
and his bell-cheeked Negro infantry
on St. Gaudens'[2] shaking Civil War relief,
propped by a plank splint against the garage's earthquake.

Two months after marching through Boston,
half the regiment was dead;
at the dedication,
William James[3] could almost hear the bronze Negroes breathe.

Their monument sticks like a fishbone
30 in the city's throat.

---

[1] "They sacrifice everything to serve the republic."   [2] Sculptor Augustus Saint-Gaudens
(1848–1907) made a bronze relief of Colonel Robert Shaw (1837–1863), who led a regiment
during the Civil War.   [3] William James (1842–1910), American psychologist and philosopher,
professor at Harvard

Its Colonel is as lean
as a compass-needle.

He has an angry wrenlike vigilance,
a greyhound's gentle tautness;
he seems to wince at pleasure,
and suffocate for privacy.

He is out of bounds now. He rejoices in man's lovely,
peculiar power to choose life and die—
when he leads his black soldiers to death,
40 he cannot bend his back.

On a thousand small town New England greens,
the old white churches hold their air
of sparse, sincere rebellion; frayed flags
quilt the graveyards of the Grand Army of the Republic.

The stone statues of the abstract Union Soldier
grow slimmer and younger each year—
wasp-waisted, they doze over muskets
and muse through their sideburns . . .

Shaw's father wanted no monument
50 except the ditch,
where his son's body was thrown
and lost with his "niggers."

The ditch is nearer.
There are no statues for the last war here;
on Boylston Street, a commercial photograph
shows Hiroshima boiling

over a Mosler Safe, the "Rock of Ages"
that survived the blast. Space is nearer.
When I crouch to my television set,
60 the drained faces of Negro school-children rise like balloons.

Colonel Shaw
is riding on his bubble,
he waits
for the blessèd break.

The Aquarium is gone. Everywhere,
giant finned cars nose forward like fish;
a savage servility
slides by on grease.

Derek Mahon

Derek Mahon (1941–   ) was born in Belfast, a northerner like many important Irish poets of our time. He has published many books of poems, of which *Poems 1962–1978* is available in the United States from the Oxford University Press, and *They Hunt by Night* from the Wake Forest University Press. He has lived much of his adult life in London, and has spent time in the United States.

The Chinese Restaurant in Portrush   (1979)

Before the holidaymakers comes the spring
Softening the sharp air of the coast
In time for the first 'invasion'.
Today the place is as it might have been,
Gentle and almost hospitable. A girl
Strides past the Northern Counties Hotel,
Light-footed, swinging a book-bag,
And the doors that were shut all winter
Against the north wind and the sea-mist
10 Lie open to the street, where one
By one the gulls go window-shopping
And an old wolfhound dozes in the sun.

While I sit with my paper and prawn chow-mein
Under a framed photograph of Hong Kong
The proprietor of the Chinese restaurant
Stands at the door as if the world were young
Watching the first yacht hoist a sail—
An ideogram on sea-cloud—and the light
Of heaven upon the mountains of Donegal;
20 And whistles a little tune, dreaming of home.

Christopher Marlowe

Christopher Marlowe (1564–1593) born the same year as Shakespeare, was a great playwright who helped establish English poetry upon the stage. Two of his best plays were *Tragedy of Doctor Faustus* and *Edward II*. He was murdered in a tavern at Deptford by a man named Ingram Frisar.

The Passionate Shepherd to His Love   (1600)

Come live with me and be my love,
And we will all the pleasures prove
That hills and valleys, dale and field,
And all the craggy mountains yield!

There will we sit upon the rocks
And see the shepherds feed their flocks,
By shallow rivers, to whose falls
Melodious birds sing madrigals.

10 There will I make thee beds of roses
With a thousand fragrant posies;
A cap of flowers, and a kirtle
Embroider'd all with leaves of myrtle;

A gown made of the finest wool
Which from our pretty lambs we pull;
Fair lined slippers for the cold,
With buckles of the purest gold;

A belt of straw and ivy buds,
With coral clasps and amber studs:

20 And if these pleasures may thee move,
Come live with me and be my love!

Thy silver dishes, for thy meat
As precious as the gods do eat,
Shall on an ivory table be
Prepared each day for thee and me.

The shepherd swains shall dance and
            sing
For thy delight each May morning.
If these delights thy mind may move,
30 Then live with me and be my love!

Sir Walter Ralegh (see also page 310) wrote an answer for the Nymph to address to the Shepherd:

The Nymph's Reply to the Shepherd   (1600)

If all the world and love were young,
And truth in every shepherd's tongue,
These pretty pleasures might me move
To live with thee and be thy love.

Time drives the flocks from field to fold
When rivers rage and rocks grow cold,
And Philomel° becometh dumb;   the nightingale
The rest complains of care to come.

The flowers do fade, and wanton fields
10 To wayward winter reckoning yields;
A honey tongue, a heart of gall,
Is fancy's spring, but sorrow's fall.

Thy gowns, thy shoes, thy beds of roses,
Thy cap, thy kirtle,° and thy posies   underdress
Soon break, soon wither, soon forgotten—
In folly ripe, in reason rotten.

Thy belt of straw and ivy buds,
Thy coral clasps and amber studs,
All these in me no means can move
20 To come to thee and be thy love.

But could youth last and love still breed,
Had joys no date nor age no need,
Then these delights my mind might move
To live with thee and be thy love.

Andrew Marvell

Andrew Marvell (1621–1678) was a poet in youth but, as he grew older, became increasingly more political than poetical. A defender of Cromwell and Milton, after the restoration of the monarchy he joined Parliament and represented his birthplace, Hull.

The Garden   (1652)

How vainly men themselves amaze
To win the palm, the oak, or bays;[1]
And their incessant labours see
Crowned from some single herb or tree,
Whose short and narrow-vergèd shade
Does prudently their toils upbraid;
While all flowers and all trees do close
To weave the garlands of repose.

10 Fair Quiet, have I found thee here,
And Innocence, thy sister dear!
Mistaken long, I sought you then
In busy companies of men.
Your sacred plants, if here below,
Only among the plants will grow:
Society is all but rude
To this delicious solitude.

No white nor red was ever seen
So amorous as this lovely green.
Fond lovers, cruel as their flame,
20 Cut in these trees their mistress' name:
Little, alas, they know or heed,
How far these beauties hers exceed!
Fair trees! wheres'e'er your barks I
    wound,
No name shall but your own be found.

When we have run our passion's
    heat,
Love hither makes his best retreat.
The gods, that mortal beauty chase,
30 Still in a tree did end their race.
Apollo hunted Daphne so,
Only that she might laurel grow;
And Pan did after Syrinx speed,
Not as a nymph, but for a reed.

What wondrous life is this I lead!
Ripe apples drop about my head;
The luscious clusters of the vine
Upon my mouth do crush their wine;
The nectarine, and curious peach,
40 Into my hands themselves do reach;
Stumbling on melons, as I pass,
Ensnared with flowers, I fall on grass.

Meanwhile the mind, from pleasure
    less,
Withdraws into its happiness:
The mind, that ocean where each kind
Does straight its own resemblance find;
Yet it creates, transcending these,
Far other worlds, and other seas;
50 Annihilating all that's made
To a green thought in a green shade.

Here at the fountain's sliding foot,
Or at some fruit-tree's mossy root,
Casting the body's vest aside,
My soul into the boughs does glide:
There like a bird it sits and sings,
Then whets, and combs its silver wings;
And, till prepared for longer flight,
Waves in its plumes the various light.

60 Such was that happy garden-state,
While man there walked without a
    mate:
After a place so pure and sweet,
What other help could yet be meet?
But 'twas beyond a mortal's share
To wander solitary there:
Two Paradises 'twere in one,
To live in Paradise alone.

[1] Laurel wreaths, symbolizing achievement in sport, politics, and poetry

How well the skilful gardener drew
70 Of flowers and herbs this dial new!
Where, from above, the milder sun
Does through a fragrant zodiac run;
And, as it works, the industrious bee

Computes its time as well as we.
How could such sweet and wholesome hours
Be reckoned but with herbs and flowers?

To His Coy Mistress   (1652)

Had we but world enough, and time,
This coyness, Lady, were no crime.
We would sit down, and think which way
To walk, and pass our long love's day.
Thou by the Indian Ganges' side
Shouldst rubies find; I by the tide
Of Humber would complain. I would
Love you ten years before the Flood;
And you should, if you please, refuse
10 Till the conversion of the Jews.
My vegetable° love should grow   vegetative
Vaster than empires, and more slow.
An hundred years should go to praise
Thine eyes, and on thy forehead gaze;
Two hundred to adore each breast;
But thirty thousand to the rest:
An age, at least, to every part,
And the last age should show your heart.
For, Lady, you deserve this state,
20 Nor would I love at lower rate.
      But, at my back, I always hear
Time's wingèd chariot hurrying near:
And yonder, all before us lie
Deserts of vast eternity.
Thy beauty shall no more be found;
Nor, in thy marble vault, shall sound
My echoing song. Then worms shall try
That long preserved virginity:
And your quaint honour turn to dust;
30 And into ashes all my lust.
The grave's a fine and private place,
But none, I think, do there embrace.
      Now, therefore, while the youthful hue
Sits on thy skin like morning dew,
And while thy willing soul transpires
At every pore with instant fires,
Now let us sport us while we may;
And now, like amorous birds of prey,
Rather at once our time devour,
40 Than languish in his slow-chapt° power.   slow-jawed
Let us roll all our strength, and all
Our sweetness, up into one ball;

And tear our pleasures, with rough strife,
Thorough° the iron gates of life.   through
    Thus, though we cannot make our sun
Stand still, yet we will make him run.

Wesley McNair

Wesley McNair (1941–   ) was born in New Hampshire and has written most of
his poems out of his sense of character connected to region. He attended the
University of New Hampshire in Keene, and has held a Fulbright Lectureship in
Chile, two National Endowment grants, and a Guggenheim fellowship. His first
book of poems, *The Faces of Americans in 1953* (1984) won the Devins Award;
The Town of No followed in 1989.

Mina Bell's Cows   (1983)

O where are Mina Bell's cows who gave no milk
and grazed on her dead husband's farm?
Each day she walked with them into the field,
loving their swayback dreaminess more
than the quickness of any dog or chicken.
Each night she brought them grain in the dim barn,
holding their breath in her hands.
O when the lightning struck Daisy and Bets,
her son dug such great holes in the yard
10 she could not bear to watch him.
And when the baby, April, growing old
and wayward, fell down the hay chute,
Mina just sat in the kitchen, crying "Ape,
Ape," as if she called all three cows,
her walleyed girls who never would come home.

Where I Live   (1983)

You will come into an antique town
whose houses move apart
as if you'd interrupted
a private discussion. This is the place
you must pass through to get there.
Imagining lives tucked in
like china plates, continue driving.
Beyond the landscaped streets,
beyond the last colonial gas station
10 and unsolved by zoning,
is a road. It will take you
to old farmhouses and trees
with car-tire swings.
Signs will announce hairdressing
and nightcrawlers.
The timothy grass will run beside you
all the way to where I live.

Archibald MacLeish

Archibald MacLeish (1892–1982) attended Yale, went to law school at Harvard, practiced law briefly, and then moved to France as an American expatriate in the 1920s. When the Great Depression hit the United States he returned to this country, where he became increasingly political. He worked for *Fortune,* wrote on political subjects, and eventually allied himself with President Franklin D. Roosevelt. He was Librarian of Congress, and, toward the end of Roosevelt's life, became an Assistant Secretary of State. When Roosevelt died, MacLeish left government. He taught at Harvard for some years, beginning in 1949, and returned to the writing of poetry.

You, Andrew Marvell   (1928)

And here face down beneath the sun
And here upon earth's noonward height
To feel the always coming on
The always rising of the night:

To feel creep up the curving east
The earthy chill of dusk and slow
Upon those under lands the vast
And ever climbing shadow grow

And strange at Ecbatan the trees
10 Take leaf by leaf the evening strange
The flooding dark about their knees
The mountains over Persia change

And now at Kermanshah the gate
Dark empty and the withered grass
And through the twilight now the late
Few travelers in the westward pass

And Baghdad darken and the bridge
Across the silent river gone

And through Arabia the edge
20 Of evening widen and steal on

And deepen on Palmyra's street
The wheel rut in the ruined stone
And Lebanon fade out and Crete
High through the clouds and overblown

And over Sicily the air
Still flashing with the landward gulls
And loom and slowly disappear
The sails above the shadowy hulls

And Spain go under and the shore
30 Of Africa the gilded sand
And evening vanish and no more
The low pale light across that land

Nor now the long light on the sea:

And here face downward in the sun
To feel how swift how secretly
The shadow of the night comes on . . .

Louis MacNeice

Louis MacNeice (1907–1963) was an English poet associated during the 1930s with W. H. Auden, who collaborated with him on *Letters from Iceland.* Born in Ireland, he lived most of his life in London, where he was a producer for the BBC.

The Sunlight on the Garden   (1937)

The sunlight on the garden
Hardens and grows cold,
We cannot cage the minute
Within its nets of gold,
When all is told
We cannot beg for pardon.

Our freedom as free lances
Advances towards its end;
The earth compels, upon it
10 Sonnets and birds descend;
And soon, my friend,
We shall have no time for dances.

The sky was good for flying
Defying the church bells
And every evil iron
Siren and what it tells:
The earth compels,
We are dying, Egypt, dying

And not expecting pardon,
20 Hardened in heart anew,
But glad to have sat under
Thunder and rain with you,
And grateful too
For sunlight on the garden.

James Merrill

James Merrill (1926–   ) attended Amherst and now alternates between a house in Greece and a house in Connecticut. He has published two novels; his books of poems have won the National Book Award and other prizes.

After Greece   (1962)

Light into the olive entered
And was oil. Rain made the huge pale stones
Shine from within. The moon turned his hair white
Who next stepped from between the columns,
Shielding his eyes. All through
The countryside were old ideas
Found lying open to the elements.
Of the gods' houses only
A minor premise here and there
10 Would be balancing the heaven of fixed stars
Upon a Doric capital. The rest
Lay spilled, their fluted drums half sunk in cyclamen
Or deep in water's biting clarity
Which just barely upheld me
The next week, when I sailed for home.

But where is home—these walls?
These limbs? The very spaniel underfoot
Races in sleep, toward what?
It is autumn. I did not invite
20 Those guests, windy and brittle, who drink my liquor.
Returning from a walk I find
The bottles filled with spleen, my room itself
Smeared by reflection on to the far hemlocks.
I some days flee in dream
Back to the exposed porch of the maidens
Only to find my great-great-grandmothers
Erect there, peering
Into a globe of red Bohemian glass.
As it swells and sinks, I call up
30 Graces, Furies, Fates, removed
To my country's warm, lit halls, with rivets forced
Through drapery, and nothing left to bear.
They seem anxious to know
What holds up heaven nowadays.
I start explaining how in that vast fire
Were other irons—well, Art, Public Spirit,
Ignorance, Economics, Love of Self,
Hatred of Self, a hundred more,
Each burning to be felt, each dedicated
40 To sparing us the worst; how I distrust them
As I should have done those ladies; how I want
Essentials: salt, wine, olive, the light, the scream—
No! I have scarcely named you,
And look, in a flash you stand full-grown before me,
Row upon row, Essentials,
Dressed like your sister caryatids
Or tombstone angels jealous of their dead,
With undulant coiffures, lips weathered, cracked by grime,
And faultless eyes gone blank beneath the immense
50 Zinc and gunmetal northern sky . . .
Stay then. Perhaps the system
Calls for spirits. This first glass I down
To the last time
I ate and drank in that old world. May I
Also survive its meanings, and my own.

John Milton

John Milton (1608–1674) was a precocious poet. He prepared himself assiduously for his poetic vocation, and in 1637 wrote the remarkable elegy "Lycidas" for a young man he had known at Cambridge. During the next twenty years he wrote a few sonnets—excellent poems—but largely he substituted politics and political action for poetry, working as Cromwell's Latin secretary. His first marriage was tempestuous, and he wrote prose works advocating divorce, which earned him considerable denunciation. He became blind while he was still Cromwell's secretary, and was assisted by several helpers, notably Andrew Marvell. After Cromwell's death and the restoration of the monarchy, he was imprisoned, released, and lived in poverty. He had begun his great work, the religious epic *Paradise Lost,* while he was chiefly engaged in politics, but he completed it in blindness and poverty. Afterward he wrote "Paradise Regained" and "Samson Agonistes." In prose, his "Areopagitica" (on freedom of the press) is his most celebrated work. See also page 93.

On His Blindness   (1655)

When I consider how my light is spent
Ere half my days in this dark world and wide,
And that one talent which is death to hide
Lodged with me useless, though my soul more bent
To serve therewith my Maker, and present
My true account, lest He returning chide,
"Doth God exact day-labor, light denied?"
I fondly ask. But Patience, to prevent
That murmur, soon replies, "God doth not need
10 Either man's work or his own gifts. Who best
Bear His mild yoke, they serve Him best. His state
Is kingly: thousands at His bidding speed,
And post o'er land and ocean without rest;
They also serve who only stand and wait."

Marianne Moore

Marianne Moore (1887–1972) was born in St. Louis, graduated from Bryn Mawr, and taught school in Pennsylvania, but lived most of her life in Brooklyn. As editor of *The Dial* from 1925 to 1929 she published many of the best modern poets. Her own poems are original and even eccentric. Her intricate descriptions are scrupulous in detail, shaped into prosaic lines that achieve a singular music. See also pages 19–20.

A Grave   (1935)

Man looking into the sea,
taking the view from those who have as much right to it as you have to it yourself,
it is human nature to stand in the middle of a thing,

but you cannot stand in the middle of this;
the sea has nothing to give but a well excavated grave.
The firs stand in a procession, each with an emerald turkey foot at the top,
reserved as their contours, saying nothing;
repression, however, is not the most obvious characteristic of the sea;
the sea is a collector, quick to return a rapacious look.
10 There are others besides you who have worn that look—
whose expression is no longer a protest; the fish no longer investigate them
for their bones have not lasted:
men lower nets, unconscious of the fact that they are desecrating a grave,
and row quickly away—the blades of the oars
moving together like the feet of water spiders as if there were no such thing as
    death.
The wrinkles progress among themselves in a phalanx—beautiful under networks of
    foam,
and fade breathlessly while the sea rustles in and out of the seaweed;
20 the birds swim through the air at top speed, emitting catcalls as heretofore—
the tortoise shell scourges about the feet of the cliffs, in motion beneath them;
and the ocean, under the pulsation of lighthouses and noise of bell buoys,
advances as usual, looking as if it were not that ocean in which dropped things are
    bound to sink—
in which if they turn and twist, it is neither with volition nor consciousness.

Thylias Moss

Thylias Moss (1954–   ) has published three books of poems including *Hosiery Seams on a Bowlegged Woman* (1983), *Pyramid of Bone* (1989), and *At Redbone's* (1990). She graduated from Oberlin College and did graduate work at the University of New Hampshire. She teaches at Phillips Academy in Andover, Massachusetts. See also page 41.

Botanical Fanaticism   (1990)

My ancestors weren't hippies, cotton
precluded fascination with flowers.
I don't remember communes, I remember
ghettos. The riots were real, not
products of hallucinogens. Free love had
been at Redbones since black unemployment
and credit saturation.

The white women my mother cleaned
for didn't notice she had changed. I guess
10 it was a small event, a resurrected African
jumping out the gap in her front teeth. I
guess it looked like a cockroach; that's
what she was supposed to have, not dignity.

My mother just couldn't get excited
about the Beatles, those mops she swilled
in ammonia everyday on their heads. Besides,
she didn't work like a dog but like a woman;
they aren't the same. The hair was growing long
for the same reasons Pinocchio's nose did.

20 I can think only of a lesbian draping
crepe paper chains over my head to make a
black Rapunzel possible; that's how a white
woman tried to lift my burdens. At the time
I didn't reject her for being lesbian or
white but for both burdens. That was when
I didn't want Ivory soap to be what
cleaned me, made me presentable to society.
All the suds I'd seen were white, they still
are but who cares? I'm more interested in
30 how soap dwindles in my hand, under the faucet.

I'm old enough to remember blocks
of ice, old enough or poor enough.
I remember chipping away at it, broken
glass all over the floor. Later in the
riots, the broken glass of looting tattled
how desperate people were to keep cool.

There are roses now in my mother's yard.
Sometimes she cuts them, sets them in Pepsi
bottles throughout her rooms. She is,
40 I admit, being sentimental. Looting her
heart. My father who planted them is gone.
That mop in the corner
is his cane growing roots.

Sunrise Comes to Second Avenue   (1990)

Daylight announces
the start of day six hours old.

We all have thankless
jobs to do. Consider

the devotion of fishes singing
hymns without voices.

The clock's hands searching
for the lost face, a place

for the Eucharist. The man
10 bedded down on the roadway,

the asphalt pope out of bread,
breath and blessings.

The streetcleaner
sweeping up confessions.

Edwin Muir

Edwin Muir (1887–1959) was born in the Orkneys, off the coast of Scotland. After his father was evicted from an island farm, young Muir grew up in the slums of Glasgow. His poetry built upon the contrast between the pastoral and the industrial. He and his wife Willa lived by their wits most of their lives, and are Kafka's translators. Muir is author of an excellent *Autobiography* as well as the neglected *Collected Poems*.

The Horses   (1952)

Barely a twelvemonth after
The seven days war that put the world to sleep,
Late in the evening the strange horses came.
By then we had made our covenant with silence,
But in the first few days it was so still
We listened to our breathing and were afraid.
On the second day
The radios failed; we turned the knobs; no answer.
On the third day a warship passed us, heading north,
10 Dead bodies piled on the deck. On the sixth day
A plane plunged over us into the sea. Thereafter
Nothing. The radios dumb;
And still they stand in corners of our kitchens,
And stand, perhaps, turned on, in a million rooms
All over the world. But now if they should speak,
If on a sudden they should speak again,
If on the stroke of noon a voice should speak,
We would not listen, we would not let it bring
That old bad world that swallowed its children quick
20 At one great gulp. We would not have it again.
Sometimes we think of the nations lying asleep,
Curled blindly in impenetrable sorrow,
And then the thought confounds us with its strangeness.
The tractors lie about our fields; at evening
They look like dank sea-monsters couched and waiting.
We leave them where they are and let them rust:
'They'll moulder away and be like other loam.'
We make our oxen drag our rusty ploughs,
Long laid aside. We have gone back
30 Far past our fathers' land.

                        And then, that evening
Late in the summer the strange horses came.
We heard a distant tapping on the road,
A deepening drumming; it stopped, went on again
And at the corner changed to hollow thunder.
We saw the heads
Like a wild wave charging and were afraid.
We had sold our horses in our fathers' time
To buy new tractors. Now they were strange to us
40 As fabulous steeds set on an ancient shield
Or illustrations in a book of knights.
We did not dare go near them. Yet they waited,
Stubborn and shy, as if they had been sent
By an old command to find our whereabouts
And that long-lost archaic companionship.
In the first moment we had never a thought
That they were creatures to be owned and used.
Among them were some half-a-dozen colts
Dropped in some wilderness of the broken world,
50 Yet new as if they had come from their own Eden.
Since then they have pulled our ploughs and borne our loads
But that free servitude still can pierce our hearts.
Our life is changed; their coming our beginning.

[handwritten annotations: Allusion to· fable / ·Genesis / ·Revelations / Eden natural liberation / · Symbols of wildness/integrity/nonviolence/life / " " ownership/technology/war/death / the Fall]

David Mura

David Mura (1952–   ) is a *sansei* (third generation Japanese-American) who
lives in St. Paul, Minnesota, where he is married to a pediatrician and teaches at
The Loft: A Place for Literature. He has published a book of poems, *After We Lost
Our Way,* and a long essay called *A Male Grief: Notes on Pornography and
Addiction.*

Grandfather and Grandmother in Love   (1989)

Now I will ask for one true word beyond
betrayal, that creaks and buoys like the bedsprings
used by the bodies that begot the bodies that begot me.
Now I will think of the moon bluing the white
sheets soaked in sweat, that heard him whisper
haiku of clover, azalea, the cry of the cuckoo;
complaints of moles and beetles,
blight and bad debts, as the *biwa*'s[1] spirit
bubbled up between them, its song quavering.
10 Now I take this word, crack it, like a seed
between the teeth, spit it out in the world

---

[1] *Biwa:* a Japanese stringed instrument.

to root in the loam of his greenhouse roses;
let it leave the sweet taste of *teriyaki,*
a grain of her rice lodged in my molars;
in my nostrils, a faint hot breath of *sake.*

Now as *otoo-san*[2], *okaa-san*[3], drift towards
each other, there reverberates the *ran*[4]
of lovers, and the ship of the past bursts
into that other world; and she, still teasing,
20 pushes him away, swats his hand, a pesky,
tickling fly, then turns to his face that
cries out laughing, as he hauls her in,
trawling the currents, gathering
a sea that seems endless, depths a boy dreams of,
where flounder, dolphin, fluorescent fins, fish
with wings spill before him glittering scales,
and letting slip the net, he dives under,
and night washes over them, slipping from
sight, just the soft shush of waves, drifting ground
30 swells, echoing the knocking tide of morning.

Thomas Nashe

Thomas Nashe (1567–1601) was a literary jack-of-all-trades—pamphleteer, playwright, poet, and author of the first adventure novel in English. Ever contentious, he wrote a comedy called "The Isle of Dogs" which attacked the government so thoroughly that Nashe spent some months in jail. This poem is said to have been written during the plague that afflicted London from 1592 to 1594.

Adieu! Farewell Earth's Bliss!   (1592)

Adieu! farewell earth's bliss!
This world uncertain is:
Fond are life's lustful joys,
Death proves them all but toys,
None from his darts can fly:
I am sick, I must die.
    Lord, have mercy on us!

Rich men, trust not in wealth!
Gold cannot buy you health;
10 Physic himself must fade,
All things to end are made,
The plague full swift goes by:
I am sick, I must die.
    Lord, have mercy on us!

Beauty is but a flower
Which wrinkles will devour;
Brightness falls from the air,
Queens have died young and fair,
Dust hath closed Helen's eye:
20 I am sick, I must die.
    Lord, have mercy on us!

Strength stoops unto the grave:
Worms feed on Hector brave;
Swords may not fight with fate;
Earth still holds ope her gate;
'Come! come!' the bells do cry.
I am sick, I must die.
    Lord, have mercy on us!

---

[2] *Otoo-san:* father. [3] *Okaa-san:* mother (Japanese couples call each other Father and Mother). [4] *Ran:* chaos.

Wit with his wantonness
30 Tasteth death's bitterness;
Hell's executioner
Hath no ears for to hear
What vain art can reply:
I am sick, I must die.
    Lord, have mercy on us!

Haste, therefore, each degree,
To welcome destiny:
Heaven is our heritage,
Earth but a player's stage,
40 Mount we unto the sky:
I am sick, I must die.
    Lord, have mercy on us!

Howard Nemerov

Howard Nemerov (1920–1991) attended Harvard before serving in the Royal Canadian Air Force and the United States Air Force in World War II. He has taught at various American universities, and is currently at Washington University in St. Louis. Over the years, he has written steadily, with considerable skill, without drawing great attention. His *Collected Poems* appeared in 1977.

Brainstorm   (1958)

The house was shaken by a rising wind
That rattled window and door. He sat alone
In an upstairs room and heard these things: a blind
Ran up with a bang, a door slammed, a groan
Came from some hidden joist, and a leaky tap,
At any silence of the wind walked like
A blind man through the house. Timber and sap
Revolt, he thought, from washer, baulk and spike.
Bent to his book, continued unafraid
10 Until the crows came down from their loud flight
To walk along the rooftree overhead.
Their horny feet, so near but out of sight,
Scratched on the slate; when they were blown away
He heard their wings beat till they came again,
While the wind rose, and the house seemed to sway,
And window panes began to blind with rain.
The house was talking, not to him, he thought,
But to the crows; the crows were talking back
In their black voices. The secret might be out:
20 Houses are only trees stretched on the rack.
And once the crows knew, all nature would know.
Fur, leaf and feather would invade the form,
Nail rust with rain and shingle warp with snow,
Vine tear the wall, till any straw-borne storm
Could rip both roof and rooftree off and show
Naked to nature what they had kept warm.

He came to feel the crows walk on his head
As if he were the house, their crooked feet
Scratched, through the hair, his scalp. He might be dead

30 It seemed, and all the noises underneath
Be but the cooling of the sinews, veins,
Juices, and sodden sacks suddenly let go;
While in his ruins of wiring, his burst mains,
The rainy wind had been set free to blow
Until the green uprising and mob rule
That ran the world had taken over him,
Split him like seed, and set him in the school
Where any crutch can learn to be a limb.

Inside his head he heard the stormy crows.

Frank O'Hara

Frank O'Hara (1926–1966) was a poet of vast influence; the naturalness of
O'Hara's language has earned him many followers. He attended Harvard and
then worked at the Museum of Modern Art in New York, where he held an
important position at the time of his accidental death in 1966. His *Collected
Poems* came out in 1971.

The Day Lady Died   (1964)

It is 12:20 in New York a Friday
three days after Bastille day, yes
it is 1959 and I go get a shoeshine
because I will get off the 4:19 in Easthampton
at 7:15 and then go straight to dinner
and I don't know the people who will feed me

I walk up the muggy street beginning to sun
and have a hamburger and a malted and buy
an ugly NEW WORLD WRITING to see what the poets
10 in Ghana are doing these days
                          I go on to the bank
and Miss Stillwagon (first name Linda I once heard)
doesn't even look up my balance for once in her life
and in the GOLDEN GRIFFIN I get a little Verlaine
for Patsy with drawings by Bonnard although I do
think of Hesiod, trans. Richmond Lattimore or
Brendan Behan's new play or *Le Balcon* or *Les Nègres*

of Genet, but I don't, I stick with Verlaine
after practically going to sleep with quandariness

20 and for Mike I just stroll into the PARK LANE
Liquor Store and ask for a bottle of Strega and
then I go back where I came from to 6th Avenue

and the tobacconist in the Ziegfeld Theatre and
casually ask for a carton of Gauloises and a carton
of Picayunes, and a NEW YORK POST with her face on it

and I am sweating a lot by now and thinking of
leaning on the john door in the 5 SPOT
while she whispered a song along the keyboard
to Mal Waldron and everyone and I stopped breathing

Sharon Olds

Sharon Olds (1942–   ), born in San Francisco, went to Stanford and Columbia,
and now teaches at New York University. Her books include *Satan Says* (1980),
The Dead and the Living (1984), and *The Gold Cell* (1987).

Sex without Love   (1984)

How do they do it, the ones who make love
without love? Beautiful as dancers,
gliding over each other like ice skaters
over the ice, fingers hooked
inside each other's bodies, faces
red as steak, wine, wet as the
children at birth whose mothers are going to
give them away. How do they come to the
come to the   come to the   God   come to the
10 still waters, and not love
the one who came there with them, light
rising slowly as steam off their joined
skin? These are the true religious,
the purists, the pros, the ones who will not
accept a false Messiah, love the
priest instead of the God. They do not
mistake the lover for their own pleasure,
they are like great runners: they know they are alone
with the road surface, the cold, the wind,
20 the fit of their shoes, their over-all cardio-
vascular health—just factors, like the partner
in the bed, and not the truth, which is the
single body alone in the universe
against its own best time.

Charles Olson

Charles Olson (1910–1970) was highly influential as a poet and literary thinker. His first publication was critical, a book about *Moby Dick* called *Call Me Ishmael*. He wrote an essay on "Projective Verse" which may be regarded as the manifesto of the Black Mountain School of American poets, loosely derived from Pound and from Zukofsky's Objectivism. His long series of *Maximus Poems* is his major poetic work.

Maximus, to Gloucester, Sunday, July 19   (1960)

and they stopped before that bad sculpture of a fisherman

—"as if one were to talk to a man's house,
knowing not what gods or heroes are"—

not knowing what a fisherman is
instead of going straight to the Bridge
and doing no more than—saying no more than—
in the Charybdises of the
Cut waters the flowers tear off
the wreathes

10 the flowers
turn
the character of the sea   The sea jumps
the fate of the flower   The drowned men are undrowned
in the eddies

of the eyes
of the flowers
opening
the sea's eyes

The disaster
20 is undone
What was received as alien
—the flower
on the water, that a man drowns
that he dies in water as he dies on earth, the impossible
that this gross fact can return to us
in this upset
on a summer day
of a particular tide

that the sensation is true,
30 that the transformations of fire are, first of all, sea—
"as gold for wares wares for gold"

Let them be told who stopped first
by a bronze idol

A fisherman is not a successful man,
he is not a famous man he is not a man
of power, these are the damned by God

whose surface bubbles
with these gimlets
which screw-in like

40 potholes, caustic
caked earth of painted
pools, Yellowstone

Park of holes
is death the diseased
presence on us, the spilling lesion

of the brilliance
it is to be alive: to walk onto it,
as Jim Bridger the first into it,

it is more true a scabious
50 field than it is a pretty
meadow

When a man's coffin is the sea
the whole of creation shall come to his funeral,

it turns out; the globe
is below, all lapis

and its blue surface golded
by what happened

this afternoon: there are eyes
in this water

60 the flowers
from the shore,

awakened
the sea

Men are so sure they know very many things,
they don't even know night and day are one

A fisherman works without reference to
that difference. It is possible he also

by lying there when he does lie, jowl
to the sea, has another advantage: it is said,

70 'You rectify what can be rectified,' and when a man's heart
cannot see this, the door of his divine intelligence is shut

        let you who paraded to the Cut today
        to hold memorial services to all fishermen
        who have been lost at sea in a year
        when for the first time not one life was lost

            radar sonar radio telephone good engines
            bed-check seaplanes goodness over and under us

        no difference
        when men come back

Gregory Orr

Gregory Orr (1947–   ) published two books of poems, *Burning the Empty Nests* and *Gathering the Bones Together,* while still in his twenties. He was born in upstate New York and attended Antioch College and Columbia University. He teaches at the University of Virginia. See also pages 28 and 34.

The Sweater   (1975)

I will lose you. It is written
into this poem the way
the fisherman's wife knits
his death into the sweater.

Wilfred Owen

Wilfred Owen (1893–1918) was a poet of the First World War. Like most young Englishmen in 1914, he had cherished a romantic notion of battle. He lived long enough—the war killed him, just a few days before the armistice—to write bitter and antiromantic poems of real modern war.

Dulce et Decorum Est[1]   (1918)

Bent double, like old beggars under sacks,
Knock-kneed, coughing like hags, we cursed through sludge,

---

[1] The Roman poet Horace wrote that it "is sweet and fitting" (*dulce et decorum est*) "to die for one's country" (*pro patria mori*). Compare Pound's poem on page 307.

Till on the haunting flares we turned our backs,
And towards our distant rest began to trudge.
Men marched asleep. Many had lost their boots,
But limped on, blood-shod. All went lame, all blind;
Drunk with fatigue; deaf even to the hoots
Of gas-shells dropping softly behind.

Gas! Gas! Quick, boys!—An ecstasy of fumbling,
10 Fitting the clumsy helmets just in time,
But someone still was yelling out and stumbling
And floundering like a man in fire or lime.—
Dim through the misty panes and thick green light,
As under a green sea, I saw him drowning.
In all my dreams before my helpless sight
He plunges at me, guttering, choking, drowning.

If in some smothering dreams, you too could pace
Behind the wagon that we flung him in,
And watch the white eyes writhing in his face,
20 His hanging face, like a devil's sick of sin;
If you could hear, at every jolt, the blood
Come gargling from the froth-corrupted lungs,
Bitter as the cud
Of vile, incurable sores on innocent tongues,—
My friend, you would not tell with such high zest
To children ardent for some desperate glory,
The old Lie: Dulce et decorum est
Pro patria mori.

Joyce Peseroff

Joyce Peseroff (1948–   ) grew up in New York City, studied writing at the University of California at Irvine, and lives outside Boston. Her most recent book is *Dog in a Lifeboat* (1991).

The Hardness Scale   (1977)

Diamonds are forever so I gave you quartz
which is #7 on the hardness scale
and it's hard enough to get to know anybody these days
if only to scratch the surface
and quartz will scratch six other mineral surfaces:
it will scratch glass
it will scratch gold
it will even
scratch your eyes out one morning—you can't be
10 too careful.

Diamonds are industrial so I bought
a ring of topaz
which is #8 on the hardness scale.
I wear it on my right hand, the way it was
supposed to be, right? No tears and fewer regrets
for reasons smooth and clear as glass. Topaz will scratch glass,
it will scratch your quartz,
and all your radio crystals. You'll have to be silent
the rest of your days
20 not to mention your nights. Not to mention
the night you ran away very drunk very
very drunk and you tried to cross the border
but couldn't make it across the lake.
Stirring up geysers with the oars you drove the red canoe
in circles, tried to pole it but
your left hand didn't know
what the right hand was doing.
You fell asleep
and let everyone know it when you woke up.
30 In a gin-soaked morning (hair of the dog) you went
hunting for geese,
shot three lake trout in violation of the game laws,
told me to clean them and that
my eyes were bright as sapphires
which is #9 on the hardness scale.
A sapphire will cut a pearl
it will cut stainless steel
it will cut vinyl and mylar and will probably
cut a record this fall
40 to be released on an obscure label known only to aficionados.
I will buy a copy.
I may buy you a copy
depending on how your tastes have changed.
I will buy copies for my friends
we'll get a new needle,
a diamond needle,
which is #10 on the hardness scale
and will cut anything.
It will cut wood and mortar,
50 plaster and iron,
it will cut the sapphires in my eyes and I will bleed
blind as 4 A.M. in the subways when even degenerates
are dreaming, blind as the time
you shot up the room with a new hunting rifle
blind drunk
as you were.
You were #11 on the hardness scale
later that night
apologetic as
60 you worked your way up
slowly from the knees

and you worked your way down
from the open-throated blouse.
Diamonds are forever so I give you softer things.

Sylvia Plath

Sylvia Plath (1932–1963) attended Smith College, and wrote with a professional
skill from an early age. She attended Cambridge University on a fellowship, where
she met and married the English poet Ted Hughes. After the birth of their second
child, when Plath and Hughes were separated, her work abandoned its skillful
surfaces and became profoundly emotional, angry, brilliant, and disturbing. There
was a brief moment of great poetry, ended by her suicide. The posthumous *Ariel*
(1965) collects her best poetry.

Lady Lazarus   (1963)

I have done it again.
One year in every ten
I manage it—

A sort of walking miracle, my skin
Bright as a Nazi lampshade,
My right foot

A paperweight,
My face a featureless, fine
Jew linen.

10 Peel off the napkin
O my enemy.
Do I terrify?—

The nose, the eye pits, the full set of
        teeth?
The sour breath
Will vanish in a day.

Soon, soon the flesh
The grave cave ate will be
At home on me

20 And I a smiling woman.
I am only thirty.
And like the cat I have nine times to
        die.

This is Number Three.
What a trash
To annihilate each decade.

What a million filaments.
The peanut-crunching crowd
Shoves in to see

30 Them unwrap me hand and foot—
The big strip tease.
Gentleman, ladies,

These are my hands,
My knees.
I may be skin and bone,

Nevertheless, I am the same, identical
        woman.
The first time it happened I was ten.
It was an accident.

40 The second time I meant
To last it out and not come back at all.
I rocked shut

As a seashell.
They had to call and call
And pick the worms off me like sticky
        pearls.

Dying
Is an art, like everything else.
I do it exceptionally well.

50 I do it so it feels like hell.
I do it so it feels real.
I guess you could say I've a call.

It's easy enough to do it in a cell.
It's easy enough to do it and stay put.
It's the theatrical

Comeback in broad day
To the same place, the same face, the
    same brute
Amused shout:

60 "A miracle!"
That knocks me out.
There is a charge

For the eyeing of my scars, there is a
    charge
For the hearing of my heart—
It really goes.

And there is a charge, a very large
    charge,
For a word or a touch
70 Or a bit of blood

Or a piece of my hair or my clothes.
So, so, Herr Doktor.
So, Herr Enemy.

I am your opus,
I am your valuable,
The pure gold baby

That melts to a shriek.
I turn and burn.
Do not think I underestimate your
80   great concern.

Ash, ash—
You poke and stir.
Flesh, bone, there is nothing there—

A cake of soap,
A wedding ring,
A gold filling.

Herr God, Herr Lucifer,
Beware
Beware.

90 Out of the ash
I rise with my red hair
And I eat men like air.

Edgar Allan Poe

Edgar Allan Poe (1809–1849) is known for his macabre, grotesque, and
mysterious stories and poems. Poe's short life was unsettled and tempestuous.
He attended the University of Virginia for a few months, leaving when he
quarreled with his grandfather over gambling debts he had contracted. He was
expelled from West Point for breaking rules, married his thirteen-year-old
cousin, and struggled to earn enough money by his writing to support himself
and his family. He is one of the first great American authors, and his literary
criticism is as original as his stories and poems.

The City in the Sea   (1827)

Lo! Death has reared himself a throne
In a strange city lying alone
Far down within the dim West,
Where the good and the bad and the
    worst and the best
Have gone to their eternal rest.
There shrines and palaces and towers
(Time-eaten towers that tremble not!)
Resemble nothing that is ours.
10 Around, by lifting winds forgot,

Resignedly beneath the sky
The melancholy waters lie.
No rays from the holy heaven come
    down
On the long night-time of that town;
But light from out the lurid sea
Streams up the turrets silently—
Gleams up the pinnacles far and free—
Up domes—up spires—up kingly
20   halls—

Up fanes—up Babylon-like walls—
Up shadowy long-forgotten bowers
Of sculptured ivy and stone flowers—
Up many and many a marvellous
    shrine
Whose wreathèd friezes intertwine
The viol, the violet, and the vine.
Resignedly beneath the sky
The melancholy waters lie:
30 So blend the turrets and shadows there
That all seem pendulous in air,
While from a proud tower in the town
Death looks gigantically down.

There open fanes and gaping graves
Yawn level with the luminous waves;
But not the riches there that lie
In each idol's diamond eye—
Not the gaily-jewelled dead
Tempt the waters from their bed;

40 For no ripples curl, alas!
Along that wilderness of glass—
No swellings tell that winds may be
Upon some far-off happier sea—
No heavings hint that winds have been
On seas less hideously serene.

But lo, a stir is in the air!
The wave—there is a movement there!
As if the towers had thrust aside,
In slightly sinking, the dull tide—
50 As if their tops had feebly given
A void within the filmy Heaven.
The waves have now a redder glow—
The hours are breathing faint and low—
And when, amid no earthly moans,
Down, down that town shall settle
    hence,
Hell, rising from a thousand thrones,
Shall do it reverence.

Alexander Pope

Alexander Pope (1688–1744), crippled by a childhood disease, was unusually small. He was precocious, beginning to write with considerable excellence at sixteen. Much of the greater work is highly allusive. Although the poetry becomes more subtle and wise, the witwork of the young Pope was never surpassed. Pope was so proficient at the couplet that he was able to translate the entire *Iliad* and *Odyssey* into these twenty-syllable units. These lines are excerpted from "An Epistle to Dr. Arbuthnot." They begin by referring to some bad poets whom Pope earlier attacked, "all such." Then Pope draws a sketch of "Atticus," by whom he intended his contemporaries to understand his admired contemporary and rival, Joseph Addison, author of essays, poems, and a tragedy called *Cato*.

Atticus   (1723)

Peace to all such! but were there one whose fires
True genius kindles, and fair fame inspires;
Blest with each talent, and each art to please,
And born to write, converse, and live with ease,
Should such a man, too fond to rule alone,
Bear, like the Turk, no brother near the throne,
View him with scornful, yet with jealous eyes,
And hate for arts that caused himself to rise;
Damn with faint praise, assent with civil leer,
10 And, without sneering, teach the rest to sneer;
Willing to wound, and yet afraid to strike,
Just hint a fault, and hesitate dislike;
Alike reserved to blame, or to commend,
A timorous foe, and a suspicious friend;

Dreading e'en fools, by flatterers besieged,
And so obliging, that he ne'er obliged;
Like Cato, give his little Senate laws,
And sit attentive to his own applause:
While wits and Templars every sentence raise,
20 And wonder with a foolish face of praise—
Who but must laugh, if such a man there be?
Who would not weep, if Atticus were he?

Ezra Pound

Ezra Pound (1885–1972) was born in Idaho, but left as an infant and grew up in the
suburbs of Philadelphia. From an early age, he determined to become a great poet
and he set out to educate himself to that end. After graduate work at the University
of Pennsylvania, he taught briefly at Wabash College in Crawfordsville, Indiana. He
was fired when he afforded a night's shelter to a homeless dancing girl and left
almost immediately for Europe, where he spent most of the rest of his life. A young
man of extraordinary generosity, he discovered or promoted writers as diverse as
Lawrence, Eliot, Joyce, and Frost. He was determinedly esthetic. After the First
World War killed off many friends—young artists of great promise—he became
increasingly embittered about social matters and turned paranoid. This
development led to his admiration for Benito Mussolini, the Italian dictator, and to
the act of broadcasting on Italian radio to American troops during the Second
World War. After the war, he was accused of treason but was judged mentally unfit
to stand trial. After many years in St. Elizabeth's Hospital in Washington, DC, under
guard, he was released as an old man to return to Italy, where he lived out his long
life. See also pages 61–62 and 106.

The River-Merchant's Wife: A Letter   (1915)

While my hair was still cut straight across my forehead
I played about the front gate, pulling flowers.
You came by on bamboo stilts, playing horse,
You walked about my seat, playing with blue plums.
And we went on living in the village of Chokan:
Two small people, without dislike or suspicion.

At fourteen I married My Lord you.
I never laughed, being bashful.
Lowering my head, I looked at the wall.
10 Called to, a thousand times, I never looked back.

At fifteen I stopped scowling,
I desired my dust to be mingled with yours
For ever and for ever and for ever.
Why should I climb the look out?

At sixteen you departed,
You went into far Ku-to-yen, by the river of swirling eddies,

And you have been gone five months.
The monkeys make sorrowful noise overhead.

You dragged your feet when you went out.
20 By the gate now, the moss is grown, the different mosses,
Too deep to clear them away!
The leaves fall early this autumn, in wind.
The paired butterflies are already yellow with August
Over the grass in the West garden;
They hurt me. I grow older.
If you are coming down through the narrows of the river Kiang,
Please let me know beforehand,
And I will come out to meet you
                          As far as Cho-fu-Sa.   (*By Rihaku*)[1]

from Hugh Selwyn Mauberley   (1920)

IV

These fought in any case,
and some believing,
          pro domo,[1] in any case . . .

Some quick to arm,
some for adventure,
some from fear of weakness,
some from fear of censure,
some for love of slaughter, in imagination,
learning later . . .
10 some in fear, learning love of slaughter;

Died some, pro patria,[2]
          non 'dulce' non 'et decor'[3] . . .
walked eye-deep in hell
believing in old men's lies, then unbelieving
came home, home to a lie,
home to many deceits,
home to old lies and new infamy;
usury age-old and age-thick
and liars in public places.

20 Daring as never before, wastage as never before.
Young blood and high blood,
fair cheeks, and fine bodies;

fortitude as never before

[1] The Japanese name for Chinese poet Li Po, who wrote the original

[1] In Latin *pro domo* means "for home." Pound is alluding to a poem by the Roman poet Horace, whom he quotes (and later contradicts), who wrote that is is "sweet and fitting" [2](*dulce et decor* [*um*]) to die "for one's country" [3](*pro patria*). Compare Wilfred Owen's poem on pages 300–301.

frankness as never before,
disillusions as never told in the old days,
hysterias, trench confessions,
laughter out of dead bellies.

V

There died a myriad,
And of the best, among them,
30 For an old bitch gone in the teeth,
For a botched civilization,

Charm, smiling at the good mouth,
Quick eyes gone under earth's lid,

For two gross of broken statues,
For a few thousand battered books.

John Crowe Ransom

John Crowe Ransom (1888–1974) grew up in Tennessee and was a Rhodes Scholar
at Oxford. A leader in the Agrarian movement (a group of Southern writers in the
late 1920s and the 1930s) he went to Kenyon College as a professor in 1937, edited
the highly successful *Kenyon Review,* and wrote criticism as well as poetry.

Captain Carpenter   (1924)

Captain Carpenter rose up in his prime
Put on his pistols and went riding out
But had got wellnigh nowhere at that time
Till he fell in with ladies in a rout.

It was a pretty lady and all her train
That played with him so sweetly but before
An hour she'd taken a sword with all her main
And twined him of his nose for evermore.

Captain Carpenter mounted up one day
10 And rode straightway into a stranger rogue
That looked unchristian but be that as may
The Captain did not wait upon prologue.

But drew upon him out of his great heart
The other swung against him with a club
And cracked his two legs at the shinny part
And let him roll and stick like any tub.

Captain Carpenter rode many a time
From male and female took he sundry harms
He met the wife of Satan crying "I'm
20   The she-wolf bids you shall bear no more arms."

Their strokes and counters whistled in the wind
I wish he had delivered half his blows
But where she should have made off like a hind
The bitch bit off his arms at the elbows.

And Captain Carpenter parted with his ears
To a black devil that used him in this wise
O Jesus ere his threescore and ten years
Another had plucked out his sweet blue eyes.

Captain Carpenter got up on his roan
30   And sallied from the gate in hell's despite
I heard him asking in the grimmest tone
If any enemy yet there was to fight?

"To any adversary it is fame
If he risk to be wounded by my tongue
Or burnt in two beneath my red heart's flame
Such are the perils he is cast among.

"But if he can he has a pretty choice
From an anatomy with little to lose
Whether he cut my tongue and take my voice
40   Or whether it be my round red heart he choose."

It was the neatest knave that ever was seen
Stepping in perfume from his lady's bower
Who at this word put in his merry mien
And fell on Captain Carpenter like a tower.

I would not knock old fellows in the dust
But there lay Captain Carpenter on his back
His weapons were the old heart in his bust
And a blade shook between rotten teeth alack.

The rogue in scarlet and grey soon knew his mind
50   He wished to get his trophy and depart
With gentle apology and touch refined
He pierced him and produced the Captain's heart.

God's mercy rest on Captain Carpenter now
I thought him Sirs an honest gentleman
Citizen husband soldier and scholar enow
Let jangling kites eat of him if they can.

But God's deep curses follow after those
That shore him of his goodly nose and ears
His legs and strong arms at the two elbows
60 And eyes that had not watered seventy years.

The curse of hell upon the sleek upstart
That got the Captain finally on his back
And took the red red vitals of his heart
And made the kites to whet their beaks clack clack.

Sir Walter Ralegh

Sir Walter Ralegh (1552?–1618) is the same man who was alleged to have spread
his cloak over a puddle that his queen might walk dry-shod. More reliably, we
know of Ralegh as adventurer, explorer, and prisoner. He was a man of action
who fought in France and who led several voyages to the New World. Three
times, on various charges, he was committed to the Tower, where he probably
wrote most of his poetry. After a failed expedition to the Orinoco, during which a
Spanish colony was raided, Ralegh was executed (a major cause of death among
Elizabethan poets). See also page 282.

Verses Written the Night Before His Execution   (1618)

Even such is time, that takes in trust
Our youth, our joys, our all we have,
And pays us but with age and dust;
Who in the dark and silent grave,
When we have wandered all our ways,
Shuts up the story of our days:
But from this earth, this grave, this dust,
My God shall raise me up, I trust.

Liam Rector

Liam Rector (1949–   ) grew up in Virginia and studied at Johns Hopkins
University. He has taught at schools and universities, directed the poetry
program at the Folger Shakespeare Library, worked for the National Endowment
for the Arts, and directed Associated Writing Programs. He now lives in Norfolk,
Virginia. His first book of poems, *The Sorrows of Architecture,* appeared in 1984.

Showing   (1984)

They showed up for awhile and they died.
They showed up for some while and they died.

They smoked a few cigarettes and were remembered
by others who showed up and died.
They played the piano; they sat reading.
They had dinner and went to the ocean.
They stared into the hospital they were born into
and they died. They remembered
years which were lost to them
10   unless they concentrated and they died.
All their fear died. All that concern over death
died for a moment and they died. All their curly hair
and the wide sky and their many walks shot up
into a memory remembered
by others who died.
All their photographs and their staring curiosity,
all their wake up and lie down, died. I knock
twice on your door, old boy.

Kenneth Rexroth

Kenneth Rexroth (1905–1982) was born in Indiana and lived for many years in
San Francisco, where he was an elder figure behind the Beat Generation.
Anarchist in politics and broad in learning, he published essays and translations
as well as original poems. See also pages 56–57.

The Signature of All Things   (1949)

My head and shoulders, and my book
In the cool shade, and my body
Stretched bathing in the sun, I lie
Reading beside the waterfall—
Boehme's "Signature of all Things."[1]
Through the deep July day the leaves
Of the laurel, all the colors
Of gold, spin down through the moving
Deep laurel shade all day. They float
10 On the mirrored sky and forest
For a while, and then, still slowly
Spinning, sink through the crystal deep
Of the pool to its leaf gold floor.
The saint saw the world as streaming
In the electrolysis of love.
I put him by and gaze through shade
Folded into shade of slender
Laurel trunks and leaves filled with sun.

20 The wren broods in her moss domed
nest.
A newt struggles with a white moth
Drowning in the pool. The hawks
scream,
Playing together on the ceiling
Of heaven. The long hours go by.
I think of those who have loved me,
Of all the mountains I have climbed,
Of all the seas I have swum in.
The evil of the world sinks.
30 My own sin and trouble fall away
Like Christian's bundle, and I watch
My forty summers fall like falling
Leaves and falling water held
Eternally in summer air.

-----

[1] *The Signature of All Things* is one of the major works of German religious mystic writer
Jakob Boehme (1575–1624), whose thought influenced such later philosophers as Hegel and
Schopenhauer.

Deer are stamping in the glades,
Under the full July moon.
There is a smell of dry grass
In the air, and more faintly,
The scent of a far off skunk.
40 As I stand at the wood's edge,
Watching the darkness, listening
To the stillness, a small owl
Comes to the branch above me,
On wings more still than my breath.
When I turn my light on him,
His eyes glow like drops of iron,
And he perks his head at me,
Like a curious kitten.
The meadow is bright as snow.
50 My dog prowls the grass, a dark
Blur in the blur of brightness.
I walk to the oak grove where
The Indian village was once.
There, in blotched and cobwebbed light
And dark, dim in the blue haze,
Are twenty Holstein heifers,
Black and white, all lying down,
Quietly together, under
The huge trees rooted in the graves.

60 When I dragged the rotten log
From the bottom of the pool,
It seemed heavy as stone.
I let it lie in the sun
For a month; and then chopped it
Into sections, and split them
For kindling, and spread them out
To dry some more. Late that night,
After reading for hours,
While moths rattled at the lamp—
70 The saints and the philosophers
On the destiny of man—
I went out on my cabin porch,
And looked up through the black forest
At the swaying islands of stars.
Suddenly I saw at my feet,
Spread on the floor of night, ingots
Of quivering phosphorescence,
And all about were scattered chips
Of pale cold light that was alive.

Charles Reznikoff

Charles Reznikoff (1894–1975), a leading Objectivist poet, was born in New York City, where he lived most of his life. He wrote poems about the people he observed in the place where he lived. He also wrote some excellent poems out of his reading about American labor history, about the holocaust, and about biblical subjects. See page 38.

A Deserter   (1921)

Their new landlord was a handsome man. On his rounds to collect rent she became
    friendly.
Finally, she asked him in to have a cup of tea. After that he came often.

Once his mouth jerked, and turning, she saw her husband in the doorway.
She thought, One of the neighbors must have told him.
She smiled and opened her mouth to speak, but could say nothing.
Her husband stood looking at the floor. He turned and went away.

She lay awake all night waiting for him.
In the morning she went to his store. It was closed.
10 She sent for his brothers and told them he had not been home. They went to the

police. Hospitals and morgues were searched. For weeks they were called to
identify drowned men.

His business had been prosperous; bank account and all were untouched. She and
their baby girl were provided for.
In a few years they heard of him. He was dead.
He had been making a poor living in a far off city. One day he stepped in front of a
street-car and was killed.

She married again. Her daughter married and had children. She named none after
her father.

Adrienne Rich

See pages 168–179.

Edwin Arlington Robinson

Edwin Arlington Robinson (1869–1935) was born in Maine, and many of his
poems use the background of small towns in New England. Most of his adult life,
he spent the summers in New Hampshire at the MacDowell Colony and the rest
of the year in a New York apartment. He wrote many book-length poems, some of
them on subjects like *Merlin* and *Lancelot*. For most readers, the best of his work
is the shorter poems of character and narrative.

Eros Turannos[1]   (1916)

She fears him, and will always ask
   What fated her to choose him;
She meets in his engaging mask
   All reasons to refuse him;
But what she meets and what she fears
Are less than are the downward years,
Drawn slowly to the foamless weirs
   Of age, were she to lose him.

Between a blurred sagacity
10   That once had power to sound him,
And Love, that will not let him be
   The Judas that she found him,
Her pride assuages her almost,

As if it were alone the cost.—
He sees that he will not be lost,
   And waits and looks around him.

A sense of ocean and old trees
   Envelops and allures him;
Tradition, touching all he sees,
20   Beguiles and reassures him;
And all her doubts of what he says
Are dimmed with what she knows of
   days—
Till even prejudice delays
   And fades, and she secures him.

[1] Love, the Tyrant

The falling leaf inaugurates
    The reign of her confusion:
The pounding wave reverberates
    The dirge of her illusion;
30 And home, where passion lived and
      died,
Becomes a place where she can hide,
While all the town and harbor side
    Vibrate with her seclusion.

We tell you, tapping on our brows,
    The story as it should be,—
As if the story of a house
    Were told, or ever could be;

We'll have no kindly veil between
40 Her visions and those we have seen,—
As if we guessed what hers have been,
    Or what they are or would be.

Meanwhile we do no harm; for they
    That with a god have striven,
Not hearing much of what we say,
    Take what the god has given;
Though like waves breaking it may be,
Or like a changed familiar tree,
Or like a stairway to the sea
50   Where down the blind are driven.

Mr. Flood's Party   (1921)

Old Eben Flood, climbing alone one night
Over the hill between the town below
And the forsaken upland hermitage
That held as much as he should ever know
On earth again of home, paused warily.
The road was his with not a native near;
And Eben, having leisure, said aloud,
For no man else in Tilbury Town to hear:

"Well, Mr. Flood, we have the harvest moon
10 Again, and we may not have many more;
The bird is on the wing, the poet says,
And you and I have said it here before.
Drink to the bird." He raised up to the light
The jug that he had gone so far to fill,
And answered huskily: "Well, Mr. Flood,
Since you propose it, I believe I will."

Alone, as if enduring to the end
A valiant armor of scarred hopes outworn,
He stood there in the middle of the road
20 Like Roland's[1] ghost winding a silent horn.
Below him, in the town among the trees,
Where friends of other days had honored him,
A phantom salutation of the dead
Rang thinly till old Eben's eyes were dim.

Then, as a mother lays her sleeping child
Down tenderly, fearing it may awake,
He set the jug down slowly at his feet

---

[1] A hero of French medieval romances who died, ambushed by Saracens, after summoning help by blowing his famous horn

With trembling care, knowing that most things break;
And only when assured that on firm earth
30 It stood, as the uncertain lives of men
Assuredly did not, he paced away,
And with his hand extended paused again:

"Well, Mr. Flood, we have not met like this
In a long time; and many a change has come
To both of us, I fear, since last it was
We had a drop together. Welcome home!"
Convivially returning with himself,
Again he raised the jug up to the light;
And with an acquiescent quaver said:
40 "Well, Mr. Flood, if you insist, I might.

"Only a very little, Mr. Flood—
For auld lang syne. No more, sir; that will do."
So, for the time, apparently it did,
And Eben evidently thought so too;
For soon amid the silver loneliness
Of night he lifted up his voice and sang,
Secure, with only two moons listening,
Until the whole harmonious landscape rang—

"For auld lang syne." The weary throat gave out,
50 The last word wavered, and the song was done.
He raised again the jug regretfully
And shook his head, and was again alone.
There was not much that was ahead of him,
And there was nothing in the town below—
Where strangers would have shut the many doors
That many friends had opened long ago.

Theodore Roethke

See pages 154–168.

Carl Sandburg

Carl Sandburg (1878–1967) became known as a poet 'n 1914, when *Poetry*
published "Chicago," later reprinted in *Chicago Poems*. Deriving from Whitman,
populist, a celebrator of the commonplace, Sandburg was a popular poet who
became the biographer of Abraham Lincoln (six volumes, awarded a Pulitzer
Prize in 1939) and toward the end of his life the author of a long novel called
Remembrance Rock.

Chicago   (1916)

Hog Butcher for the World,
Tool Maker, Stacker of Wheat,
Player with Railroads and the Nation's Freight Handler;
Stormy, husky, brawling,
City of the Big Shoulders:
They tell me you are wicked and I believe them, for I have seen your painted
    women under the gas lamps luring the farm boys.
And they tell me you are crooked and I answer: Yes, it is true I have seen the
    gunman kill and go free to kill again.
10 And they tell me you are brutal and my reply is: On the faces of women and
    children I have seen the marks of wanton hunger.
And having answered so I turn once more to those who sneer at this my city, and I
    give them back the sneer and say to them:
Come and show me another city with lifted head singing so proud to be alive and
    coarse and strong and cunning.
Flinging magnetic curses amid the toil of piling job on job, here is a tall bold
    slugger set vivid against the little soft cities;
Fierce as a dog with tongue lapping for action, cunning as a savage pitted against
    the wilderness,
20   Bareheaded,
    Shoveling,
    Wrecking,
    Planning,
    Building, breaking, rebuilding,
Under the smoke, dust all over his mouth, laughing with white teeth,
Under the terrible burden of destiny laughing as a young man laughs,
Laughing even as an ignorant fighter laughs who has never lost a battle,
Bragging and laughing that under his wrist is the pulse, and under his ribs the heart
    of the people,
30   Laughing!
Laughing the stormy, husky, brawling laughter of Youth, half-naked, sweating, proud
    to be Hog Butcher, Tool Maker, Stacker of Wheat, Player with Railroads and
    Freight Handler to the Nation.

Yvonne Sapia

Yvonne Sapia (1946–   ) was born in New York City and moved to Florida when she was ten. She has published two collections of her poetry, *The Fertile Crescent* (1983) and *Valentino's Hair* (1987). She teaches at Lake City Community College in Florida.

Vikram Seth

Vikram Seth (1952–   ), born in India, has spent much of his life in England, the United States, and China. He is an economist as well as a poet and essayist. He has written a novel in verse called *The Golden Gate* (1987), and two collections of briefer poems—*The Humble Administrator's Garden* (1985) and *All You Who Sleep Tonight* (1990).

Anne Sexton

Anne Sexton (1928–1974) did not begin to write poems until she was in her late twenties, attending poetry workshops. Then she wrote prolifically and with great energy for many years, combating psychosis and an urge to suicide. Her books include *To Bedlam and Part Way Back* (1960), *Live or Die* (1967), and *The Awful Rowing Towards God* (1975).

Wanting to Die   (1966)

Since you ask, most days I cannot remember.
I walk in my clothing, unmarked by that voyage.
Then the almost unnameable lust returns.

Even then I have nothing against life.
I know well the grass blades you mention,
the furniture you have placed under the sun.

But suicides have a special language.
Like carpenters they want to know *which tools*.
They never ask *why build*.

10 Twice I have so simply declared myself,
have possessed the enemy, eaten the enemy,
have taken on his craft, his magic.

In this way, heavy and thoughtful,
warmer than oil or water,
I have rested, drooling at the mouth-hole.

I did not think of my body at needle point.
Even the cornea and the leftover urine were gone.
Suicides have already betrayed the body.

Still-born, they don't always die,
20 but dazzled, they can't forget a drug so sweet
that even children would look on and smile.

To thrust all that life under your tongue!—
that, all by itself, becomes a passion.
Death's a sad bone; bruised, you'd say,

and yet she waits for me, year after year,
to so delicately undo an old wound,
to empty my breath from its bad prison.

Balanced there, suicides sometimes meet,
raging at the fruit, a pumped-up moon,
30 leaving the bread they mistook for a kiss,

leaving the page of the book carelessly open,
something unsaid, the phone off the hook
and the love, whatever it was, an infection.

William Shakespeare

William Shakespeare (1564–1616) is the greatest poet of the language. About him,
we do not know as much as we would like. He was born in Stratford-upon-Avon, son
of a glovemaker who became mayor of his town. Apparently Shakespeare attended
school in Stratford, and in 1582 married Anne Hathaway, who was eight years his
senior. They had three children; one son named Hamnet died in childhood. At
some point in the decade after his marriage, Shakespeare moved to London alone
and became an actor. He began writing for the stage about 1590. His sonnets are
almost as celebrated as his plays. See also pages 38, 39 and 104–105.

They that have power to hurt and will do none   (1609)

They that have power to hurt and will do none,
That do not do the thing they most do show,
Who, moving others, are themselves as stone,
Unmoved, cold, and to temptation slow,—
They rightly do inherit heaven's graces
And husband nature's riches from expense;
They are the lords and owners of their faces,
Others but stewards of their excellence.
The summer's flower is to the summer sweet,
10 Though to itself it only live and die:
But if that flower with base infection meet,
The basest weed outbraves his dignity:
    For sweetest things turn sourest by their deeds;
    Lilies that fester smell far worse than weeds.

Percy Bysshe Shelley

Percy Bysshe Shelley (1792–1822) was expelled from Oxford in 1811 for writing a pamphlet in defense of atheism. That year he married his first wife, who was sixteen, from whom he separated three years later. She killed herself. He married Mary Wollstonecraft—author of *Frankenstein*—in 1814 and spent much of the rest of his life in Italy. He was friendly with Byron and acquainted with Keats. In Italy, in the last three years of his life, he wrote his best poems, including "Ode to the West Wind." On July 8, 1822, he was shipwrecked in a storm while sailing off the Italian coast and drowned.

Ode to the West Wind   (1820)

1

O wild West Wind, thou breath of Autumn's being,
Thou, from whose unseen presence the leaves dead
Are driven, like ghosts from an enchanter fleeing,

Yellow, and black, and pale, and hectic red,
Pestilence-striken multitudes: O thou,
Who chariotest to their dark wintry bed

The wingèd seeds, where they lie cold and low,
Each like a corpse within its grave, until
Thine azure sister of the Spring shall blow

10 Her clarion o'er the dreaming earth, and fill
(Driving sweet buds like flocks to feed in air)
With living hues and odours plain and hill:

Wild Spirit, which art moving everywhere;
Destroyer and preserver; hear, oh, hear!

2

Thou on whose stream, 'mid the steep sky's commotion,
Loose clouds like earth's decaying leaves are shed,
Shook from the tangled boughs of Heaven and Ocean,

Angels of rain and lightning: there are spread
On the blue surface of thine airy surge,
20 Like the bright hair uplifted from the head

Of some fierce Mænad, even from the dim verge
Of the horizon to the zenith's height,
The locks of the approaching storm. Thou dirge

Of the dying year, to which this closing night
Will be the dome of a vast sepulchre,
Vaulted with all thy congregated might

Of vapours, from whose solid atmosphere
Black rain, and fire, and hail will burst: oh, hear!

3

Thou who didst waken from his summer dreams
30 The blue Mediterranean, where he lay,
Lulled by the coil of his crystálline streams,

Beside a pumice isle in Baiæ's bay,
And saw in sleep old palaces and towers
Quivering within the wave's intenser day,

All overgrown with azure moss and flowers
So sweet, the sense faints picturing them! Thou
For whose path the Atlantic's level powers

Cleave themselves into chasms, while far below
The sea-blooms and the oozy woods which wear
40 The sapless foliage of the ocean, know

Thy voice, and suddenly grow gray with fear,
And tremble and despoil themselves: oh, hear!

4

If I were a dead leaf thou mightest bear;
If I were a swift cloud to fly with thee;
A wave to pant beneath thy power, and share

The impulse of thy strength, only less free
Than thou, O uncontrollable! If even
I were as in my boyhood, and could be

The comrade of thy wanderings over Heaven,
50 As then, when to outstrip thy skyey speed
Scarce seemed a vision; I would ne'er have striven

As thus with thee in prayer in my sore need.
Oh, lift me as a wave, a leaf, a cloud!
I fall upon the thorns of life! I bleed!

A heavy weight of hours has chained and bowed
One too like thee: tameless, and swift, and proud.

5

Make me thy lyre, even as the forest is:
What if my leaves are falling like its own!
The tumult of thy mighty harmonies

60 Will take from both a deep, autumnal tone,
Sweet though in sadness. Be thou, Spirit fierce,
My spirit! Be thou me, impetuous one!

Drive my dead thoughts over the universe
Like withered leaves to quicken a new birth!
And, by the incantation of this verse,

Scatter, as from an unextinguished hearth
Ashes and sparks, my words among mankind!
Be through my lips to unawakened earth

The trumpet of a prophecy! O, wind,
70 If Winter comes, can Spring be far behind?

Sir Philip Sidney

Sir Philip Sidney (1554–1586) died fighting for England against Spain, and none
of his considerable work appeared until after his death. In his generation, he was
widely admired and became the subject of several elegies, most notably
Spenser's. He was loved not only for his talent and his intelligence but also for
the nobility of his character. According to legend, while he was dying he refused
a cup of water, sending it to the wounded man beside him, claiming "Thy
necessity is greater than mine."

from Astrophel and Stella   (1591)

With how sad steps, O Moon! thou climb'st the skies!
How silently, and with how wan a face!
What! may it be, that even in heavenly place
That busy archer° his sharp arrows tries?   Cupid
Sure, if that long-with-love-acquainted eyes
Can judge of love, thou feel'st a lover's case;
I read it in thy looks; thy languish'd grace,
To me that feel the like, thy state descries.
Then, even of fellowship, O Moon, tell me,
10 Is constant love deem'd there but want of wit?
Are beauties there as proud as here they be?
Do they above love to be loved, and yet
    Those lovers scorn whom that love doth possess?
    Do they call virtue there ungratefulness?

Leslie Marmon Silko

Leslie Marmon Silko (1948–   ) is a poet and fiction writer—a
storyteller—who grew up on a Laguna Pueblo Reservation in New Mexico, in a
house of rock and adobe. Besides her poetry, she has written the screen play for
the Marlon Brando film, *Black Elk,* a book of short stories (*Storyteller,* 1981), and
a novel (*Ceremony,* 1977).

Where Mountain Lion Lay Down with Deer   (1973)

I climb the black rock mountain
    stepping from day to day
                silently.

I smell the wind for my ancestors
        pale blue leaves
        crushed wild mountain smell.
Returning
    up the gray stone cliff
    where I descended
10   a thousand years ago.
Returning to faded black stone.
    where mountain lion lay down with deer.
It is better to stay up here
               watching wind's reflection
               in tall yellow flowers.
The old ones who remember me are gone
        the old songs are all forgotten
and the story of my birth.
How I danced in snow-frost moonlight
20   distant stars to the end of the Earth,
How I swam away
        in freezing mountain water
        narrow mossy canyon tumbling down
               out of the mountain
                  out of the deep canyon stone
        down
          the memory
             spilling out
             into the world.

Charles Simic

Charles Simic (1938–   ) was born in Yugoslavia and came to the United States in 1949. He lives in New Hampshire and has published many books of poems. *The World Doesn't End* (1989) received the Pulitzer Prize in 1990, when he published his most recent volume, *Gods and Devils.*

Fork   (1971)

This strange thing must have crept
Right out of hell.
It resembles a bird's foot
Worn around the cannibal's neck.

As you hold it in your hand,
As you stab with it into a piece of meat,
It is possible to imagine the rest of the bird:
Its head which like your fist
Is large, bald, beakless and blind.

Shelley   (1990)

for M. Follain

Poet of the dead leaves driven like ghosts,
Driven like pestilence-stricken multitudes,
I read you first
One rainy evening in New York City,

In my atrocious Slavic accent,
Saying the mellifluous verses
From a battered, much-stained volume
I had bought earlier that day
In a second-hand bookstore on Fourth Avenue
10   Run by an initiate of the occult masters.

The little money I had being almost spent,
I walked the streets my nose in the book.
I sat in a dingy coffee shop
With last summer's dead flies on the table.
The owner was an ex-sailor
Who had grown a huge hump on his back
While watching the rain, the empty street.
He was glad to have me sit and read.
He'd refill my cup with a liquid dark as river Styx.

20   Shelley spoke of a mad, blind, dying king;
Of rulers who neither see, nor feel, nor know;
Of graves from which a glorious Phantom may
Burst to illumine our tempestuous day.

I too felt like a glorious phantom
Going to have my dinner
In a Chinese restaurant I knew so well.
It had a three-fingered waiter
Who'd bring my soup and rice each night
Without ever saying a word.

30   I never saw anyone else there.
The kitchen was separated by a curtain
Of glass beads which clicked faintly
Whenever the front door opened.
The front door opened that evening
To admit a pale little girl with glasses.

The poet spoke of the everlasting universe
Of things . . . of gleams of a remoter world
Which visit the soul in sleep . . .
Of a desert peopled by storms alone . . .

40   The streets were strewn with broken umbrellas
Which looked like funereal kites

This little Chinese girl might have made.
The bars on MacDougal Street were emptying.
There had been a fist fight.
A man leaned against a lamp post arms extended
    as if crucified,
The rain washing the blood off his face.

In a dimly lit side street,
Where the sidewalk shone like a ballroom mirror
50 At closing time—
A well-dressed man without any shoes
Asked me for money.
His eyes shone, he looked triumphant
Like a fencing master
Who had just struck a mortal blow.

How strange it all was . . . The world's raffle
That dark October night . . .
The yellowed volume of poetry
With its Splendors and Glooms
60 Which I studied by the light of storefronts:
Drugstores and barbershops,
Afraid of my small windowless room
Cold as a tomb of an infant emperor.

Louis Simpson

Louis Simpson (1923–   ) was born in Jamaica and grew up there, coming to
the United States when he was seventeen. He left Columbia College to enter
the U.S. Army during the Second World War and received his citizenship at
Berchtesgaden. He has published a novel, a textbook, several volumes of
criticism, and numerous books of poems. *At the End of the Open Road* (1963)
won a Pulitzer Prize. His *Collected Poems* appeared in 1988, and a *Selected Prose*
in 1989. See also pages 84 and 86–87.

Walt Whitman at Bear Mountain   (1960)

". . . life which does not give the preference to any other life, of any previous
period, which therefore prefers its own existence . . ."

                                         —*Ortega y Gasset*

Neither on horseback nor seated,
But like himself, squarely on two feet,
The poet of death and lilacs
Loafs by the footpath. Even the bronze looks alive
Where it is folded like cloth. And he seems friendly.

'Where is the Mississippi panorama
And the girl who played the piano?
Where are you, Walt?
The Open Road goes to the used-car lot.

10 'Where is the nation you promised?
These houses built of wood sustain
Colossal snows,
And the light above the street is sick to death.

'As for the people—see how they neglect you!
Only a poet pauses to read the inscription.'

'I am here,' he answered.
'It seems you have found me out.
Yet, did I not warn you that it was Myself
I advertised? Were my words not sufficiently plain?

20 'I gave no prescriptions,
And those who have taken my moods for prophecies
Mistake the matter.'
Then, vastly amused—'Why do you reproach me?
I freely confess I am wholly disreputable.
Yet I am happy, because you have found me out.'

A crocodile in wrinkled metal loafing . . .

Then all the realtors,
Pickpockets, salesmen, and the actors performing
Official scenarios,
30 Turned a deaf ear, for they had contracted
American dreams.

But the man who keeps a store on a lonely road,
And the housewife who knows she's dumb,
And the earth, are relieved.

All that grave weight of America
Cancelled! Like Greece and Rome.
The future in ruins!
The castles, the prisons, the cathedrals
Unbuilding, and roses
40 Blossoming from the stones that are not there . . .

The clouds are lifting from the high Sierras,
The Bay mists clearing;
And the angel in the gate, the flowering plum,
Dances like Italy, imagining red.

In the Suburbs   (1963)

There's no way out.
You were born to waste your life.
You were born to this middleclass life

As others before you
Were born to walk in procession
To the temple, singing.

Christopher Smart

Christopher Smart (1722–1771) wrote the long poem excerpted below when he was insane. It was his habit, in his madness, to go down on his knees in a crowded street and ask other people to pray with him. Samuel Johnson, apprised of Smart's eccentricities, avowed that he would as soon pray with Kit Smart as with any man.

from Jubilate Agno[1]   (1763)

For I will consider my Cat Jeoffry.
For he is the servant of the Living God, duly and daily serving him.
For at the first glance of the glory of God in the East he worships in his way.
For is this done by wreathing his body seven times round with elegant
    quickness.
For then he leaps up to catch the musk,° which is the blessing of   catnip (?)
    God upon his prayer.
For he rolls upon prank to work it in.
For having done duty and received blessing he begins to consider himself.
10 For this he performs in ten degrees.
For first he looks upon his fore-paws to see if they are clean.
For secondly he kicks up behind to clear away there.
For thirdly he works it upon stretch with the fore-paws extended.
For fourthly he sharpens his paws by wood.
For fifthly he washes himself.
For sixthly he rolls upon wash.
For seventhly he fleas himself, that he may not be interrupted upon the beat.
For eighthly he rubs himself against a post.
For ninthly he looks up for his instructions.
20 For tenthly he goes in quest of food.
For having considered God and himself he will consider his neighbor.
For if he meets another cat he will kiss her in kindness.
For when he takes his prey he plays with it to give it chance.
For one mouse in seven escapes by his dallying.
For when his day's work is done his business more properly begins.

[1] Rejoice in the Lamb

For he keeps the Lord's watch in the night against the adversary.
For he counteracts the powers of darkness by his electrical skin and glaring
    eyes.
For he counteracts the Devil, who is death, by brisking about the life.
30 For in his morning orisons he loves the sun and the sun loves him.
For he is of the tribe of Tiger.
For the Cherub Cat is a term of the Angel Tiger.
For he has the subtlety and hissing of a serpent, which in goodness he
    suppresses.
For he will not do destruction if he is well-fed, neither will he spit without
    provocation.
For he purrs in thankfulness, when God tells him he's a good Cat.
For he is an instrument for the children to learn benevolence upon.
For every house is incomplete without him and a blessing is lacking in the
40   spirit.
For the Lord commanded Moses concerning the cats at the departure of the
    Children of Israel from Egypt.
For every family had one cat at least in the bag.
For the English Cats are the best in Europe.

W. D. Snodgrass

William DeWitt Snodgrass (1926–   ) was born in Pennsylvania and attended
the Writer's Workshop at Iowa, where he wrote his first book, *Heart's Needle*
(1959), which won the 1960 Pulitzer Prize. Credited by Robert Lowell with the
invention of confessional verse, Snodgrass in his own work has moved on to the
dramatic monologue. In 1987 he published his *Selected Poems.*

April Inventory (1959)

The green catalpa tree has turned
All white; the cherry blooms once more.
In one whole year I haven't learned
A blessed thing they pay you for.
The blossoms snow down in my hair;
The trees and I will soon be bare.

The trees have more than I to spare.
The sleek, expensive girls I teach,
Younger and pinker every year,
10 Bloom gradually out of reach.
The pear tree lets its petals drop
Like dandruff on a tabletop.

The girls have grown so young by now
I have to nudge myself to stare.
This year they smile and mind me how

My teeth are falling with my hair.
In thirty years I may not get
Younger, shrewder, or out of debt.

The tenth time, just a year ago,
20 I made myself a little list
Of all the things I'd ought to know,
Then told my parents, analyst,
And everyone who's trusted me
I'd be substantial, presently.

I haven't read one book about
A book or memorized one plot.
Or found a mind I did not doubt.
I learned one date. And then forgot.
And one by one the solid scholars
30 Get the degrees, the jobs, the dollars.

And smile above their starchy collars.
I taught my classes Whitehead's[1]
   notions;
One lovely girl, a song of Mahler's.[2]
Lacking a source-book or promotions,
I showed one child the colors of
A luna moth and how to love.

I taught myself to name my name,
To bark back, loosen love and crying;
40 To ease my woman so she came,
To ease an old man who was dying.
I have not learned how often I
Can win, can love, but choose to die.

I have not learned there is a lie
Love shall be blonder, slimmer,
   younger;
That my equivocating eye

Loves only by my body's hunger;
That I have forces, true to feel,
50 Or that the lovely world is real.

While scholars speak authority
And wear their ulcers on their sleeves,
My eyes in spectacles shall see
These trees procure and spend their
leaves.
There is a value underneath
The gold and silver in my teeth.

Though trees turn bare and girls turn
wives,
60 We shall afford our costly seasons;
There is a gentleness survives
That will outspeak and has its reasons.
There is a loveliness exists,
Preserves us, not for specialists.

Lobsters in the Window   (1963)

First, you think they are dead.
Then you are almost sure
One is beginning to stir.
Out of the crushed ice, slow
As the hands of a schoolroom clock,
He lifts his one great claw
And holds it over his head;
Now, he is trying to walk.

But like a run-down toy;
10 Like the backward crabs we boys
Splashed after in the creek,
Trapped in jars or a net,
And then took home to keep.
Overgrown, retarded, weak,
He is fumbling yet
From the deep chill of his sleep

As if, in a glacial thaw
Some ancient thing might wake
Sore and cold and stiff
20 Struggling to raise one claw
Like a defiant fist;
Yet wavering, as if
Starting to swell and ache
With that thick peg in the wrist.

I should wave back, I guess.
But still in his permanent clench
He's fallen back with the mass
Heaped in their common trench
Who stir, but do not look out
30 Through the rainstreaming glass,
Hear what the newsboys shout,
Or see the raincoats pass.

---

[1] Alfred North Whitehead (1861–1947), English philosopher and mathematician   [2] Gustave Mahler (1860–1911), Austrian composer and conductor, wrote several songs and song cycles in addition to nine monumental symphonies.

Gary Snyder

Gary Snyder (1930–   ) grew up on the West Coast and attended Reed College. He did graduate work in Oriental languages at Berkeley and has lived many years in Japan, studying Zen Buddhism in Kyoto. Now he lives in a house of his own construction called Kitkitdizze, north of Sacramento, and practices the life he preaches. See also page 49.

Above Pate Valley   (1959)

We finished clearing the last
Section of trail by noon,
High on the ridge-side
Two thousand feet above the creek—
Reached the pass, went on
Beyond the white pine groves,
Granite shoulders, to a small
Green meadow watered by the snow,
Edged with Aspen—sun
10 Straight high and blazing
But the air was cool.
Ate a cold fried trout in the
Trembling shadows. I spied
A glitter, and found a flake

Black volcanic glass—obsidian—
By a flower. Hands and knees
Pushing the Bear grass, thousands
Of arrowhead leavings over a
Hundred yards. Not one good
20 Head, just razor flakes
On a hill snowed all but summer,
A land of fat summer deer.
They came to camp. On their
Own trails. I followed my own
Trail here. Picked up the cold-drill,
Pick, singlejack, and sack
Of dynamite.
Ten thousand years.

Cathy Song

Cathy Song (1955–   ) lives in Honolulu, Hawaii, where she was born. A graduate of Wellesley College and Boston University, she has published two collections of her poems. *Picture Bride* appeared in the Yale Younger Poets Series in 1983, and *Frameless Windows, Square of Light* in 1988.

A Small Light   (1988)

When the man comes home he takes off his hat
and looks up at the leaves of the tree.
The light annoints each leaf as it sinks into the sea.
The tree shimmers like a thousand mirrors,
the suddenness of birds in flight.
A child is sleeping in the house.
The house rises and falls with each breath
as if the house were made of cloth.
Tacked to the walls is the sound of the clock
10 which keeps the house from floating away.
A curtain divides the bed and the sink.

A woman lies on the bed and feels
the house fall into itself, the window fill with leaves.
Her body fills with sleep
as if sleep were a dream of water.
The sound of the clock grows smaller
like a light in a window you pass at night.
The child opens her eyes to a dream of water.
A web in the window is sunlight
20 seen from the inside of water.
Floating in the window, it is barely there,
like her breath, like hair.
She understands what can't be seen
can still be broken.
She holds her breath as though her breath
could break. When the tree hauls its leaves
in shadows across the room,
the web stretches like an accordian,
but silent, elastic, made of skin.
30 A dead stream is a river of leaves.
All day the wind stirs a parched soup,
a kindling of matchsticks and leaves,
the size of the child's hand.
Some part of the tree is always dying.
Somewhere it is always raining leaves
and a child, closing the door on the falling
walls of a house, walks away,
her slight dress sinking into the dry river,
hair, a small light, touching each leaf.

Gary Soto

Gary Soto (1952–   ) was born in Fresno, California, and teaches at the
University of California, Berkeley. He has published seven books of poetry,
including *Black Hair* (1985) and *Who Will Know Us* (1990), and several
collections of essays and reminiscences.

Robert Southwell

Robert Southwell (1561?–1595), a Catholic, wrote most of his devotional poetry
in prison, where he was tortured and finally executed.

The Burning Babe   (1592)

As I in hoary winter's night stood shivering in the snow,
Surprised I was with sudden heat, which made my heart to glow;
And lifting up a fearful eye to view what fire was near,

A pretty Babe all burning bright, did in the air appear,
Who scorchèd with excessive heat, such floods of tears did shed,
As though His floods should quench His flames which with His tears were fed;
Alas! quoth He, but newly born, in fiery heats I fry,
Yet none approach to warm their hearts or feel my fire but I!
My faultless breast the furnace is, the fuel wounding thorns,
10 Love is the fire, and sighs the smoke, the ashes shame and scorns;
The fuel Justice layeth on, and Mercy blows the coals,
The metal in this furnace wrought are men's defilèd souls,
For which, as now on fire I am to work them to their good,
So will I melt into a bath to wash them in My blood:
With this He vanished out of sight, and swiftly shrank away,
And straight I callèd unto mind that it was Christmas-day.

William Stafford

William Stafford (1914–   ) was born in Kansas and has lived most of his life in the Pacific Northwest. His *Stories That Could Be True: Poems New and Collected* appeared in 1977, only fifteen years after his first collection, *Travelling Through the Dark*, won the National Book Award. His poetry is quiet, reticent, reserved, compassionate, and ultimately happy.

Travelling Through the Dark   (1960)

Travelling through the dark I found a deer
dead on the edge of the Wilson River road.
It is usually best to roll them into the canyon:
that road is narrow; to swerve might make more dead.

By glow of the tail-light I stumbled back of the car
and stood by the heap, a doe, a recent killing;
she had stiffened already, almost cold.
I dragged her off; she was large in the belly.

My fingers touching her side brought me the reason—
10 her side was warm; her fawn lay there waiting,
alive, still, never to be born.
Beside that mountain road I hesitated.

The car aimed ahead its lowered parking lights;
under the hood purred the steady engine.
I stood in the glare of the warm exhaust turning red;
around our group I could hear the wilderness listen.

I thought hard for us all—my only swerving—,
then pushed her over the edge into the river.

Wallace Stevens

Wallace Stevens (1879–1955) is one of the finest of American poets. He attended Harvard, tried his luck as a journalist, and went to New York University Law School. After practicing some years in New York City, he took a job with the legal department of Hartford Accident and Indemnity, an insurance company, and eventually moved to Hartford, thus becoming known as "the insurance man who is a poet." His poetry has a delicacy, a Frenchified elegance, and a nice concern for matters epistemological. There seemed to be a clear and sustained break between the poetry he wrote and the life he lived. Perhaps they came together in Florida, which like many Connecticut businessmen he visited and which entered his poems as a place of unsurpassable bright lushness. See also page 12.

The Emperor of Ice-Cream   (1922)

Call the roller of big cigars,
The muscular one, and bid him whip
In kitchen cups concupiscent curds.
Let the wenches dawdle in such dress
As they are used to wear, and let the boys
Bring flowers in last month's newspapers.
Let be be finale of seem.
The only emperor is the emperor of ice-cream.

Take from the dresser of deal,
10 Lacking the three glass knobs, that sheet
On which she embroidered fantails once
And spread it so as to cover her face.
If her horny feet protrude, they come
To show how cold she is, and dumb.
Let the lamp affix its beam.
The only emperor is the emperor of ice-cream.

The Snow Man   (1921)

One must have a mind of winter
To regard the frost and the boughs
Of the pine-trees crusted with snow;

And have been cold a long time
To behold the junipers shagged with ice,
The spruces rough in the distant glitter

Of the January sun; and not to think
Of any misery in the sound of the wind,
In the sound of a few leaves,

10 Which is the sound of the land
Full of the same wind
That is blowing in the same bare place

For the listener, who listens in the snow,
And, nothing himself, beholds
Nothing that is not there and the nothing that is.

Sunday Morning   (1915)

I

Complacencies of the peignoir, and late
Coffee and oranges in a sunny chair,
And the green freedom of a cockatoo
Upon a rug mingle to dissipate
The holy hush of ancient sacrifice.
She dreams a little, and she feels the dark
Encroachment of that old catastrophe,
As a calm darkens among water-lights.
The pungent oranges and bright, green wings
10 Seem things in some procession of the dead,
Winding across wide water, without sound.
The day is like wide water, without sound,
Stilled for the passing of her dreaming feet
Over the seas, to silent Palestine,
Dominion of the blood and sepulchre.

II

Why should she give her bounty to the dead?
What is divinity if it can come
Only in silent shadows and in dreams?
Shall she not find in comforts of the sun,
20 In pungent fruit and bright, green wings, or else
In any balm or beauty of the earth,
Things to be cherished like the thought of heaven?
Divinity must live within herself:
Passions of rain, or moods in falling snow;
Grievings in loneliness, or unsubdued
Elations when the forest blooms; gusty
Emotions on wet roads on autumn nights;
All pleasures and all pains, remembering
The bough of summer and the winter branch.
30 These are the measures destined for her soul.

III

Jove in the clouds had his inhuman birth.
No mother suckled him, no sweet land gave
Large-mannered motions to his mythy mind
He moved among us, as a muttering king,
Magnificent, would move among his hinds,
Until our blood, commingling, virginal,
With heaven, brought such requital to desire
The very hinds discerned it, in a star.

Shall our blood fail? Or shall it come to be
40 The blood of paradise? And shall the earth
Seem all of paradise that we shall know?
The sky will be much friendlier then than now,
A part of labor and a part of pain,
And next in glory to enduring love,
Not this dividing and indifferent blue.

IV

She says, "I am content when wakened birds,
Before they fly, test the reality
Of misty fields, by their sweet questionings;
But when the birds are gone, and their warm fields
50 Return no more, where, then, is paradise?"
There is not any haunt of prophecy,
Nor any old chimera of the grave,
Neither the golden underground, nor isle
Melodious, where spirits gat them home,
Nor visionary south, nor cloudy palm
Remote on heaven's hill, that has endured
As April's green endures; or will endure
Like her remembrance of awakened birds,
Or her desire for June and evening, tipped
60 By the consummation of the swallow's wings.

V

She says, "But in contentment I still feel
The need of some imperishable bliss."
Death is the mother of beauty; hence from her,
Alone, shall come fulfilment to our dreams
And our desires. Although she strews the leaves
Of sure obliteration on our paths,
The path sick sorrow took, the many paths
Where triumph rang its brassy phrase, or love
Whispered a little out of tenderness,
70 She makes the willow shiver in the sun
For maidens who were wont to sit and gaze
Upon the grass, relinquished to their feet.
She causes boys to pile new plums and pears
On disregarded plate. The maidens taste
And stray impassioned in the littering leaves.

VI

Is there no change of death in paradise?
Does ripe fruit never fall? Or do the boughs
Hang always heavy in that perfect sky,
Unchanging, yet so like our perishing earth,
80 With rivers like our own that seek for seas
They never find, the same receding shores

That never touch with inarticulate pang?
Why set the pear upon those river-banks
Or spice the shores with odors of the plum?
Alas, that they should wear our colors there,
The silken weavings of our afternoons,
And pick the strings of our insipid lutes!
Death is the mother of beauty, mystical,
Within whose burning bosom we devise
90 Our earthly mothers waiting, sleeplessly.

VII

Supple and turbulent, a ring of men
Shall chant in orgy on a summer morn
Their boisterous devotion to the sun,
Not as a god, but as a god might be,
Naked among them, like a savage source.
Their chant shall be a chant of paradise,
Out of their blood, returning to the sky;
And in their chant shall enter, voice by voice,
The windy lake wherein their lord delights,
100 The trees, like serafin, and echoing hills,
That choir among themselves long afterward.
They shall know well the heavenly fellowship
Of men that perish and of summer morn.
And whence they came and whither they shall go
The dew upon their feet shall manifest.

VIII

She hears, upon that water without sound,
A voice that cries, "The tomb in Palestine
Is not the porch of spirits lingering.
It is the grave of Jesus, where he lay."
110 We live in an old chaos of the sun,
Or old dependency of day and night,
Or island solitude, unsponsored, free,
Of that wide water, inescapable.
Deer walk upon our mountains, and the quail
Whistle about us their spontaneous cries;
Sweet berries ripen in the wilderness;
And, in the isolation of the sky,
At evening, casual flocks of pigeons make
Ambiguous undulations as they sink,
120 Downward to darkness, on extended wings.

Mark Strand

Mark Strand (1934–   ) was born in Canada and went to college in the United States, where he has settled. He lives in Salt Lake City and teaches at the University of Utah. In 1990–1991 he was Poet Laureate of the United States and, in 1990, republished his *Selected Poems* as well as a new collection called *The Continuous Life*. He has also written books of art criticism, short stories, and children's books.

Always   (1990)
for Charles Simic

Always so late in the day
In their rumpled clothes, sitting
Around a table lit by a single bulb,
The great forgetters were hard at work.
They tilted their heads to one side, closing their eyes.
Then a house disappeared, and a man in his yard
With all his flowers in a row.
The great forgetters wrinkled their brows.
Then Florida went and San Francisco
10 Where tugs and barges leave
Small gleaming scars across the Bay.
One of the great forgetters struck a match.
Gone were the harps of beaded lights
That vault the rivers of New York.
Another filled his glass
And that was it for crowds at evening
Under sulphur yellow streetlamps coming on.
And afterwards Bulgaria was gone, and then Japan.
"Where will it stop?" one of them said.
20 "Such difficult work, pursuing the fate
Of everything known," said another.
"Down to the last stone," said a third,
"And only the cold zero of perfection
Left for the imagination." And gone
Were North and South America,
And gone as well the moon.
Another yawned, another gazed at the window:
No grass, no trees . . .
The blaze of promise everywhere.

The End   (1990)

Not every man knows what he shall sing at the end,
Watching the pier as the ship sails away, or what it will seem like
When he's held by the sea's roar, motionless, there at the end,
Or what he shall hope for once it is clear that he'll never go back.

When the time has passed to prune the rose or caress the cat,
When the sunset torching the lawn and the full moon icing it down
No longer appear, not every man knows what he'll discover instead.
When the weight of the past leans against nothing, and the sky

Is no more than remembered light, and the stories of cirrus
10   And cumulus come to a close, and all the birds are suspended in flight,
Not every man knows what is waiting for him, or what he shall sing
When the ship he is on slips into darkness, there at the end.

Alfred, Lord Tennyson

Alfred, Lord Tennyson (1809–1892), who began to publish poems before he was twenty, matured in technical accomplishment early. After his great friend Arthur Hallam died in 1833, Tennyson matured in other ways, beginning his long, elegiac "In Memoriam." In Tennyson's character, there was a quarrel between a personal predilection for melancholy and the Victorian duty to be optimistic and progressive. For much of his life, Victorian optimism won out; he is the poet of his age. When he speaks the philosophy of imperialism, as in "Ulysses," he speaks it with eloquence and vigor. In his more private poems, sweetness and fire remain as public gusto vanishes.

Ulysses   (1833)

It little profits that an idle king,
By this still hearth, among these barren crags,
Matched with an agèd wife, I mete and dole
Unequal laws unto a savage race,
That hoard, and sleep, and feed, and know not me.
I cannot rest from travel: I will drink
Life to the lees: all times I have enjoyed
Greatly, have suffered greatly, both with those
That loved me, and alone; on shore, and when
10   Through scudding drifts the rainy Hyades
Vext the dim sea: I am become a name;
For always roaming with a hungry heart
Much have I seen and known; cities of men
And manners, climates, councils, governments,
Myself not least, but honored of them all;
And drunk delight of battle with my peers,
Far on the ringing plains of windy Troy.
I am a part of all that I have met;
Yet all experience is an arch wherethro'
20   Gleams that untraveled world, whose margin fades
For ever and for ever when I move.
How dull it is to pause, to make an end,

To rust unburnished, not to shine in use!
As though to breathe were life. Life piled on life
Were all too little, and of one to me
Little remains: but every hour is saved
From that eternal silence, something more,
A bringer of new things; and vile it were
For some three suns to store and hoard myself,
30 And this gray spirit yearning in desire
To follow knowledge like a sinking star,
Beyond the utmost bound of human thought.

This is my son, mine own Telemachus,
To whom I leave the scepter and the isle—
Well-loved of me, discerning to fulfill
This labor, by slow prudence to make mild
A rugged people, and through soft degrees
Subdue them to the useful and the good.
Most blameless is he, centered in the sphere
40 Of common duties, decent not to fail
In offices of tenderness, and pay
Meet adoration to my household gods,
When I am gone. He works his work, I mine.

There lies the port; the vessel puffs her sail:
There gloom the dark broad seas. My mariners,
Souls that have toiled, and wrought, and thought with me—
That ever with a frolic welcome took
The thunder and the sunshine, and opposed
Free hearts, free foreheads—you and I are old;
50 Old age hath yet his honor and his toil;
Death closes all: but something ere the end,
Some work of noble note, may yet be done,
Not unbecoming men that strove with Gods.
The lights begin to twinkle from the rocks:
The long day wanes: the slow moon climbs: the deep
Moans round with many voices. Come, my friends,
'Tis not too late to seek a newer world.
Push off, and sitting well in order smite
The sounding furrows; for my purpose holds
60 To sail beyond the sunset, and the baths
Of all the western stars, until I die.
It may be that the gulfs will wash us down:
It may be we shall touch the Happy Isles,
And see the great Achilles, whom we knew.
Though much is taken, much abides; and though
We are not now that strength which in old days
Moved earth and heaven; that which we are, we are;
One equal temper of heroic hearts,
Made weak by time and fate, but strong in will
70 To strive, to seek, to find, and not to yield.

The Eagle   (1851)

He clasps the crag with crooked hands;
Close to the sun in lonely lands,
Ringed with the azure world, he stands.

The wrinkled sea beneath him crawls;
He watches from his mountain walls,
And like a thunderbolt he falls.

Dylan Thomas

Dylan Thomas (1914–1953) grew up in Wales and wrote prose and poetry about his childhood. He began early to write excellent lyrical poetry, and published his first book when he was only nineteen. At least half of his *Collected Poems* was written or drafted before he was twenty-two. Continually in debt and an alcoholic, he lived a life with less and less poetry in it. The sparse later work remained high in quality, like the play *Under Milk Wood,* finished just as he died at the age of thirty-nine.

This Bread I Break   (1939)

This bread I break was once the oat,
This wine upon a foreign tree
Plunged in its fruit;
Man in the day or wind at night
Laid the crops low, broke the grape's joy.

Once in this wind the summer blood
Knocked in the flesh that decked the vine,
Once in this bread
The oat was merry in the wind;
10 Man broke the sun, pulled the wind down.

This flesh you break, this blood you let
Make desolation in the vein,
Were oat and grape
Born of the sensual root and sap;
My wine you drink, my bread you snap.

Fern Hill   (1946)

Now as I was young and easy under the apple boughs
About the lilting house and happy as the grass was green,
    The night above the dingle starry,
        Time let me hail and climb
    Golden in the heydays of his eyes,

And honoured among wagons I was prince of the apple towns
And once below a time I lordly had the trees and leaves
      Trail with daisies and barley
    Down the rivers of the windfall light.

10 And as I was green and carefree, famous among the barns
About the happy yard and singing as the farm was home,
    In the sun that is young once only,
      Time let me play and be
    Golden in the mercy of his means,
And green and golden I was huntsman and herdsman, the calves
Sang to my horn, the foxes on the hills barked clear and cold,
    And the sabbath rang slowly
    In the pebbles of the holy streams.

All the sun long it was running, it was lovely, the hay
20 Fields high as the house, the tunes from the chimneys, it was air
    And playing, lovely and watery
      And fire green as grass.
    And nightly under the simple stars
As I rode to sleep the owls were bearing the farm away,
All the moon long I heard, blessed among stables, the night-jars
    Flying with the ricks, and the horses
      Flashing into the dark.

And then to awake, and the farm, like a wanderer white
With the dew, come back, the cock on his shoulder: it was all
30   Shining, it was Adam and maiden,
      The sky gathered again
    And the sun grew round that very day.
So it must have been after the birth of the simple light
In the first, spinning place, the spellbound horses walking warm
    Out of the whinnying green stable
      On to the fields of praise.

And honoured among foxes and pheasants by the gay house
Under the new made clouds and happy as the heart was long,
    In the sun born over and over,
40   I ran my heedless ways,
    My wishes raced through the house high hay
And nothing I cared, at my sky blue trades, that time allows
In all his tuneful turning so few and such morning songs
    Before the children green and golden
      Follow him out of grace,

Nothing I cared, in the lamb white days, that time would take me
Up to the swallow thronged loft by the shadow of my hand,
    In the moon that is always rising,
      Nor that riding to sleep
50   I should hear him fly with the high fields
And wake to the farm forever fled from the childless land.

Oh as I was young and easy in the mercy of his means,
  Time held me green and dying
  Though I sang in my chains like the sea.

Do not go gentle into that good night   (1952)

Do not go gentle into that good night,
Old age should burn and rave at close of day;
Rage, rage against the dying of the light.

Though wise men at their end know dark is right,
Because their words had forked no lightning they
Do not go gentle into that good night.

Good men, the last wave by, crying how bright
Their frail deeds might have danced in a green bay,
Rage, rage against the dying of the light.

10 Wild men who caught and sang the sun in flight,
And learn, too late, they grieved it on its way,
Do not go gentle into that good night.

Grave men, near death, who see with blinding sight
Blind eyes could blaze like meteors and be gay,
Rage, rage against the dying of the light.

And you, my father, there on the sad height,
Curse, bless, me now with your fierce tears, I pray.
Do not go gentle into that good night.
Rage, rage against the dying of the light.

Edward Thomas

Edward Thomas (1878–1917) was Robert Frost's great English friend, a freelance writer of prose whom Frost teased and encouraged into poetry. Thomas came to poetry late, wrote furiously in his brief poetic life, and was killed in World War I.

The Owl   (1915)

Downhill I came, hungry, and yet not starved;
Cold, yet had heat within me that was proof
Against the North wind; tired, yet so that rest
Had seemed the sweetest thing under a roof.

Then at the inn I had food, fire, and rest,
Knowing how hungry, cold, and tired was I.

All of the night was quite barred out except
An owl's cry, a most melancholy cry

Shaken out long and clear upon the hill,
10 No merry note, nor cause of merriment,
But one telling me plain what I escaped
And others could not, that night, as in I went.

And salted was my food, and my repose,
Salted and sobered, too, by the bird's voice
Speaking for all who lay under the stars,
Soldiers and poor, unable to rejoice.

Charles Tomlinson

Charles Tomlinson (1927–   ) was born in an industrial English town and
attended Cambridge. He teaches at Bristol and is a painter as well as a poet. In
some of his poetry he has learned from American sources, especially Wallace
Stevens and the Black Mountain poets.

Paring the Apple   (1958)

There are portraits and still-lifes.

And there is paring the apple.

And then? Paring it slowly,
From under cool-yellow
Cold-white emerging. And. . . ?

The spring of concentric peel
Unwinding off white,
The blade hidden, dividing.

There are portraits and still-lifes
10 And the first, because 'human'

Does not excel the second, and
Neither is less weighted
With a human gesture, than paring the
      apple
With a human stillness.

The cool blade
Severs between coolness, apple-rind
Compelling a recognition.

Jean Toomer

Jean Toomer (1894–1967) wrote in *Cane* a combination of poetry and prose that
was an early contribution to the literature of the black American.

Reapers   (1923)

Black reapers with the sound of steel on stones
Are sharpening scythes. I see them place the hones
In their hip-pockets as a thing that's done,

And start their silent swinging, one by one.
Black horses drive a mower through the weeds,
And there, a field rat, startled, squealing bleeds,
His belly close to ground. I see the blade,
Blood-stained, continue cutting weeds and shade.

John Updike

John Updike (1932–   ) grew up in Pennsylvania, attended Harvard and
Oxford, and worked for a while at *The New Yorker,* where his stories and poems
first appeared. He writes articles and reviews, stories and poems, and he is best
known as a novelist. Some of his many novels are *Rabbit Run* (1960), *The
Centaur* (1963), *Couples* (1968), *Rabbit Redux* (1971), and *Rabbit at Rest* (1991).

Ex-Basketball Player   (1958)

Pearl Avenue runs past the high-school lot,
Bends with the trolley tracks, and stops, cut off
Before it has a chance to go two blocks,
At Colonel McComsky Plaza. Berth's Garage
Is on the corner facing west, and there,
Most days, you'll find Flick Webb, who helps Berth out.

Flick stands tall among the idiot pumps—
Five on a side, the old bubble-head style,
Their rubber elbows hanging loose and low.
10 One's nostrils are two S's, and his eyes
An E and O. And one is squat, without
A head at all—more of a football type.

Once Flick played for the high-school team, the Wizards.
He was good: in fact, the best. In '46
He bucketed three hundred ninety points,
A county record still. The ball loved Flick.
I saw him rack up thirty-eight or forty
In one home game. His hands were like wild birds.

He never learned a trade, he just sells gas,
20 Checks oil, and changes flats. Once in a while,
As a gag, he dribbles an inner tube,
But most of us remember anyway.
His hands are fine and nervous on the lug wrench.
It makes no difference to the lug wrench, though.

Off work, he hangs around Mae's luncheonette.
Grease-gray and kind of coiled, he plays pinball,
Smokes those thin cigars, nurses lemon phosphates.
Flick seldom says a word to Mae, just nods
Beyond her face toward bright applauding tiers
30 Of Necco Wafers, Nibs, and Juju Beads.

Derek Walcott

Derek Walcott (1930–   ) was born in Saint Lucia in the West Indies, and now lives in Massachusetts. He teaches at Boston University. Walcott has published many collections, including a *Collected Poems: 1948–1984* and, most recently, *Omeros* (1990).

Sea Grapes   (1971)

That sail in cloudless light
which tires of islands,
a schooner beating up the Caribbean

for home, could be Odysseus
home-bound through the Aegean,
just as that husband's

sorrow under the sea-grapes, repeats
the adulterer's hearing Nausicaa's name
in every gull's outcry.

10   But whom does this bring peace? The classic war
between a passion and responsibility
is never finished, and has been the same

to the sea-wanderer and the one on shore,
now wriggling on his sandals to walk home,
since Troy sighed its last flame,

and the blind giant's boulder heaved the trough
from which The Odyssey's hexameters come
to finish up as Caribbean surf.

The classics can console. But not enough.

Robert Penn Warren

Robert Penn Warren (1905–   ) attended Vanderbilt University and then Oxford University as a Rhodes scholar. He was the youngest member of the Fugitive Group of Southern writers, along with Allen Tate and John Crowe Ransom. Author with Cleanth Brooks of *Understanding Poetry,* a most influential textbook, he is an eminent critic and novelist—*All the King's Men* won the Pulitzer Prize for fiction in 1947—as well as a poet. His books of poems have earned him Pulitzer Prizes and a National Book Award.

Gold Glade   (1957)

Wandering, in autumn, the woods of boyhood,
Where cedar, black, thick, rode the ridge,

Heart aimless as rifle, boy-blankness of mood,
I came where ridge broke, and the great ledge,
Limestone, set the toe high as treetop by dark edge

Of a gorge, and water hid, grudging and grumbling,
And I saw, in mind's eye, foam white on
Wet stone, stone wet-black, white water tumbling,
And so went down, and with some fright on
10 Slick boulders, crossed over. The gorge-depth drew night on,

But high over high rock and leaf-lacing, sky
Showed yet bright, and declivity wooed
My foot by the quietening stream, and so I
Went on, in quiet, through the beech wood:
There, in gold light, where the glade gave, it stood.

The glade was geometric, circular, gold,
No brush or weed breaking that bright gold of leaf-fall.
In the center it stood, absolute and bold
Beyond any heart-hurt, or eye's grief-fall.
20 Gold-massy in air, it stood in gold light-fall,

No breathing of air, no leaf now gold-falling,
No tooth-stitch of squirrel, or any far fox bark,
No woodpecker coding, or late jay calling.
Silence: gray-shagged, the great shagbark
Gave forth gold light. There could be no dark.

But of course dark came, and I can't recall
What county it was, for the life of me.
Montgomery, Todd, Christian—I know them all.
Was it even Kentucky or Tennessee?
30 Perhaps just an image that keeps haunting me.

No, no! in no mansion under earth,
Nor imagination's domain of bright air,
But solid in soil that gave it its birth,
It stands, wherever it is, but somewhere.
I shall set my foot, and go there.

Walt Whitman

Walt Whitman (1819–1892) is the first great American poet. He is also one of the greatest innovators in the history of the art. His long, loose rhythms derive in part from the King James version of the Bible and in part from the expansive gestures of nineteenth-century political oratory. But largely they seem Whitman's own creation.

Born on Long Island, son of a carpenter who was also a farmer, Whitman was sporadically educated, became a newspaper editor, and created himself as a poet. The first edition of *Leaves of Grass,* which through subsequent editions became a collection of his life's work, appeared in 1855. Emerson praised him, but few other early readers had the imagination to understand that his writing was poetry at all. Not only was his work innovative; in its broad sensuality and in its hints at homoeroticism, it was shocking. Emily Dickinson's comment, in a letter to Thomas Wentworth Higginson, tells the tale: "You speak of Mr. Whitman—I never read his Book—but was told that he was disgraceful—"

Out of the Cradle Endlessly Rocking   (1881)

Out of the cradle endlessly rocking,
Out of the mocking-bird's throat, the musical shuttle,
Out of the Ninth-month midnight,
Over the sterile sands and the fields beyond, where the child leaving his bed
    wandered alone, bareheaded, barefoot,
Down from the showered halo,
Up from the mystic play of shadows twining and twisting as if they were alive,
Out from the patches of briers and blackberries,
From the memories of the bird that chanted to me,
10 From your memories sad brother, from the fitful risings and fallings I heard,
From under that yellow half-moon late-risen and swollen as if with tears,
From those beginning notes of yearning and love there in the mist,
From the thousand responses of my heart never to cease,
From the myriad thence-aroused words,
From the word stronger and more delicious than any,
From such as now they start the scene revisiting,
As a flock, twittering, rising, or overhead passing,
Borne hither, ere all eludes me, hurriedly,
A man, yet by these tears a little boy again,
20 Throwing myself on the sand, confronting the waves,
I, chanter of pains and joys, uniter of here and hereafter,
Taking all hints to use them, but swiftly leaping beyond them,
A reminiscence sing.

Once Paumanok,
When the lilac-scent was in the air and Fifth-month grass was growing,
Up this seashore in some briers,
Two feathered guests from Alabama, two together,
And their nest, and four light-green eggs spotted with brown,
And every day the he-bird to and fro near at hand,
30 And every day the she-bird crouched on her nest, silent, with bright eyes,
And every day I, a curious boy, never too close, never disturbing them,
Cautiously peering, absorbing, translating.

Shine! shine! shine!
Pour down your warmth, great sun!
While we bask, we two together.

Two together!
Winds blow south, or winds blow north.
Day come white, or night come black,
Home, or rivers and mountains from home,
40 *Singing all time, minding no time,*
While we two keep together.

Till of a sudden,
May-be killed, unknown to her mate,
One forenoon the she-bird crouched not on the nest,
Nor returned that afternoon, nor the next,
Nor ever appeared again.

And thenceforward all summer in the sound of the sea,
And at night under the full of the moon in calmer weather,
Over the hoarse surging of the sea,
50 Or flitting from brier to brier by day,
I saw, I heard at intervals the remaining one, the he-bird,
The solitary guest from Alabama.

Blow! blow! blow!
Blow up sea-winds along Paumanok's shore:
I wait and I wait till you blow my mate to me.

Yes, when the stars glistened,
All night long on the prong of a moss-scalloped stake,
Down almost amid the slapping waves,
Sat the lone singer wonderful causing tears.

60 He called on his mate,
He poured forth the meanings which I of all men know.

Yes my brother I know,
The rest might not, but I have treasured every note,
For more than once dimly down to the beach gliding,
Silent, avoiding the moonbeams, blending myself with the shadows,
Recalling now the obscure shapes, the echoes, the sounds and sights after their
    sorts,
The white arms out in the breakers tirelessly tossing,
I, with bare feet, a child, the wind wafting my hair,
70 Listened long and long.

Listened to keep, to sing, now translating the notes,
Following you my brother.

Soothe! soothe! soothe!
Close on its wave soothes the wave behind,
And again another behind embracing and lapping, every one close,
But my love soothes not me, not me.

Low hangs the moon, it rose late.
It is lagging—O I think it is heavy with love, with love.
O madly the sea pushes upon the land,
80 *With love, with love.*

O night! do I not see my love fluttering out among the breakers?
What is that little black thing I see there in the white?

Loud! loud! loud!
Loud I call to you, my love!

High and clear I shoot my voice over the waves,
Surely you must know who is here, is here,
You must know who I am, my love.

Low-hanging moon!
What is that dusky spot in your brown yellow?
90 *O it is the shape, the shape of my mate!*
O moon do not keep her from me any longer.

Land! land! O land!
Whichever way I turn, O I think you could give me my mate back again if you only
        would.
For I am almost sure I see her dimly whichever way I look.

O rising stars!
Perhaps the one I want so much will rise, will rise with some of you.

O throat! O trembling throat!
Sound clearer through the atmosphere!
100 *Pierce the woods, the earth,*
Somewhere listening to catch you must be the one I want.

Shake out carols!
Solitary here, the night's carols!
Carols of lonesome love! death's carols!
Carols under that lagging, yellow, waning moon!
O under that moon where she droops almost down into the sea!
O reckless despairing carols.

But soft! sink low!
Soft! let me just murmur.
110 *And do you wait a moment you husky-noised sea,*
For somewhere I believe I heard my mate responding to me,
So faint, I must be still, be still to listen,
But not altogether still, for then she might not come immediately to me.

Hither my love!
Here I am! Here!
With this just-sustained note I announce myself to you.
This gentle call is for you my love, for you.

Do not be decoyed elsewhere,
That is the whistle of the wind, it is not my voice,
120   *That is the fluttering, the fluttering of the spray.*
Those are the shadows of leaves.

O darkness! O in vain!
O I am very sick and sorrowful.

O brown halo in the sky near the moon, drooping upon the sea!
O troubled reflection in the sea!
O throat! O throbbing heart!
And I singing uselessly, uselessly all the night.

O past! O happy life! O songs of joy!
In the air, in the woods, over fields,
130   *Loved! loved! loved! loved! loved!*
But my mate no more, no more with me!
We two together no more.

The aria sinking,
All else continuing, the stars shining,
The winds blowing, the notes of the bird continuous echoing,
With angry moans the fierce old mother incessantly moaning,
On the sands of Paumanok's shore gray and rustling,
The yellow half-moon enlarged, sagging down, drooping, the face of the sea almost
      touching,
140   The boy ecstatic, with his bare feet the waves, with his hair the atmosphere dallying,
The love in the heart long pent, now loose, now at last tumultuously bursting,
The aria's meaning, the ears, the soul, swiftly depositing,
The strange tears down the cheeks coursing,
The colloquy there, the trio, each uttering,
The undertone, the savage old mother incessantly crying,
To the boy's soul's questions sullenly timing, some drowned secret hissing,
To the outsetting bard.

Demon or bird! (said the boy's soul,)
Is it indeed toward your mate you sing? or is it really to me?
150   For I, that was a child, my tongue's use sleeping, now I have heard you,
Now in a moment I know what I am for, I awake,
And already a thousand singers, a thousand songs, clearer, louder and more
      sorrowful than yours,
A thousand warbling echoes have started to life within me, never to die.

O you singer solitary, singing by yourself, projecting me,
O solitary me listening, never more shall I cease perpetuating you,
Never more shall I escape, never more the reverberations,
Never more the cries of unsatisfied love be absent from me,
Never again leave me to be the peaceful child I was before what there in the night,
160   By the sea under the yellow and sagging moon,
The messenger there aroused, the fire, the sweet hell within,
The unknown want, the destiny of me.

O give me the clue! (it lurks in the night here somewhere,)
O if I am to have so much, let me have more!

A word then, (for I will conquer it,)
The word final, superior to all,
Subtle, sent up—what is it?—I listen;
Are you whispering it, and have been all the time, you sea-waves?
Is that it from your liquid rims and wet sands?

170   Whereto answering, the sea,
        Delaying not, hurrying not,
        Whispered me through the night, and very plainly before daybreak,
        Lisped to me the low and delicious word death,
        And again death, death, death, death,
        Hissing melodious, neither like the bird nor like my aroused child's heart,
        But edging near as privately for me rustling at my feet,
        Creeping thence steadily up to my ears and laving me softly all over,
        Death, death, death, death, death.

        Which I do not forget,
180   But fuse the song of my dusky demon and brother,
        That he sang to me in the moonlight on Paumanok's gray beach,
        With the thousand responsive songs at random,
        My own songs awaked from that hour,
        And with them the key, the word up from the waves,
        The word of the sweetest song and all songs,
        That strong and delicious word which, creeping to my feet,
        (Or like some old crone rocking the cradle, swathed in sweet garments, bending
              aside,)
        The sea whispered me.

A Farm Picture   (1865)

Through the ample open door of the peaceful country barn,
A sunlit pasture field with cattle and horses feeding,
And haze and vista, and the far horizon fading away.

Cavalry Crossing a Ford   (1865)

A line in long array where they wind betwixt green islands,
They take a serpentine course, their arms flash in the sun—hark to the musical
      clank,
Behold the silvery river, in it the splashing horses loitering stop to drink,
Behold the brown-faced men, each group, each person a picture, the negligent rest
      on the saddles,
Some emerge on the opposite bank, others are just entering the ford—while,
Scarlet and blue and snowy white,
The guidon flags flutter gayly in the wind.

Richard Wilbur

Richard Wilbur (1921–   ) was born in New Jersey and has lived in the eastern
United States. During World War II, he fought in Italy and France; he began
writing poems in the Army. His work is decorative, skillful, aimed to please and
to enlighten rather than to shock or to overwhelm. He is one of the few poets of
his generation who has not undergone violent change, in work and private life,
which has earned him the disapproval of critics. In 1988, he published his *New
and Collected Poems,* which won him his second Pulitzer Prize. See also pages 48
and 88.

Still, Citizen Sparrow   (1950)

Still, citizen sparrow, this vulture which you call
Unnatural, let him but lumber again to air
Over the rotten office, let him bear
The carrion ballast up, and at the tall

Tip of the sky lie cruising. Then you'll see
That no more beautiful bird is in heaven's height,
No wider more placid wings, no watchfuller flight;
He shoulders nature there, the frightfully free,

The naked-headed one. Pardon him, you
10 Who dart in the orchard aisles, for it is he
Devours death, mocks mutability,
Has heart to make an end, keeps nature new.

Thinking of Noah, childheart, try to forget
How for so many bedlam hours his saw
Soured the song of birds with its wheezy gnaw,
And the slam of his hammer all the day beset

The people's ears. Forget that he could bear
To see the towns like coral under the keel,
And the fields so dismal deep. Try rather to feel
20 How high and weary it was, on the waters where

He rocked his only world, and everyone's.
Forgive the hero, you who would have died
Gladly with all you knew; he rode that tide
To Ararat;[1] all men are Noah's sons.

---

[1] The mountain on which Noah's Ark landed

William Carlos Williams

William Carlos Williams (1883–1963) knew Ezra Pound at the University of Pennsylvania when they were students. Williams went on to become a medical doctor, living most of his life in suburban Rutherford, New Jersey, where he practiced medicine, specializing in obstetrics. His poetry was resolute in its use of the American idiom. Followers have turned his theory and his practice into one of the main schools of contemporary American poetry. See also pages 10, 25, and 68.

This Is Just to Say   (1938)

I have eaten
the plums
that were in
the icebox

and which
you were probably

saving
for breakfast

Forgive me
10 they were delicious
so sweet
and so cold

Spring and All   (1922)

By the road to the contagious hospital
under the surge of the blue
mottled clouds driven from the
northeast—a cold wind. Beyond, the
waste of broad, muddy fields
brown with dried weeds, standing and
    fallen

patches of standing water
the scattering of tall trees

10 All along the road the reddish
purplish, forked, upstanding, twiggy
stuff of bushes and small trees
with dead, brown leaves under them
leafless vines—

Lifeless in appearance, sluggish
dazed spring approaches—

They enter the new world naked,
cold, uncertain of all
save that they enter. All about them
20 the cold, familiar wind—

Now the grass, tomorrow
the stiff curl of wildcarrot leaf

One by one objects are defined—
It quickens: clarity, outline of leaf

But now the stark dignity of
entrance—Still, the profound change
has come upon them: rooted they
grip down and begin to awaken

William Wordsworth

William Wordsworth (1770–1850) attended Cambridge, afterward touring Europe
on foot and living for a year in France when the revolutionary society was at its
most exciting. Back in England, he continued to write poems, and in 1795 began
his long and close friendship with Samuel Taylor Coleridge. The two poets, with
Wordsworth's sister Dorothy and with Coleridge's wife, lived near each other for
a time, and Wordsworth and Coleridge published *Lyrical Ballads* in 1798, a
collection of poetry by both of them, including Coleridge's "Rime of the Ancient
Mariner" and Wordsworth's "Lines Written Above Tintern Abbey." The year of
publication provides as good a date as any for the beginning of the romantic
movement in English literature. Two years later, reprinting the volume,
Wordsworth added prose "observations" in which he defended his own theory of
poetry, deriving his language from rustic life. His imagery also derived from
rustic life, and his poems were at first denounced as obscure and meaningless.
Later, he became one of the most popular poets of the English tradition. In his
long life, he wrote prolifically; most of his best work is early.

Ode: Intimations of Immortality from Recollections of Early Childhood   (1806)

> The Child is father of the Man;
> And I could wish my days to be
> Bound each to each by natural piety.

I

There was a time when meadow, grove, and stream,
The earth, and every common sight,
     To me did seem
    Apparelled in celestial light,
The glory and the freshness of a dream.
It is not now as it hath been of yore;—
    Turn whereso'er I may,
      By night or day,
The things which I have seen I now can see no more.

II

10   The Rainbow comes and goes,
    And lovely is the Rose,
    The moon doth with delight
Look round her when the heavens are bare,
    Waters on a starry night
    Are beautiful and fair;
  The sunshine is a glorious birth;
  But yet I know, where'er I go,
That there hath past away a glory from the earth.

III

Now, while the birds thus sing a joyous song,
20   And while the young lambs bound

As to the tabor's sound,
To me alone there came a thought of grief:
A timely utterance gave that thought relief,
    And I again am strong:
The cataracts blow their trumpets from the steep;
No more shall grief of mine the season wrong;
I hear the Echoes through the mountains throng,
The Winds come to me from the fields of sleep,
    And all the earth is gay;
30   Land and sea
  Give themselves up to jollity,
    And with the heart of May
Doth every Beast keep holiday;—
    Thou Child of Joy,
Shout round me, let me hear thy shouts, thou happy
    Shepherd-boy!

IV

Ye blessèd Creatures, I have heard the call
  Ye to each other make; I see
The heavens laugh with you in your jubilee;
40   My heart is at your festival,
    My head hath its coronal,
The fulness of your bliss, I feel—I feel it all.
    Oh evil day! if I were sullen
    While Earth herself is adorning,
      This sweet May-morning,
    And the Children are culling
      On every side,
    In a thousand valleys far and wide,
    Fresh flowers; while the sun shines warm,
50 And the Babe leaps up on his Mother's arm:—
    I hear, I hear, with joy I hear!
    —But there's a Tree, of many, one,
A single Field which I have looked upon,
Both of them speak of something that is gone:
    The Pansy at my feet
    Doth the same tale repeat:
Whither is fled the visionary gleam?
Where is it now, the glory and the dream?

V

Our birth is but a sleep and a forgetting:
60 The Soul that rises with us, our life's Star,
    Hath had elsewhere its setting,
      And cometh from afar:
    Not in entire forgetfulness,
    And not in utter nakedness,
But trailing clouds of glory do we come
    From God, who is our home:

Heaven lies about us in our infancy!
Shades of the prison-house begin to close
      Upon the growing Boy,
70 But He beholds the light, and whence it flows,
      He sees it in his joy;
The Youth, who daily farther from the east
      Must travel, still is Nature's Priest,
      And by the vision splendid
      Is on his way attended;
At length the Man perceives it die away,
And fade into the light of common day.

VI

Earth fills her lap with pleasures of her own;
Yearnings she hath in her own natural kind,
80 And, even with something of a Mother's mind,
      And no unworthy aim,
      The homely Nurse doth all she can
To make her Foster-child, her Inmate Man,
      Forget the glories he hath known,
And that imperial palace whence he came.

VII

Behold the Child among his new-born blisses,
A six years' Darling of a pigmy size!
See, where 'mid work of his own hand he lies,
Fretted by sallies of his mother's kisses,
90 With light upon him from his father's eyes!
See, at his feet, some little plan or chart,
Some fragment from his dream of human life,
Shaped by himself with newly-learnèd art;
      A wedding or a festival,
      A mourning or a funeral;
        And this hath now his heart,
      And unto this he frames his song.
        Then will he fit his tongue
To dialogues of business, love, or strife;
100   But it will not be long
      Ere this be thrown aside,
      And with new joy and pride
The little Actor cons another part;
Filling from time to time his "humorous stage"
With all the Persons, down to palsied Age,
That Life brings with her in her equipage;
      As if his whole vocation
      Were endless imitation.

VIII

Thou, whose exterior semblance doth belie
110   Thy Soul's immensity;

Thou best Philosopher, who yet dost keep
Thy heritage, thou Eye among the blind,
That, deaf and silent, read'st the eternal deep,
Haunted for ever by the eternal mind,—
      Mighty Prophet! Seer blest!
      On whom those truths do rest,
Which we are toiling all our lives to find,
In darkness lost, the darkness of the grave,
Thou, over whom thy Immortality
120 Broods like the Day, a Master o'er a Slave,
A Presence which is not to be put by;
Thou little Child, yet glorious in the might
Of heaven-born freedom on thy being's height,
Why with such earnest pains dost thou provoke
The years to bring the inevitable yoke,
Thus blindly with thy blessedness at strife?
Full soon thy Soul shall have her earthly freight,
And custom lie upon thee with a weight,
Heavy as frost, and deep almost as life!

IX

130   O joy! that in our embers
       Is something that doth live,
       That nature yet remembers
       What was so fugitive!
The thought of our past years in me doth breed
Perpetual benediction: not indeed
For that which is most worthy to be blest;
Delight and liberty, the simple creed
Of Childhood, whether busy or at rest,
With new-fledged hope still fluttering in his breast:—
140   Not for these I raise
       The song of thanks and praise;
     But for those obstinate questionings
     Of sense and outward things,
     Fallings from us, vanishings;
     Blank misgivings of a Creature
Moving about in worlds not realised,
High instincts before which our mortal Nature
Did tremble like a guilty Thing surprised:
      But for those first affections,
150   Those shadowy recollections,
    Which, be they what they may,
Are yet the fountain-light of all our day,
Are yet a master-light of all our seeing;
    Uphold us, cherish, and have power to make
Our noisy years seem moments in the being
Of the eternal Silence: truths that wake,
      To perish never:
Which neither listlessness, nor mad endeavour,
      Nor Man nor Boy,

160 Nor all that is at enmity with joy,
  Can utterly abolish or destroy!
    Hence in a season of calm weather
      Though inland far we be,
  Our Souls have sight of that immortal sea
      Which brought us hither,
    Can in a moment travel thither,
  And see the Children sport upon the shore,
  And hear the mighty waters rolling evermore.

X

  Then sing, ye Birds, sing, sing a joyous song!
170   And let the young Lambs bound
      As to the tabor's sound!
  We in thought will join your throng,
      Ye that pipe and ye that play,
      Ye that through your hearts today
      Feel the gladness of the May!
  What though the radiance which was once so bright
  Be now for ever taken from my sight,
    Though nothing can bring back the hour
  Of splendour in the grass, of glory in the flower
180   We will grieve not, rather find
      Strength in what remains behind;
      In the primal sympathy
      Which having been must ever be;
      In the soothing thoughts that spring
      Out of human suffering;
      In the faith that looks through death,
  In years that bring the philosophic mind.

XI

  And O, ye Fountains, Meadows, Hills, and Groves,
  Forebode not any severing of our loves!
190 Yet in my heart of hearts I feel your might;
  I only have relinquished one delight
  To live beneath your more habitual sway.
  I love the Brooks which down their channels fret,
  Even more than when I tripped lightly as they;
  The innocent brightness of a new-born Day
      Is lovely yet;
  The Clouds that gather round the setting sun
  Do take a sober colouring from an eye
  That hath kept watch o'er man's mortality;
200 Another race hath been, and other palms are won.
  Thanks to the human heart by which we live,
  Thanks to its tenderness, its joys, and fears,
  To me the meanest flower that blows can give
  Thoughts that do often lie too deep for tears.

The World Is Too Much with Us   (1807)

The world is too much with us; late and soon,
Getting and spending, we lay waste our powers:
Little we see in Nature that is ours;
We have given our hearts away, a sordid boon!
The sea that bares her bosom to the moon;
The winds that will be howling at all hours,
And are up-gathered now like sleeping flowers;
For this, for everything, we are out of tune;
It moves us not.—Great God! I'd rather be
10 A pagan suckled in a creed outworn;
So might I, standing on this pleasant lea,
Have glimpses that would make me less forlorn;
Have sight of Proteus rising from the sea;
Or hear old Triton blow his wreathèd horn.

Charles Wright

Charles Wright (1935–   ) comes from Virginia and lives in Charlottesville,
where he teaches at the University of Virginia.

Virgo Descending   (1975)

Through the viridian (and black of the burnt match),
Through ox-blood and ochre, the ham colored clay,
Through plate after plate, down
Where the worm and the mole will not go,
Through ore-seam and fire seam,
My grandmother, senile and 89, crimpbacked, stands
Like a door ajar on her soft bed,
The open beams and bare studs of the hall
Pink as an infant's skin in the floating dark;
10 Shavings and curls swing down like snowflakes across her face.

My aunt and I walk past. As always, my father
Is planning rooms, dragging his lame leg,
Stroke-straightened and foreign, behind him,
An aberrant 2-by-4 he can't fit snug.
I lay my head on my aunt's shoulder, feeling
At home, and walk on.
Through arches and door jambs, the spidery wires
And coiled cables, the blueprint takes shape:
My mother's room to the left, the door closed;
20 My father's room to the left, the door closed—

Ahead, my brother's room, unfinished;
Behind, my sister's room, also unfinished.
Buttresses, winches, block-and-tackle: the scale of everything
Is enormous. We keep on walking. And pass
My aunt's room, almost complete, the curtains up,
The lamp and the medicine arranged
In their proper places, in arm's reach of where the bed will go . . .
The next one is mine, now more than half done,
Cloyed by the scent of jasmine
30 White-gummed and anxious, their mouths sucking the air dry.

Home is what you lie in, or hang above, the house
Your father made, or keeps on making,
The dirt you moisten, the sap you push up and nourish . . .
I enter the living room, it, too, unfinished, its far wall
Not there, opening on to a radiance
I can't begin to imagine, a light
My father walks from, approaching me,
Dragging his right leg, rolling his plans into a perfect curl.
That light, he mutters. that damned light.
40 We can't keep it out. It keeps on filling your room.

James Wright

James Wright (1927–1980) grew up among the coal mines and steel mills of Ohio
and attended Kenyon College, where he studied with John Crowe Ransom. His
first book was *The Green Wall,* which made him the Yale Younger Poet in 1957.
This Journey appeared posthumously in 1982. In 1990, his publishers issued his
collected poems under the title *Above the River.* See also pages 28–29 and 30–31.

The First Days   (1974)
Optima dies prima fugit[1]

The first thing I saw in the morning
Was a huge golden bee ploughing
His burly right shoulder into the belly
Of a sleek yellow pear
Low on a bough.
Before he could find that sudden black honey
That squirms around in there
Inside the seed, the tree could not bear any more.
The pear fell to the ground
10 With the bee still half alive

[1] "The best day is the first to flee," a line from the Roman poet Virgil, who was born near
Mantua

Inside its body.
He would have died if I hadn't knelt down
And sliced the pear gently
A little more open.
The bee shuddered, and returned.
Maybe I should have left him alone there,
Drowning in his own delight.
The best days are the first
To flee, sang the lovely
20 Musician born in this town
So like my own.
I let the bee go
Among the gasworks at the edge of Mantua.

Jay Wright

Jay Wright (1935–   ) was born in New Mexico and lives in New Hampshire,
which he sometimes leaves to teach at Yale University. His *Selected Poems* was
published by Princeton University Press in 1987, and *Elaine's Book* in 1988. He
has received a Fellowship from the MacArthur Foundation.

Meta-A and the A of Absolutes   (1976)

I write my God in blue.
I run my gods upstream on flimsy rafts.
I bathe my goddesses in foam, in moonlight.
I take my reasons from my mother's snuff breath,
or from an old woman, sitting with a lemonade,
at twilight, on the desert's steps.
Brown by day and black by night,
my God has wings that open to no reason.
He scutters from the touch of old men's eyes,
10 scutters from the smell of wisdom, an orb
of light leaping from a fire.
Press him he bleeds.
When you take your hand to sacred water,
there is no sign of any wound.
And so I call him supreme, great artist,
judge of time, scholar of all living event,
the possible prophet of the possible event.
Blind men, on bourbon, with guitars,
blind men with their scars dulled by kola,
20 blind men seeking the shelter of a raindrop,
blind men in corn, blind men in steel,
reason by their lights that our tongues
are free, our tongues will redeem us.

Speech is the fact, and the fact is true.
What is moves, and what is moving is.
We cling to these contradictions.
We know we will become our contradictions,
our complex body's own desire.
Yet speech is not the limit of our vision.
30 The ear entices itself with any sound.
The skin will caress whatever tone
or temperament that rises or descends.
The bones will set themselves to a dance.
The blood will argue with a bird in flight.
The heart will scale the dew from an old chalice,
brush and thrill to an old bone.
And yet there is no sign to arrest us
                  from the possible.
We remain at rest there, in transit
40 from our knowing to our knowledge.
So I would set a limit where I meet my logic.
I would clamber from my own cave
into the curve of sign, an alphabet
of transformation, the clan's cloak of reason.
I am good when I am in motion,
when I think of myself at rest
in the knowledge of my moving,
when I have the vision of my mother at rest,
in moonlight, her lap the cradle of my father's head.
50 I am good when I trade my shells,
and walk from boundary to boundary,
unarmed and unafraid of another's speech.
I am good when I learn the world
through the touch of my present body.
I am good when I take the cove of a cub
                  into my care.
I am good when I hear the changes in my body
echo all my changes down the years,
when what I know indeed is what I would
60   know in deed.
I am good when I know the darkness of all light,
and accept the darkness, not as sign, but as my body.
This is the A of absolutes,
the logbook of judgments,
the good sign.

Thomas Wyatt

Sir Thomas Wyatt (1503–1542) was ambassador for Henry VIII—and several times imprisoned by him in the Tower of London for alleged offenses. Wyatt brought the sonnet to England, imitating the form used by Italian poets. When the music of English verse had vanished for a hundred years after Chaucer's death, Wyatt's lyrics and sonnets began its restoration.

They Flee from Me   (1535)

They flee from me, that sometime did me seek,
With naked foot, stalking in my chamber.
I have seen them, gentle, tame, and meek,
That now are wild, and do not remember
That sometime they put themselves in danger
To take bread at my hand, and now they range,
Busily seeking with a continual change.

Thankèd be fortune, it hath been otherwise
Twenty times better; but once, in special,
10   In thin array, after a pleasant guise,
When her loose gown from her shoulders did fall,
And she me caught in her arms long and small,
Therewithal sweetly did me kiss,
And softly said, "Dear heart, how like you this?"

It was no dream; I lay broad waking.
But all is turned, thorough my gentleness,
Into a strange fashion of forsaking;
And I have leave to go, of her goodness,
And she also to use new-fangledness.
20   But since that I so kindely° am served,   naturally
I would fain know what she hath deserved.

William Butler Yeats

William Butler Yeats (1865–1939), born in Dublin, grew up largely in Ireland in an Anglo-Irish family. Both his father and his brother were well-known artists. Yeats published his first collection of poetry when he was twenty-four and wrote continually until his death fifty years later. Considered by many the greatest of modern poets, Yeats was a leader in the Irish renaissance, playwright and founder of the Abbey Theatre, an Irish patriot and a denouncer of nationalism, a mystic and skeptic—a man of passion and conflict whose poetry derived from passionate conflict. In 1919, he acquired Thoor Ballylee, an ancient Norman tower in the west of Ireland that became a feature and a fixture in his poetry. He became a senator of independent Ireland and was awarded the Nobel Prize for literature in 1923. He made his best books of poems after receiving the prize: *The Tower* in 1928 and the posthumous *Last Poems* in 1940. See also page 112.

Who Goes with Fergus?

Who will go drive with Fergus[1] now,
And pierce the deep wood's woven shade,
And dance upon the level shore?
Young man, lift up your russet brow,
And lift your tender eyelids, maid,
And brood on hopes and fear no more.

And no more turn aside and brood
Upon love's bitter mystery;
For Fergus rules the brazen cars,
10   And rules the shadows of the wood,
And the white breast of the dim sea
And all dishevelled wandering stars.

The Magi   (1914)

Now as at all times I can see in the mind's eye,
In their stiff, painted clothes, the pale unsatisfied ones
Appear and disappear in the blue depth of the sky
With all their ancient faces like rain-beaten stones,
And all their helms of silver hovering side by side,
And all their eyes still fixed, hoping to find once more,
Being by Calvary's turbulence unsatisfied,
The uncontrollable mystery on the bestial floor.

The Second Coming   (1921)

Turning and turning in the widening gyre°   spiral
The falcon cannot hear the falconer;
Things fall apart; the centre cannot hold;

[1] Legendary king who renounced his throne to become an itinerant poet

Mere anarchy is loosed upon the world,
The blood-dimmed tide is loosed, and everywhere
The ceremony of innocence is drowned;
The best lack all conviction, while the worst
Are full of passionate intensity.

Surely some revelation is at hand;
10   Surely the Second Coming is at hand.
The Second Coming! Hardly are those words out
When a vast image out of *Spiritus Mundi*°   soul of the world
Troubles my sight: somewhere in sands of the desert
A shape with lion body and the head of a man,
A gaze blank and pitiless as the sun,
Is moving its slow thighs, while all about it
Reel shadows of the indignant desert birds.
The darkness drops again; but now I know
That twenty centuries of stony sleep
20   Were vexed to nightmare by a rocking cradle,
And what rough beast, its hour come round at last,
Slouches towards Bethlehem to be born?

Sailing to Byzantium   (1927)

I

That is no country for old men. The young
In one another's arms, birds in the trees
—Those dying generations—at their song,
The salmon-falls, the mackerel-crowded seas,
Fish, flesh, or fowl, commend all summer long
Whatever is begotten, born, and dies.
Caught in that sensual music all neglect
Monuments of unageing intellect.

II

An aged man is but a paltry thing,
10   A tattered coat upon a stick, unless
Soul clap its hands and sing, and louder sing
For every tatter in its mortal dress,
Nor is there singing school but studying
Monuments of its own magnificence;
And therefore I have sailed the seas and come
To the holy city of Byzantium.

III

O sages standing in God's holy fire
As in the gold mosaic of a wall,
Come from the holy fire, perne° in a gyre,   wind or unwind
20   And be the singing-masters of my soul.
Consume my heart away; sick with desire

And fastened to a dying animal
It knows not what it is; and gather me
Into the artifice of eternity.

IV

Once out of nature I shall never take
My bodily form from any natural thing,
But such a form as Grecian goldsmiths make
Of hammered gold and gold enamelling
To keep a drowsy Emperor awake;
30 Or set upon a golden bough to sing
To lords and ladies of Byzantium
Of what is past, or passing, or to come.

Leda and the Swan   (1924)

A sudden blow: the great wings beating still
Above the staggering girl, her thighs caressed
By the dark webs, her nape caught in his bill,
He holds her helpless breast upon his breast.

How can those terrified vague fingers push
The feathered glory from her loosening thighs?
And how can body, laid in that white rush,
But feel the strange heart beating where it lies?

A shudder in the loins engenders there
10 The broken wall, the burning roof and tower
And Agamemnon dead.
                              Being so caught up,
So mastered by the brute blood of the air,
Did she put on his knowledge with his power
Before the indifferent beak could let her drop?

Among School Children   (1928)

I

I walk through the long schoolroom questioning;
A kind old nun in a white hood replies;
The children learn to cipher and to sing,
To study reading-books and history,
To cut and sew, be neat in everything
In the best modern way—the children's eyes
In momentary wonder stare upon
A sixty-year-old smiling public man.

II

I dream of a Ledaean body, bent
10 Above a sinking fire, a tale that she

Told of a harsh reproof, or trivial event
That changed some childish day to tragedy—
Told, and it seemed that our two natures blent
Into a sphere from youthful sympathy,
Or else, to alter Plato's parable,
Into the yolk and white of the one shell.

III

And thinking of that fit of grief or rage
I look upon one child or t'other there
And wonder if she stood so at that age—
20   For even daughters of the swan can share
Something of every paddler's heritage—
And had that color upon cheek or hair,
And thereupon my heart is driven wild:
She stands before me as a living child.

IV

Her present image floats into the mind—
Did Quattrocento finger fashion it
Hollow of cheek as though it drank the wind
And took a mess of shadows for its meat?
And I though never of Ledaean kind
30   Had pretty plumage once—enough of that,
Better to smile on all that smile, and show
There is a comfortable kind of old scarecrow.

V

What youthful mother, a shape upon her lap
Honey of generation had betrayed,
And that must sleep, shriek, struggle to escape
As recollection or the drug decide,
Would think her son, did she but see that shape
With sixty or more winters on its head,
A compensation for the pang of his birth,
40   Or the uncertainty of his setting forth?

VI

Plato thought nature but a spume that plays
Upon a ghostly paradigm of things;
Solider Aristotle played the taws
Upon the bottom of a king of kings;[1]
World-famous golden-thighed Pythagoras
Fingered upon a fiddle-stick or strings
What a star sang and careless Muses heard:
Old clothes upon old sticks to scare a bird.

---

[1] Aristotle tutored Alexander the Great.

VII

Both nuns and mothers worship images,
50 But those the candles light are not as those
That animate a mother's reveries,
But keep a marble or a bronze repose.
And yet they too break hearts—O Presences
That passion, piety or affection knows,
And that all heavenly glory symbolize—
O self-born mockers of man's enterprise;

VIII

Labor is blossoming or dancing where
The body is not bruised to pleasure soul,
Nor beauty born out of its own despair,
60 Nor blear-eyed wisdom out of midnight oil.
O chestnut-tree, great-rooted blossomer,
Are you the leaf, the blossom or the bole?
O body swayed to music, O brightening glance,
How can we know the dancer from the dance?

Crazy Jane Talks with the Bishop   (1933)

I met the Bishop on the road
And much said he and I.
'Those breasts are flat and fallen now,
Those veins must soon be dry;
Live in a heavenly mansion,
Not in some foul sty.'

'Fair and foul are near of kin,
And fair needs foul,' I cried.
'My friends are gone, but that's a truth

10 Nor grave nor bed denied,
Learned in bodily lowliness
And in the heart's pride.

'A woman can be proud and stiff
When on love intent;
But Love has pitched his mansion in
The place of excrement;
For nothing can be sole or whole
That has not been rent.'

Louis Zukofsky

Louis Zukofsky (1904–1978) is one of the founders of Objectivism, a school of poets that declared the poem itself an object, and natural objects the material of poetry. He began as a follower of Ezra Pound, published widely in the 1930s, and then survived in obscurity until a group of younger poets, following a similar esthetic, rediscovered him in the 1960s.

"In Arizona"   (1965)

In Arizona
      (how many years in the mountains)
The small stumped bark of a tree

Looks up
      in the shape of an adored pup

The indians do not approach it
The round indian tents
          remain where they are
The tanned whites
10   are never seen by it
And one can imagine its imploring eyes

The skies
      it seems to look up to
          blue
The same sun that warms the desert
Warms what one
          can imagine to be its ears.

Writing About Poems

1. General Advice

One way to learn about anything is to write about it. You can test your ability to read poems by writing essays that explain or argue or compare or evaluate. Writing a paper, you clarify your ideas—to yourself and to others—as you describe how you understand. If your goal in studying poetry is to arrive at sound taste and just discrimination, you should write papers on poems in order to examine and clarify the means by which you arrive at your judgments.

For general advice, there is none better at the start than *use your intelligence.* (1) Many people beginning to write about literature feel that they should show themselves responding ("I cried when I finished this sonnet") instead of applying their brains and looking closely at the words in front of them. Second, *be forthright* in stating an opinion; learn by making a thesis and (2) defending it, even if later you discover that you have erred. A noncommittal paper usually has less to say than a paper that is vigorous but mistaken. Third, while writing and revising a paper, continually *question whether it serves the* (3) *poem* written about. Do not digress into subjects that lead away from the work itself. Writing about Theodore Roethke's poem "Orchids," one student displayed only botanic research into the flower; another who read up on Roethke's life offered information about the poet's childhood in a greenhouse. Neither served the poem itself.

A. Ways of Writing about Poems

1. Concentration on the Text

Most teachers, when they assign papers, ask their students to concentrate on the text—not on the lives of the authors, or the authors' historical eras, or the context of literary history or influence. Most assignments ask for an explication, an analysis, or a comparison and contrast.

a. Explication

The word *explication* originally meant "unfolding." When you explicate a literary work, you unfold its intricate layers of theme and form, showing its construction as if you were spreading it out on a table. In writing about poetry, you should most often use the tool of explication, because poems are usually dense and concentrated; take the poem word by word or line by line. Explication's goal is to lay out in critical prose everything the author has done in a short poem or brief passage of a longer poem; the best explication goes the furthest toward that goal.

Explication does not concern itself with the poet's life or times; it treats the work of art almost as if it were anonymous. The poet's historical period, however, may determine the definitions of words. If the work is a century or more old, the meanings of some of its words will have changed. Because your task, as explicator, is to make explicit what the author *may* have put into the work—not assuming conscious intentions, but aware of possibilities—keep in mind the time when the work was written and the altering definitions of words. Thus, when an eighteenth-century writer like Alexander Pope speaks of "science," the word means something like "general knowledge" and not the curriculum you study as chemistry, physics, and biology. To determine the meaning of a word in a particular era, consult the *Oxford English Dictionary* (see page 16).

Use common sense when explicating. It is tempting to go too far, to follow particular words down rabbit holes into Wonderland, using ingenuity more than intelligence. One student explicated a couplet of Robert Frost:

> The old dog barks backward without getting up.
> I can remember when he was a pup.

Desperate to write four hundred words about two lines—and having chosen the wrong poem to write four hundred words about—the student noticed that Frost had elsewhere written about Sirius the Dog Star, and that *dog* was "God" spelled backward. In four hundred words, the student confused astrology and theology into a pair of lines about aging and the passage of time. The general advice must govern your explication as well as the work of all other critics: write so that you make sense of the whole work considered; do not entertain fascinating improbabilities.

For an example of explication, look again at the poems explained in the first chapter—Frost's "Stopping by Woods on a Snowy Evening" and Williams's "so much depends." These explications are longer and more detailed than most teachers will expect from students beginning a study of literature, but they give notions of method and range. When you explain a poem or a passage in poetry, you should attend to form as well as to content; you must not simply indicate intellectual understanding by paraphrase, but account for the shape and sound of a poem as well as its paraphrasable content.

Paraphrase is a necessary *part* of explication; it is not the whole thing. Many critics beginning an explication find it useful to summarize the action and theme of the poem as a prelude, giving a brief account of the whole before concentrating on the parts. This summary is like the beginning of a speech in a debate, which states the general conclusion the argument will lead to. With explication as with argument, the proof is in the pudding. The step-by-step explanation of the use and function of particular words is the pudding of explication.

To write a paper of explication, always pick a poem that pleases you, one that you find fascinating. Don't choose something you do not respond to, or something about which you find little that is intriguing. It is all right (it is possibly even good tactics) if something in the poem either displeases you or remains puzzling. When you have chosen a poem to write about, or narrowed your choices down to a few, you should read and reread and reread. Read with a pencil or pen in hand, taking notes both of your observations about the poem and your puzzlements. After many readings, with note-taking, refresh your mind about the elements of poetry and reread again, to notice matters you have possibly ignored. Everyone is naturally more sensitive to certain elements than to others. Perhaps you will find yourself sensitive to the poem's structure as argument, if it is a poem that structures an argument. Perhaps you need to look harder to pick up the poem's images and their connections. Use the elements of poetry, as noted in the chapters of this text, as a checklist of suggestions on what to look for. Not all poems will satisfy all items on the checklist of chapters. But it is your task as explicator to make yourself aware of everything that is there.

Here is a paper by a student named Mary Lois Goldberg, who picked a short poem by Robert Frost for explication.

Mistaking Snow

Only eight lines long, Robert Frost's "A Patch of Old Snow" appears as slight as it is brief. Close reading of the poem, however, reveals that its off-hand manner or tone conceals something more serious than first appears. In this disparity between appearance and reality, between apparent lightness and real seriousness, we see a poem typical of Frost.

The title gives us no problem, because the poem's primary subject is simply "a patch of old snow." Somebody might try to work something out of the dictionary definition of "patch" as a "piece of material . . . to conceal or reinforce . . ."[1] Perhaps the poem in its playful tone acts as a concealment of its own seriousness— but really I don't think the title expresses an idea of hiding. The snow is "a patch" because it is smaller than the earth it lies on.

One of the first things I noticed about this poem was its rhyme, which is really good! They are rhymes which you would never expect. First, a verb with an -ed ending—"guessed," which we pronounce the same as "guest" really—is rhymed with the noun "rest." Just because they are spelled differently, and maybe because they are different parts of speech, they seem as if they should not go together, but they do. Then the second rhyme is a rhyme of two syllables, which is unusual in itself: "overspread it" and "read it." Although the parts of speech are the same—a verb followed by a pronoun object—the first of the verbs has three syllables and the second has one. This difference contributes to the surprise of the rhyme, and the surprise gives part of the poem's pleasure.

---

[1] *American Heritage Dictionary,* William Morris, ed., American Heritage Publishing Co. Inc. & Houghton Mifflin Co.: Boston, 1969.

The poem is written not only in rhyme but in meter. The first and third lines of each stanza have three feet and the second and fourth have two. (Trimeter and dimeter). Some of the feet are three-syllable (˘˘ ´) and some are two-syllable (˘´). I don't know whether to call the meter anapestic or iambic. Here is my scansion:

Thĕre's ă pátch | ŏf oĺd snów | ĭn ă córnĕr

Thăt Ĭ shóuld | hăve guéssed

Wăs ă blów | ăwăy páp | ĕr thĕ ráin

Hăd bróught | tŏ rést.

Ĭt ĭs spéck | lĕd wĭth gríme | ăs íf

Smăll prínt | ŏvĕrspréad ĭt

Thĕ néws | ŏf ă dáy | I've fŏrgóttĕn—

Ĭf Ĭ év | ĕr reád ĭt.

Thirteen of the twenty feet are anapestic and seven are iambic; maybe we should call the meter anapestic with iambic tendencies. Of the eight lines, *half* have feminine endings, including the last line of the poem.

Having written all this about meter, I am not sure what to say about it. I wonder if the tentativeness or uncertainty of the meter—all those extra syllables, or all those syllables cut away—might combine with the surprise of the rhyme to pull you along feeling that you are not just sure where you are going. But with the direct (if surprising) rhyme, and the foot-numbers staying the same, when you come to the end you know that this is the only place you could have come to.

Each stanza is composed of one sentence, and each sentence also seems tentative or uncertain at first, and finally conclusive. Frost built the sentences so that they stick together (which is like the direct rhyme and count of feet) but so that it's hard to see how they stick together (which is like the witty rhymes and mixed feet). The "I should have guessed" in the second line is an interruption to "that . . . was"—except that without the interruption the sentence would not make any sense because it would mix present and past tenses. Therefore the sentence looks at first as if it were careless or off-hand, but when you put it together, you see that all the parts fit and are necessary.

Finally I want to talk about the meaning or theme in the poem, and I come to it only now because I think that the poem needs its own sound-shape and sentence-shape to say what it has to say. The statement of the poem is easy enough to paraphrase: I see a piece of snow and at first I think it is a piece of newspaper because it looks like one, but it is a small matter anyhow. But the poem seems to me to imply something more.

There are two things I want to notice, one in each stanza. First is "paper," which could be wrapping paper or waxpaper but turns out to be newspaper. I think that the delay in discovering the kind of paper is a teasing which is like the surprise of the rhymes. Then in the second stanza, "speckled with grime" is an accurate image for old snow—and when I notice this I suddenly realize that this poem about something visible has hardly any images in it. The title, "A Patch of Old Snow," is an image, but not a vivid one. If this poem does not end in description, then what does it end in?

I think this poem is about a casual, unremarkable visual mistake—and then it says, "So what; it doesn't matter." At first the poet reports that he "should have guessed" that a clump of old snow was a piece of paper. We give easy assent to the comparisons: yes, in April a piece of dirty snow does look like a newspaper. Then in the second stanza Frost explains that grime is speckled on snow *as* print overspreads paper, almost as if he needs to say: look; this mistake was easy to make! Then, as if he felt that he had protested too much, he says that the newspaper (which does not exist except as a mental error) probably did not have any news important to him anyway, because he would have forgotten it. As his withdrawal seems complete, he withdraws further: "If I ever read it." He has made a mistake and explained, and then said it's not worth worrying about, but at the same time he has shown himself worrying about it—a lot!

Another student in the same class decided that *patch* was a key word, that it implied diminishment, concealment, and despair in the poem—and wrote a good paper to defend her ideas.

b. Analysis

To analyze something is to separate it into parts, in order to understand it. Explication deals exhaustively with something small; analysis deals with a part of something—perhaps the repetition of certain phrases in D. H. Lawrence's "Bavarian Gentians" or Robert Frost's characterization in "The Death of the Hired Man." Attending to one part of a poem, an analyst must relate that part to the work as a whole. In analysis, you thus use summary or paraphrase to establish the whole of which you analyze a part. If an analysis fails to relate part to whole, the paper will seem pointless. Your readers want to know not only that the poet repeats the word *blue* twenty-seven times in thirty-nine lines but what this repetition accomplishes in the poem.

When you write about poems of any length, analysis allows you to limit your topic. Never try to analyze a whole long work, any more than you would try to explicate a whole long work. Find ways to limit your topic by analysis— by the isolation of parts. No one can write a decent six-hundred-word theme on the whole of Adrienne Rich's "From an Old House in America." Nor would an analysis of the theme of that poem be possible in less than several thousand words. Analysis discovers part within part. It would be possible to analyze the role of place in that poem.

When you consider writing an analytical paper, you begin by thinking analytically about what you have read. Looking at several poems by Robert Frost, fascinated by "Design" with its white flower that should have been blue, you might analyze "Color in Three Poems by Robert Frost." Thinking about this subject, you must come to some sort of conclusion. For an analytical paper to hold together, it will assert and defend a *thesis* that can usually be reduced to a single sentence. A thesis is not the same as a topic—"Robert Frost Using Colors"—nor should it merely describe or report: "Robert Frost often uses imagery of color in his poetry . . . ." Instead, it must conclude and assert a purpose: "For Robert Frost, in these poems, color disguises reality and suggests a malignancy of matter or maker."

In the text of *To Read a Poem,* many poems or passages are analyzed for one element—for the use of language, imagery, metaphor, allusion, symbolism, rhythm, assonance, alliteration, and meter. For examples, look at the metaphorical analysis of a Shakespearean sonnet on pages 36–37, or the analysis of allusion in Louise Bogan's epigram on pages 55–56.

Students writing analytical papers often limit their topics by concentrating on one part of an element. Theodore Roethke's "The Meadow Mouse" (pages 167–168) includes so many images that "Imagery in 'The Meadow Mouse'" would make a long paper; one student narrowed it to "'My Thumb of a Child': Infant Images in 'The Meadow Mouse.'" Writing about Frost's "Stopping by Woods on a Snowy Evening," a student might analyze "The Tone of Frost's Speaker," or "Frost's Smart Horse in 'Stopping by Woods . . .,'" or "Images of Cold and Comfort." Dealing with a longer poem, a writer might isolate one character: "The Characterization of the Hired Man in Frost's 'Death of the Hired Man'"; or analyze a part of theme: "Definitions of 'Home' in Frost's 'Death of the Hired Man.'"

Writing analysis, remain aware that everything is related to everything else. If you speak of images, it is hard not to mention metaphor, because many images make metaphors. Discussing the metaphorical structure of a sonnet, you will notice that some of the linkage among metaphors is accomplished by images. Sometimes you can lose track of your topic by noticing too closely the interrelationships of many elements. You need, sometimes, to mention a rhyme when you are discussing characterization, if the rhyme makes a point of character. But you should not be sidetracked into a discussion of rhyme just because the subject comes up. You must keep watch, as you write, that you do not lose track. A clear thesis can be the North Star that guides readers through the wilderness of analysis.

In making a thesis, look for an element that has relevance to the whole poem. Some students fall into an analysis that records accurately some facts about a poem but stops short of showing the relevance of these facts. A formal analysis of a sonnet that only discloses the existence of sonnet form would be too trivial to be a true analysis. However, a good analytical paper might show how sonnet form reflected itself in the poem's shapely argument, sorting itself out into the quatrains (if the sonnet is Shakespearean) and into octave and sestet.

Here is Mark O'Malley's analysis of Theodore Roethke's "The Meadow Mouse." (The poem is on pages 167–168.)

"My Thumb of a Child": Infant Images in "The Meadow Mouse"

In Theodore Roethke's "The Meadow Mouse," the speaker finds a tiny mouse, feeds it and protects it, then finds it missing and worries over it. At the beginning, the poem seems to be a simple, affectionate story about caring for a little animal; by the end the poet raises the emotional pitch, and we feel pity for everything—human as well as animal, adult as well as infantile—"innocent, hapless, forsaken."

This emotional widening, this enlargement of compassion, derives from Roethke's skillful and touching uses of imagery associated with infancy, that era of life (whether of man or beast) that most demands our protectiveness. The poem is full of images, and many of them suggest the miniature. In the first stanza we have the adjectives "baby," "little," "small," "little" again, and finally "miniscule." Contrasts of size emphasize the mouse's tininess and connect his tininess to infancy. He is "cradled" in my hand: in relation to this mouse, my hand is in shape and size like a cradle to a baby. When his whiskers are compared to those of a "cartoon mouse," perhaps we recollect small children watching cartoons; at any rate, the notion of a "cartoon mouse" belongs to the world of the child.

At the beginning of the second stanza occurs the most touching contrast of size. In relation to a big animal (horse, cow), the mouse is like a bottle top to a watering trough. This mouse is little! Then the mouse is described anatomically as if his body were distorted like a human baby's, where the head is proportionately large and the stomach puffs out after eating: "His belly big / as his head."

In the second part of the poem, when the mouse is discovered missing, we find the most startling image of smallness and infancy: "My thumb of a child . . . ." I think that the image works two ways; first, this mouse is no bigger than a child's thumb—thus we insist on the small while continuing to associate the mouse with childhood. Or, second, we could paraphrase it: "This child the size of my [grown-up] thumb." (We have heard this kind of language before: the phrase "this dog of an infidel" or "my prince of a friend" equates dog and infidel, prince and friend.) In this second reading, the mouse becomes "this child," almost the speaker's child, as anxiety increases tenderness.

Toward the end of the poem we read of another baby animal, "the nestling fallen"; this ends the series of images of infancy. From the alternate baby animal the poem moves to the presumably adult turtle and to the presumably human "paralytic stunned in the tub," and finally to the general lamentation of the great concluding line. The many images of infancy begin and sustain the pity which becomes general at the end.

c. Comparison and Contrast

A third kind of paper is the comparison and contrast of two texts, usually in connection with a specific theme, a formal device, or a technical element of the genre. A teacher might invite a comparison of Shakespeare's use of the sonnet form with Robert Frost's, for instance. (When you compare two objects, you make notes of likeness and unlikeness; henceforth we will speak only of comparing, implying contrast.) The process of comparison requires analysis of each work and recognition of similarities and differences in the matters analyzed. (If necessary, review the remarks on analysis.)

In writing comparison and contrast, your troubles are likely to be structural. You may generate the materials for a decent analysis of two different poems, but then find it difficult to organize these materials. Here is a passage from a student's draft:

In the sonnet by Shakespeare every four lines is a whole separate idea, then the last two lines is another unit that is complete to itself. In Milton's the first part is eight lines and the second is six, without further subdivision. Shakespeare's rhyming separates the parts, not just the ideas. Milton's rhyming is more difficult, using just two rhymes in the octave (ABBAABBA) but therefore making the eight lines a smooth whole. Shakespeare . . .

These rapid oscillations are nervous; the reader's head snaps back and forth, as if watching a ping-pong game. Which poet is which, and who has the serve?

In a short paper of comparison, you may be able to write a paragraph or two of similarities, add a paragraph or two of dissimilarities, and reach a conclusion in the final paragraph. But such simplicity of structure is rare. More likely, you will need to make a structure something like this:

1. Statement of comparability

2. First similarity
   Work A
   Work B

3. Second similarity
   Work A
   Work B

4. First dissimilarity
   Work A
   Work B

5. Second dissimilarity
   Work A
   Work B

6. Conclusion based on evidence: thesis

Sometimes the grammar of a complex sentence can avoid the ping-pong monotony of compounds. Instead of saying "Work A is seven stanzas of 11 lines making the whole poem 77 lines long, and Work B is 13 stanzas of six lines each which makes 78 lines in all," you can sound more various: "While Work A displays its 77 lines in seven stanzas of 11 lines each, Work B spreads its 76 lines into 19 four-line stanzas."

A different structure takes a topic and then looks at each work two ways:

First item (like the use of color symbolism)
   Similarities between Works A and B
   Dissimilarities between Works A and B

Second item (like the means used for indicating symbolism)
   Similarities between Works A and B
   Dissimilarities between Works A and B

The material you collect for a paper determines its best form. Always decide on a thesis before writing. If you start writing in the sweet hope that a thesis will solidify from the air of your prose, you will write a disorganized paper.

Find the differences between two works that have obvious similarities: the two sonnets are each fourteen lines long, each within iambic pentameter, each rhymed throughout—and then the differences begin: structure of thought, rhyme, rhythm, metaphor, diction. One paper might end by asserting that, despite all the differences between them, these two sonnets share many qualities. Another might, with equal justice, argue that the differences outweigh the similarities. The conclusions will supply the writers' theses.

You illustrate analyzed elements of poems by comparing and contrasting them. Sometimes you will find, within one poet's work, a habit of writing or thinking: "Emily Dickinson's Imagery of Animals." Such a paper might compare and contrast elements in three or four of Dickinson's poems, to investigate her use of animal images. Not only images, but structural devices, recurrent symbols, and themes may provide material for comparative analysis.

You may also contrast two or more poets. "Poets and Flowers: Two Strategies in Roethke and Frost" compares Frost's "Design" with Roethke's "Orchids." Any comparison and contrast, within one poet's work or among different poets, will require separate analyses or small explications, and judgment on likeness or difference.

2. Concentration on Context

Sometimes, in studying poetry and in writing papers about it, your concentration will be not so much on the text as on the context of the work—the historical, personal, or literary backgrounds out of which the poem came. This kind of criticism usually suggests cause and effect: the work has characteristics that derive from causes or sources in the author's society, personal life, or reading. To establish these characteristics, a critic must usually analyze or explicate; but then, having described these characteristics, the writer will shift emphasis from text to context.

a. History and Society

Whatever people do, they express the times they live in. When poets write, they reflect their own era by deploring it, by celebrating it, or even by writing to escape it. Social criticism sometimes supports philosophical positions. Some critics find literary form and content dominated and determined by economics; this criticism draws a line of causation from economic force to literary result. Other social criticism relates literature to theories of nationality and national history. Often, the social or historical critic tries to illuminate meaning by understanding the social and historical conditions under which older work was written, helping the modern reader to understand how it seemed to its contemporaries. When we read ancient poetry, we would be ignorant if we identified a queen as a figure resembling Queen Elizabeth II.

Because this sort of criticism requires historical knowledge, when you write about the historical sources of a text, you must do research. In the library, you can find, for example, what critics and historians have discovered about the relationship of Elizabethan culture to the sonnet sequence by researching books that give backgrounds to different literary periods, setting forth the dominating philosophical, political, and religious ideas of an era. Basil Willey's *Eighteenth Century Background* is an example. But you need not write about remote times when you write social or historical papers. You could connect some poems by William Butler Yeats with the political situation of Yeat's Ireland by readings in the history of modern Ireland.

b. Biography

If a work of art cannot help but reflect its era, equally it cannot help but reflect the life of the man or woman who wrote it.

This statement is easy enough to make, but demonstrating the connection between life and work is often difficult. Things are subtler than they seem. For instance, a poet may speak of himself overtly—Yeats wrote the line "I, the poet William Yeats . . ."—yet make statements that are not historically true. If you take the poet's word, you are often deceived. Writers frequently make up a self to speak from, and make great literature out of this fabrication. Walt Whitman constructed a character called "Walt Whitman" who was rough, manly, vigorous, brave, and noisy; apparently, the man himself was shy, and, when he read his poems aloud, spoke so softly that no one could hear him past the first row. On the other hand, T. S. Eliot proclaimed the impersonality of the artist, said that literature was a flight from personality, and proclaimed these doctrines when he had written "The Waste Land," which critics have begun to understand as the most personal of poems. By noticing disparities between the poet's proclamations and realities, you can begin to investigate the biographical context.

A student who undertakes biographical criticism should therefore take warning. Perhaps no other approach to literature requires more sophistication. Like historical criticism, it requires research as well as subtlety, psychological acumen, and modesty. The last quality may be the most urgent; you may suspect a biographical connection and suggest it by inference, but you seldom *know*. You will know only the obvious: reading a biography of D. H. Lawrence, you can trace his imagery of flowers to the landscape he grew up in; but if you derive his ideas of evil from a childhood experience, you must be very careful.

c. The Literary History

If a literary work is a big river, many tributaries help to form it. There is the language an author grows up among, the common speech; there are the politics, economics, and social structure of a poet's historical period and social class; there are a poet's own psyche, upbringing, relationships with parents and siblings, even inheritance of characteristics. Another large tributary is the poetry that the poet has learned from.

Everything a writer has read—like everything that has happened in his or her life—can contribute to the work done. As athletes learn their moves from watching other athletes, as a guitar player learns chords from another musician, writers learn their craft from observing, analyzing, and loving earlier literary work. For this reason, literature has a history, a sequence if not a progress. (Progress would imply that literature was getting better all the time, a proposition difficult to support.)

To write a paper in literary history, a critic must know earlier literature—not usually a requirement in an introductory course.

Although this discussion has separated the approaches to literature's context in order to describe them, they are not mutually exclusive. To write about influence on Keats, read his letters and consult his biographers. Use explication and analysis, within the historical or biographical or literary methods, to establish claims about the text discussed. It is most important to know what you are doing when you are doing it, and not to confuse your methods.

3. Common Pitfalls in Writing about Poetry
A few common errors of method occur again and again.

a. The Personal Error
Many of the pitfalls that threaten you when you write about poetry take one shape: not regarding the work itself or its context, but some irrelevant matter from the outside. One of the most frequent irrelevancies is personal histories and beliefs.

To write a theme about your personal experience can be a fine thing, but such a theme is *not* about literature. Perhaps because it seems easier to write of personal experience, many people fall into the personal error. Taking the title of D. H. Lawrence's "Bavarian Gentians," they tell about their experience of gardens. Writing about Robert Frost's "Stopping by Woods on a Snowy Evening," they confide that they respond to this poem with special pleasure because they are so fond of horses.

Even without personal narrative, there is danger of sanctifying personal response. It is a commonly held notion in the modern world that one person's opinion is as good as anybody else's. The defense of misreading is usually a smug "That is how *I* see it, and everyone is entitled to a personal opinion." Democratic and egalitarian as the idea appears, it is an idea held to only so long as it is convenient. The same student who holds that his opinion of Plato is as worthy as his philosophy professor's is unlikely to consider his professor's opinion of automobile repair as good as his own. Although there are many possible ways to understand a poem, it is demonstrable that some interpretations are wrong; the text denies them. No one should go to jail for having a wrong opinion—but *opinions can be wrong.* Poetry is not a series of cloud shapes into which everyone can imagine all sorts of castles.

Be governed by the text. Learn to submit to the text, to test all ideas and interpretations to the scrutiny of the text, and to discard ideas that do not fit. This attitude requires humility before the fact of literature and expels or denies the conceit that says "Whatever *I* discover in the text is right for *me.*" There is more of I/me in such reading than there is of poetry.

b. The Historical Error
A less egotistical fallacy that equally impedes good reading is biographical and historical error: looking past a work of the imagination to find events, in the poet's life or times, or which the poem is a representation or to which it responds. This error uses the text as a pretext for discourse, not about the work of art but about history or biography. I do not mean to attack good criticism that legitimately connects a work and a life, on a work and the artist's times. Too often, readers pick on some portion of a poem, trust it as a piece of reality, and run away from literature to speak of history or biography. Yeats's poem "The Second Coming" (pages 363–364) speaks of a time of chaos and

turbulence, when "the center does not hold. / Mere anarchy is loosed upon the world . . . ." One student, noticing Yeats's dates (1865–1939) decided that Yeats was referring to the Great War of 1914–1918, and wrote:

> As Yeats predicted, the great empires came apart, the German and especially the Austro-Hungarian, but really it was not "mere anarchy" because out of parts of these empires Czechoslovakia was created, and the Treaty of Versailles which followed the war determined exactly who had authority over what territory. It is true that the League of Nations . . .

The historical error has run away with the paper, and the student has taken a few lines from the poem as a text for a summary of world history. Information is used not to illuminate the poem but to escape from it. As a matter of fact, this poem was written after World War I at the time of the Civil War in Ireland.

Never assume, when the poet uses *I,* that the poet speaks in his or her own person. First, many poets like Robert Browning write dramatic monologue, in which they assume the mask (sometimes called a *persona*) of an imagined or historical personage; the poem resembles a speech from a play. Second, as we observed earlier, writers often make up a self, called by their own names, that remains an imaginary and unhistorical creature.

Uninformed guesses are as likely to be wrong as right. When a writer undertakes a work, some of the material doubtless comes from the author's experience and observation, as true as a photograph or a verbatim account; other material is doubtless imagined, made up in the service of a truth-telling broader than representation. For the most part, readers cannot determine what is imagined and what reported, and it does not matter. The job of readers is not to determine one from the other but to read the whole as a work of art.

c. The Error of Influence

The error of influence blights some papers in literary history. There is a logical fallacy for which there is a Latin phrase, *post hoc ergo propter hoc:* "after the fact, therefore on account of the fact," describing the human tendency to mistake sequence for cause and effect. Many poor themes assume an influence because of tenuous evidence. Even when the influence is genuine, it is not always important. It may be useful to notice that Robert Frost learned this or that from Wordsworth, or that Robert Creeley is indebted to the example of William Carlos Williams. In each case, the causes are clear and the effects significant. But it does not follow that every literary phenomenon can usefully be discussed in terms of literary genealogy. Walt Whitman's style was a shock to the literary world it assaulted. We have learned that it derives partly from old Hebrew poetry translated by the scholars of the King James version of the Bible. Yet, for the most part, Whitman's style remains Whitman's invention. Anyone asserting literary influence ought to ask the question: If what I assert is true, what of it? It seems true enough, for instance, that the style of D. H. Lawrence's poetry altered after he had read Walt Whitman . . . but what of it? One student, noticing not only the influence but the background suggested by Whitman's style, came up with a notion of connection:

Lawrence's rhythm and his use of parallel constructions changed only after he had studied Whitman in order to write his celebrated essay upon him. Such a fact, true enough, is merely a detail of influence. Whitman's rhythms apparently unleashed something in Lawrence, but what did they unleash? I want to suggest a connection which I cannot demonstrate. We know that much of Whitman's grammar, and therefore rhythm, came from the translations of Hebrew poetry, in its parallel syntactic structures, as rendered by the King James translators of the seventeenth century. We know from Lawrence's fiction and essays that he grew up listening to Bible readings and biblical oratory. Especially in his late work about the Book of Revelation, he reveals how essential to his emotional youth were the accents of prophecy. I suggest that Whitman affected Lawrence's poetry by way of the Bible. Whitman's rhythms showed Lawrence how to tap a source of feeling in himself.

Notice that this student takes a subject that has a factual base, and uses biographical information and inference. We know that Lawrence read Whitman with great attention because Lawrence wrote a famous essay about him. Sometimes, influence-hunters have argued the influence of X on Y where it has been virtually certain that Y was wholly unaware of X, or could not possibly have read more than a story or two. Even more embarrassing, on occasion a critic has described the influence of A on B—when B died before A was born.

4. Reading the Critics

If you are asked to write about history, biography, or literary influence, you are expected to use the library, to read historians, biographers, critics, and scholars. This raises an important question: If you explicate or analyze only (neither requires background information), how much should you use the library, how much should you refer to critics who have published analyses and explications of the poems you are writing about?

Some teachers find it useful to ask their students to check out the critics, to test their own notions against the published work of professionals. Other teachers ask their students *not* to consult critics; some even forbid the practice. Many teachers feel that reading professional criticism inhibits their students and keeps them from developing their own ideas, from making mistakes and learning to correct their mistakes, from finding their own ways to evaluate and interpret. With an exaggerated respect for the printed word, these teachers argue, students become passive when they read critics; they assume that published work must be correct and parrot it back in their own papers. On the other hand, students doing their own work, without help or interference from professional critics and knowing that fellow students are also working alone, do their best work.

B. Writing the Theme

1. Before Writing: Getting Ideas

Whether a topic is assigned or free, gather ideas as the first stage of the paper-writing process, long before beginning a first draft.

Generally, you will know which poems you are to write about. If you have a choice, pick the poem that fascinates you most, even if you feel you do not understand it thoroughly. It is a deadly mistake to pick something uninterest-ing because you think it is simple or easy. If you are not interested, you will never write well about it. After you choose the poem or poems, undertake a series of thorough readings, pencil in hand. If the book is your own, you can write in the margins or underline. (If the book belongs to a library or some-one else, *do not make a mark on it.*) Some notes will spill over the page, and you should keep a notebook beside you when you read. At first, you should not look for anything in particular, but take note of everything that strikes you—a pun, a piece of wit, a linebreak, a rhyme, an ambiguity, a curious tone, a word to look up, a striking image, a puzzling repetition. Make note not only of what you enjoy but of what puzzles or annoys you. Read aggres-sively, demanding of each word or line that it reveal its function and useful-ness. Note big and note little, note outside and inside. If a poem is fourteen lines long, remember that it can be embarrassing to write five pages on a brief poem without having mentioned that it is a sonnet.

Read, taking notes, for one long session, then put the theme out of your mind for a day before returning to read it again. You will be astonished at how much thinking you do when you do not know you are thinking.

The next stage is to assemble notes toward a conclusion. If you are writing an explication, you may use all the notes that continue to look sensible, that contribute to understanding and elucidating the meaning and form of the text. If you are writing analysis, you will need to narrow the topic, which will probably mean discarding many notes. Look for a topic large enough to be worth the time and effort, small enough to be handled in the space assigned.

2. Writing and Revising

Notes make a blueprint for constructing a paper. It helps to make an informal outline, a recognition of what needs to follow what, in order to demonstrate a thesis. These notes can be numbered in a notebook, or trans-ferred to three-by-five-inch cards and stacked in order, or cut from long sheets and piled in appropriate groupings. Probably many notes will refer to lines of the text, because the heart of literary criticism is intelligent quota-tion. No amount of good argument will persuade a reader so much as a brief, accurate example: an image; a rhyme. Any paper will need to assert a thesis, list occasions, and exemplify.

Always try to spend at least one day away from your paper, between a draft and a revision. Revising, check for good, complete sentences, fresh language, logic, accurate quotation, and correct spelling; *try for conciseness.* You have probably used too many adjectives; you may find that you can drop a whole paragraph here and there. If you leave big margins in typing a first draft, or type it triple-space, you will be grateful for the correcting space. Revising, fill out paragraphs that remain thin; find more reasons, more examples, and bol-ster your points. Examine the order of ideas, arguments, and examples.

3. Manuscript Form

Teachers sometimes require particular form for papers. In the absence of other directions, the notes that follow should serve in most circumstances.

a. **Paper, Margins, etc.**

Use 8¹/₂-by-11-inch-paper.

Type if you can, double-space. Avoid erasable typing paper, which smudges. If you write by hand, use paper with deep lines, or write every other line on narrow-lined paper. Use only one side of a piece of paper.

Put your name, your teacher's name, your class and section number, and the date in the upper right-hand corner of your paper.

Leave margins of 1¹/₄ inches at top, bottom, and sides. Always make a copy—a carbon or a photocopy—before you hand your paper in.

Number your pages.

Staple your pages together in the upper left-hand corner.

b. **Titles**

Put quotation marks around titles of poems shorter than book length ("Stopping by Woods on a Snowy Evening"). A book-length poem's title is underlined (The Iliad). Note that titles underlined in papers will be *italicized* in print.

c. **Quotations**

Use quotation marks around excerpts from literature that you quote within a sentence and paragraph:

> When William Carlos Williams looked at a primitive piece of farm machinery, he saw something which he made important through the power of his seeing; he saw it "glazed with rain / water . . ." He saw it "beside the white / chickens . . ." But seeing was not the only sense the doctor . . .

(Use a /, when quoting a poem, to indicate a linebreak.) When you separate a quotation from a sentence and paragraph—indenting it and typing it single-space—do not use quotation marks. You will have indicated quotation by the spacings of the typography:

> When William Carlos Williams looked at a primitive piece of farm machinery, he saw something important because of the power of his seeing:
>
> glazed with rain
> water
>
> beside the white
> chickens
>
> But seeing was not the only sense that the doctor employed in making his poems. . . .

These two ways of quoting are appropriate to different lengths of quotation. When you are quoting only a few words, include the quotation within the paragraph, and put quotation marks around it. When you quote more than a few words, indent the quotation, single-space it, and omit quotation marks—except when the quoted passage itself has already used quotation marks.

d. Footnotes

When you clearly quote from the text under discussion, as in an explication, there is no point in footnoting.

Often, you can note the source of a quotation, without a footnote, in the text of the paper: "Not until the fifth line does Frost use an image of sight . . ." When you find it awkward to include such information in the flow of sentences, a parenthesis can be used; sometimes it is easiest, if there is likely to be any confusion, simply to footnote a reference. Always be certain that the reader knows what he or she is reading.

When you quote or paraphrase from a critic, scholar, biographer, or historian—or even from the *Encyclopaedia Britannica—always footnote your sources.* If you take full notes when you read and remain scrupulous in noting the sources of your ideas or words, no one will ever accuse you of plagiarism (stealing, borrowing, or otherwise appropriating other people's ideas or sentences).

To quote from a book, copy the quotation accurately, put quotation marks around it, and put a number slightly higher than the line of words:[1]. Number sequentially throughout your paper; do not begin a new series of numbers on each page. Footnoting a book, give this information in this order: author's name, book's title, edition number if any, city and publisher, date, and the number of the page quoted from. Here is one example:

[1] X. J. Kennedy, *Literature,* 2nd ed. (Boston: Little, Brown, 1979), pp. 1386–1387.

When quoting from a magazine article, use the volume number and date (in place of the edition number), city, publisher, and date. Here is an example:

[12] Howard Norman, "Dry Tomb," *Westigan Review,* vol. 3, no. 4 (Fall 1978), 10.

When referring, later in the paper, to a source quoted earlier, you can shorten the reference to the writer's name and give the different page number:

Kennedy, 1385.

If you refer to two different books by Kennedy, or two or more poems by Norman, you must use full footnote form, and, in further references, distinguish between the two sources by quoting title as well as author.

e. Bibliography

When you have consulted books or magazines in order to write a paper, list everything consulted in your *bibliography* (a separate section at the end of the paper). List material consulted, even if you have not footnoted the source as a quote or a paraphrase. Arrange the list alphabetically by the authors' last name. List anonymous works alphabetically by title.

A book:

Newman, Edwin, *Strictly Speaking.* New York: Warner Books, 1975.

An article in a book:

Hamill, Pete. "The Language of the New Politics." In *Language in America.* Ed. Neil Postman, Charles Weingartner, and Terence P. Moran. New York: Pegasus, 1969.

An article in a magazine:

Middleton, Christopher. "Notes on a Viking Prow," *PN Review,* 10, Vol. 6, No. 2, 6–8.

An anonymous article from an encyclopedia:

"Geisha." *The Columbia Encyclopedia.* 1963.

Acknowledgments

The American Bible Association, "The Lord is My Shepherd" from *The Book of Psalms* in Today's English Version. Copyright © 1976 by and reprinted by permission of The American Bible Society.

A. R. Ammons, "Working with Tools" from *Briefings: Poems Small and Easy* by A. R. Ammons. Copyright © by A. R. Ammons. Reprinted by permission of W. W. Norton & Company, Inc.

John Ashbery, "Rivers and Mountains" from *Rivers and Mountains* by John Ashbery. Copyright © 1962, 1963, 1964, 1966 by John Ashbery. Reprinted by permission of Georges Borschardt, Inc.

Margaret Atwood, "You Are Happy" from *You Are Happy* by Margaret Atwood. Copyright © 1974 by Margaret Atwood. Reprinted by permission of Phoebe Laramore, Inc.

W. H. Auden, "In Memory of W. B. Yeats," "Musee Des Beaux Arts" and "The Unknown Citizen" from *W. H. Auden: Collected Poems,* by W. H. Auden, compiled and edited by Edward Mendelson. Copyright 1940, renewed 1968 by W. H. Auden. Reprinted by permission of Random House, Inc.

Jimmy Santiago Baca, "Perfecto Flores" from *Black Mesa Poems* by Jimmy Santiago Baca. Copyright © 1982 by Jimmy Santiago Baca. Reprinted by permission of Curbstone Press.

Imamu Amiri Baraka, "Careers" from *Selected Poetry of Imamu Amiri Baraka/ Leroy Jones* by Imamu Amiri Baraka. Copyright © 1979 by Imamu Amiri Baraka. Reprinted by permission of William Morrow & Company.

Wendell Berry, "The Wild Geese" from *The Country of Marriage* by Wendell Berry. Copyright © 1971 by Wendell Berry. Reprinted by permission of Harcourt Brace Jovanovich, Inc.

John Berryman, "Dream Song #16," and "Dream Song #312" from *The Dream Songs* by John Berryman. Copyright © 1959, 1962–1969, by John Berryman. Reprinted by permission of HarperCollins.

Elizabeth Bishop, "The Monument" and "The Fish" from *The Complete Poems, 1927–1979* by Elizabeth Bishop. Copyright © 1939 by Elizabeth Bishop. Copyright © 1979, 1983 by Alice Helen Methfessel. Reprinted by permission of Farrar, Straus and Giroux, Inc.

Robert Bly, "The Dead Seal Near McClure's Beach" from *Morning Glory* by Robert Bly. Copyright © 1975 by and reprinted by permission of Robert Bly. "Hunting Pheasants in a Cornfield" from *Silence in the Snowy Fields,* by Robert Bly. Published by Wesleyan University Press. Copyright © 1962 by and reprinted by permission of Robert Bly.

Louise Bogan, 'Cartography" and "To an Artist, to Take Heart" from *The Blue Estuaries* by Louise Bogan. Copyright © 1937, 1964, 1965, 1968 by Louise Bogan. Reprinted by permission of Farrar Straus and Giroux, Inc.

Gwendolyn Brooks, "The Bean Eaters" and "We Real Cool" from *The Blacks* by Gwendolyn Brooks. Copyright © 1987 by Gwendolyn Brooks. Published by The David Company, Chicago. Reprinted by permission of Gwendolyn Brooks.

David Budbill, "What I Heard at the Discount Department Store" from *Judevine: The Complete Poems* by David Budbill. Copyright © 1991 by and reprinted by permission of David Budbill.

Tom Clark, "Poem" from *Stones* by Tom Clark. Copyright © by and reprinted by permission of Tom Clark.

Lucille Clifton, "good times," "my dream about the cows" and "my dream about the poet" from *Good Woman: Poems and A Memoir, 1969-1980*, by Lucille Clifton. Copyright © 1987 by Lucille Clifton. Reprinted by permission of Boa Editions, Ltd.

Gregory Corso, "Marriage" from *The Happy Birthday of Death* by Gregory Corso. Copyright © 1960 by Gregory Corso. Reprinted by permission of New Directions Publishing Corporation.

Sam Cornish, "Brother of the Streets" by Sam Cornish. Copyright © by and reprinted by permission of Sam Cornish.

Hart Crane, from "The Bridge," and "Voyages I and II" from *The Complete Poems and Selected Prose and Poetry of Hart Crane* by Hart Crane. Copyright © 1933, 1958, 1966 by and reprinted by permission of Liveright Publishing Corporation.

Robert Creeley, "For My Mother Genevieve Jules Creeley" and "The Rain" from *Collected Poems of Robert Creeley, 1945–1975,* by Robert Creeley. Copyright © 1983 by The Regents of the University of California. Reprinted by permission of The University of California Press.

Countee Cullen, "For a Lady I Know" from *On These I Stand* by Countee Cullen. Copyright © 1925 by Harper & Brothers, renewed 1953 by Ida M. Cullen. Reprinted by permission of GRM Associates, Inc., Agents for the Estate of Ida M. Cullen.

e.e. cummings, "l)a" from *Complete Poems 1913–1962* by e.e. cummings. Copyright © 1958 by e.e. cummings. Reprinted by permission of Harcourt Brace Jovanovich, Inc. "Poem, or Beauty Hurts Mr. Vinal" from *Is 5 Poems* by e.e. cummings. Copyright © 1926 by Boni Liveright, renewed 1953 by e.e. Cummings. Reprinted by permission of Liveright Publishing Corporation.

J. V. Cunningham, Two epigrams by J. V. Cunningham. Copyright © by J. V. Cunningham. Reprinted by permission of Ohio University Press, Athens.

James Dickey, "The Heaven of Animals" from *Drowning with Others* by James Dickey. Copyright © 1961 by James Dickey. Originally published in *The New Yorker.* Reprinted by permission of Wesleyan University Press.

Emily Dickinson, "After great pain, a formal feeling comes—," "The first Day's Night had come—," "Me from Myself—to banish—," "My Life had stood—A Loaded Gun—," "The Province of the Saved," and "A still—Volcano—Life—" from *The Complete Poems of Emily Dickinson,* by Emily Dickinson, edited by Thomas H. Johnson. Copyright 1914, 1929, 1935, 1942 by Martha Dickinson Bianchi, renewed 1957, 1963 by Mary L. Hampson. Reprinted by permission of Little Brown and Company. "Because I could not stop for Death—," "He fumbles at your Soul—," "He put a Belt around my life—," "I cannot live with You—," "I'm ceded—I've stopped being Theirs—," "I felt a Cleaving in my Mind—," "I heard a Fly buzz—when I died—," "I would not paint—a picture—," "A narrow Fellow in the Grass" "Much Madness is divinest Sense—," "Severer Service of myself," "The Soul has Bandaged moments—," from *The Poems of Emily Dickinson,* by Emily Dickinson, edited by Thomas H.

Johnson, Cambridge, Mass. Copyright © 1951, 1955, 1979, 1983 by the President and Fellows of Harvard College. Reprinted by permission of Belknap, Harvard University Press/The Trustees of Amherst College.

David Dooley, "How I Wrote It" from *The Volcano Inside* by David Dooley. Copyright © 1988 by and reprinted by permission of David Dooley.

H. D., "Heat" and "Sea Rose" from *Selected Poems of H. D.,* by H. D. (Hilda Doolittle). Copyright © 1957 by Norman Holmes Pearson. Reprinted by permission of New Directions Publishing Corporation.

Edward Dorn, "On the Debt My Mother Owed to Sears Roebuck" by Edward Dorn. Copyright © by and reprinted by permission of Edward Dorn.

Rita Dove, "Horse and Tree" and "Lint" from *Grace Notes, Poems* by Rita Dove. Copyright © 1989 by Rita Dove. Reprinted by permission of W. W. Norton, Inc.

Alan Dugan, "On Hurricane Jackson" from *New and Collected Poems: 1961–1983* by Alan Dugan. Copyright © 1961 by Alan Dugan. Reprinted by permission of The Ecco Press.

Robert Duncan, "Poetry, A Natural Thing" from *The Opening of the Field* by Robert Duncan. Copyright © 1960 by Robert Duncan. Reprinted by permission of New Directions Publishing.

Richard Eberhart, "The Groundhog" from *Collected Poems 1930–1976* by Richard Eberhart. Copyright © 1960 by Richard Eberhart. Reprinted by permission of Oxford University Press.

Russell Edson, "Bringing a Dead Man Back to Life" from *The Intuitive Journey and Other Works* by Russell Edson. Copyright © 1976 by Russell Edson. Reprinted by permission of HarperCollins, Inc.

T. S. Eliot, "The Love Song of J. Alfred Prufrock" and "Journey of the Magi" from *Collected Poems 1909–1962* by T. S. Eliot. Copyright © by T. S. Eliot. Reprinted by permission of Harcourt Brace Jovanovich, Inc./Faber and Faber, Ltd.

William Empson, "Villanelle" from *Collected Poems of William Empson* by William Empson. Copyright © 1949 by William Empson. Reprinted by permission of Harcourt Brace Jovanovich, Inc./Chatto & Windus.

Louise Erdrich, "Owl" from *Baptism of Desire* by Louise Erdrich. Copyright © 1989 by Louise Erdrich. Reprinted by permission of HarperCollins.

Martin Espada, "Latin Night at the Pawnshop" and "The Savior is Abducted in Puerto Rico" from *Rebellion is the Circle of a Lover's Hands* by Martin Espada. Copyright © 1990 by Martin Espada. Reprinted by permission of Curbstone Press.

Ian Hamilton Finlay, "Homage to Malevich" from *Poems to Hear and See* by Ian Hamilton Finlay. Copyright © 1971 by Ian Hamilton Finlay. Reprinted by permission of Macmillan Publishing Co., Inc.

Robert Francis, "Hogwash" and "Three Woodchoppers" from *Robert Francis Collected Poems, 1936–1975* by Robert Francis. Copyright © 1944, 1965, 1972, 1976 by Robert Francis. Reprinted by permission of University of Massachusetts Press, Amherst.

Robert Frost, "Acquainted with the Night," "After Apple-Picking," "Birches," "Design," "To Earthward," "Ends," "The Gift Outright," "Home Burial," "The Most of It," "Mowing," "The Need of Being Versed in Country Things," "Once by the Pacific," "The Pasture," "The Road Not Taken", and "The Silken Tent" from *The Poetry of Robert Frost,* by Robert Frost, edited by Edward Connery Lathem. Copyright 1923, © 1969 by Holt, Rinehart and Winston, Inc.; 1936, 1951 by Robert Frost; and 1964 by Lesley Frost Ballentine. Reprinted by permission of Henry Holt and Company, Inc. "The Draft Horse" from *The Poetry of Robert Frost,* by Robert Frost, edited by Edward Connery Lathem. Copyright 1923, 1928, 1930, 1934, 1939, © 1967, 1969, by Holt, Rinehart and Winston. Copyright 1935, 1942, 1951, © 1956, 1958, 1962 by Robert

Frost. Copyright © 1964, 1967, 1970 by Lesley Frost Ballantine. Reprinted by permission of Henry Holt, and Company, Inc. "In White" from *The Dimensions of Robert Frost* by Robert Frost, edited by Reginald L. Cook. Copyright © 1958 by Robert Frost/Reginald Cook. Reprinted by permission of Henry Holt and Company, Inc. "Out, Out" from *The Poetry of Robert Frost* by Robert Frost, edited by Edward Connery Latham. Copyright 1916, 1944 by Robert Frost, renewed © 1969 by Holt, Rinehart and Winston, Inc. Reprinted by permission of Henry Holt and Company, Inc. "Stopping by Woods on a Snowy Evening" from *The Poetry of Robert Frost,* by Robert Frost, edited by Edward Connery Lathem. Copyright 1923, renewed 1951 by Robert Frost. Reprinted by permission of Holt, Rinehart and Winston, Inc.

Mavis Gallant, "Acceptance of Their Ways" from *My Heart is Broken* by Mavis Gallant. Copyright © 1957 by Mavis Gallant. Reprinted by permission of Georges Borchardt, Inc.

Allen Ginsberg, "America" by Allen Ginsberg. Copyright © 1956, 1959 by Allen Ginsberg. "First Party at Ken Kesey's with Hell's Angels" from *Collected Poems, 1947–1980,* by Allen Ginsberg. Copyright © 1965, 1984 by Allen Ginsberg. Reprinted by permission of HarperCollins.

Louise Gluck, "Gratitude" from *The House on Marshland* by Louise Gluck. Copyright © 1971–1975 by Louise Gluck. Reprinted by permission of The Ecco Press.

Edward Gorey, From "The Listing Attic" from *Amphigory* by Edward Gorey. Copyright © 1972 by Edward Gorey. Reprinted by permission of Candida Donadio & Associates, Inc.

Robert Graves, "In Broken Images" from *Robert Graves: Collected Poems 1975* by Robert Graves. Copyright © 1975 by Robert Graves. Reprinted by permission of A. P. Watt Ltd., and the Executors of the Estate of Robert Graves.

Thom Gunn, "On the Move" from *The Sense of Movement* by Thom Gunn. Copyright © by Thom Gunn. Reprinted by permission of Thom Gunn.

John Haines, "And When the Green Man Comes" and "To Turn Back" from *Winter News* by John Haines. Copyright © 1961, 1964 by John Haines. Reprinted by permission of Wesleyan University Press/University Press of New England.

Donald Hall, "My Son, My Executioner" and "Names of Horses" from *Old and new Poems* by Donald Hall. Copyright © 1990 by Donald Hall. Reprinted by permission of Ticknor & Fields, a Houghton Mifflin Co.

Thomas Hardy, "During Wind and Rain," "Epitaph on a Pessimist," "The Oxen" and "Transformations" from *The Complete Poems of Thomas Hardy,* by Thomas Hardy, edited by James Gibson. Published by MacMillan, 1978.

Robert Hayden, "Middle Passage" from *Angle of Ascent, New and Selected Poems* by Robert Hayden. Copyright © 1970, 1972, 1975 by Robert Hayden. Reprinted by permission of Liveright Publishing Corporation.

Seamus Heaney, "A Drink of Water" and "Song" from *Field Work* by Seamus Heaney. Copyright © 1976, 1979 by Seamus Heaney. "Iron Spike" from "Shelf of Life" from *Station Island* by Seamus Heaney. Copyright © 1985 by Seamus Heaney. Reprinted by permission of Farrar Straus & Giroux, Inc.

Anthony Hecht, "The Dover Bitch: A Criticism of Life" from *The Hard Hours* by Anthony Hecht. Copyright © 1967 by Anthony Hecht. Reprinted by permission of Atheneum Publishers, Inc.

Geoffrey Hill, "Merlin" and "Orpheus and Euridice" from *Somewhere Is Such a Kingdom* by Geoffrey Hill. Copyright © 1975 by Geoffrey Hill. Reprinted by permission of Andre Deutsch Ltd.

Linda Hogan, "The Rainy Season" by Linda Hogan. Copyright © by and reprinted by permission of Linda Hogan.

Garrett Hongo, "The Legend" from *The River of Heaven* by Garrett Hongo. Copyright © 1988 by Garrett Hongo. Reprinted by permission of Alfred A. Knopf, Inc.

Langston Hughes, "Bad Luck Card," "Homecoming" and "Hope" from *Selected Poems of Langston Hughes,* by Langston Hughes. "Bad Luck Card," copyright © 1927 by Alfred A. Knopf, Inc.; "Homecoming," copyright © 1959 by Langston Hughes; and "Hope," copyright 1942 by Alfred A. Knopf, Inc., and renewed 1970 by Anna Bontemps and George Houston Bass. Reprinted by permission of Alfred A. Knopf, Inc.

Ted Hughes, "Thrushes" from *New Selected Poems* and from *Lupercal* by Ted Hughes. Copyright © 1959 by Ted Hughes. Reprinted by permission of HarperCollins/Faber and Faber Ltd.

Richard Hugo, "Degrees of Gray in Philipsburg" from *The Lady in Kicking Horse Reservoir, Poems by Richard Hugo,* by Richard Hugo. Copyright © 1973 by Richard Hugo. Reprinted by permission of W. W. Norton & Company, Inc.

Randall Jarrell, "Eighth Air Force" from *Selected Poems* by Randall Jarrell. Copyright © 1947, 1967 by Mrs. Randall Jarrell. Reprinted by permission of Farrar Straus Giroux, Inc.

Robinson Jeffers, "Hurt Hawks" from *The Selected Poetry of Robinson Jeffers,* by Robinson Jeffers. Copyright 1928, renewed 1956 by Robinson Jeffers. Reprinted by permission of Random House, Inc.

Donald Justice, "Counting the Mad" from *Summer Anniversaries* by Donald Justice. Copyright © 1957 by Donald Justice. Reprinted by permission of Wesleyan University Press.

X. J. Kennedy, "In a Prominent Bar in Secaucus One Day" by X. J. Kennedy. Copyright © by and reprinted by permission of X. J. Kennedy.

Galway Kinnell, "The Bear" from *Body Rags* by Galway Kinnell. Copyright © 1967 by Galway Kinnell. Reprinted by permission of Houghton Mifflin Company.

Etheridge Knight, "Hard Rock Returns to Prison from the Hospital of the criminally Insane" from *Poems from Prison* by Etheridge Knight. Copyright © 1968 by Etheridge Knight. Reprinted by permission of Broadside/Crummell Press.

Yusef Komunyakaa, "Facing It" from *Dien Cai Dau* by Yusef Komunyakaa. Copyright © 1988 by Yusef Komunyakaa. Reprinted by permission of Wesleyan University Press/University Press of New England.

Philip Larkin, "Aubade" and "Mr. Bleaney" from *The Whitsun Weddings* by Philip Larkin. Copyright © by the Estate of Philip Larkin. Reprinted by permission of Faber and Faber Ltd.

D. H. Lawrence, "Bavarian Gentians," "Piano" and "The Song of a Man Who Has Come Through" from *The Complete Poems of D. H. Lawrence,* collected and edited by Vivian de Sola Pinto and F. Warren Roberts. Copyright © 1964, 1971 by Angelo Ravagli and C. Montague Weekley, Executors of the Estate of Frieda Lawrence Ravagli. Reprinted by permission of Viking Penguin, a Division of Penguin USA.

Denise Levertov, "October" and "The World Outside" from *Poems 1960–1967* by Denise Levertov. Copyright © 1962, 1964 by Denise Levertov Goodman. Reprinted by permission of New Directions Publishing Corporation.

Philip Levine, "Salami" from *They Feed They Lion* by Philip Levine, published by Atheneum. Copyright © 1972 by and reprinted by permission of Philip Levine.

Vachel Lindsay, "The Flower-Fed Buffaloes" from *Going to the Stars* by Vachel Lindsay. Copyright © 1926, renewed 1954 by Elizabeth C. Lindsay. Reprinted by permission of Hawthorn Books, Inc.

Li-Young Lee, "Between Seasons," and "Eating Alone" from *Rose* by Li-Young Lee. Copyright © 1986 by Li-Young Lee. Reprinted by permission of Boa Editions, Ltd.

"From Blossoms" from *Rose* by Li-Young Lee. Copyright © 1986 by Li-Young Lee. Reprinted by permission of BOA Editions, Ltd.

John Logan, "The Picnic" from *Only The Dreamer Can Change the Dream* by John Logan. Copyright © 1981 by John Logan. Reprinted by permission of John Logan/The Ecco Press.

Audre Lorde, "Hanging Fire" *The Black Unicorn* by Audre Lorde. Copyright © by Audre Lorde. Reprinted by permission of W. W. Norton, Inc.

Robert Lowell, "After the Surprising Conversions" and "New Year's Day" from *Lord Weary's Castle* by Robert Lowell. Copyright 1946, 1974 by Robert Lowell. Reprinted by permission of Harcourt Brace Jovanovich, Inc. "For the Union Dead" from *For The Union Dead* by Robert Lowell. Copyright © 1960 by Robert Lowell. Reprinted by permission of Farrar Straus & Giroux. "Skunk Hour" from *Life Studies* by Robert Lowell. Copyright © 1956 by Robert Lowell. Reprinted by permission of Farrar Straus & Giroux.

Archibald MacLeish, "You, Andrew Marvell" from *New and Collected Poems 1917– 1976* by Archibald MacLeish. Copyright © 1976 by Archibald MacLeish. Reprinted by permission of Archibald MacLeish.

Louis MacNeice, "The Sunlight on the Garden" from *The Collected Poems of Louis MacNeice* by Louis MacNeice. Copyright © by Louis MacNeice. Reprinted by permission of Faber and Faber Ltd.

Derek Mahon, "The Chinese Restaurant in Portrush" from *Poems 1962–1978* by Derek Mahon. Copyright © 1979 by Derek Mahon. Reprinted by permission of Oxford University Press.

Wesley McNair, "Mina Bell's Cows" from *The Faces of Americans in 1853* by Wesley McNair. Copyright © 1983 by and reprinted by permission of Wesley McNair. "Where I Live" from *The Faces of Americans in 1853* by Wesley McNair. Copyright © 1983 by and reprinted by permission of Wesley McNair.

James Merrill, "After Greece" from *Water Street* by James Merrill. Copyright © 1962 by James Merrill. Reprinted by permission of Atheneum Publishers, Inc.

Marianne Moore, "A Grave" and "Silence" from *Collected Poems* by Marianne Moore. Copyright © 1935 by Marianne Moore, renewed 1963 by Marianne Moore and T. S. Eliot. Reprinted by permission of Macmillan Publishing Co., Inc.

Thylias Moss, "Botanical Fanaticism," "Sunrise comes to Second Avenue" and "November and Aunt Jemima" from *At Redbones* by Thylias Moss. Copyright © by Thylias Moss. Reprinted by permission of Thylias Moss/Cleveland State University Poetry Center.

Edwin Muir, "The Horses" from *The Collected Poems of Edwin Muir* by Edwin Muir. Copyright © by Edwin Muir. Reprinted by permission of Faber and Faber Ltd.

David Mura, "Grandfather and Grandmother in Love" from *After We Lost Our Way* by David Mura. Copyright © 1989 by David Mura. Reprinted by permission of E. P. Dutton, an imprint of New American Library, a division of Penguin Books USA Inc.

National Council of the Churches of Christ in the USA, "The Lord Is My Shepherd" from *the Revised Standard Version of The Bible*. Copyright © 1946, 1952, 1971, by and reprinted by permission of the Division of Christian Education of the National Council of the Churches of Christ in the USA.

Howard Nemerov, "Brainstorm" from *The Collected Poems of Howard Nemerov* by Howard Nemerov. Copyright © 1977 by and reprinted by permission of Howard Nemerov.

Pablo Neruda, "The Burial in the East" and "Ode to My Socks" from *Neruda and Valejo: Selected Poems,* edited and translated by Robert Bly. Published by Beacon

Press. Copyright © 1967, 1976 by and reprinted by permission of Robert Bly. "Taking the Hands" by Robert Bly. Copyright © by and reprinted by Robert Bly.

Frank O'Hara, "The Day Lady Died" from *Lunch Poems* by Frank O'Hara. Copyright © 1964 by Frank O'Hara. Reprinted by permission of City Lights, Inc.

Sharon Olds, "Sex Without Love" from *The Dead and The Living* by Sharon Olds. Copyright © 1983 by Sharon Olds. Reprinted by permission of Alfred A. Knopf, Inc.

Charles Olson, "Maximus, to Gloucester, Sunday, July 19" from *The Maximus Poems* by Charles Olson. Copyright © 1960 by Charles Olson. Reprinted by permission of Corinth Books, Inc.

Gregory Orr, "All Morning" and "The Sweater" from *Gathering The Bones Together* by Gregory Orr. Copyright © 1975 by and reprinted by permission of Gregory Orr. "Washing My Face" from *Burning the Empty Nests* by Gregory Orr. Copyright © 1973 by and reprinted by permission of Gregory Orr.

Joyce Peseroff, "The Hardness Scale" from *The Hardness Scale* by Joyce Peseroff. Copyright © by Joyce Peseroff. Reprinted by permission of The Alice James Poetry Cooperative, Inc.

Sylvia Plath, "Lady Lazarus" from *The Collected Poems of Sylvia Plath,* edited by Ted Hughes. Copyright © 1963 by Ted Hughes. Reprinted by permission of HarperCollins.

Ezra Pound, "The Bath Tub," "Hugh Selwyn Mauberly," "The Return" and "The River-Merchant's Wife: A Letter" from *Personae* by Ezra Pound. Copyright © 1926 by Ezra Pound. Reprinted by permission of New Directions Publishing Corporation.

John Crow Ransom, "Captain Carpenter" from *The Selected Poetry of John Crow Ransom,* Third Edition, by John Crow Ransom. Copyright © 1924 by John Crow Ransom. Reprinted by permission of Alfred A. Knopf, Inc.

Liam Rector, "Showing" from *The Sorrows of Architecture* by Liam Rector. Copyright © 1984 by Liam Rector. Reprinted by permission of Dragon Gate, Inc.

Kenneth Rexroth, "Proust's Madeleine" and "The Signature of All Things" from *Collected Shorter Poems* by Kenneth Rexroth. Copyright © 1949, 1963 by Kenneth Rexroth. Reprinted by permission of New Directions Publishing Corporation.

Charles Reznikoff, "Holding the Stem" and "A Deserter" from *The Complete Poems 1937–1975* by Charles Reznikoff. Copyright © 1941 by Charles Reznikoff. Reprinted with permission of Black Sparrow Press, Inc.

Adrienne Rich, "Aunt Jennifer's Tigers," "Living Memory," "After Twenty Years," "From an Old House in America," "A Marriage in the Sixties" and "Women" from *Twenty-One Love Poems* by Adrienne Rich. Copyright © 1981, 1984 by Adrienne Rich. Reprinted by permission of W. W. Norton & Company, Inc.

Edwin Arlington Robinson, "Eros Turannos" and "Mr. Flood's Party" from *Collected Poems* by Edwin Arlington Robinson. Copyright © 1916 by Edwin Arlington Robinson, renewed 1944 by Ruth Nivison. Reprinted by permission of Macmillan Publishing Co.

Theodore Roethke, "Big Wind," "Cuttings," "Dolor," "Elegy for Jane," "I Knew a Woman," "Journey to the Interior," "The Lost Son," "Orchids," "Sloth," and "The Visitant" from *The Collected Poems of Theodore Roethke* by Theodore Roethke. Copyright © 1972 by Hearst Magazines Inc., 1963 by Beatrice Roethke, Administratrix of the Estate of Theodore Roethke. Reprinted by permission of Doubleday, a division of Bantam Doubleday Dell Publishing Group, Inc.

Carl Sandburg, "Chicago" from *Chicago Poems* by Carl Sandburg. Copyright © 1916 by Holt, Rinehart and Winston, copyright 1944 by Carl Sandburg. Reprinted by permission of Harcourt Brace Jovanovich, Inc.

Yvonne Sapia, "Valentino's Hair" from *Valentino's Hair* by Yvonne Sapia. Copyright © 1987 by Yvonne Sapia. Reprinted by permission of Northeastern University Press, Boston.

Vikram Seth, "God's Love" from *All you Who Sleep Tonight* by Vikram Seth. Copyright © 1990 by Vikram Seth. Reprinted by permission of Faber & Faber, Inc.

Anne Sexton, "Wanting to Die" from *Live or Die* by Anne Sexton. Copyright © 1966 by Anne Sexton. Reprinted by permission of Houghton Mifflin Company.

Leslie Marmon Silko, "When Mountain Lion Lay Down with Deer" by Leslie Marmon Silko. Copyright © by and reprinted by permission of Leslie Marmon Silko.

Charles Simic, "Fork" from *Dismantling the Silence* by Charles Simic. Copyright © by Charles Simic. Reprinted by permission of George Braziller, Inc. "Shelley" from *The Book of Gods and Devils* by Charles Simic. Copyright © 1990 by Charles Simic. Reprinted by permission of Harcourt Brace Jovanovich, Inc.

Louis Simpson, "Early in the Morning" from *The Good News of Death and Other Poems* by Louis Simpson. Copyright 1950, 1951, 1952, 1953, 1953, 1954, 1955 by Louis Simpson. Reprinted by permission of Charles Scribner's Sons. "In the Suburbs" and "Walt Whitman at Bear Mountain" from *At the End of the Open Road* by Louis Simpson. Copyright © by Louis Simpson. Reprinted by permission of Wesleyan University Press/University Press of New England. "To the Western World" from *A Dream of Governors* by Louis Simpson. Copyright © by Louis Simpson. Reprinted by permission of Wesleyan University Press/University Press of New England.

W. D. Snodgrass, "April Inventory" and "Lobsters in the Window" from *After Experience* by W. D. Snodgrass. Copyright © 1963 by W. D. Snodgrass. Reprinted by permission of Soho Press.

Gary Snyder, "Above Pate Valley" and "Hay for the Horses" from *Riprap* by Gary Snyder. Copyright © 1959, 1965 by Gary Snyder. Published by North Point Press. Reprinted by permission of Farrar Straus & Giroux, Inc.

Cathy Song, "A Small Light" from *Frameless Windows, Squares of Light* by Cathy Song. Copyright © by Cathy Song. Reprinted by permission of W. W. Norton, Inc.

Gary Soto, "Sun" by Gary Soto. Copyright © by and reprinted by permission of Gary Soto.

William Stafford, "Travelling through the Dark" from *Stories That Could Be True* by William Stafford. Copyright © 1960 by William Stafford. Reprinted by permission of HarperCollins.

Wallace Stevens, "Disillusionment at Ten O'Clock," "The Emperor of Ice-Cream," "The Snow Man" and "Sunday Morning" from *The Collected Poems of Wallace Stevens* by Wallace Stevens. Copyright © 1923, renewed 1951 by Wallace Stevens. Reprinted by permission of Alfred A. Knopf, Inc.

Mark Strand, "Always" and "The End" from *The Continuous Life* by Mark Strand. Copyright © 1990 by Mark Strand. Reprinted by permission of Alfred A. Knopf, Inc.

Dylan Thomas, "Do Not Go Gently into That Good Night," "Fern Hill," and "This Bread I Break" from *Poems of Dylan Thomas* by Dylan Thomas. Copyright © 1945 by The Trustees for The Copyrights of Dylan Thomas. Reprinted by permission of New Directions Publishing Corporation/David Higham Associates Limited.

Edward Thomas, "The Owl" from *Collected Poems* by Edward Thomas. Copyright © 1974 by Edward Thomas. Reprinted by permission W. W. Norton & Company, Inc.

Charles Tomlinson, "Paring the Apple" from *Seeing is Believing* by Charles Tomlinson. Copyright © 1958, 1960 by Charles Tomlinson. Published by McDowell Oglesby, OUP. Reprinted by permission of Charles Tomlinson, Gloustershire, England.

Jean Toomer, "Reapers" from *Cane* by Jean Toomer. Copyright © 1923 by Boni & Liveright, renewed 1951 by Jean Toomer. Reprinted by permission of Liveright Publishing Corporation.

John Updike, "Ex-Basketball Players" from *The Carpentered Hen and Other Tame Creatures* by John Updike. Copyright © 1957, 1982 by John Updike. Reprinted by permission of Alfred A. Knopf, Inc., a Division of Random House, Inc.

Derek Walcott, "Sea Grapes" from *Sea Grapes* by Derek Walcott. Copyright © 1976 by Derek Walcott. Reprinted by permission of Farrar Straus & Giroux, Inc.

Robert Penn Warren, "Gold Glade" from *Promises: Poems 1954–1956* by Robert Penn Warren. Copyright © 1957 by Robert Penn Warren. Reprinted by permission of Random House, Inc.

Richard Wilbur, "Museum Piece," "Still, Citizen Sparrow" and "Tywater" from *Ceremony and Other Poems.* Copyright © 1950 and renewed 1978 by Richard Wilbur, reprinted by permission of Harcourt Brace Jovanovich, Inc.

William Carlos Williams, "Nantucket," "Poem" ("as the Cat"), "The Red Wheelbarrow," "So Much Depends," "Spring and All" and "This is Just to Say" from *Collected Earlier Poems* by William Carlos Williams. Copyright 1938 by and reprinted by permission of New Directions Publishing Corporation.

Charles Wright, "Virgo Descending" from *Bloodlines* by Charles Wright. Copyright © 1975 by Charles Wright. Reprinted by permission of Wesleyan University Press.

James Wright, "A Blessing" and "The First Days" from *To a Blossoming Pear Tree* by James Wright. Copyright © 1974, 1979 by James Wright. Reprinted by permission of Farrar Straus & Giroux, Inc. "Lying in a Hammock at William Duffy's Farm in Pine Island, Minnesota" from *Collected Poems* by James Wright. Copyright © 1961 by James Wright. Reprinted by permission of Wesleyan University Press/University Press of New England.

Jay Wright, "Meta-A and A of Absolutes" from *Selected Poems of Jay Wright,* pp. 175–176, by Jay Wright, edited by R. B. Stepto. Copyright © 1987 by Jay Wright. Reprinted by permission of Princeton University Press.

William Butler Yeats, "The Apparitions," "Among School Children," four versions of "Cradle Song," "Crazy Jane Talks with the Bishop," two versions of "The Lamentation of the Old Pensioner," "Leda and the Swan," two versions of "London," "The Magi," "Sailing to Byzantium," "The Second Coming," and "Who Goes With Fergus" from *The Poems of W. B. Yeats: A New Edition* by William Butler Yeats, edited by Richard J. Finneran. Copyright © 1940 by Georgie Yeats, renewed 1968 by and reprinted by permission of Bertha Georgie Yeats, Michael Butler Yeats and Anne Yeats/Macmillan, London, Ltd.,/A. P. Watt, Ltd.

Louis Zukofsky, "In Arizona" from *Collected Short Poems 1923–1964* by Louis Zukofsky. Copyright © 1971 by Louis Zukofsky. Reprinted by permission of Paul Zukofsky, CZ Publications, Inc.

Photo Credits

John Keats (p. 124), Emily Dickinson (p. 139), and Robert Frost (p. 144)/ Bettmanns; Theodore Roethke (p. 168)/Office of Information Services, University of Washington, Seattle; Adrienne Rich (p. 168)/Wide World Photos.

Index

Tender, semi-, 215

Tennyson, Alfred, Lord, 93, *337*

"The Eagle," 339

"Ulysses," 337–338

Terrifying are the attent sleek thrushes on the lawn, 256

Tetrameter, 78

That is no country for old men . . ., 364

That sail in cloudless light, 344

"That time of year thou mayest in me behold" (Shakespeare), 39

That's my last Duchess painted on the wall, 199

The barred owls scream in the black pines, 232

The blue jay scuffling in the bushes follows, 239

The broken pillar of the wing jags from the clothed shoulder, 259

The buzz saw snarled and rattled in the yard, 97

The Child is father of the man, 353

"The first Day's Night had come—" (Dickinson), 140

The first thing I saw in the morning, 359

The flower-fed buffaloes of the spring, 274

The good grey guardians of art, 48

The grass people bow, 240

The green catalpa tree has turned, 327

The house had gone to bring again, 151

The houses are haunted, 12

The house was shaken by a rising wind, 295

The land was ours before we were the land's, 20

The Lord is my shepherd, 116–117

The old South Boston Aquarium stands, 279

The people along the sand, 153

"The Province of the Saved" (Dickinson), 141

The sea is calm tonight, 182

The shattered water made a misty din, 151

"The Soul has Bandaged moments—" (Dickinson), 141

The sunlight on the Garden, 287

The time you won your town in the race, 255

The tongue that mothered such a metaphor, 17

The water turns, 185

The whiskey on your breath, 156

The women are walking to town, 252

The world is too much for us; late and soon, 358

Their new landlord was a handsome man . . ., 312

Theme, 381–382

There are portraits and still-lifes, 342

There are those to whom place is unimportant, 165

There was never sound beside the wood but one, 145

There's no way out, 326

These fought in any case, 307

Thesis, and topic, 373–374, 376

They eat beans mostly, this old yellow pair, 198

"They Flee from Me" (Wyatt), 362

They lean over the path, 39

They sing their dearest songs—, 18

They showed up for awhile and they died, 310

"They that have power to hurt and will do none" (Shakespeare), 318

"This Bread I Break" (Thomas), 339

"This Is Just to Say" (Williams), 352

"This Living Hand" (Keats), 138

This one was put in a jacket, 261

This strange thing must have crept, 322

This urge, wrestle, resurrection of dry sticks, 154

This was Mr. Bleaney's room . . ., 267

Thomas, Dylan, *339*

"Do not go gentle into that good night," 341

"Fern Hill," 339–341

"This Bread I Break," 339

Thomas, Edward, *341*

"The Owl," 341–342

Thou still unravished bride of quietness, 137

Though there are wild dogs, 251

"Three Woodchoppers" (Francis), 235

Through the ample open door of the peaceful country barn, 350

"Thrushes" (Hughes), 256–257

Title, of poem, 2